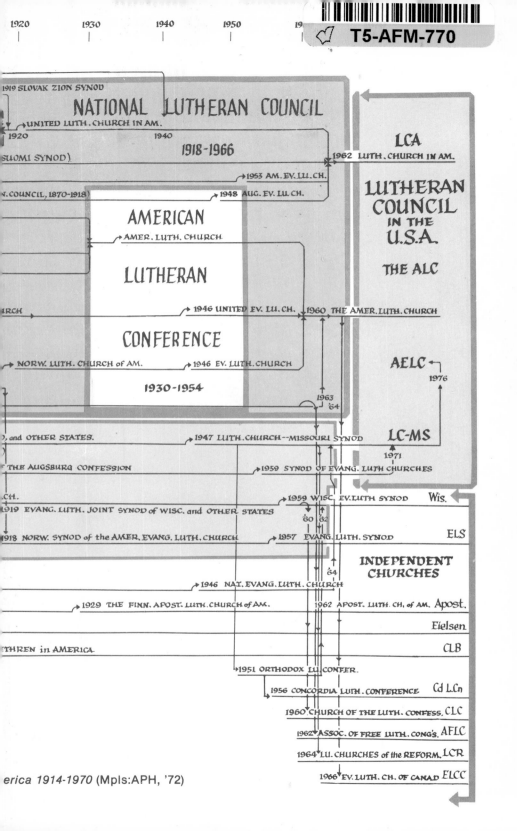

erica 1914-1970 (Mpls:APH, '72)

THE RISE OF
WORLD LUTHERANISM

THE RISE OF
WORLD LUTHERANISM

AN AMERICAN PERSPECTIVE

E. CLIFFORD NELSON

FORTRESS PRESS   PHILADELPHIA

Biblical quotations from the Revised Standard Version of the Bible, copyrighted 1946, 1952, © 1971, 1973 by the Division of Christian Education of the National Council of the Churches of Christ in the U.S.A., are used by permission.

The photographs in this book were obtained from the Archives of Cooperative Lutheranism, Lutheran Council in the U.S.A. New York City.

Library of Congress Cataloging in Publication Data

Nelson, E. Clifford, 1911–
The rise of world Lutheranism.

Includes bibliographical references and index.
1. Lutheran Church—History—20th century.
2. Christian union—Lutheran Church.
3. Lutheran World Federation—History.
I. Title.
BX8018.N37   284.1'09'04   80–2376
ISBN 0-8006-0661-2   AACR2

8570C81   Printed in the United States of America   1–661

In Memoriam

Carl E. Lund-Quist
1908–1965

Executive Secretary
Lutheran World Federation
1951–1960

Contents

Foreword

A careful study of the history of global Lutheran relations prior to the formation of the Lutheran World Federation was envisioned by the federation's Department of Theology as early as 1965. The title of this book indicates the magnitude and significance of the task. A part of the task has already been undertaken by Bengt Wadensjö, who offers a Scandinavian interpretation in *Toward a World Lutheran Communion: Developments in Lutheran Cooperation up to 1929* (Uppsala: Verbum, 1970). A second study, a two-volume work entitled *Die Lutherische Kirche: Geschichte und Gestalten* (Gütersloh: Gerd Mohn, 1976), is written from a German point of view. The second volume of that study, *Vom Lutherischen Weltconvent zum Lutherischen Weltbund*, is by Kurt Schmidt-Clausen, executive (general) secretary of the Lutheran World Federation from 1961 to 1965. It is fitting that an American perspective now be written.

No one is better qualified to write this history than E. Clifford Nelson. As has been said about another story and another book, he has lived a part of the history he writes. Not only has he taught history in the schools of the church during most of his career, but he has also been involved in the life and work of the Lutheran World Federation. He served as director of the Third Lutheran World Assembly at Minneapolis in 1957. He has been a member of several federation committees and was an associate editor of *The Lutheran World* for eight years. At the Fourth Lutheran World Assembly in Helsinki in 1963, he delivered a key lecture entitled "The One Church and the Lutheran Churches," a superb exposition of Lutheran ecclesiology and the Lutheran commitment to ecumenism.

The questions of Lutheran ecclesiology which Nelson posed at Helsinki are raised again by this history. What is the church? Is

Lutheranism more than just a confessional movement within the church catholic? When, how, and why is the Lutheran church a church? What is the worldwide Lutheran movement to be called, and what is its ecclesiological significance? These questions give the book a major theme and provide dramatic coherence to the complex history of Lutheranism from its beginnings in the Reformation through the era of the Lutheran World Convention.

This book would perhaps never have been written without a substantial grant for research. As the present executive secretary of the Lutheran World Federation, I wish to express the thanks of the federation to the Lutheran Brotherhood insurance company of Minneapolis, Minnesota, which made the project financially possible.

The book is dedicated to the memory of Carl E. Lund-Quist, executive (general) secretary of the Lutheran World Federation from 1951 to 1960. A close friend and colleague of Nelson, Lund-Quist was the successor of the federation's first executive secretary, Sylvester C. Michelfelder, and he served with great distinction until poor health forced him to resign. Lund-Quist established the basic patterns and direction of the work of the Lutheran World Federation. Most of the present departments came into existence under his administration. He bequeathed the work of a quiet and dedicated churchman to his successors, and his guiding spirit can still be felt in the halls of the federation's headquarters in Geneva.

Nelson's study is remarkably relevant to the present situation of the Lutheran World Federation and to its problems. For the light this book sheds on questions about the role of the federation in the ecumenical movement, about the relation of the federation to the World Council of Churches, and about the nature and quality of the life of the Lutheran community within the federation, and for its presentation of a comprehensive study of organized world Lutheranism, the global family of Lutherans will be grateful. This book is a rich and lasting resource.

CARL H. MAU, JR.
Executive Secretary
Lutheran World Federation

Geneva, Switzerland

Preface

The Indian poet and Nobel prize winner Rabindranath Tagore once wrote, "Emancipation from the bondage of the soil is no freedom for the tree." This figure may be at the heart of the "roots syndrome" that has ignited so much of recent American interest in personal, family, and institutional heritage. The present book reflects the desire of the Lutheran World Federation to set forth its prehistory and its confessional particularity in the context of ecclesiastical ecumenism and religious pluralism. It has no desire for the illusory freedom of a tree "emancipated from the bondage of the soil." Moreover, Lutherans, like others, are discovering the wisdom of another Tagore aphorism, "History slowly smothers its truth, but hastily struggles to revive it in the terrible penance of pain."[1] This wisdom has produced a conscious effort among leaders of world Lutheranism to avoid penitential pain and to secure the freedom that knowledge of one's history provides.

During the summer of 1947, the First Assembly of the Lutheran World Federation was held at Lund, Sweden. Its predecessor, the Lutheran World Convention (established in 1923), barely survived the withering effects of a worldwide depression and the spiritual and physical devastation of political totalitarianism and World War II. But survive it did. Immediately the federation began to think about its roots as a global institution. The minutes of the executive committee meeting at Lund on July 7, 1947 (recorded by Carl E. Lund-Quist, to whose memory this book is dedicated) report a suggestion "that a committee on the history of the Lutheran Church and the Lutheran World Federation be included in the list of commissions to be set up."

---

1. The Tagore quotations are from *Fireflies* (New York: Macmillan Co., 1933), pp. 150, 243.

This proposal was never realized, but its concerns have been illustrated by the publication in 1929, 1952, 1957, 1963, and 1977 of books dealing with the Lutheran churches throughout the world. It was not until a decade ago, however, that the Lutheran World Federation specifically charged its Department of Theology (later Department of Studies) to initiate bibliographical and archival research that might lead to scholarly publications on the prehistory of the federation (see LWF, *Reports 1963–1969* [Geneva, 1970], p. 164).

Almost from the beginning, organized world Lutheranism recognized three "centers" or groupings of churches: Germany (or Central Europe), Scandinavia, and North America. It seemed natural, therefore, that historical studies be approached from the perspectives of each center. The studies that have resulted reflect these three angles of vision. The Scandinavians were the first to enter the field. Bengt Wadensjö, *Toward a World Lutheran Communion: Developments in Lutheran Cooperation up to 1929* (Uppsala: Verbum, 1970), sees the story of world Lutheranism through Scandinavian (Swedish) eyes, concluding with a report of the Copenhagen assembly in 1929. The German interpretation of the prehistory is a two-volume work, *Die Lutherische Kirche: Geschichte und Gestalten* (Gütersloh: Gerd Mohn, 1976). The first volume, *Wege zur Einheit der Kirche in Luthertum*, had four authors: Wilhelm Kahle, Gottfried Klapper, Wilhelm Maurer, and Martin Schmidt. The second volume, *Vom Lutherischen Weltkonvent zum Lutherischen Weltbund*, was written by Kurt Schmidt-Clausen, former executive secretary of the Lutheran World Federation (1961–65) and now Landessuperintendent of Osnabrück. The story that unfolds narrates and interprets the fortunes and misfortunes of world Lutheranism from Eisenach 1923 to Lund 1947. As planned, Schmidt-Clausen's work provides the German view of global Lutheranism.

The present volume has benefited richly from the Scandinavian and German chronicles, and it attempts, as its title indicates, to reflect the third "center" of early world Lutheranism by adding the American dimension.

I was informed about the LWF project by the Department of Theology in 1968 and did some preliminary research in 1971. This continued on a deeper level during a sabbatical leave in the academic year 1974–75. Following retirement in 1976, I was able to devote some large segments of time to the task and completed the manuscript in the summer of 1979.

What I have written has been under a twofold constraint: (1) the knowledge that, extensive as my investigations have been, my research—like housewives' work—was never done; and (2) the caution of the Danish Ogden Nash, Piet Hein:

> Long-winded writers I abhor,
>   and glib, prolific chatters;
> give me the ones who tear and gnaw
>   their hair and pens to tatters:
> who find their writing such a chore
>   they only write what matters.[2]

Despite Hein's caveat, the opulence of the archival and library material and the desire to weave it into a somewhat intelligible and readable story have produced what is obviously a long and detailed narrative. Others must judge whether the result falls under the rubric of "what matters" or under the judgment of Luther's words on egocentric verbosity: "If you imagine that . . . your book, teaching, or writing, is a great achievement . . . then, my dear reader, feel your ears. If you do so properly, you will discover that you have a splendid pair of big, long, shaggy jackass ears."[3]

It is pleasant to acknowledge one's indebtedness to the many persons who assisted in the preparation of this volume. The list of individuals and groups is both quantitatively and qualitatively impressive.

First, I must mention those who were responsible for getting the project under way. In 1973, Lloyd Svendsbye, dean of St. Olaf College, nudged me into serious study of the topic. This nudging was subsequently supported by encouragement from the U.S. National Committee of the Lutheran World Federation, which was prepared to administer a substantial research subsidy received from the Lutheran Brotherhood insurance company of Minneapolis.

These actions propelled me into a half-dozen years of research and writing, which soon put me in debt to an army of librarians, archivists,

---

2. Piet Hein, *Grooks* (Cambridge, Mass.: MIT Press, 1966), p. 45.

3. See Luther's introduction to the Wittenberg edition (1539) of his writings in *D. Martin Luthers Werke* (Weimar: Hermann Böhlaus Nachfolger, 1914), 50:660.

professors, and research and editorial assistants. It is a pleasant duty to single out a few for special mention. Among these are Archivist Joan Olson and Librarian Forrest Brown and his staff at Rølvaag Memorial Library, St. Olaf College, Northfield, Minnesota; Helen Knubel and Alice Kendrick at the Archives of Cooperative Lutheranism, the Lutheran Council in the U.S.A., New York City. Although the bulk of my research took place in Northfield and New York, I found staffs of libraries and archives in other places unfailingly helpful and resourceful. Among these were the Luther-Northwestern Seminaries Library, St. Paul; the Krauth Memorial Library at Philadelphia Lutheran Seminary, Philadelphia; the Wartburg Seminary Library, Dubuque; the American Lutheran Church Archives, Dubuque; the Lutheran Church in America Archives, Lutheran School of Theology, Chicago; the National Archives, Copenhagen; the Bethel Institute Archives, Bielefeld; the archives of the Church of Hannover and the German National Committee of the Lutheran World Federation in Hannover; the archives of the Church of Bavaria in Nürnberg; and the archives of the Lutheran World Federation and the World Council of Churches in Geneva.

I am grateful to Carl Mau, Jr., executive secretary of the Lutheran World Federation, Geneva, for writing the Foreword and reading the manuscript with a critical eye. Others who prepared critiques were E. Theodore Bachmann, Princeton Junction, N.J.; Lloyd Svendsbye, Eugene L. Fevold, and Gerhard Förde, Luther-Northwestern Seminaries, St. Paul; and Sidney A. Rand, former president of St. Olaf College, Northfield, and U.S. Ambassador to Norway.

Manuscript editing was in the always competent hands of Alma Roisum, St. Paul, and Todd W. Nichol, Berkeley. St. Olaf College Professor Emerita Charlotte Jacobson, who early on organized the massive research materials into a manageable system, produced the book's index. Oberkirchenrat Gottfried Klapper, Hannover, provided books and historical data, organized my 1974 research trips in Germany, and arranged for two days of taped interviews with the late Bishop Hanns Lilje.

Concluding thanks are reserved for my wife, Lois, who listened to the reading of every syllable and reacted with gentle candor. Moreover, when both research and writing seemed to be mired in futility, she spoke the right word of encouragement. It was often a virtuoso performance of matching wit and will and daily routine to the shifting moods of a less-than-inspired but grateful author-husband.

E. CLIFFORD NELSON
Emeritus Professor
St. Olaf College

Chronology

1530	Augsburg Confession of Lutherans before the emperor, Charles V.
1555	Peace of Augsburg. Imperial recognition of two confessional communities, Roman Catholic and Lutheran, according to the principle *cuius regio eius religio*.
1580	The Book of Concord, the confessional writings of the Evangelical Lutheran church.
ca. 1608	Hohenzollerns in Lutheran Brandenburg-Prussia become Calvinist (Reformed).
1648	Treaty of Westphalia. Imperial recognition of three confessional communities: Catholic, Lutheran, Calvinist (Reformed).
1701	Calvinist Hohenzollern Elector Frederick unites Brandenburg-Prussia into the kingdom of Prussia, a Lutheran state with a Calvinist monarch.
1748	First American Lutheran Synod: Ministerium of Pennsylvania.
1815	Prussian territories enlarged by the Congress of Vienna.
1817	Calvinist King Frederick William III (1797–1840), as *summus episcopus* of Lutheran Prussia, creates the "Evangelical Christian Church," popularly known as the Old Prussian Union.
1820	Formation of the Evangelical Lutheran General Synod of the United States of North America.
1847	Formation of the Missouri Synod.
1852	King Frederick William IV (1840–61) alters the Prussian Union from a doctrinal union to an "administrative union" of Lutherans and Reformed.

1863 Formation of the General Synod of the Evangelical Lutheran Church in the Confederate States of America; later, United Synod, South.

1866 Prussia annexes Schleswig-Holstein, Hannover, and other territories. Lutheran Hannover and Schleswig-Holstein keep their church government independent of the Prussian Union.

1867–68 Formation of the General Evangelical Lutheran Conference (AELK) in Hannover.

1867 Formation of the General Council of the Evangelical Lutheran Church of North America by withdrawal from the General Synod.

1917 Merger of three Norwegian-American synods into the Norwegian Lutheran Church of America, June 6–10.
Formation of the National Lutheran Commission for Soldiers' and Sailors' Welfare (NLCSSW), October 19.

1918 Formation of the National Lutheran Council (NLC), September 6.
Merger of the General Synod, the General Council, and the United Synod, South into the United Lutheran Church in America, November 18.
NLCSSW commission to Europe, autumn 1918 to spring 1919.

1919 NLC commission to Europe, summer and autumn; urges (November 6) a world Lutheran "federation."

1920 "Washington Declaration of Principles" adopted by the United Lutheran Church in America.

1920–22 American and German discussions about a world Lutheran conference.

1922 Official call (November 15) for the Lutheran World Convention (LWC) at Eisenach in 1923.

1923 First Lutheran World Convention, Eisenach, August 19–26.
Executive committee: John A. Morehead, Lars W. Boe, Ludwig Ihmels, Wilhelm von Pechmann, Per Pehrsson, Alfred Th. Jørgensen.

1925 Life and Work Conference in Stockholm, August 19–30.
"Minneapolis Theses" draws Ohio, Iowa, and the Norwegians into a bloc within the NLC, November 18.

1927	Faith and Order Conference in Lausanne, August 3–21.
1929	Second Lutheran World Convention at Copenhagen, June 26 – July 4.
	LWC executive committee meets in Örebro, Sweden, July 6. Wilhelm von Pechmann's resignation.
	New York stock market crash and the Great Depression.
1930	Merger of Ohio, Iowa, Buffalo, and Texas synods into American (German) Lutheran Church, August 11.
	Formation of the American Lutheran Conference (the American Lutheran Church, the Norwegian Lutheran Church of America, the Augustana Synod, the United Danish Evangelical Lutheran Church, and the Lutheran Free Church) within the National Lutheran Council, October 29–31.
	August Marahrens and Hans Meiser replace Ludwig Ihmels and Wilhelm von Pechmann on LWC executive committee.
1933	Hitler and the Nazis win control in Germany. "Church struggle" (*Kirchenkampf*) with Nazis begins.
	Election and defeat of Friederich von Bodelschwingh as Reich bishop, May–June.
	LWC executive committee meets in Hannover, November.
1934	Synod of Barmen. The Confessing Church's two wings: (1) Evangelical Confessing Churches and (2) Evangelical Lutheran Confessing Churches.
1935	The Third Lutheran World Convention at Paris, October 13–20. August Marahrens succeeds John A. Morehead as president.
1936	Death of John A. Morehead, June.
	LWC executive committee meets in New York, September 29–October 6. Election of Hanns Lilje as executive secretary. Publication of "Lutherans and Ecumenical Movements."
1937	Oxford Life and Work Conference and Edinburgh Faith and Order Conference.
	LWC executive committee meets in Amsterdam. Constitutional drafts for world Lutheranism.
	Nazis immobilize German church.

"American Section" of LWC begins to assume responsibility for LWC continuity.

1938   LWC executive committee meets in Uppsala, May 21–25. Constitutional and ecumenical issues come to the fore.

Lutherans urge "confessional representation" in World Council of Churches.

Plans for Fourth Lutheran World Convention in Philadelphia in 1940.

Erling Eidem replaces Per Pehrsson on LWC executive committee. Hanns Lilje's trip to the United States to assist in plans for Philadelphia assembly.

1939   LWC executive committee meets in Waldenburg, Saxony, May 20–25.

Nazi invasion of Poland. Start of World War II, September.

1940   Philadelphia convention canceled. August Marahrens and Hanns Lilje remain as president and executive secretary, respectively.

Nazi invasion of Denmark and Norway, April. Eivind Berggrav begins leadership of Norwegian church resistance to Nazis.

American Lutheran Emergency Appeal for Orphaned Missions.

1941   Bombing of Pearl Harbor; the United States enters World War II.

Lutheran World Action appeals begin for wartime services to military personnel, orphaned missions, refugees, and prisoners of war.

1942   Death of Lars W. Boe, December.

1944   LWC American Section's postwar planning for survey of European needs and appointment of Geneva representative, January.

Allies land in Normandy, D-Day, June 6.

Assassination attempt on Hitler, July 20. Arrests include Hanns Lilje.

1945   American Lutheran fact-finding team to England, Sweden, and Switzerland, February–April (Peter O. Bersell, Ralph H. Long, Lawrence Meyer).

Allied victory in Europe, May.

Sylvester C. Michelfelder is American Lutheran representative in Geneva, July.

August Marahrens resigns presidency of LWC, October 31.

Second Lutheran team (Franklin Clark Fry, Johan A. Aasgaard, Ralph H. Long) to Europe, November–December.

Unofficial meeting of LWC executive committee in Copenhagen, December 16–17.

Erling Eidem elected temporarily to replace Marahrens.

Treysa (German Church) Conference, August 27–September.

1946   First official postwar LWC executive committee meets in Uppsala, July 24–26. August Marahrens's resignation officially accepted; Erling Eidem elected president; Hanns Lilje's resignation accepted; Sylvester C. Michelfelder elected secretary of the committee. Abdel Ross Wentz's draft of Lutheran World Federation constitution received. Confessional representation in World Council of Churches pressed. Decision to hold First Assembly of LWF in Lund in summer of 1947.

1947   August Marahrens resigns as bishop of Hannover; Hanns Lilje succeeds him.

LWC executive committee meets in Lund, June 28–29. Lilje elected to the committee. Agenda for the LWF assembly approved, including constitutional draft.

First Assembly of the Lutheran World Federation, in Lund, June 30–July 6. Adoption of constitution with amendments; election of Anders Nygren to succeed Erling Eidem as president; election of Sylvester C. Michelfelder as executive secretary.

THE RISE OF
WORLD LUTHERANISM

Introduction

The story of the birth and early life of what we now call global Lutheranism is intensely dramatic and immensely complicated. The dramatis personae alone is formidable. As in a nineteenth-century Russian novel, the characters move in and out in such numbers that they leave one bewildered and exhausted. To be sensitive to the drama without losing the thread of the plot as it unfolds through the centuries places heavy demands on the historian's ability to reconstruct the past imaginatively while simultaneously reporting the data uncovered by research. The task is to establish each event in relationship to antecedent events and at the same time to interpret each event as in some way reflecting the impingement of the contemporary milieu. This kind of undertaking is, of course, fraught with the dangers of romantic subjectivism and the vulnerability of even the most painstaking research.

The circumstances affecting Lutheranism from the time of the Reformation to the present are complex, perhaps even unique. It is our hope that, in attempting to unravel the tangled threads, the story can be told so that the inherent drama will become self-evident and the complexities an exciting detective narrative.

Since the Reformation there has been no internationally structured Lutheran church, only Lutheran churches resulting from geographical and political barriers, the emigration of Europeans to the New World, and the establishment of indigenous churches in the Third World. The sixteenth century gave rise to the religio-political agreement *cuius regio eius religio* ("whose the region, his the religion," or the religion of the sovereign is the religion of the people). The churches within the cultural barriers of their historical origins therefore developed their own ethos and cultivated their own idiosyncrasies, so that Saxon

1

Lutherans had no structural ties to Hannoverian Lutherans, Bavarian Lutherans were strangers to Pomeranian Lutherans, and Scandinavian Lutherans were unrelated structurally not only to German Lutherans but also to one another. In urging loyalty to their own political rulers, the churches, often unconsciously, were influenced by rivalries with neighboring kings and rulers. This, in turn, accounted for the growing tensions between politically aggressive Prussia and a German kingdom like Hannover and a non-German kingdom like Denmark, and the bitterness of the Norwegians resulting from Norway's forcible separation from Denmark and transfer to the Swedish crown in 1814 by the post-Napoleonic European powers.

Crossing the Atlantic in search of "freedom" in the New World, the European emigrants carried with them many of the fetters that characterized their life in the Old World. Their traditional cultural and ecclesiastical insularity was compounded by new problems emerging on the frontier. The fundamental fact, however, is that certain intangible ties gave a "spiritual" unity to Lutherans. Foremost among these was the theological content of the Lutheran confessions. There was also the fact that they expressed their piety, individual and corporate, in similar ways, and that they responded to the secular world with basically the same missionary and ethical motives. This spiritual unity was nurtured by the circulation of theological literature and the power of a common liturgical and hymnological tradition translated from the homeland of the Reformation.

Content with spiritual unity, Lutherans on both sides of the Atlantic saw no need for an international ecclesiastical framework to provide a forum for the multilingual and geographically separated churches to address common problems, to express interdependence, and to cooperate in achieving goals defined by the evangelical legacy bequeathed to all of them by Luther's *theologia crucis*. In fact, the word "church" was limited empirically to local congregations and national bodies— "St. John's Church" or "the Church of Sweden," for example. Globally the concept "church" was a Platonic reality whose "shadows" appeared parochially and nationally. Without regarding the strong confessional warning against the heresy of "dreaming" of the church as a Platonic "idea," and neglectful of the affirmation that "this church actually exists, made up of true believers and righteous men scattered throughout the world,"[1] this ecclesiological idealism has persisted as a stubborn ingredient of inter-Lutheran relations into the 1980s. This is clearly evident in American Lutheranism, where in some quarters "spiritual" unity is heralded as the justification for corporate independence and disunity. The distinction between unity and union comes close to saying that unity is of God, union is of man. The latter, it is argued, can be "negotiated, and, if desired, postponed by men."[2]

The problem of structural Lutheran unity was compounded by the shattering effect of two world wars in the twentieth century. Perhaps no religious body was as grievously wounded by these two horrors as the Lutheran family. One need only recall the strong anti-German sentiment in America during World War I, and similar feeling in Scandinavia during and after World War II. But it was the two wars which astonishingly became the instruments that finally gave birth to a global Lutheran self-consciousness that in time produced the Lutheran World Federation, thus transcending four hundred years of discrete existence. However, the development of a full-orbed Lutheran ecclesiology remains unfinished business in this last quarter of the twentieth century. Corroborating witness to this fact has been the nervous reluctance to recognize the ecclesial dimension of Lutheranism at the global level.

Except for Chapter 1, the book is arranged chronologically. Chapter 1 introduces the reader to "the end," the establishment of the Lutheran World Federation in 1947.[3] The remaining chapters deal with Lutheran unity movements in Europe and America and how they

---

1. See "Apology of the Augsburg Confession," in *The Book of Concord*, trans. and ed. Theodore G. Tappert (Philadelphia: Fortress Press, 1958), p. 171.

2. The difficulty seems to lie in the inability of some church leaders to deal with the dialectical relationships that pervade the topics of Lutheran theology. For example: one must distinguish between Holy Scripture and the word of God but not separate them; one must distinguish between faith and works, justification and sanctification, but not separate them; one must distinguish between the kingdom of God and the church, but not separate them; one must distinguish between the body of Christ and the empirical church, but not separate them; one must distinguish between spiritual unity and corporate union, but not separate them.

3. In Chapter 1, I have tried to employ the common literary device of previewing the end at the beginning. The New Testament, for example, sees the story of Israel, notably the Exodus, in the light of the "exodus" accomplished by Christ (Luke 9:31). The new Exodus helps us understand the ancient Exodus. It was a British theologian—Alan Richardson, I believe—who observed that all understanding of our past involves seeing the significance of the beginning from the end.

were to converge after World War I; preparations for the Eisenach conference and the formation of the Lutheran World Convention in 1923; the second world assembly at Copenhagen in 1929 and the third convention in Paris in 1935; world Lutheranism in the Nazi era; World War II and the postwar reconstruction leading to the transformation of the Lutheran World Convention into the Lutheran World Federation. The study interprets topics and events as they appear in the chronicle. A brief Epilogue raises the question of the federation's self-understanding as it anticipated the future after the Lund assembly in 1947.

1

The Lutheran World Assembly: Lund 1947

The time was ten o'clock, Monday morning, June 30, 1947. The place was Cathedral Square, Lund, Sweden. The occasion was the constituting convention of the Lutheran World Federation (LWF). Many may have been recalling a somewhat similar event twenty-four years earlier: Eisenach 1923, and the formation of the Lutheran World Convention (LWC) by churchmen who had yearned for a worldwide communion of Lutherans. The years between 1923 and 1947 had spawned immense problems for all Christians, and Lutherans gathering now at Lund were hoping to revive and reshape the Lutheran World Convention, which had almost been destroyed by the experiences of a global economic depression, the fascination of disillusioned peoples with the ideologies of Communism, Fascism, and Nazism, and the horrors of a second world war. These were stark realities that would have to be addressed. Eivind Berggrav of Oslo, the primate of Norway, assessed the postwar situation in a paradoxical and prophetic manner shortly after Lund: "It is not likely that there will be a new war, but there will be no peace. We shall for years to come have a non-war, always anxiety, no security, every day a new fear. We do not know where it is to end."[1]

Approximately six hundred delegates and visitors from more than thirty nations were assembled. The well-dressed and well-fed Swedes and Americans, having read and heard much about the effects of war

1. Eivind Berggrav, "Only the Shooting Has Stopped," *The Lutheran*, July 23, 1947, p. 13.

upon the minds and bodies of people, expected to see the representatives from the war-stricken countries exhibiting emaciated bodies and shabby clothing. Although enough of the marks of struggle and survival remained to provoke thoughtful compassion among Americans and others, the massive programs of relief and rehabilitation had already begun to take hold. This was evident in many of the delegates from Germany, Scandinavia, and Eastern Europe, who revealed a buoyant spirit of joy and gratitude that transformed, without erasing, the reminders of profound suffering. Although ill-dressed, several of the clergymen carried battered handbags that contained their "Sunday best" clothes, the solemn and dignified black suits which had lasted them through the war years. They had worn them now at the opening service of Holy Communion in the Lund cathedral.

Erling Eidem, archbishop of Uppsala, having been elected chairman of the executive committee of the Lutheran World Convention in 1946, began the sermon at that service by quoting from Colossians: "Put on then, as God's chosen ones, holy and beloved, compassion, kindness, lowliness, meekness, and patience, forbearing one another . . . and forgiving each other; as the Lord has forgiven you, so you also must forgive. And above all these put on love, which binds everything together in perfect harmony" (3:12–14). The preacher continued: "We are truly brothers. . . . Of this [Christ] reminds us, when He today invites us to partake of the Sacrament of His Body and His Blood."[2] The text and sermon were clearly directed to the sensitive situation of 1947.

Following the service the delegates and visitors gathered at high noon in the Great Hall of the Academic Union as chimes sounded from the cathedral's magnificent fourteenth-century clock, *Horologium mirabile Lundense*. The tune was that of the medieval Christmas hymn "In Dulci Jubilo," and as it played, carved figures of the Three Kings emerged to greet the Christ. It was Christmas in midsummer, a fortuitous reminder that the name which drew men and women together from all corners of the world was Immanuel, God-with-us. Despite the long years of war that had divided the world so bitterly and Lutherans so tragically, here was a sign, a portent of a new

2. *The Lutheran*, July 16, 1947, p. 4.

opportunity for the church. Even the weather smiled on the assembly. The warmth of midsummer—the Scandinavians had just celebrated St. Hans's Day—was a welcome contrast to the severity of the past winter, when Siberian winds and bitter cold had plunged millions of people into untold suffering.

When the chimes in the cathedral had concluded their jubilant rendition of "Now Sing We, Now Rejoice," Erling Eidem stood at the chairman's place in the Great Hall, clapped his hands, and called the assembly to order. He made a brief address of welcome in which he applied the moving words of 1 Peter 1:3–7 to the event that was now unfolding. The text spoke of faith and hope, and the divine love in which they were rooted: "God begat us again to a living hope. . . . Ye have been put to grief in manifold trials, that the proof of your faith . . . may be found unto praise and glory. . . ." As always, God was speaking to people in their existential situation; therefore, the archbishop, as prophet, pastor, and minister of God, used these words to underscore the profound significance of the moment. The fact that the years since the last convention (Paris 1935) had been marked by "war, destruction and bloodshed, violence, torture and oppression, hate, lying-propaganda, and enmity" made it important for the assembly to proclaim that Christ "is stronger than all the powers of darkness." This evangelical confession, at the heart of the Lutheran heritage, was a powerful reminder that Lutherans belonged together in order to make this confession with one voice. But, the archbishop warned, "any Lutheran egotism" must not be allowed to foster "indifference toward our Christian sister churches." Moreover, he said, the assembly must not entertain unrealistic expectations, "either in the form of declarations of principle or in the solving of many practical problems." Nonetheless, this assembly must be viewed as "a beginning to which God would give His blessing."[3]

Despite the hectic details and pleasant confusion of getting a large

---

3. The full text of Eidem's "Address of Welcome" and "Communion Sermon" is in *Proceedings of the Lutheran World Federation . . . Lund, Sweden, June 30 –July 6, 1947* (Philadelphia: United Lutheran Publication House, 1948), pp. 109–14 (hereafter referred to as *Proceedings . . . Lund . . . 1947*). One of the American church papers observed that this assembly was the first large world gathering of Christians open to the public press. The comment was not a boastful marking of a "first" but rather a stress on openness and necessary publicity in facing world problems. *The Lutheran*, July 23, 1947, p. 5.

convention under way, the assembly acted with dispatch to bring "The Lutheran World Federation" into official existence by the adoption on July 1 of the proposed constitution.[4] This action was described later by Abdel Ross Wentz as "a turning point in the history of world Lutheranism."[5]

Two addresses by Americans quickly focused the attention of delegates and visitors on the paramount issues with which world Lutheranism had heretofore been struggling and which the years since 1939 had served to exacerbate in a calamitous way. These two presentations, summarized below, launched the assembly into consideration of its theme and overarching concern, "The Lutheran Church in the World Today."

The first address was the official report of the executive secretary, Sylvester C. Michelfelder, and the second was the keynote speech by Ralph H. Long, executive director of the National Lutheran Council and member of the American Section of the Lutheran World Convention, New York. Both speakers looked back to the origins of the Lutheran World Convention at Eisenach and surveyed the intervening years. If Lutherans at Lund were to approach their common problems with intelligence as well as compassion, they seemed to say, they must recognize that virtually every issue before them had its own history. In other words, despite the holocaust of World War II, Lund was not a beginning *de novo*. Ever since the difficult days following World War I, certain specific problems had surfaced and continued to clamor for attention. The external circumstances had obviously altered during the past quarter century, but the basic issues remained as the working agenda for Lund. It is this fact that emerges with astonishing clarity when one reads the reports and resolutions of Lund over against Lund's prehistory, the account of Lutherans seeking to work together in an international organization whose arms embraced peoples and their needs around the world. The story will show that some of these basic issues were addressed in a grand fashion, others with hesitation and even extreme caution, and still others with ambivalence.

From the vantage point of the present, an observer can perceive that

---

4. *Proceedings . . . Lund . . . 1947*, p. 21.
5. *The Encyclopedia of the Lutheran Church*, ed. Julius Bodensieck (Minneapolis: Augsburg Publishing House, 1965), 2:1425.

the issues were identified in the official proceedings, notably in the reports of Michelfelder and Long, the reports of the three discussion sections, and in post-Lund reflections by churchmen who had participated in the assembly. By looking at these records the "red threads" of specifically Lutheran concerns, in seeking to be a global fellowship marked by evangelical fidelity, are readily evident.[6]

The first issue was what Michelfelder called "a real desire throughout the Lutheran Church of the whole world for fellowship and unity." This desire had expressed itself at Eisenach (1923), Copenhagen (1929), and Paris (1935). Since World War II it had emerged again in an official proposal to adopt a constitutional draft reorganizing the former Lutheran World Convention (which purposely had no constitution) into a new structure to be called "The Lutheran World Federation." Unity was an important consideration at Eisenach, but a firm structural expression of that unity was not deemed an urgent necessity until 1947.

The second issue was "the rescue of the needy who had suffered from the war." Once again this was not a new problem. After World War I, American Lutherans had energetically sought to dramatize the plight of the peoples all but crushed by the dislocations that characterized the economic, political, and moral scene of the 1920s. With eyes on Poland, Russia, and Germany, Lutherans sought to consolidate their strengths in hopes of ministering effectively to their co-religionists in Europe as well as in the so-called orphaned missions of Africa and Asia. A quarter century later, at Lund, Michelfelder could say, "No Protestant church in Europe has suffered so much as our own Lutheran churches in Norway, Finland, Denmark, Poland, Czechoslovakia, Austria, Hungary, Romania, Yugoslavia, France, Holland, Italy, and Germany." And what he said was undeniably true. Billions of dollars of value had been wiped out by the destruction of church properties. Even more overwhelming was the problem posed by ten

---

6. Sylvester C. Michelfelder, "Report of the Executive Secretary, June 30, 1947," in *Proceedings . . . Lund . . . 1947*, pp. 35–41; Ralph H. Long, "The Place of the Lutheran World Federation in the World Today," in ibid., pp. 125–39; "Report of Sections," in ibid., pp. 44–92; G. Elson Ruff, "Questions Were Answered at Lund," *The Lutheran*, October 22, 1947, pp. 17–20; and Thaddaeus F. Gullixson, "Achievements at Lund in Retrospect after One Year," *Lutheran Church Quarterly* 21 (October 1948): 383–86.

million war refugees and displaced persons. Relief, resettlement, rehabilitation—these were key words. Although the needs of 1947 were staggering, they were not totally new.

The third issue addressed at Lund was likewise familiar, but now it manifested itself with a new importunity. The modern ecumenical movement—a plant whose roots were deep in the missionary soil of the nineteenth century and whose blossoms began to appear at the famous World Missionary Conference at Edinburgh in 1910—forced Lutherans to ask such questions as "What is the relation between confessional particularity and ecumenical universality?" and "What are 'the essentials of a catholic spirit'?" and "Will Lutheran identity be eroded by participation in the ecumenical movement?" At Eisenach, Ludwig Ihmels of Saxony had spoken on the topic "The Ecumenical Character of the Lutheran Church." The president of the United Lutheran Church, Frederick H. Knubel, had sounded the same theme in his lecture "That They All May Be One—What Can the Lutheran Church Contribute to This End?"

Thus, from 1910 to 1947 the ecumenical question was never far from the deliberations and thoughts of the church's leaders and theologians. The executive committee of the Lutheran World Convention, meeting at New York in 1936, drafted a remarkable document entitled "Lutherans and Ecumenical Movements."[7] Stressing both universality ("the one holy catholic and apostolic church") and particularity (Lutheran confessional identity), the statement provided guidelines for wholehearted participation in the ecumenical movement on the basis of the evangelical consciousness that permeated the Lutheran confessions. Of special note was the fact that this vigorous support of *confessional identity* within the ecumenical community emerged from the leadership of the United Lutheran Church, often labeled "the liberal wing" of American Lutheranism.

At Lund in 1947, in full consciousness that the World Council of Churches ("in process of formation") would be holding its constituting assembly at Amsterdam in 1948, Lutherans had thus equipped themselves for genuine participation and confessional presence in the

7. *The Lutheran World Almanac and Encyclopedia 1934–1937* (New York: NLC, 1937), 36–38. The statement was largely the work of Abdel Ross Wentz of Gettysburg Seminary, and Hanns Lilje, executive secretary of the LWC.

ecumenical movement. This is why lecturers at Lund could say sincerely, "Our provincialism must come to an end" (Michelfelder) and "We must not apply a Lutheran egotism toward our sister churches" (Eidem). At the same moment, and with the same sincerity and without inconsistency, they would state that "the Lutheran Church must witness to 'The Truth' as never before. . . .We will not surrender our [confessions] for any temporary advantages no matter how tempting they may be" (Michelfelder) and that "those who oppose the consolidation of churches of the same faith are not truly ecumenical" (Long). Thus, for world Lutherans the issue of ecumenism stretched back at least to 1923 and perhaps further. Certainly Lund was neither a gathering of ecumenical "enthusiasts" nor an assembly of "triumphalists" genuflecting before the statue of Luther and waving the flag of "ultraconfessionalism."

No doubt there were other ecclesio-theological issues in the prologue to Lund, but we must now take note of the fact that the era of 1923–47 was characterized by attitudes as well as issues. In fact, attitudes and issues were often so intertwined that distinctions are difficult to make. Nonetheless, it is quite clear today that foremost among the attitudes were certain *fears* harbored by persons in all the churches—fears, suspicions, and even hatreds that the offal from years of isolation, warfare, national pride, and idiosyncratic theological traditionalism served to fertilize. As we shall see, these fears were acutely present in the LWC years 1923, 1929, and 1935. And it was recognized that the era of World War II did nothing to lessen an apprehensive attitude. For example, a group of Americans aboard ship on the way to Lund found themselves musing about such potentially enervating and divisive fears as hypernationalism, exclusivist confessionalism, and strident Americanism.[8]

We are seeking to point out that just as there was a continuity between Eisenach and Lund in the realm of issues and ideas, so there was a continuity in the realm of emotions, attitudes, and fears. The fears were to some degree overblown, but nevertheless they were smolderingly present. Neither Eisenach nor Lund, nor the intervening years, was able to remove persisting apprehensions about a potentially

8. *The Lutheran*, October 22, 1947, pp. 18–19.

imperialistic world Lutheranism; and neither were they able to quiet the anxious concerns that some churches entertained about other churches. A few of these fears deserve mention.

First, there was the fear of an international organization. Most often expressed by Americans, but not limited to them, this attitude led the early leaders of the "world Lutheran movement" (as it was often referred to by John A. Morehead, Lars W. Boe, and Frederick H. Knubel) to seek to remove or circumvent the fear by asserting that the planned conference in Eisenach would be a one-time, nonrecurring convention. We shall seek to identify the causes of this fear later on, but for the time being it should be noted that some American church leaders were voicing reservations about an international ecclesiastical organization at the same time that American politicians were undercutting Woodrow Wilson's dream of a League of Nations.

Although the pressures of circumstances led to a jettisoning of the "nonrecurring event" concept, the hesitations about a Lutheran "superchurch" with headquarters in Geneva were only partially hidden in the constitutional definition of 1947. The Lutheran World Federation was to be an agency, "a free association of Lutheran churches" (Article III, 1). The implicit assertion in the explicit definition makes it clear that for the founding fathers only a local congregation and a national body possessed an ecclesiological character. The fear of granting churchly significance to a world organization, like so many other fears, was not only irrational but also hardly consistent with the Lutheran doctrine of the nature of the church. Nevertheless, prominent leaders from 1923 through 1947 to the present were saying, "The Lutheran World Federation . . . is and must remain 'a free association of Lutheran churches.' "[9]

Second, there was a fear of nationalism. Prior to Eisenach, nationalistic interests were frequently seen to be thwarting attempts to reconcile or to transcend traditional antagonisms. How could Poles, Germans, and Frenchmen sit at the same table? Germans were wondering out loud how long they would have to suffer the indignities of the Versailles Treaty and to what depths Frenchmen and Americans might push them in their insistence on "war guilt." Germans feared that

9. Thaddaeus F. Gullixson, *Lutheran Church Quarterly* 21 (October 1948): 386.

world Lutheranism would be "an American show," while Americans feared that world Lutheranism would suffocate from German theology. And Scandinavians, divided by their own nationalisms, had neither the desire nor the aggressive skills to dominate any world organization.

By 1947 the nationalisms were surging with unmitigated power. The bitterness and cruelty of Nazi occupation of Poland, France, Holland, Czechoslovakia, Austria, Denmark, and Norway were not easily set aside. Moreover, German memories of Allied bombing of places like Berlin, Hamburg, and Dresden could not be buried beneath the rubble. The haunting question among many at Lund was "Can the fellowship of faith transcend the scars of war?" Fortunately, at Lund the attitude of recrimination was almost totally absent when the non-Germans met their wartime enemies; likewise, it should be noted that German delegates, meeting at Hamburg on the way to Lund, had agreed they would not talk about their concerns unless they were asked.[10] Thus the long-feared confrontation that might tear world Lutheranism further apart was avoided.

A third fear was theological in nature. Ever since before Eisenach, some Europeans, especially the Swedes, had looked upon the Lutheran World Convention as an agency for theologically illiterate Americans to mobilize the forces of Lutheran conservatism and thus to build a bastion of confessional imperialism with a worldwide scope. Exhibit A, it was said, was the absence of any front-rank theologian in the formation of plans for a world Lutheran movement. Some Danish Lutherans, who liked to think of their church as a folk church, were not acutely conscious of their church as "Lutheran" and tended to ally themselves with the Swedes, who thought in a similar vein. The Norwegians, almost totally preoccupied with internal theological conflict, were less-than-interested spectators. The German Lutherans, by virtue of their history, were divided between "self-conscious Lutherans" and "Union Lutherans," but on the whole they gave support to a confessionally oriented international Lutheranism. The Americans, though lacking any theological giants, were not to be reckoned as theological babes-in-the-woods whose lack of sophistica-

10. *The Lutheran,* October 8, 1947, p. 13.

tion would force them to desire a mighty international fortress from within which they could parrot "Lutheranism" without being challenged. This image of Americans hardly corresponded to reality. As a matter of fact, it was the allegedly "liberal" Eastern American Lutherans who pushed for an international expression of Lutheranism, not as a defensive alliance but as an evangelically confessional voice within the church catholic. But the Americans did have some real fears. They had witnessed the erosion of Reformation theology in the Anglo-American Protestant tradition; they had watched the bitter struggle between fundamentalists and modernists; and they wondered how long evangelical Lutheranism could survive in the land of religious liberty without being unequivocally confessional. Therefore, they looked expectantly for support from their fellow Lutherans in Central and Northern Europe. It was a great and mighty reassurance to them when at Lund the new president of the Lutheran World Federation urged not a retreat to "safety" but a forward movement to a new look at Luther. Anders Nygren said: "Now the great question arises as to whether the Lutheran Church can recover its original testimony, or if she can speak only in secularized terms. Our task is clear: we must give testimony of the Gospel—Luther's testimony—to the present world. This, therefore, must be our watchword: 'Always forward toward Luther.' "[11]

Nygren's concern lest the church speak "only in secularized terms" must be related to what a moment earlier he had designated "the spirit of secularization." He saw the secularization of the church as beginning with the loss of early Christianity's transcendent, eschatological perspective. By the time of the Enlightenment the "Lutheran Church also . . . lost its eschatological dynamic." Its theology and preaching, he declared, had been drawn into the general process of secularization.

Although Nygren and others optimistically asserted that World War II had demonstrated the bankruptcy of secularism, its demise was greatly exaggerated. Despite this misjudgment, Nygren's picture of the corrosive power of secularism was accurate. In recognition of this, theologians since the nineteenth century had used "secularism" as an

11. *Proceedings . . . Lund . . . 1947*, p. 140.

umbrella term to cover a whole mélange of threatening "isms," the ascendancy of any one of which led quite naturally to a new fear. Therefore, in concluding this prologue, it is appropriate to mention a few of the "isms" under secularism that church leaders assessed as genuine occasions for fear. One was, of course, theological liberalism, with its secularization of the biblical theme of "the kingdom of God." Many Lutherans considered this a genuine cause for alarm and resisted everything that had the odor of liberalism, including the "liberal" rejection of verbal inspiration and inerrancy of the Bible. This, of course, was far from Nygren's 1947 denouncement of the de-eschatologizing of the New Testament, and, likewise, it was hardly in the mind of Charles M. Jacobs in 1923, when he drafted the Eisenach statement on the authority of the Holy Scriptures. But despite dubious definitions and unwarranted extensions of the term "liberalism," it constituted a genuine fear.

Secularism had other identifying marks, and these were likewise judged fearsome. There was, for example, the fear of aggressive political ideologies. In the early 1920s it was Marxist communism ("Bolshevism"). In the 1930s and 1940s it was Hitlerite Nazism. And in the years after World War II it was once again Marxism. The materialism that marked American culture in the so-called Roaring Twenties and the unabashed hedonism of Berlin and Hamburg during the unheroic days of the Weimar Republic were not the fantasies of pietistic and puritanical imaginations. They were only too real. At Lund this fear of secularism no doubt lay behind the words of Michelfelder: "The world is aflame . . . materialism, secularism, nihilism, and new 'isms' are declaring war on the Christian Church. . . . There must be a clear sound of the trumpet and fearless advance to meet the foe."[12]

The purpose of the introductory survey above is to alert the reader that the prehistory of the Lutheran World Federation is the history of the Lutheran World Federation writ small. To use a Dickensian phrase, "not to put too fine a point on it," the ecclesio-theological issues and emotional attitudes present in the pre- and post-Eisenach

---

12. Ibid., p. 39.

(1923) era moved in and out of the story to its *terminus ad quem,* Lund (1947). For this reason we can without strain or affectation inscribe over the First Assembly of the Lutheran World Federation the words "What is past is prologue."

We turn now to look with American eyes and biases to the origins of "the world Lutheran movement" and to examine its fortunes through the more than half a century that experienced World War I, the economic stranglehold of the Great Depression, the power of international and national socialism, the vast devastation of World War II, and the monstrous birth of the Nuclear Age.

2

The European Roots of International Lutheranism

The emergence of Lutheranism in the context of rising nationalism in the late Middle Ages has often been noted. For four hundred years after the Reformation, Lutherans lived apart from one another as well as from other Christians—Protestants, Roman Catholics, and Eastern Orthodox. Ultimately, however, politically and ecclesiastically separated Lutherans on both sides of the Atlantic gradually came to the conviction that an international expression of Lutheranism was desirable. The events leading to the First Assembly of the Lutheran World Convention in Eisenach in 1923 illuminate the circumstances and processes by which the two strands of Lutherans—European and American—were brought together. In order to understand the shape of subsequent events, it appears wise to begin with an examination of Lutheranism in Europe.

THE ROLE OF LUTHER IN THE POST-REFORMATION ERA

During the summer of 1971, a short trip through East Germany brought the writer to Dresden, a historical cultural center featuring museums, opera, theater, and architecture on a grand scale. He had read about the splendor of the *Frauenkirche,* built originally in the thirteenth century and completely redone in Renaissance baroque between 1726 and 1738 by the renowned architect Georg Bähr. The octagonal structure, with a dome fashioned after St. Peter's in Rome, was described by its detractors as "that religious opera house." It was nevertheless in one sense a remarkable symbol of a society and culture

Dresden, Germany, 1945: The Reitschel statue of Martin Luther, at the site of the Frauenkirche, survived the Allied bombing of the city in February.

---

that seemed so permanent in 1900. At the end of World War I, the colossal edifice remained unscarred, but only as a monument to a past grandeur. In 1971 when he sought it out, camera in hand, the writer knew that the massive British and American firebombing of Dresden in February 1945 had reduced that church building and most of the city to a vast pile of rubble beneath which many of the 135,000 dead were buried. (The atom bomb at Hiroshima killed 75,000.)[1] By a strange happenstance the heroic Reitschel statue of Martin Luther (erected in 1885) which stood in front of the *Frauenkirche* had survived the fourteen hours and ten minutes of exploding horror raining down from above the cloud cover. Thus it came about that the

1. For accounts of the *Frauenkirche* and Dresden before and after World War II see Leo Woerl, ed., *Illustrierter Führer . . . Dresden* (Leipzig: Woerls Reisebücherverlag, 1909); Sophus Ruge, *Dresden und die Sächsische Schweiz* (Bielefeld and Leipzig: Velhagen & Klasing, 1913); and David Irving, *The Destruction of Dresden* (New York: Holt, Rinehart & Winston, 1964).

lens of the writer's camera was focused not on a building. not on a grass- and weed-covered mound of rubble, but on a statue that stood as a forlorn figure in a Communist-ruled city.

Some might be inclined to interpret this as a symbol of hope or as a reminder of a voice crying in the wilderness. Surely that is one way of viewing the phenomenon; it is especially attractive, of course, to those seeking homiletical aids and eschatological interpretations. However, it seems more appropriate for our purposes to see the statue's survival not so much as a sign of divine protection—there must have been hundreds of Luther statues destroyed—as an accidental reminder of the immense prestige of Luther's personality. Goethe once said, "The Germans were no nation till the time of Luther."[2] Luther's statue and his face were as familiar in Germany as George Washington's and Abraham Lincoln's are in America. But Luther was more than a national figure; he was a religious hero. Despite his oft-quoted disclaimer ("I pray you leave my name alone, and do not call yourselves Lutherans but evangelicals"), the dissident Catholics in Germany of the First Reich[3] came to be called Lutherans shortly after the Reformation.[4]

The history of what to call the renewed church of the Reformation documents an oscillation between the words "evangelical" and "Lutheran." It is necessary to review the long and complicated story if the reader is not to be bewildered by what may seem to be pettiness and even arrogance on the part of those involved and needless inclusion of extraneous materials on the part of the writer. It is doubly needful to understand sympathetically the emergence of the specifically *Lutheran* world community alongside the modern ecumenical movement and the German church struggle against Hitler. In the decades and centuries that followed the creative events of the Reformation, the

2. Quoted by Heinrich Bornkamm, *Luther und der deutsche Geist* (Tübingen: J. C. B. Mohr, 1934), p. 15.

3. The First Reich lasted from Charlemagne (800) through Charles V to 1806, when Napoleon destroyed the last remnants of the Holy Roman Empire of the Germans. The Second Reich was the handiwork of Otto von Bismarck and was officially proclaimed in 1871 and destroyed by the Allies in 1918. The Third Reich, created by Hitler in 1933, was destroyed in 1945.

4. "Lutheran" was a *Schimpfname* (a term of jest or insult) that Catholics used in referring to the evangelicals. The confessions shun the name "Lutheran," preferring "evangelical" or "churches of the Augsburg Confession." See *Die Religion in Geschichte und Gegenwart*, 3d ed. (Tübingen, 1957–65), 4:531–32.

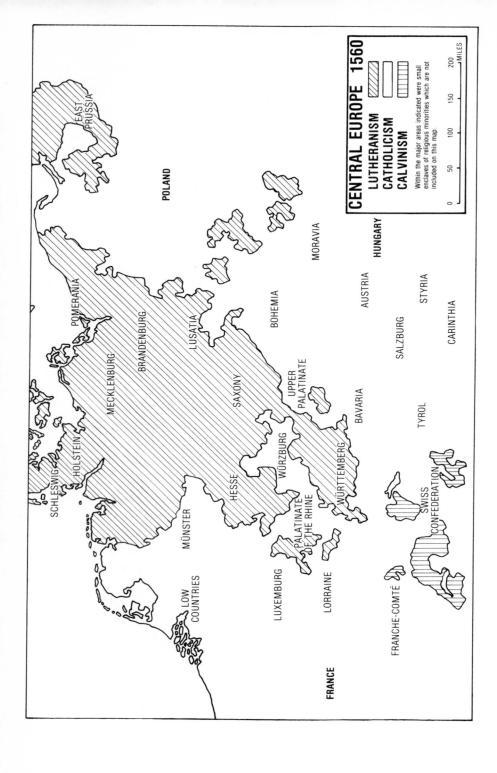

CENTRAL EUROPE 1560

LUTHERANISM

CATHOLICISM

CALVINISM

Within the major areas indicated were small enclaves of religious minorities which are not included on this map.

0   50   100   150   200
MILES

EAST PRUSSIA

POLAND

POMERANIA

MECKLENBURG

BRANDENBURG

LUSATIA

SCHLESWIG

HOLSTEIN

MÜNSTER

SAXONY

BOHEMIA

MORAVIA

AUSTRIA

HUNGARY

SALZBURG

STYRIA

CARINTHIA

HESSE

WÜRZBURG

UPPER PALATINATE

BAVARIA

TYROL

SWISS CONFEDERATION

WÜRTTEMBERG

PALATINATE OF THE RHINE

LUXEMBURG

LORRAINE

FRANCHE-COMTÉ

LOW COUNTRIES

FRANCE

Lutherans were bedeviled by wars, theological controversies on three fronts, and church-state problems that threatened the continuing vitality and integrity of the Reformer's cause.

TERRITORIAL CONFESSIONALISM

The use of the word "Lutheran" accelerated after the Peace of Augsburg (1555), when the legislative action of the Diet recognized as law the principle *cuius regio eius religio* ("whose the region, his the religion," or the religion of the sovereign is the religion of the people), which had been enunciated earlier at the Diet of Speyer (1526). This bit of ecclesio-imperial politics is usually noted as the origin of what came to be known as "territorial confessionalism," by which a particular "confession," either Catholic or Lutheran, became the juridical confession of the state, thereby greatly enhancing the churchly power of the prince. "Territorial confessionalism" and the role of the prince in church affairs were accepted with relative ease, because "territorialism" (not "confessional" territorialism) had existed in the German empire ever since the Golden Bull of 1356, which was regarded as the fundamental law for the conduct of imperial elections. In effect this meant that the pope and the curia in Rome, especially during the fifteenth century, realistically recognized that the future lay with the German territorial princes, and therefore permitted the growth of the Germanic *Eigenkirche* (the prince was the ruler in his "own church"). Territorialism was far advanced in Luther's Saxony, as witnessed by the power and influence of Elector Frederick the Wise, whom Gerhard Ritter describes as the archetypal "pious German prince" concerned about his own church.[5] "Territorialism" was a late medieval phenomenon that became "territorial *confessionalism*" only after Speyer (1526) and Augsburg (1555). Between 1555 and 1648 the only religions receiving imperial legitimacy were Lutheran and Catholic, but with the Peace of Westphalia (1648) at the end of the Thirty Years' War, the Calvinists ("Reformed") were likewise recognized.

5. Gerhard Ritter, *Die Neugestaltung Europas im 16. Jahrhundert* (Berlin: Verlag des Druckhauses Tempelhof, 1950), p. 60. Cf. Lewis W. Spitz, "Luther's Ecclesiology and His Concept of the Prince as *Notbischof*," *Church History* 22 (June 1953): 113–15. For a careful account of the medieval concept of *Eigenkirche* see *Die Religion in Geschichte und Gegenwart*, 2:356–57.

Of these far-reaching developments we underscore a few. First, the religio-political presupposition of the Holy Roman Empire, namely, the relationship of church and state as two sides of one coin, was in reality continued, but only on a national (e.g., Scandinavia) or territorial (Germany) basis. The principle of *cuius regio eius religio* had destroyed the medieval concept of "one church, one empire." The one imperial church and the one churchly empire were gone.

A second result was the grievous distortion of Luther's understanding of the evangelical nature of "confession/s." The "confession" for Luther was a dynamic act of witness to the gospel and thus a safeguard for the church in its proclamation. Hence the Augsburg Confession and other confessional statements were "the spirit-effected witness to the truth by brothers and fathers in the faith."[6] A confessional document, then, is to be understood in relation to the act of confessing the faith. The tragedy for Lutheranism was that the imperial edict gave a *legal* cast to the confessional documents. From 1555 they were "law," and as such they were in practice severed from the confessional act; the confessions had become juridical, political, constitutional documents whose validity rested on the power of human decree. Many of the confessional conflicts in subsequent decades and centuries were variations on the theme "evangelical" versus "legal."[7]

A third result of the imperial *cuius regio* principle for Lutherans was the unanticipated rigidity of subsequent ecclesiastical structure. When Luther turned to the evangelical princes of Germany and asked them to assume episcopal duties (e.g., the authorization and implementing of "visitations," the appointing of governing consistories and ecclesiastical superintendents, and the provision for general oversight), he did so with the firm conviction that they should be merely "emergency bishops" (*Notbischöfe*) as the leading lay persons in their territories. This was to be an ad hoc, flexible arrangement, intended

6. Friedrich W. Kantzenbach, "The Reformation's Power to Organize the Church and Confessional Lutheranism from 1530 to 1648," in *The Lutheran Church: Past and Present,* ed. Vilmos Vajta (Minneapolis: Augsburg Publishing House, 1977), p. 31.
7. One might think that the break with territorial confessionalism which occurred in America as a result of the First Amendment might have caused a return to Luther's concept of confession as an evangelical statement related to the act of confessing the faith. Confessional legalism, however, was often evident in the interpretation of the confessional article in denominational constitutions. The conflict in the Missouri Synod between 1959 and 1977 is a case in point.

only to bridge the difficult days of separation from Roman papal and episcopal authority. He reasoned that, given time, the evangelical church could and would set up its own episcopal government independent of secular authorities. Far from being an uncritical and obsequious subject of the prince to whom he would gladly surrender control of the churches, he pointed out very frankly that the elector [of Saxony] "is not commanded to teach and rule spiritually . . . ; as a secular ruler [he is] to maintain things so that . . . disorder does not arise among the subjects."[8] Luther made no attempt to disguise his awareness of the personal failings of many "Christian princes." He said in his justly famous tract "On Secular Authority" (1523) that genuinely pious princes were "rare birds"; they were most often "the biggest fools or the most crafty knaves on earth."[9] Moreover, he said, the great danger was that the secular lords sought to be popes and bishops, thus misusing their office and arrogating to themselves duties that God had not given them.[10]

However low Luther's opinion of rulers may have been, he did call on them to act as Christian brothers in that time of emergency. As often happens, the taste of ecclesiastical power served only to whet the appetites of the princes. Thus, when Luther died without having devised an ecclesiastical government in accordance with his evangelical concerns, the princes, armed with the *nihil obstat* of the imperial *cuius regio* principle ceased to be "emergency bishops" and took to themselves the title of *summus episcopus* (supreme bishop). This had the long-run effect of establishing a mode of relationship between church and state that persisted in Germany until the end of World War I and in Scandinavia until the present.[11]

A fourth result of the *cuius regio* principle was the rising problem of distinctions among the "evangelicals" after the Treaty of Westphalia in

---

8. "Instructions for the Visitors of Parish Pastors in Electoral Saxony," *Luther's Works*, American Edition (Philadelphia: [Muhlenberg] Fortress Press, 1958), 40:271–73.

9. *D. Martin Luthers Werke*, Kritische Gesamtausgabe (Weimar, 1883–), 11:263ff., 267–68. English translation in *Works of Martin Luther* (Philadelphia: A. J. Holman, 1930), 3:252–55, 257–58.

10. "Sermons on the Gospel of John," in *Luther's Works*, American Edition (St. Louis: Concordia Publishing House, 1957), 22:228.

11. Helpful discussions of these developments are found in Ivar Asheim and Victor Gold, eds., *Episcopacy in the Lutheran Church?* (Philadelphia: Fortress Press, 1970), chaps. 3, 4, 5. See also Andrew L. Drummond, *German Protestantism since Luther* (London: Epworth Press, 1951), pp. 173–277.

1648. The treaty, as noted, recognized both Lutherans and Calvinists; they were imperially legitimated representatives of the non-Roman evangelical churches. Prior to 1648 the term "evangelical" was used primarily as a designation for the followers of Luther. In common parlance the words "evangelical" and "Lutheran" were synonymous. Moreover, the desire of Luther to have the churches of the Reformation be known not as Lutheran but as Evangelical was consciously or unconsciously implemented. After 1648, however, with the imperial recognition of the Reformed church, the term "evangelical" was no longer equated with "Lutheran." It was broadened to mean Lutherans, Calvinists, and perhaps even the so-called "left wing" of the Reformation. All claimed to have been "liberated" from Rome by the gospel. But it was just at this point, namely, the use of the term "evangel," that problems arose. What is the evangel? And what is evangelical? And how do evangelicals safeguard the proclamation of the evangel? Lacking anything comparable to a Roman *magisterium* (i.e., teaching authority, the means of speaking to and for the whole church), the Lutherans and Calvinists utilized their confessional writings as instruments for identifying their particular understanding of the content of the evangel and as weapons in the seventeenth-century theological polemic that was waged between the two groups. It was not strange that the conflict within the evangelical ranks tended to sharpen the confessional differences, especially since both sides were using the Bible as an inerrant "paper pope," verbally inspired. The result for the Lutherans particularly was a genuine distaste for being lumped into an undifferentiated ecclesiastical mass known simply as "evangelicals." They therefore insisted, "We are indeed evangelicals, but we are *Lutheran* evangelicals."

THEOLOGY IN CONFLICT, 1600–1800

A major change in the religious, theological, and ecclesiastical climate occurred between 1600 and 1800. The traditional way to mark this change has been to describe the influence of pietism, rationalism, and the church-state relationship. Before sketching these influences, we must remind ourselves that the century following the Reformation is generally known as the Age of Scholastic Orthodoxism, both Protestant and Catholic. It is also known as the Age of Absolutism, when temporal authorities were accorded absolute powers. It was the age of the absolute authority of kings, the absolute authority of the pope and the church, the absolute authority of the Bible—forgetting that the only absolute is God.

In keeping with the climate of the age, Lutherans deemed it necessary to build a massive intellectual defense of their faith, the documents of which became the standards of orthodoxy. Simultaneously, Calvinists stressed their Calvinism, Catholics their Catholicism, and Anglicans their Anglicanism. In a short time two latently important religious groups would have to be added to this list: (1) the Anglo-American Puritans, who were concerned about the ecclesiological question "What is the true (pure) church?" and (2) the Anglo-American Methodists, who sought to revive the religious content of the word "evangelical." Thus the Western religious world was sharply differentiated confessionally.

Reaction to scholasticism and absolutism occurred in three eighteenth-century movements: religious pietism, theological rationalism, and politically encouraged ecumenism. Each served in its own way to blunt the confessional consciousness of the churches but did not achieve the desired church unity. Pietism, a movement of religious renewal, revolted against scholastic arguments, definitions, and orthodoxisms and encouraged experiential religion. Although it is true that the scholastic method of the seventeenth-century theologians tended to stifle religion and to support a rigid formalism, there were many individuals in the Age of Orthodoxy in whom the currents of personal religion ran deep. Not all had forgotten Luther's wisdom: "The heart of religion lies in its personal pronouns." This was evident in the magnificent hymnody of such prepietistic, orthodox Lutherans as Martin Rinkhart ("Now Thank *We* All *Our* God"), Paul Gerhard ("Oh How Shall *I* Receive Thee?"), and others. But pietism's pitting of "heart religion" against "head religion" naturally led to a disenchantment with the intellectualism of scholastic orthodoxy's dogmatic and legalistic confessionalism. Conclusion: it is better to be "evangelical" than "Lutheran." An earlier motto became popular: *"In necessariis unitas, in non necessariis libertas, in omnibus caritas"* (In essentials unity, in nonessentials liberty, in all things charity).[12] Many Lutherans, however, saw a danger in such an attitude. More and more they concluded that the word "evangelical" conveyed the sense of inclusiveness (pan-Protestantism) rather than precision of definition and concern for the theological content of the word. This was the genesis of a problem that was to reappear in the nineteenth century, when "neo-confessional" Lutherans who, like Luther, loved the word "evangelical," became restive and nervous about being classified simply as evangelicals.

The second movement that undercut Lutheran self-consciousness was the Enlightenment. Described by Ernst Troeltsch (1865–1923) as "Neo-Protestantism"—as differentiated from the "Old Protestantism" of the sixteenth and seventeenth centuries—this was an intellectually elitist movement that decried confessionalism of any kind. Evangelical Protestants as well as Roman Catholics were judged equally obscurantist. Pietistic "enthusiasts," scholastic orthodoxists (Lutheran or Calvinistic), and papal traditionalists all felt the withering scorn of the rationalists, who proclaimed "liberation" from the oppression of irrational dogma. Paradoxically, the Age of the Enlightenment produced its own brand of dogmatic orthodoxy called "natural religion" or "enlightened religion." The new religion maintained that its beliefs in "God, virtue, and immortality" should be universally acceptable because they were demonstrable by human reason. It was argued that just as Christianity in the ancient church found it necessary to Hellenize its doctrines, so contemporary Protestantism must allow itself to be refashioned by the elements of modern culture (*Kulturprotestantismus*). The teachings of "Old Protestantism" about revelation, biblical authority, sin and grace, and atonement and forgiveness were repugnant to modern people. Evangelicals were quick to point out that according to "enlightened religion," God was an impersonal, absentee lord, Jesus was an exemplar of virtue, and the human spirit—not the Holy Spirit—would lead into all truth. Thus the ranks of

---

12. This aphorism is ascribed to Peter Meiderlin (1582–1651), a German Lutheran theologian (pseudonym: Rupertus Meldenius) who was distressed by the controversies over orthodoxy. See *The New Schaff-Herzog Encyclopedia of Religious Knowledge* (New York, 1908–12), 7:287.

conservatives tended to close under rationalism's attack, but the overall effect of "enlightened Neo-Protestantism" was to minimize confessional particularity.[13]

PRINCES AND TERRITORIAL CHURCH UNITY

By the end of the eighteenth and the beginning of the nineteenth century, the pendulum that had been swinging between "evangelical" and "Lutheran" had settled for the moment on "evangelical." This is to say that, although the great strongholds of Lutheranism—like the German *Landeskirchen* (territorial churches) of Saxony, Hannover, Schleswig-Holstein, and Mecklenburg and the Scandinavian state churches—were constitutionally Lutheran, the influence of rationalism and to a lesser extent pietism dulled the confessional consciousness of these Lutheran churches. The French Revolution and the Napoleonic era altered the mood of the Western world to such an extent that by the time of the Congress of Vienna (1815) an era of "restorationism" was evident. The excesses of the earlier period gave way to a yearning for stability, peace, and the rule of law. Awareness of this new state of mind helps us to understand, for example, the Roman church's increasing sensitivity to nineteenth-century movements that seemed to be undercutting Catholic traditions and papal authority. The promulgation of the dogma of papal infallibility (1870) was the end result of the mood of Catholic "restorationism."

Lutheranism, like Catholicism, was simultaneously undergoing a resurgence of concern over its identity. Chief among the problems were the persistence of rationalism, the rise of idealist philosophy, the application of the historical-critical method in biblical study, the emergence of Marxism and Darwinism, and the rapid spread of secularism. Strangely enough, a new form of pietism, known in Germany as the *Erweckungsbewegung,* an "awakening," in which both Lutherans and Calvinists participated, proved to be the catalyst for a revived Lutheranism which was opposed to the two other major

13. For a brief but helpful discussion of the Troeltschian terminology "Old" and "Neo-Protestantism" see Theodore G. Tappert, "Neo-Protestantism," in *Twentieth-Century Encyclopedia of Religious Knowledge* (Grand Rapids: Baker, 1955), 2:792; cf. Gerhard Ritter, "Protestantism," in ibid., pp. 914–20.

institutional expressions of religion, Calvinism and Romanism. However, all three—Lutherans, Calvinists, and Romanists—found themselves on the same side against the other nineteenth-century movements that seemed to threaten classical Christianity: the new science, the Marxist theories, "Neo-Protestant" liberalism, and increasing secularism. Each church opposed these hostile forces by itself; common enemies did not produce common cause or joint action. For our purposes, however, it is well to note that a revival of Lutheran confessionalism occurred in this context.

An additional development contributing to the increase of Lutheran self-consciousness was the politically encouraged religious unity led largely by the rulers of Prussia, the Hohenzollern princes. The majority of the north and central German provinces were Lutheran, which, according to the *cuius regio* principle, meant that they had Lutheran rulers. Sooner or later, however, the question was to arise: What happens when a Lutheran territory suddenly finds itself without a Lutheran prince? What if the ruler is a Calvinist or perhaps even a Catholic? An instructive instance of this occurred in the strongly Lutheran province of Brandenburg-Prussia (after 1701 the kingdom of Prussia) ruled by the house of Hohenzollern.[14] As early as the seventeenth century, Elector John Sigismund (1572–1619) had become a Calvinist for military and political reasons. Despite the *cuius regio* principle, the elector wisely did not force his Lutheran constituency to follow him into the Reformed church. He was quite aware that his subjects, including his wife, Anna, would strenuously oppose attempts to Calvinize the domain. Nevertheless, the elector insisted that in addition to his own right to be a Calvinist, toleration be granted other Calvinists. Moreover, the Berlin Cathedral (the elector's church) would henceforth be Reformed, not Lutheran. These events indicated that a breach had now occurred in monolithic territorial confessionalism.

Although the Prussians remained Lutherans even under such strong Calvinist rulers as Elector Frederick William (1640–88), called "The

14. For a careful work on Prussia see J. A. R. Marriott and C. Grant Robertson, *The Evolution of Prussia* (London: Oxford University Press, 1917). Helpful articles on Brandenburg and Prussia are found in *Encyclopaedia Britannica*, 11th ed. (Cambridge: University Press, 1910) vols. 4 and 22.

Great Elector," and his son Frederick I, the first king of Prussia (1688–1713), there was an increased Calvinist presence in the population. For example, the Great Elector had welcomed the French Huguenots (Calvinists), who were refugees from Louis XIV and his revocation of the Edict of Nantes (1685). This strong influx—estimated at about one million—did much to strengthen and vitalize the Reformed church, not only in Berlin and Prussia but in other German principalities as well.[15]

The "Prussianization" of the Lutherans under the Hohenzollerns, including the Lutheran pietist Frederick William I (1713–40) and the rationalist admirer of the French Enlightenment, Frederick the Great (1740–86), reached a royal climax in the first quarter of the nineteenth century. This came about after Prussia's war with Napoleon in the years 1806–7. Prussia had been so thoroughly defeated and disgraced by Napoleon that the Hohenzollern political dreams seemed all but dashed. The next few years (1808–15), however, became a turning point, a regeneration of Prussian pride and patriotism; out of the depths of humiliation Prussia was being reborn politically, militarily, and culturally.[16] After helping to defeat Napoleon at Waterloo, Prussia received at the Congress of Vienna (1815) large territorial acquisitions, more than doubling its population.

A major hindrance to Prussia's potential power and leadership in Germany, however, was the internal problem posed by the lack of religious unity among Protestants. Unity negotiations between the Lutherans and Calvinists, conducted ever since the Reformation, were often tedious and even acrimonious, and in the end unsuccessful.[17] When faced with their chief political rivals, the Catholic Hapsburgs of Austria, the Hohenzollerns perceived this religious disunity as a definite political liability. Under these circumstances a strong Germany under Prussian leadership could best be hastened by a royal

15. The large Reformation monument in Geneva includes the likeness of the Great Elector who, incidentally, is given more prominence than Luther.

16. The Peace of Tilsit (1807) had deprived Prussia of the University of Halle. In this circumstance and as a part of the program of national regeneration led by Baron von Stein (1757–1831), it was decided in 1809 to found the University of Berlin, which rapidly became renowned for the remarkable faculty recruited by Wilhelm von Humboldt, the minister for cultural affairs.

17. The painful story is told in detail in Jürgen L. Neve, *The Lutherans in the Movements for Church Union* (Philadelphia: Lutheran Publication House, 1921).

decree bringing about union of Lutherans and Calvinists and calling it the "Evangelical Christian Church." If this could be accomplished, a religiously united Protestant Prussia would be powerful enough to win hegemony over the equally ambitious Hapsburgs of Austria.

This is the background against which we must assess the fateful actions of Frederick William III (1797–1840), who dissolved the partially autonomous church government and placed it squarely under a government department, which the king controlled through his minister for cultural affairs, Wilhelm von Humboldt.[18] The king was admittedly a deeply religious person, a Calvinist pietist who valued the *Erweckungsbewegung* for its emphasis on personal piety as well as its contribution to the moral and national renewal of Prussia. In fact, both the king's pietism and his inherited Hohenzollern state church policy were factors in the decision to decree a union of Lutherans and Calvinists in Prussia.[19] The historic proclamation occurred in 1817 in the form of a royal edict, or "order-in-cabinet."[20] The edict, dated September 27, was issued one month before the tricentennial celebration of the Reformation (October 31) and was calculated to capitalize on the romantic milieu surrounding that observance. On Reformation Day the king himself would participate in a joint Lutheran-Reformed service of Holy Communion to be held at the royal Garrison Church at Potsdam.

According to Jürgen L. Neve, the program for achieving an "Evangelical Christian Church" (popularly called the "Prussian Union Church"), included eight measures.[21] Most significant were those that dealt with church government (Lutherans and Reformed were placed under the authority of one department of the state; the act merely acknowledged the fait accompli of 1808); the liturgy (a common

18. "The pope in Rome had never more power over his church than was now vested in the hands of the Reformed king of Prussia as bishop of the Lutheran church in his domain" (ibid., p. 116).

19. Some interpreters maintain that the pietism of leading figures in the house of Hohenzollern and pietists within the Prussian aristocracy and the Potsdam bureaucracy were powerful in shaping the Prussian tradition. See Ritter, "Protestantism," p. 917. Cf. A. Hauck, "Ecclesiastical Union in Germany," *New Schaff-Herzog Encyclopedia*, 12:79–81.

20. The text of the decree is to be found in Gerhard Ruhbach, ed., *Kirchenunionen im-19. Jahrhundert* (Gütersloh: Gerd Mohn, 1967), pp. 34–35.

21. *The Lutherans*, pp. 117–18.

Communion service with the breaking of the bread to signify acceptance of the Union); and the de-confessionalizing of the two churches (the Union meant neither a capitulating of the Reformed to the Lutherans nor vice versa, but rather that both should form one revived evangelical church in which pastors would subscribe only to the Reformation confessions insofar as they agreed with one another). The conference of Berlin pastors, with Friedrich Schleiermacher [22] presiding, was the first to adopt the Union; others followed, especially in the Rhineland and the Palatinate.

OPPOSITION TO THE PRUSSIAN UNION

At first there seemed to be general approval of, or at least no overt opposition to, the Prussian Union. This was due, no doubt, to the royal assurance that congregations would not be forced to join the Union. Trouble arose, however, when the king, who fancied himself something of a liturgical scholar, prepared a new order of worship (*Agenda*) for Prussia. Filled with Romanticism's affection for the past, he reworked the Lutheran Brandenburg Order of 1640 and promptly made its use obligatory. He reasoned that a common liturgy would be a symbol of the Union, a sign that differing confessions could celebrate the sacrament together. This act, more than anything else, stirred up opposition to the Union among both the Reformed and the Lutherans.

The Reformed had several reasons for resisting the Union. First, there was the usual Calvinist charge that Lutherans had not gone far enough in rejecting Romanism. The new royal liturgy and the medieval ceremonial trappings (e.g., chanting, candles, crucifixes) that accompanied it were a case in point. In the eyes of the anti-Union Calvinists, even the Berlin Cathedral, long since a Reformed church, had not been sufficiently cleansed of its Lutheran-Catholic appointments. Zealous Calvinists now felt constrained to remedy this failure

---

22. Friedrich Schleiermacher (1768–1834), a young professor at the pietistic University of Halle, moved to Berlin when Prussia lost Halle (1807). One of the founders of the University of Berlin, he became a luminary on the brilliant Berlin faculty. Originally a strong advocate of the Prussian Union (his book *The Christian Faith* [1821] was the dogmatics of the Prussian Union), he came to disapprove of the Prussian king's attempt to impose the royal liturgy on the churches.

by tearing the cathedral's altar crucifix from its place and throwing it into the river Spree. There were additional grounds for resistance. Why, for example, must the Reformed be forced to follow the Lutheran-Catholic enumeration of the Ten Commandments? And by what right did a Prussian king override the presbyterian and synodical government of the Calvinist church?

The Lutherans were even more distrustful of and opposed to the edict of 1817. Their dissatisfaction also centered on the liturgy, particularly on the formula for Holy Communion. Two main objections were raised. First, the common celebration of the Lord's Supper was seen as an expression of church fellowship without prior agreement on the meaning of the gospel. The Lutherans insisted that for the unity of the Christian church the gospel must be preached in its purity and the sacraments administered according to this gospel (Augsburg Confession, Article VII). To use the Lord's Supper as a means to promote unity in the gospel was to put the cart before the horse. In the second place, they objected to the formula of distribution. The new liturgy required that the minister use the words "Christ our Lord said: Take and eat. . . ." These words might suggest to the communicant that he was at liberty to interpret Christ's words as he pleased. In the controversy that followed, the retention of this formula became the shibboleth of the Prussian Union, whereas the Lutherans inserted their doctrinal concerns into the celebration by using the words "This is the *true* body. . . ."

The Lutheran opposition found expression in a new "Ninety-Five Theses" published by the foremost preacher in northern Germany, Klaus Harms, a former friend and disciple of Schleiermacher. In the seventy-fifth thesis he said: "As a poor maiden the Lutheran Church is now to be made rich by being married. Do not perform the ceremony over Luther's bones. They will become alive at it, and then—woe to you!"[23] The Harms prophecy was being quickly fulfilled, and leaders

---

23. The English translation has slightly "laundered" the German: "Als eine arme Magd möchte man die luth. Kirche jetzt *durch eine Kopulation* reich machen. Vollziehet den Akt ja nicht über Luthers Gebein! Es wird lebendig davon und damit—Wehe euch!" *Real-Encyclopedie für protestantische Theologie und Kirche* (Leipzig, 1877–88), 5:619. For an English translation see *The Lutheran Cyclopedia*, ed. Henry Eyster Jacobs and John A. W. Haas (New York, 1899), pp. 512–14.

of the Lutheran opposition multiplied. Henrik Steffens, like Harms a former friend and associate of Schleiermacher, rallied to the Lutheran cause, as did the Silesian professors Johann Gottfried Scheibel and Georg P. E. Huschke. Many Lutherans in Silesia, Saxony, Pomerania, and Brandenburg left the Prussian church and sought to emigrate. Branded as rebels and denied emigration, the Lutherans were harassed by the police and many were imprisoned. Among the latter was Johannes A. A. Grabau, who was finally permitted to lead a large colony of "Old Lutherans" to America, where he became the "father" of the Buffalo Synod.

The Prussian king was flooded with protests that the Union was neither "united" nor "evangelical" but an ill-founded caesaropapal partnership, certainly not a church. Unwilling to risk the unity of Prussia by continuing insistence on the amalgamation of the two Protestant churches, King Frederick William III, and later his son Frederick William IV (1840–61), issued "orders in cabinet" (1834 and 1852) that relaxed tensions and preserved the Prussian church as an "administrative union" of two confessions governed by a "supreme ecclesiastical council" (*Oberkirchenrat*) empowered to represent the whole Evangelical national church and to maintain and protect the rights of the differing confessions.[24] The Prussian universities feared that the royal concessions would encourage the dissolution of the Union, but Frederick William IV promised to support the institution his father had sought so vigorously to establish.

To understand subsequent developments that led to growing international Lutheran solidarity, it is necessary now to point out some of the far-reaching effects of the Prussian experiment in caesaropapal ecumenism. In the first place, the conflict over the Union caused the Lutherans to reexamine their tradition and thus give birth to the nineteenth-century confessional movement.

In the second place, the large German states that appeared in the nineteenth century and whose antecedents were mainly Lutheran now followed the Prussian example of unifying the Protestant churches within their territories. This was not difficult, because many of the states had been incorporated into Prussia. Eventually more than

24. For the texts of the 1834 and 1852 "orders in cabinet" see Rubach, ed. *Kirchenunionen*, pp. 36–43.

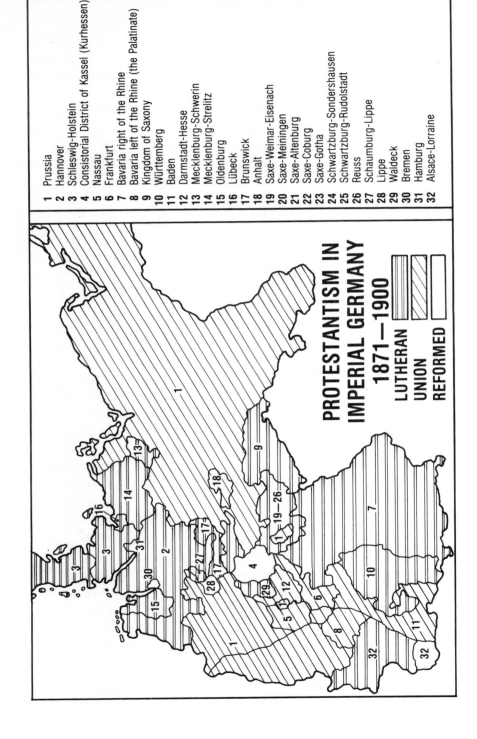

PROTESTANTISM IN IMPERIAL GERMANY 1871—1900

LUTHERAN
UNION
REFORMED

1 Prussia
2 Hannover
3 Schleswig-Holstein
4 Consistorial District of Kassel (Kurhessen)
5 Nassau
6 Frankfurt
7 Bavaria right of the Rhine
8 Bavaria left of the Rhine (the Palatinate)
9 Kingdom of Saxony
10 Württemberg
11 Baden
12 Darmstadt-Hesse
13 Mecklenburg-Schwerin
14 Mecklenburg-Strelitz
15 Oldenburg
16 Lübeck
17 Brunswick
18 Anhalt
19 Saxe-Weimar-Eisenach
20 Saxe-Meiningen
21 Saxe-Altenburg
22 Saxe-Coburg
23 Saxe-Gotha
24 Schwartzburg-Sondershausen
25 Schwartzburg-Rudolstadt
26 Reuss
27 Schaumburg-Lippe
28 Lippe
29 Waldeck
30 Bremen
31 Hamburg
32 Alsace-Lorraine

half of Germany's Lutherans were siphoned off into territorial "Union" churches. The hopes expressed by informal Lutheran associations in Silesia, Brandenburg, Pomerania, and Saxony for the reestablishment of the Lutheran church were not realized.

In the third place, protesting "Lutheran Free Churches" were established within the territory of the Union. The first of these was the Evangelical Lutheran ("Old Lutheran") Church, whose center was Breslau in Silesia. Persecution of the church ended in 1845, when a "general concession" provided governmental recognition and permission to exist as a "free church" independent of the state. A second Lutheran free church originated (1846) in Nassau and Saxony in protest of both rationalism and unionism. Five other free churches appeared in the second half of the nineteenth century in principalities stretching from Hamburg in the north to Baden in the southwest.[25]

A fourth result was associated with the geographical expansion of Prussia in the third quarter of the nineteenth century. Under the powerful leadership of the pietistic chancellor, Otto von Bismarck, who shared the Hohenzollerns' belief in their divine mission for Germany, Prussia engaged in a policy of unabashed aggrandizement by war and diplomacy. As a result of this policy, Prussia acquired in 1866 the kingdom of Hannover, the provinces of Hesse-Cassel, Hesse-Nassau, Frankfurt, and the duchies of Schleswig-Holstein and Lauenburg. The largest of these accessions were the Lutheran states of Hannover and Schleswig-Holstein, both of which succeeded in keeping their church government independent of Prussian Union control. Their success, coupled with the fact that the Lutheran churches in the south of Germany, namely, Bavaria and Württemberg, had not become unionized along the lines of the Prussian Union, provided the non-Prussian Lutherans with a base from which to consolidate an uncompromised confessional church. Leaders of Prussia had frankly revealed their plans for absorbing the churches of the recently conquered lands into the Prussian Union. One of them wrote: "He . . . who resists the development and expansion of the Union negates the results of the

---

25. For details, see "Free Churches (Lutheran)," in *The Encyclopedia of the Lutheran Church*, ed. Julius Bodensieck (Minneapolis: Augsburg Publishing House, 1965), 2:885–86.

German Reformation and misconceives thoroughly the mission of Germany with regard to the Church."[26] Words of this nature served only to stiffen the non-Prussian Lutheran will to resist the encroachments of the Union. Voices were soon heard saying, "To be sure, we wish the unity of the church, but not under the aegis of the Supreme Ecclesiastical Council of Prussia!"[27]

Recognizing that the attempt to force non-Prussian Lutherans into a merger along the lines of the Prussian Union had little prospect of success, the German church diet (*Der deutsche evangelische Kirchentag*), meeting at Wittenberg in 1848, proposed a "Protestant federation." Adolph G. C. von Harless and other Lutheran leaders rejected the pan-Protestant idea on the grounds that a federation was not compatible with Lutheran principles. Lutherans themselves must draw together to assert their identity.[28]

THE GENERAL EVANGELICAL LUTHERAN CONFERENCE

It was in this atmosphere that a small group of prominent Lutherans, thirty-one in number, met in Hannover, October 30–31, 1867, to discuss the formation of a general conference of Lutherans for all of Germany, Die Allgemeine Evangelisch-Lutherische Konferenz (General Evangelical Lutheran Conference [AELK]).[29] Although the confreres were Lutheran "confessionalists," they were by no means of one theological mind. In fact, there were representatives of all three parties within the neo-confessional movement: repristinationists, high

26. Quoted in Neve, *The Lutherans*, p. 134.
27. The watchword of the Lutherans became *"Nur nicht unter den Evangelischen Oberkirchenrat"* (ibid.).
28. *Evangelisches Kirchen Lexikon* (Göttingen: Vandenhoeck & Ruprecht, 1956, 1961), 1:1194. A contrasting and favorable response was given, interestingly, by the General Synod of the Lutheran Church in America. See Richard C. Wolf, *Documents of Lutheran Unity in America* (Philadelphia: Fortress Press, 1966), pp. 313–14. It has been suggested that political as well as confessional motives hastened the Lutheran consolidation. See "Hannover," in *Evangelisches Kirchen Lexikon*, 2:19.
29. The definitive history of the AELK is Paul Fleisch, *Für Kirche und Bekenntnis: Geschichte der Allgemeinen Evangelisch-Lutherischen Konferenz* (Berlin: Lutherisches Verlagshaus, 1956). For a brief English summary of the AELK, see Alfred Th. Jørgensen, Paul Fleisch, and Abdel Ross Wentz, eds., *The Lutheran Churches of the World* (Minneapolis: Augsburg Publishing House, 1929), pp. 421–24. See also Bengt Wadensjö, *Toward a World Lutheran Communion: Developments in Lutheran Cooperation up to 1929* (Uppsala: Verbum, 1970), pp. 17–36.

PROTESTANT
GERMANY
1948

SCHLESWIG-HOLSTEIN
Eutin
Lübeck
POMERANIA
MECKLENBURG
Hamburg
Bremen
SCHAUMBURG-LIPPE
OLDENBURG
HANNOVER
BERLIN-BRANDENBURG
CHURCH PROVINCE SAXONY
LIPPE
ANHALT
BRUNSWICK
SILESIA
WESTPHALIA
SAXONY
RHINELAND
KURHESSEN-WALDECK
THURINGIA
HESSE-NASSAU
THE PALATINATE
BAVARIA
WÜRTTEMBERG
BADEN

LUTHERAN CHURCHES
United Evangelical Lutheran
Church of Germany
Other Lutheran Churches

Members of the Lutheran World
Federation (with the addition of
Pomerania)

UNITED CHURCHES
Evangelical Church of the Union
(formerly the Old Prussian Union)
Other United Churches

REFORMED CHURCHES
Territorial Church of Lippe
(with Lutheran congregations,
mainly in the cities)
Evangelical-Reformed Church
of Northwest Germany

church "New Lutherans," and "Erlangen" theologians.[30] What bound them together was their common concern to preserve a distinctly Lutheran presence within the Second German Reich, which was now rapidly taking shape, and to prevent a supine and bland "evangelicalism" in German Protestantism from following meekly upon German political unification. Realizing that the state Lutheran churches could not act as corporate units in these circumstances, the ad hoc group at Hannover decided that the AELK would be constituted of individuals, both clerical and lay, drawn from all the German territorial churches. There would be periodic public conventions of the conference, but the administrative leadership would rest in a "Smaller Conference" (*engere Konferenz*) within which there would be an executive committee.

The founding convention of the AELK, held in Hannover July 1–2, 1868, brought together 1,500 persons under the leadership of such well-known theologians as Theodor Kliefoth (Mecklenburg), Adolph G. C. von Harless (Erlangen), C. E. Luthardt (Leipzig), and Gerhard Uhlhorn (Hannover). The conference held assemblies at intervals of several years, published a periodical, *Die Allgemeine Evangelisch-Lutherische Kirchenzeitung,* and continued to promote its aim to strengthen "the entire Evangelical Lutheran Church in all of her parts . . . especially in the preservation of the true teaching of the gospel . . . and the waging of a battle against unbelief, false and worldly Christianity and unionism."[31]

The AELK remained an effective though sometimes controversial organization through the remainder of the nineteenth century. It survived World War I, the Weimar Republic, Hitler's Third Reich, and finally went out of existence when the United Evangelical Lutheran Church (Vereinigte Evangelisch-Lutherische Kirche Deutschland [VELKD]) was established in 1948.

Several observations must be made about the significance of the

---

30. Fleisch, *Für Kirche und Bekenntnis,* pp. 5–6. For discussions of the Lutheran confessional movement in Germany, see Friedrich W. Kantzenbach, "Das Bekenntnis Problem in der Lutherischen Theologie des 19. Jahrhunderts," *Neue Zeitschrift für Systematische Theologie* 4 (1962): 243–317; and idem, *Gestalten und Typen des Neuluthertums* (Gütersloh: Gerd Mohn, 1968). Cf. Holsten Fagerberg, "Neuluthertum," *Die Religion in Geschichte und Gegenwart,* 4:536–40.

31. Jørgensen et al., eds., *Lutheran Churches,* p. 422.

AELK in anticipation of its role in the formation and development of the Lutheran World Convention at Eisenach in 1923. First, the founding of the conference, much like the Anglican Oxford Movement, was a testimony to the rising awareness that church independence and confessional integrity could be seriously compromised by the state. The parallels between the English and German movements are astonishing. Especially noteworthy is the fact that both arose out of the conviction that the church *qua* church must be free of domination by civil authorities.

Second, the AELK, though overwhelmingly German (membership included some Scandinavians), recognized that a Lutheran confessional church transcended political boundaries and national and provincial concerns. Its international interests brought about contact with Lutherans in America and Scandinavia. Shortly after the Hannover assembly (1868), the conference was in correspondence with Charles W. Schaeffer, president of the General Council of the Evangelical Lutheran Church of North America (organized in 1867). The American body, like the AELK, was a part of the nineteenth-century neo-confessional movement. The General Council followed up the initial contact by asking Sigmund Fritschel of the Iowa Synod to represent the General Council at the second AELK assembly in Leipzig (1870). Representatives of the churches of Sweden and Norway, as well as of the French Lutherans, were also present at Leipzig.[32] Informal ties between the AELK and the General Council were continued until the outbreak of war in 1914. Between 1909 and 1915, this relationship led the General Council to propose a world federation of Lutheranism—unrealizable, of course, when World War I began.[33] The significance of this gesture must not be overlooked, however, because American Lutherans, having undertaken postwar relief in 1918–19, turned again to the AELK and raised the question of holding a convention of world Lutherans, realized at Eisenach in 1923.

Third, because of the AELK's growing consciousness of contempo-

---

32. Fleisch, *Für Kirche und Bekenntnis*, p. 12. Cf. Wadensjö, *Toward a World Lutheran Communion*, p. 20; and Herman Fritschel, *Biography of Sigmund and Gottfried Fritschel* (Milwaukee, 1951), pp. 107–8.

33. Wolf, *Documents*, pp. 315–18. Cf. General Council, *Minutes . . . 1871*, pp. 6, 42–44. A historical summary of relationships is to be found in General Council, *Minutes . . . 1903*, pp. 177–78.

rary culture its activities thrust it beyond a legalistic preoccupation with confessionalism, anti–Prussian Unionism, and anti-Romanism.

At its first conference outside Germany, held at Lund, Sweden, in 1901, the AELK recognized that a tremendous cultural change had occurred in the Western world and that confessional Lutherans must take cognizance of the rapidly developing secularism generated by industrialization, urbanization, and scientific, social, and philosophical positivism. The main address at Lund, delivered by Norwegian theologian Thorvald Klaveness (1844–1915), was a frontal attack on the confessional orthodoxy being repristinated in both Germany and Scandinavia. Klaveness charged that Lutheran pastors and theologians were giving homiletical and theological answers before they were aware of the questions. Many in his audience were shocked, but they quickly recovered to accuse him of liberalism. Especially sharp criticism was voiced by some German theologians and by his own countrymen, who at the moment were engaged in an internecine conflict that shortly brought about the formation of the Free Theological Faculty (Oslo) known as *Menighedsfakulteten*. Despite valiant support at Lund by Swedish bishop Gottfrid Billing, Klaveness discovered that his position was unacceptable among scholastic Lutherans, notably those of a pietistic-orthodox orientation.

On the other hand, it must be recognized that the leadership of the AELK, as demonstrated by Erlangen and Leipzig professor Ludwig Ihmels (1858–1933), had been engaged in precisely the same issue as that raised by Klaveness: How can evangelical, confessional Lutherans best address modern culture? When Norwegians learned that Klaveness and the AELK leaders in Germany and Sweden were raising the same issue, they concluded prematurely that the AELK was "liberal." This conclusion led to a discrediting of the organization, especially among Norwegian pietistic orthodoxists, who quickly classified the AELK as an opponent of "true Christianity."[34] In actuality, al-

34. For details on these developments see Eivind Berggrav, *Norske Kirkeprofiler* (Oslo: Land og Kirke, 1946), pp. 9–83; and John Nome, *Brytningstid* (Oslo: Lutherstiftelsen, 1958), pp. 9–151. Cf. also Einar Molland, *Church Life in Norway 1800–1950*, trans. Harris Kaasa (Minneapolis: Augsburg Publishing House, 1957), pp. 66–92; and the theological journal edited by Eivind Berggrav, *Kirke og Kultur* 28 (1921): 117–22. Fleisch describes the Klaveness debate as a "storm" (*Für Kirche und Bekenntnis*, pp. 32–33).

though the AELK was profoundly cognizant of the theological threat posed by contemporary secularism, it was by no means prepared—as its detractors feared—to jettison its Lutheran raison d'être.

A fourth observation deals with the role of "Union" Lutherans in the AELK. This issue became a neuralgic point in 1907. From the beginning in 1868, it had been agreed that since the AELK was an association of individuals, not churches, Lutherans within the Prussian Union state church should be granted membership along with the majority of members from the "intact" Lutheran state churches (such as Hannover). Compounding the problem was the fact that Lutherans from the conservative Free Churches, who were cool toward the "Union" Lutherans, were granted full voting privileges in the "Smaller Conference," whereas the "Union" Lutherans possessed only "advisory" votes. An explosive situation developed in 1907, when the AELK, under the leadership of Ludwig Ihmels, granted full membership and full voting privileges in the Smaller Conference to the "Union" Lutherans. Since the Smaller Conference administered policy for the AELK, this action was interpreted by Free Church individuals as a threat to confessional Lutheranism. In protest of the 1907 decision, the Free Church members of the Smaller Conference, together with a number of members from the Lutheran state churches, resigned from the AELK and in 1908 established "the Lutheran League" (*Lutherischer Bund*).[35]

The significance of these events is to be seen in the light of the cultural shock that the late nineteenth century and early twentieth century produced. The Lutheran confessional movement could not isolate itself by refusing to take notice of cultural changes (like the opponents of Klaveness). Confessional Lutherans began to realize that "unionism" was not the only enemy; in fact, even more threatening was the potentially overwhelming tidal wave of secularism.[36]

The Americans reflected several attitudes. Certainly one was the

---

35. Fleisch, *Für Kirche und Bekenntnis*, pp. 55–59, 68.
36. American Lutheran reaction, as reflected in the conservative General Council, was cautious if not unsympathetic. Prior to 1907, the General Council had decided to invite the AELK to meet in the United States, thus dramatically demonstrating the international character of the AELK. But having learned of the AELK's 1907 decision, the General Council withdrew its invitation and subsequently registered an official protest without going so far as to break off relations. Wolf, *Documents*, pp. 315–18.

American version of neo-confessionalism, which was conditioned to a great extent by the fact that many Lutherans in America, notably the Missouri Synod, considered the General Council confessionally unstable, a situation that led the council to take no actions that might be interpreted as confessionally unsound. Closely related to this was the fact that Americans had not yet fully comprehended the change in theological climate reflected in Ludwig Ihmels, the AELK president and the last of the great representatives of Lutheran "Erlangen" theology. Theodore E. Schmauk, president of the General Council, and Adolph Spaeth, chairman of the council's committee on relations with the AELK, were essentially "old Lutherans" who either mistrusted or did not understand the Erlangen brand of neo-confessionalism. In any case, it was not until Charles M. Jacobs (Philadelphia), whose studies under Albert Hauck at Leipzig had introduced him to Ihmels's theology, replaced the ailing Schmauk as the theological spokesman for the Americans after World War I, that German and American confessionalism were on the same wavelength. This explains why Ihmels and Jacobs were able to work so harmoniously in shaping the Lutheran World Convention at Eisenach in 1923.

SECULARISM

We have already noted the onrushing and widespread secularism that characterized much of the latter part of the nineteenth century. Some leaders in the church not only raised their voices in warning but also provided a new and confessionally based orientation to the intellectual currents of the age. An outstanding example of this kind of leadership was Ludwig Ihmels, whose theological writings and ecclesiastical statesmanship placed him in the front ranks of those who looked beyond the immediate alarm caused by the historical-critical study of the Scriptures, the attraction of optimistic evolution, and the theoretical Marxist criticism of religion. He perceived that these were symptoms of a pervasive cultural change that threatened to alienate intellectuals and the laboring class from the church. He was asking the question Klaveness had asked at Lund: How can Lutheran confessional theology be set in constructive relation to contemporary culture? Central to his thought was the problem of religious assurance, which he argued was of primary concern precisely because modern secularism appeared to be destroying the traditional religious supports, one of which was scholastic orthodoxy's (Catholic and Protestant) static view of revelation as a body of verbally inspired truth. Ihmels countered the latter with a dynamic understanding: revelation as the redemptive acts of God to which the Bible bears witness.[37]

Ihmels's voice was not the only one raised to warn Christians of the weakness of a scholastic defense in the face of burgeoning secularism. But the voices were too few, the fears of the "orthodox" were too great, and the new secularism was too attractive to prevent a mounting indifference to the role of the church among the intellectuals who shaped cultural life and the workers who provided the manpower for expanding industry.

Ragnar Askmark, a contemporary Swedish churchman, has described the situation in the Scandinavian countries. What occurred there may be assumed to be typical of Central Europe, England, and America.[38] The literary movement against the church in Scandinavia was led by such men as Georg Brandes (1842–1927), a Danish Jew; Henrik Ibsen (1828–1906) and Bjørnstjerne Bjørnson (1832–1910) in Norway; and August Strindberg (1849–1912) in Sweden. These spokesmen for the new culture believed that the theories and findings of scholars like Feuerbach, Darwin, Marx, and Nietzsche were creating a society that would be forced to admit that "God is dead" and so is the church. By and large, intellectuals were won to this view, and as their enchantment with it grew, so did their snobbery toward Christianity and the church. Askmark comments, "To be educated and to be a Christian [were] considered contradictory terms."

The literary intelligentsia soon discovered that their naturalist philosophy of life was welcomed by those who were interested in

---

37. See Ludwig Ihmels, *Wie werden wir der christlichen Wahrheit gewiss?* (Leipzig, 1900); and idem, *Die christliche Wahrheitsgewissheit* (Leipzig, 1901). For an English translation and evaluation of Ihmels, see "Ludwig Ihmels and the Erlangen School of Theology," in Ludwig Ihmels, "Christian Certainty," trans. and ed. Dorris A. Flesner, unpublished manuscript. See also Friedrich W. Kantzenbach, "Von Ludwig Ihmels bis zu Paul Althaus," *Neue Zeitschrift für systematische Theologie und Religionsphilosophie* 11, no. 1 (1969): 94–111.

38. Ragnar Askmark, "The Scandinavian Churches," in *Lutheran Churches of the World*, ed. Carl E. Lund-Quist (Minneapolis: Augsburg Publishing House, 1957), pp. 101–9.

social and political problems. Early socialism looked upon these anti-Christian literary figures as allies and companions in creating a modern secularized society. Thus religious and political extremism worked hand in hand and regarded the church as their common enemy. Although by tradition the people made use of the church for baptism, confirmation, marriage, and funerals, church attendance and other acts of religious devotion were reckoned ridiculous and absurd. Among both intellectuals and the laboring class, staying away from worship became "almost a matter of principle."

We have already observed that relatively few church leaders were prepared to meet this attack; on the whole, the ecclesiastical reaction was one of fear and uncertainty that sought safety in retreating to pietistic and orthodoxist formulas of the seventeenth century. The problem lay in the concept of truth, which theologians and anti-Christians defined in ways that they deemed to be mutually exclusive. Both failed to see that the word "truth" by itself had no inherent meaning apart from its use within a frame of reference. Scientists, historians, and philosophers used the word to refer to accuracy (*Richtigkeit*) of facts, correctness of propositions, and logical relationships. Christianity, judged by these criteria, was not "true." Churchmen, on the other hand, pointed to the "truth" of doctrinal propositions whose verity was ultimately guaranteed by an inspired and verbally inerrant Bible. Those few theologians who addressed the question within a biblical, but not biblicistic, frame of reference recognized that in the Bible the question of truth is not a matter of accuracy in the relationship between facts, propositions, and ideas (*Richtigkeit*) but the relationship between persons, ultimately the relationship between God and humankind, as defined in the person and work of Christ who called himself "the Truth" (*Wahrheit*). For Luther, if not for some Lutherans, the truth in Christ did not negate the truth discoverable by rational, investigative means. For him these two aspects followed from his doctrine concerning God's right-hand activity (the gospel of forgiveness in Christ) and his left-hand activity (the law of creation).

Regrettably, most Lutherans, when driven to the defense of the truth of Christianity, failed to use the resources of Lutheran theology and thus were clumsy and ill-prepared to meet the challenge. They were like actors on a stage without lines to speak, or if they had lines, what emerged seemed to be merely mumbo jumbo. The conclusion of the secularists—both intellectuals and workers—was that the church had forfeited its right to speak. Followers of Georg Brandes in Denmark expressed the sentiments of secular humanism by saying, "We weave the shroud for the one they call our Lord."[39] It was a genuinely fearsome thing, therefore, when secularism seemed to be tolling the death knell of confessional Christianity.

Thus, when seeking to evaluate the Lutheran witness in the world shortly before the outbreak of World War I, one can hardly avoid the conclusion that it was largely of a defensive nature. Lutherans on both sides of the Atlantic could well be driven together by the common enemies that were now identifiable. There was, of course, the traditional Roman Catholic threat to evangelical Lutheranism. There was also the enemy of "unionism" according to the Prussian pattern, now complicated by an urgent call for a united Protestant or ecumenical witness to the world (the World Missionary Conference, Edinburgh 1910). Neo-Protestant liberalism or modernism was yet another threat. Added to this list, and thought to be the most dangerous, were Marxist socialism and secular humanism.

We have traced the rise of these issues in connection with our chronicle of continental Lutheranism. During the nineteenth century to 1914, hundreds of thousands of Lutheran emigrants, driven by economic and religious motives, found their way to the New World, in whose soil they planted "free churches." Each developed its own idiosyncratic ethos, thus compounding the problem of inter-Lutheran relationships both nationally and internationally. We turn in the next chapter to a survey of Lutheranism in America after World War I.

39. Quoted in ibid., p. 102.

3

American Lutherans at the End of World War I

"The guns of August" (1914) were silenced by the armistice of November 11, 1918. During the week of the cease-fire in Europe, three Eastern American Lutheran church bodies of German and colonial traditions held their final meetings in preparation for the merger that became the United Lutheran Church in America. Two months earlier, on September 6, 1918, representatives of ten American churches formally organized an agency to be known as the National Lutheran Council. One year earlier, June 9 – 10, 1917, two months after the American entry into World War I, the first Protestant merger of the twentieth century occurred in St. Paul, Minnesota, when three Midwestern immigrant bodies united to form the Norwegian Lutheran Church of America. Thus, in less than a year and a half American Lutherans were experiencing the first fruits of a movement toward unity that had been present since the first immigrants arrived in the seventeenth and eighteenth centuries. The high tide of the transatlantic migration from Germany and Scandinavia had taken place in the nineteenth century; by 1914 it had all but ceased.

THE IMMIGRANT CHURCHES

The immigrants found American freedom an intoxicating experience, and they luxuriated in it. Ecclesiastically they may have lived unwisely, but never frivolously. The church bodies that they established were serious manifestations of convictions that circumstances in their homelands tended to suppress. Consequently, when the New World permitted the immigrants to express their concerns, the churches embodying these concerns became more numerous than both the established churches and the free churches that they had left behind in "the old country." Although ethnic differences were a major reason accounting for American Lutheran denominations, ethnicity was not the complete explanation. America provided freedom for diversity *within* the ethnic groupings; theological, religious, and even geographical idiosyncrasies were now at liberty to be incarnated in structures and incorporated before the law of the land. The Norwegians, to take but one ethnic example, had foliated into no less than twelve independent bodies prior to World War I. The Lutheran family was so bewildering that outsiders, when forced to characterize these people, were reduced to making vague and whimsical generalizations about these "foreigners": they were really more Catholic than Protestant; they were reluctant to accept American ways; they kept to themselves; they were doctrinally inflexible; some were as puritanic and pietistic as "American Evangelicals," while others were liberal on such matters as alcoholic beverages but theologically conservative. It was all very confusing.

Ironically, it was hardly less bewildering to the Lutherans themselves. They too found self-understanding difficult; to make sense out of the luxuriant growth of synods, councils, conferences, and nationwide ecclesiastical bodies was all but impossible. Each group went about its task of organizing congregations, building schools, colleges, and seminaries, caring for those of their own in need, and contributing money and personnel to missionary work in Africa and Asia, especially during the last quarter of the nineteenth century. The very intensity and seriousness with which each of the churches addressed its own "identity problem" and its own sense of missionary responsibility in the New World made the path to Lutheran unity a rugged obstacle course.

THE ERA OF WORLD WAR I

Although America entered World War I at a relatively late stage, like the rest of the combatants the United States experienced the long-range results of the war. Hardly any major area of American life remained unaltered by the cataclysmic events of 1914–18. The ecclesiastical arena was no exception. The events surrounding and following the war catapulted Lutherans into the twentieth century with such force and velocity that the years between 1917 and 1920 were to become one of the most significant eras in Lutheran history. If we are to understand the role of Americans in the movement toward world Lutheran solidarity, symbolized by the founding of the Lutheran World Convention in 1923, we must single out for attention a few fairly obvious but easily overlooked circumstances that shaped the postwar era.

One of the primary facts, as already noted, was the end of immigration, despite a brief flurry in the early 1920s. This meant a vast change for Lutherans, who had expended immense energies before 1914 in the task of gathering the immigrants into the ecclesiastical fold. Now there were new demands, new opportunities, and new questions. How could peoples of diverse ethnic roots become *American* Lutherans? How could descendants of colonial Eastern Lutherans who fought as Americans in the War of Independence relate themselves to Midwestern bilingual Lutherans who were but a generation or two removed from their European forebears? How were the various churches to respond to the pressures for church unity which the new situation thrust upon them? How were they to repair broken contacts with brethren in Europe? How could they best carry on relief work among both allies and former enemies, who had suffered so much as a consequence of the war? What about war-orphaned mission fields in Africa and Asia? Could Americans help to sustain them, in addition to carrying the responsibility for their own fields of work? How could their long-held convictions be enfleshed in new institutions, Lutheran and non-Lutheran, without compromise?

It is clear that the new situation was compounded of a large assortment of ingredients, sociological, cultural, historical, theological, and ecclesiastical. In trying to sort them out, it is perhaps best to begin by a simple listing of the Lutheran church bodies in existence in America around 1914.

Lutheran Church Bodies around 1914

At the outbreak of World War I, American Lutherans had organized themselves largely around doctrinal and ethnic issues. The spiritual descendants of the colonial Lutherans were in three main bodies: the General Synod, the General Council, and the United Synod, South. The descendants of the German immigrants of the mid-nineteenth century were federated in the Synodical Conference, made up primarily of the Missouri Synod and the Wisconsin Synod. Other Midwestern German Lutherans were the Joint Synod of Ohio, the Buffalo Synod, and the Iowa Synod. The Norwegian Lutherans found themselves in three main bodies and three smaller groups: the Hauge Synod, the Norwegian Synod, the United Norwegian Church, the Lutheran Free Church, the Church of the Lutheran Brethren, and the Eielsen Synod. The Swedes were united in the Augustana Synod. The Danes flowed in two streams: the United Danish Lutheran Church and the Danish Evangelical Lutheran Church. The Finns were divided three ways: the Suomi Synod, the Finnish National Lutheran Church, and the Finnish Apostolic Lutheran Church. The Slovaks called their group the Slovak Evangelical Lutheran Church; and finally, the Icelanders were simply organized as the Icelandic Synod. In all there were twenty-two church bodies with a membership of approximately two million in the United States and Canada.

In the postwar years, the issues that rose to the surface were (1) the acculturation of the hyphenated Lutherans (e.g., German-Lutherans), (2) the struggle for domestic Lutheran church unity, (3) the administration of relief among victims of the war, and (4) the resumption of prewar contacts, tentative though they may have been, with Lutherans in Europe.

Acculturation or "Americanization"

World War I hastened the widespread use of English by Lutherans. This was part and parcel of the "Americanization" process, by which Lutherans labored to remove the "foreign" stigma they felt "Yankee" Americans had attached to them. Even those Lutherans who had long thought of themselves as fully Americanized were indiscriminately placed in this category. Although Eastern Lutherans of the colonial tradition had taken great strides in making the transition to speaking English, American Lutheranism as a whole was still engaged in the so-called language struggle; 80 percent of all Lutherans still used one or another of about thirty languages. Some indication of the hold that foreign languages had on Lutherans is given by the percentage of congregations using a European mother-tongue to some degree in the years just prior to World War I:

United Synod of the South	5.0%	⎫
General Synod	20.0%	
Joint Synod of Ohio	87.0%	
		German
		and
General Council (including Augustana)	92.0%	Swedish (Augustana)
Synodical Conference (Missouri and Wisconsin)	97.0%	⎭
Norwegian Synod	99.0%	
United Norwegian Church	99.5%[1]	

In most of the churches the debate over language was not whether English should be introduced but when and to what extent it should be used. Many reasoned that it would be a mistake to deprive people of their "religious language" (mother tongue) by a too hasty transition to English. Others argued that a rapid swing to English might be inimical to the preservation of Lutheran liturgical traditions and an open invitation to un-Lutheran, perhaps even heretical, theological notions. With World War I, the popular prejudice against German extended to other languages as well. Foreign ways of dress and diet led an extreme advocate of Theodore Roosevelt's "100 percent Americanism" to ask rhetorically, "What kind of American consciousness can grow in an atmosphere of sauerkraut and Limburger cheese?"[2] Among the many who experienced this attitude was a Danish-American who wrote:

> I was under no pressure to speak Danish at home but I continued to do so most of the time so my grandparents would understand what I was talking

1. E. Clifford Nelson, ed., *The Lutherans in North America* (Philadelphia: Fortress Press, 1975), p. 366.
2. Quoted in Carl Malmberg, *America Is Also Scandinavian* (New York: G. P. Putnam's Sons, 1970), p. 66.

about. When I was ten, however, World War I broke out, and soon we found that Danish was a language to avoid. Most people in the Wisconsin town where we lived could not distinguish Danish from German, even if it had occurred to them to do so.[3]

As narrow and provincial as much pro-Americanism was, it nevertheless became sufficiently widespread to deprive a whole generation of American students of the advantages of foreign-language study. It would be a mistake, however, to say that World War I was the sole cause of the cultural transition in the churches. Actually such transition was a process that had been going on for decades. Already in the eighteenth century, children of German parents in Pennsylvania and New York were clamoring for the adoption of American ways and language. This resulted in some instances in generational conflict, and churches experienced bitter controversy between the "old" and the "new."[4] "Hansen's Law" (the third generation tries to remember what the second generation tries to forget) was being experienced before it was formulated. The reluctance of the elders to introduce English alienated large numbers of young people, and thousands left foreign-language Lutheran congregations and joined "American" denominations (Presbyterian, Methodist, Episcopalian) or lost themselves in the world of the churchless. George H. Gerberding, writing in 1914, said:

> Ours is the most polyglot Protestant church in America. We like to boast that the Gospel is preached in Lutheran pulpits in more languages than were heard on the day of Pentecost. . . . But while these many tongues are on the one hand our glory, they are on the other hand our heavy cross.[5]

Thus it was that, even before World War I, the immigrant churches faced a difficult twofold missionary task: reaching the first generation in the language they knew best, and retaining the second generation which, in its eagerness to become "American," placed a high priority on the use of English in church, school, and home.

Leaders of the more Americanized branches of Lutheranism urged

3. Quoted in ibid., p. 71. Malmberg has a good summary of this attempt to eliminate all "un-American" influences; see pp. 119–22.
4. See Marcus L. Hansen, "The Problem of the Third Generation Immigrant," in *Augustana Historical Society Publications,* vol. 8, pt. 1 (Rock Island, Ill., 1938).
5. *Problems and Possibilities* (Columbia, S.C.: Lutheran Board of Publication, 1914), p. 171.

those who were reluctant to introduce English not to repeat the
mistakes of the past. It was not true, they argued, that "true Lutheranism" could not survive in the English tongue. "We Lutherans from the
East," wrote Gerberding, "had a century and a half of history behind
us. We had made our mistakes. . . . It is a tragic story. We did not
want the [Lutherans] of the West to repeat the suicidal blunders of
Germans and Swedes in the East. We wanted to help them save their
children in the Lutheran Church."[6] Suspicion of the motives of those
whose slogan was "The Faith of the Fathers in the Language of the
Children" was eventually overcome, and foreign-language church
bodies soon organized an "association," "conference," "district," or
"synod," the main responsibility of which was to promote the use of
English. By 1917 most of the churches had established English-
language periodicals and had published English liturgies, hymnals,
and catechisms. Even the most ardent advocates of change assumed
that the process of transition would extend over many years—certainly
another generation at least—but World War I accelerated the change
beyond all expectations. "Virtually over night," said the historian of
the Augustana Synod, "the congregations . . . made the transition
from Swedish to English."[7] In fact, so rapid was the changeover that
the synodical president felt obligated in 1921 to urge the setting aside
of "one or two congregations . . . in the large cities as exclusively Swedish churches" for those who still preferred the mother
tongue.[8]

In 1917 the merger of three Norwegian Lutheran bodies had been
made possible in part by the agreement to christen the new body the
"Norwegian Lutheran Church of America." The following year the
pro-American feeling was running so high that some leaders began
agitation to eliminate the word "Norwegian" from the name of the
church.[9] The opposition to the change that developed postponed
action until 1946, although in actuality the language transition was

6. George H. Gerberding, *Reminiscent Reflections of a Youthful Octogenarian*
(Minneapolis: Augsburg Publishing House, 1928), p. 155.

7. Everett Arden, *Augustana Heritage* (Rock Island, Ill.: Augustana Press, 1963), p.
246.

8. Ibid., p. 247.

9. "The Change of Name," *Lutheran Church Herald*, May 17, 1918, p. 305.

almost completed by 1930.[10] The story was similar among the Danish Lutherans and the German Missouri Synod.[11]

The effect of World War I upon the churches was not limited to "Americanization," nor was "Americanization" limited to patriotic feelings or to a rapid switch to the English language. The alteration in American Lutheran church life was to reach into theological attitudes, which forced this question: If we all speak English and we all teach the gospel according to the Lutheran confessions, is there any genuine reason for maintaining our ecclesiastical separateness? The question of Lutheran unity would ultimately lead to a search for ways in which Lutherans could participate in the emerging ecumenical movement. Before surveying the attitudes and achievements of the movement toward church unity, we must give a short description of theological attitudes and social thought prevalent among Lutherans of this era.

Theological Stance and Social Thought

Despite the diversity among American Lutherans at the outbreak of World War I, there was a remarkable underlying homogeneity about them. This homogeneous quality was most visible in the attitude that all the church bodies assumed over against the new intellectual climate of the nineteenth century. The "evangelical liberalism" and "scientific modernism"[12] that disturbed and polarized several Protestant denominations were stoutly resisted by Lutherans. When this "new theology" was later wedded to what was called "the Social Gospel," Lutherans of all varieties protested that the "new" was a dangerous distortion of the biblical message.

In order to understand the theological travail of American Lutheranism in the years after World War I, it is necessary to make a rapid survey of theological thought in nineteenth-century American Luther-

10. E. Clifford Nelson, *The Lutheran Church among Norwegian-Americans* (Minneapolis: Augsburg Publishing House, 1960), 2:250.

11. Paul C. Nyholm, *The Americanization of the Danish Lutheran Churches in America* (Copenhagen: Institute for Danish Church History, 1963), pp. 292–322; Everette Meier and Herbert T. Mayer, "The Process of Americanization," in *Moving Frontiers*, ed. Carl Meyer (St. Louis: Concordia Publishing House, 1964), pp. 380–81.

12. For a brief discussion of these two distinct, but often equated, movements see Winthrop S. Hudson, *Religion in America* (New York: Scribner's, 1965), pp. 269–77, esp. p. 274 n. 16.

anism. In the early years of that exciting era, Lutherans faced a crisis compounded by the threat of rationalism and the seduction of "Americanization" via revivalism. Religious indifference during the first years of the young republic was judged by Protestant churches as a massive threat to spiritual life and morals. The Second Awakening and the Great Revival in the West were consequently welcomed as means by which to defeat the enemy and to preserve an evangelical witness in America. When Lutherans added their strength to this effort, they tended to minimize the distinctly Lutheran confessional principle and to embrace some of the emphases of American "evangelicalism."[13] This attitude was to be seen in the positions advocated by Samuel S. Schmucker, president of the Lutheran seminary at Gettysburg and the most influential American Lutheran theologian of the era.[14] The movement that resulted from his leadership was given the descriptive title "American Lutheranism"[15] and, ironically, was detected as being un-Lutheran not only by Schmucker's opponent, Charles Porterfield Krauth, but also by the staunchly Reformed theologians of Mercersburg, John Nevin and Philip Schaff. The Mercersburg men charged Schmucker with being neither Lutheran nor Calvinist in his view of Holy Communion, that his was a denatured Lutheranism hardly distinguishable from the Zwinglianism of contemporary American "evangelicalism."[16]

This "American Lutheranism" was overcome eventually by a growing interest in recently imported German neo-confessionalism that arrived in three ways: (1) by the translation of German Lutheran theological literature and its subsequent use in the General Synod just at the time the controversy over "American Lutheranism" was reach-

13. For an insightful examination of "American Evangelicalism" see Leigh Jordahl, "The American Evangelical Tradition and Culture Religion," *Dialog* 4 (Summer 1965): 188–93. Cf. William G. McLoughlin, ed., *The American Evangelicals, 1800–1900* (New York: Harper & Row, 1968).

14. See Samuel S. Schmucker, *The American Lutheran Church, Historically, Doctrinally, and Practically Delineated* . . . (Springfield, Ohio: D. Harbaugh, 1851); and *Fraternal Appeal to the American Churches, with a Plan for Catholic Union, on Apostolic Principles* (1838; reprint ed., Philadelphia: Fortress Press, 1965). Cf. Abdel Ross Wentz, *Pioneer in Christian Unity: Samuel Simon Schmucker* (Philadelphia: Fortress Press, 1967).

15. For a discussion see Vergilius Ferm, *The Crisis in American Lutheran Theology* (New York: Century Co., 1927).

16. See James H. Nichols, *Romanticism in American Theology: Nevin and Schaff at Mercersburg* (Chicago: University of Chicago Press, 1961), pp. 92–93.

ing a climax; (2) by the mass immigration of German and Scandinavian Lutherans at mid-century; and (3) by a revival of interest in the Lutheran liturgical tradition circa 1860–90. This neo-confessionalism became a movement to combat religious indifference, not by the methods of "American evangelicalism" but by a repristination of the scholasticism of the seventeenth-century Lutheran dogmaticians and by a continuing emphasis on pietistic orthodoxy, the latter especially among Scandinavians.

The problem facing American Lutherans was that they could see no other options. The historically oriented biblical hermeneutics of the so-called Erlangen school were largely unknown or, if known, regarded with suspicion.[17] This was to be expected in the Missouri Synod, whose leaders asserted that the Erlangen theology "pierced the hands and feet of Christianity" and "stabbed it through the heart," not least in its "denial of the verbal inspiration and inerrancy of Scripture."[18] Although some of the professors in seminaries of the General Synod and General Council were ready to admit, even before World War I, the necessity of moving beyond biblical literalism, they were generally skittish about theological novelty. An exception to this pattern was Carl J. Sodergren of the Augustana Synod (a part of the General Council until 1918), whose views were considered dangerously liberal by some of his colleagues. He wrote in 1914 about the Bible and evolution: "The time has arrived, it appears, for someone to say that the theory of evolution is not necessarily atheistic, and that it might be quite consistent with the Bible and with Christian belief in God as the Creator of heaven and earth."[19] Sodergren, however, was but one of a small and untypical number of American Lutheran theologians who were open to the new insights.

17. The hallmarks of Erlangen theology were: fidelity to the Lutheran confessions understood historically; exposition of the Bible, not as a compendium of verbally inspired proof texts, but as witness to God's redemptive activity in history; and the affirmation of the personal, inner experience of new-birth and justification by faith as the controlling principle of systematic theology. See Otto W. Heick, *A History of Christian Thought* (Philadelphia: Fortress Press, 1966), 2:203–16; and "Erlangen Schule," *Die Religion in Geschichte und Gegenwart*, 3d ed. (Tübingen, 1957–65), 2:566–67. For Missouri's view see Franz Pieper, *Christian Dogmatics* (St. Louis: Concordia Publishing House, 1950–53), 1:ix, 160–86.

18. See Friedrich Bente, "Vorwort," *Lehre und Wehre* 50 (January 1904): 14.

19. *The Lutheran Companion*, December 26, 1914; cited in Arden, *Augustana Heritage*, p. 285.

On the whole, Lutheranism in America looked upon scholars who used the historical-critical approach to the Bible as subversives. The "Social Gospel" of such Protestants as Washington Gladden and Walter Rauschenbusch was rejected outright by Lutherans as "a different gospel" (Gal. 1:6–7). There was a genuine fear that to affirm it was to substitute sociology for theology and to secularize Christianity. Very few would have disagreed with reports from the General Synod and the General Council that the main task of the church was "the faithful preaching of the Gospel, and . . . [the] bringing [of] individual members of society to a saving knowledge of Jesus Christ . . ."; "His relation to society is through the individual soul and through the community of saints . . . but He is not . . . a reformer of its evils, or an adjuster of its economic distresses." [20]

As far as the church as a whole was concerned, the theological-social climate of American Lutheranism remained relatively unchanged. The congregations rested in indolent satisfaction with "the received faith," a confession of the Lutheran tradition interpreted in large measure according to the canons of the seventeenth century. The problems of American Lutheranism, it was reasoned, were basically not theological but rather practical and immensely urgent. Unchurched immigrants and second- or third-generation Lutherans, new missions in city and country, colleges and seminaries, hospitals and orphanages, missions in Africa and Asia, and, of course, "Americanization"—these were "the real problem." In the light of the pressing task to establish the church in the American setting, there was little time to reflect on the "new theology" or the role of the church in a society rapidly being urbanized and industrialized.

LUTHERAN UNITY, 1917–25

Despite Lutheranism's common front in the matters mentioned above, organizational unity was a long way from being achieved. The ever-present problem of ethnic origins, and the estrangement between "Eastern Lutherans" and the immigrant churches of the Midwest,

20. General Synod, *Minutes . . . 1913*, pp. 150–51; and General Council, *Minutes . . . 1911*, p. 228. Cited by Fred W. Meuser, in Nelson, ed., *Lutherans in North America*, pp. 386–87.

delayed Lutheran unity for decades. The Eastern Lutherans' brush with "American Lutheranism" led other Lutherans to regard them as confessionally indifferent because of their attitudes toward "unionism," freemasonry, and chiliasm. The Midwestern Lutherans failed to understand that these were not the concerns of liberal theology. Even the confessionally indifferent groups of individuals remaining in the old General Synod were not "liberals" in the sense of nineteenth-century German theology.

By the 400th anniversary of the Reformation (1917) the question of church unity was "in the air." Spokesmen for the cause were present in several quarters, and they would not be denied. Major steps in the direction of Lutheran unity were taken in the late war years (1917–18). The merger of three Norwegian-background bodies into the Norwegian Lutheran Church of America (1917), the reunion of Eastern Lutherans into the United Lutheran Church in America (1918), and the formation of a cooperative agency, the National Lutheran Council (1918) were all events of far-reaching importance. Influences from these developments continued to flow into the life of American Lutheranism and the ecumenical movement.

The Formation of the Norwegian Lutheran Church of America [21]

Norwegian immigrants began arriving in the Midwest in 1839. By 1890 those who had been gathered into the church were to be found in three "synods": Hauge's Norwegian Evangelical Lutheran Synod in America (1846 and 1876), the Synod for the Norwegian Evangelical Lutheran Church in America (1853), and the United Norwegian Lutheran Church in America (1890). The latter suffered two schisms in the decade after its founding, the Lutheran Free Church (1897) and the Church of the Lutheran Brethren (1900). Despite these setbacks the United Church lost none of its enthusiasm for ultimate merger of Norwegian Lutherans in America. Year after year it extended overtures to the other churches and arranged conferences for the purpose of resolving differences. The Norwegian Synod, strongly influenced

---

21. For a detailed discussion of the Norwegian Lutheran union movement see Nelson, *The Lutheran Church among Norwegian-Americans*, 2:183–225.

by the Missouri Synod, with which it had been in fellowship from 1872 to 1883 (in the Synodical Conference), rejected the overtures for doctrinal reasons. The Hauge Synod, reflecting pietistic and low-church concerns, feared that some of its emphases, such as preaching by laymen, would be jeopardized if not lost in a large union of churches. Then in 1905, quite unexpectedly, the Haugeans reversed themselves, appointed a union committee, and invited the United Church and the Norwegian Synod to do the same.[22] Fruitful conferences were held until 1908, when negotiations were threatened by the long-standing and troublesome question of election (predestination), in which the Norwegian Synod held the Missourian viewpoint. Despite the efforts of Hans G. Stub, president of the Norwegian Synod, to make room for both the Missourian and anti-Missourian interpretations of election, the discussions reached an impasse in 1910. Nevertheless, proponents of union on both sides revived the discussions by the expedient of appointing completely new committees, which, with considerable encouragement from laymen, finally reached a "settlement" (*opgjør*) in 1912. Both the United Church and the Norwegian Synod (the Hauge Synod had stepped aside but supported the United Church) agreed that although there were two interpretations of the doctrine of election each could be accepted as orthodox.

With this theological barrier removed, the three churches were able to work out practical and constitutional matters over the next few years and bring about the merger known as the Norwegian Lutheran Church of America (NLCA). Its first president, Hans G. Stub, combined great gifts of leadership with a pronounced tilt toward the Missouri Synod. Despite his sympathies for Missourianism, he allowed himself to be elected president of the National Lutheran Council (1918) and became a supporter of the Lutheran World Convention. The impact of his strong personality on the new half-million-member church would become unmistakable during the eight years of his presidency (1917–25). Other leading Norwegian-American personalities, like Lauritz Larsen (1882–1923) and Lars W. Boe (1875–1942), were to become familiar names in American and world Lutheranism.

22. The same invitation went out to the Eielsen Synod (earlier Haugeans who refused to participate in a synodical reorganization in 1876), the Lutheran Brethren, and the Lutheran Free Church. Only the latter responded, saying it was interested in cooperation but not merger.

A small party within the former Norwegian Synod rejected the merger and in 1918 formed the Norwegian Synod of the American Evangelical Lutheran Church. Casting its lot with the Missouri and Wisconsin synods in the Synodical Conference, it declared that its purpose was to preserve orthodox Lutheranism among the Norwegians in America. In the early 1950s it changed its name to the Evangelical Lutheran Synod.

The Reunion of the Muhlenberg Tradition:
"Eastern Lutherans"[23]

The ecclesiastical descendants of the "patriarch" of colonial Lutheranism, Henry M. Muhlenberg, were divided into three general groups by the 1860s: the General Synod, the General Council, and the United Synod, South. Following overtures made by the General Synod in the 1870s, the General Council proposed an informal conference for "all Lutherans who accept the Unaltered Augsburg Confession." Two "Free Lutheran Diets" (1877 and 1878) revealed that the three Eastern general bodies, from which attendance was primarily drawn, were of a common mind. In terms of confessional stance the General Synod was considered "left," the General Council "right," and the United Synod, South "middle," but as contacts increased there was a perceptible movement toward a common confessional attitude.

While the three groups were moving together theologically, they were working toward common forms for worship. By 1888 a joint committee had produced The Common Service, which was based on "the common consent of the pure Lutheran liturgies of the sixteenth century. . . ." When there was no complete agreement among these liturgies, "the consent of the largest number of those of greatest weight" would be determinative.[24] Although the new service was initially opposed in numerous congregations of the General Synod, which was less liturgical (but more "Americanized") than the other two bodies, by 1917 when a common hymnal was adopted to take its place alongside the new liturgy most of Eastern Lutheranism was using the *Common Service Book*. Its preface declared, "This book

---

23. For a detailed discussion of the formation of the United Lutheran Church in America see Abdel Ross Wentz, *A Basic History of Lutheranism in America*, rev. ed. (Philadelphia: Fortress Press, 1964), pp. 140–68, 221–39, 269–85.

24. Ibid., pp. 225–26.

. . . witnesses to the essential strength and spiritual oneness of the
Lutheran Church in America." It is worth noting that church bodies in
the Midwest—especially the Missouri Synod, the Augustana Synod,
the Joint Synod of Ohio, and the Norwegian Lutheran Church of
America—soon made The Common Service available to their congregations.

The new spirit of goodwill and cooperation, created and promoted
by "Free Diets" and joint work on common worship, led to formal (the
"Free Diets" had been just that, free and informal) discussions by
official representatives of the churches. In response to a proposal by
the General Council, the first General Conference of Lutherans in
America was held in 1898. This was followed by similar conferences in
1902 and 1904. The total impact of such meetings was the growing
conviction that the confessional condition for unity (Augsburg Confession, Article VII: "For the true unity of the church it is enough to agree
concerning the teaching of the Gospel and the administration of the
sacraments") was present and therefore should be implemented. This
did not come without fear of "confessionalism" on the part of some in
the General Synod.[25] The whole issue, however, was pressed by the
General Council's insistence that closer relationships depended on the
General Synod's unequivocal affirmation that the Bible *is* (not merely
contains) the Word of God and that the Lutheran confessions are a
correct exhibition of the faith and doctrine of the church.[26] The
General Synod acquiesced to General Council wishes and thus
prepared the way for the merger of 1918. Its action also, for the first
time, placed all Lutherans in America on virtually the same confessional basis.[27]

Theological and liturgical advances had been supplemented by a
history of cooperation between the three synods in home and foreign
missionary enterprises. Moreover, lay people of the various groups had

25. See especially John W. Richard, *The Confessional History of the Lutheran
Church* (Philadelphia: Lutheran Publication Society, 1909). Richard, together with his
colleague at Gettysburg Seminary, Milton Valentine, was fearful of a "repristination"
theology.
26. See Theodore Schmauk's comments quoted in George S. Sandt, *Theodore
Emanuel Schmauk, D.D., L.L.D.: A Biographical Sketch* (Philadelphia: United Lutheran Publication House, 1921), pp. 176–78; cf. pp. 133–36.
27. For an account of development in the General Synod see Wentz, *Basic History*,
pp. 230–32.

learned to know one another in a variety of organizations that crossed synodical lines. In fact, it was the enthusiasm of laymen for organic unity that helped to spark the actual merger. The occasion was the intersynodical preparation for the 400th anniversary of the Reformation. A joint committee had been making arrangements for the celebration since 1914. The lay people on this committee in 1917 spearheaded a move for "immediate and organic union." The entire committee responded favorably to a resolution that the three synods "together with all other bodies one with us in our Lutheran faith" merge as soon as possible into an organization "to be known as the United Lutheran Church in America."[28] The reaction was prompt and overwhelmingly favorable. The presidents appointed a joint committee that produced a constitution for submission to the synods in 1918. "Beginning on November 11, 1918, the day of the armistice in Europe," says Wentz, "each general body held an adjourned meeting in New York City, completed its business . . . and then, November 14–16, joined . . . the first convention of the United Lutheran Church in America [ULCA]."[29] The new church, numbering about one million baptized members, elected Frederick H. Knubel of the General Synod over Theodore E. Schmauk of the General Council as its first president. Schmauk, as noted earlier, was known in Germany through his contacts with the Allgemeine Evangelisch-Lutherische Konferenz (AELK). Knubel wisely resumed Schmauk's war-broken relationship with the AELK and gave American leadership in the movement to form the Lutheran World Convention.

It was hoped that the preamble of the ULCA constitution would set the stage for further union by inviting all Lutherans who subscribed to the confessional position stated in the constitution to unite in one Lutheran Church in America.[30] Other Lutherans, however, did not respond favorably. The Augustana Synod, which had been a national rather than geographic synod in the General Council, did not participate in the merger, preferring to preserve its identity without cutting

---

28. Ibid., p. 272.
29. Ibid., p. 273.
30. For further details on the formation of the church see the account in *The Lutheran World Almanac and Encyclopedia 1921* (New York: NLC, 1920), pp. 76–83; and ULCA, *Minutes . . . 1918*, pp. 37–42, 63–68, 90–92.

off the possibility of continuing friendly relations with the new church. The Norwegian Lutheran Church, having just consummated its own merger, was hardly prepared to consider the invitation seriously. The Synodical Conference, under the strong leadership of the Missouri Synod, maintained that there were confessional differences between it and the new body. The Joint Synod of Ohio preferred a pan-Lutheran federation to organic merger, and the Iowa Synod continued to feel uneasy about the Eastern Lutherans. The invitation by the United Lutheran Church, considered by its framers as a gesture of goodwill toward other Lutherans, was actually regarded by not a few Midwestern Lutherans as an arrogant affront.

Despite the lack of response from other Lutherans, the United Lutheran Church moved into the new era with great enthusiasm and rejoiced that after more than sixty years of separation the churches of the Muhlenberg tradition were reunited. The church stood ready to take its place in the postwar world and to give leadership in both American and international Lutheranism and in the emerging ecumenical movement.

Solidarity: The Joint Synod of Wisconsin and Other States

There were some Germans in the Midwest whose history in the nineteenth century revealed a move from the left to the right on the "scale of orthodoxy." Three synods (Wisconsin, 1850; Michigan, 1860; and Minnesota, 1880) traced their roots to leaders who were not "strict constructionists" with regard to the norms of confessionalist Lutheranism. The largest of these, Wisconsin, participated in the organization of the General Council (1867), but within less than a decade (1871) it had withdrawn because the council was judged to be doctrinally inadequate. The Michigan Synod, also a member of the General Council, withdrew in 1888. The Minnesota Synod, originally a part of the General Synod, moved into the General Council in 1867. The latter proved to be unsatisfactory and led to Minnesota's withdrawal in 1871.

These three synods, with common German ancestry and growing theological conservatism, found it expedient in 1892 to enter a loose federation, the Joint Synod of Wisconsin, Minnesota, Michigan, and

Other States, which in the same year became a part of the larger federation, the Missouri Synod–dominated Synodical Conference.[31] By 1904 a fourth synod (Nebraska) had become a part of the 1892 federation. These four bodies, three-fifths of whose membership was contributed by the Wisconsin Synod, dissolved their loose federation in 1919 and formed an organic merger called the Evangelical Lutheran Joint Synod of Wisconsin and Other States (later shortened to the Wisconsin Evangelical Lutheran Synod). After World War I, and especially after World War II, this church grew increasingly critical of its sister church in the Synodical Conference, the Missouri Synod. In the early 1960s Wisconsin, together with the Evangelical Lutheran (Norwegian) Synod, found it necessary to disavow fellowship with the Missouri Synod for the latter's deviations from the standards of "true Lutheranism."[32]

GROWING COOPERATION

One of the sad facts of Lutheran history on the North American continent has been the operation of what has been called the "calamity theory" in the movement toward cooperation and unity.[33] A few optimists from time to time said that closer fellowship was at hand. As a matter of fact, it was only in the face of dire necessity, external pressures, and threatening crises that Lutherans began to close ranks. Ironically, this confessionally oriented ecclesiastical family found itself drawn together more often by common disaster than by common confession.

Lutheran churches were suddenly confronted in wartime with the necessity of caring for the spiritual needs of their young members in

31. The Synodical Conference was begun by the Missouri and Ohio synods because the General Council was considered too lax. For the next decade it was the largest general association of Lutherans in North America. Wentz, *Basic History*, pp. 217–18.

32. This brief account of the Wisconsin Synod is based on ibid., pp. 262–68. Cf. John Philipp Koehler, *The History of the Wisconsin Synod*, ed. and with intro. by Leigh D. Jordahl (Mosinee, Wis.: Protestant Conference, 1970).

33. The most recent account of the National Lutheran Council is Frederick K. Wentz, *Lutherans in Concert* (Minneapolis: Augsburg Publishing House, 1968); Wentz uses this expression (p. 95), which was first used by E. Theodore Bachmann in *The Lutheran Churches of the World*, ed. Abdel Ross Wentz (Geneva: LWF, 1952), p. 30, and also in his *The Epic of Faith* (New York: NLC, 1952), p. 15.

the armed services. The crisis nature of the situation did not permit the luxury of arguing old differences. Moreover, the government was unwilling to deal with major denominations individually, preferring that churches work through the Young Men's Christian Association or the Federal Council of Churches. Unwilling, for both theological and practical reasons, to join other Protestants in using these agencies, and certainly unwilling to leave young Lutherans in military service spiritually unshepherded, there remained no other course but to unite in common action. The result was the formation of the National Lutheran Commission for Soldiers' and Sailors' Welfare (NLCSSW) on October 19, 1917.[34]

The National Lutheran Commission for Soldiers' and Sailors' Welfare

When the United States entered the war, all Lutherans, whether they supported this participation or not (prior to 1917 many Lutherans were pro-German), now became concerned about the welfare of Lutheran servicemen. Within three weeks of America's entry into the war, the Inner Mission Board of the General Synod invited similar boards of the General Council and the United Synod, South to form a United Inner Mission. Organized in May 1917, the agency immediately sought the cooperation of the Iowa and Ohio synods, as well as that of the Norwegians.

Seven Lutheran church bodies, including Missouri, were represented at an October 19, 1917, meeting called by the United Inner Mission to organize one central board for Lutheran wartime service. Six more quickly joined, but Missouri's representative could not commit his church to membership in the new National Lutheran Commission for Soldiers' and Sailors' Welfare. In view of the scathing

---

34. For details of the commission's work, see NLCSSW, *Reports of . . . Annual Meeting, October 16, 1918* and *Annual Meeting, November 4, 1919* (New York: NLCSSW, 1918, 1919). An account of the origins of the NLCSSW is in the 1918 report, pp. 17–21. This includes an "Agreement" with the Synodical Conference. Additional valuable primary materials on the NLCSSW are in Helen Knubel, "The National Lutheran Commission for Soldiers' and Sailors' Welfare: As Revealed Largely through the Official Correspondence," *Concordia Historical Institute Quarterly* 40 (October 1967): 127–28. Of special significance are Helen Knubel's insights on the roles of her father, Frederick H. Knubel; Lauritz Larsen, secretary of the NLCSSW and late executive director of the NLC; and Jacob A. O. Stub, son of Hans G. Stub and president of the Lutheran Brotherhood of America. Cf. also Fred W. Meuser, in Nelson, ed., *Lutherans in North America*, pp. 401–3.

attacks that Missouri Synod papers were making on all planning for the United Lutheran Church merger of 1918, even the presence of a Missouri representative was surprising. Representatives of the others had no qualms about committing their churches to a well-defined program of cooperation. The NLCSSW was by far the most inclusive organization of Lutherans to this point in American history.[35] Even the Synodical Conference maintained a carefully delineated working agreement with it, especially in matters that required a single Lutheran approach to governmental or military units.[36] Full cooperation was established with the organization of lay people, the Lutheran Brotherhood of America, which continued to build and equip "Lutheran centers" for servicemen. President of the NLCSSW for its relatively short life span was Frederick H. Knubel, the Manhattan pastor who had been chairman of the General Synod's Inner Mission Board and of the United Inner Mission. He was soon to be elected president of the United Lutheran Church. His leadership, which combined spiritual depth, theological insight, and great executive ability, was a key factor in the success of the commission.

Through the program of the Commission for Soldiers' and Sailors' Welfare no area of wartime service to Lutherans was ignored. Chaplains were recruited and equipped; pastors of congregations near military installations were appointed as camp pastors; field secretaries were appointed to visit all bases so that every Lutheran young man had some opportunity for pastoral contact; churches near camps were given interest-free loans to provide proper facilities; workers were assigned to the centers built by laymen of the Lutheran Brotherhood of America; chaplain services were provided for military hospitals and camps for interned aliens.[37] Christian literature for servicemen was provided virtually free of charge; mail contact was maintained with all

---

35. Member churches: Danish Lutheran, General Council, General Synod, Icelandic Synod, Iowa Synod, Lutheran Brethren, Lutheran Free Church, Norwegian Lutheran Church, Joint Synod of Ohio, Suomi Synod, United Danish Church, United Synod, South. Fred W. Meuser's excellent summary of the NLCSSW's activity is found in Nelson, ed., *Lutherans in North America*, pp. 401–3.

36. For "Agreement with the Synodical Conference" and "Agreement with the Lutheran Brotherhood" see the NLCSSW's 1918 annual report, pp. 19–21. For a full report on Missouri's Church Board for Army and Navy, U.S.A., see Missouri Synod, *Synodal-Bericht . . . 1920*, pp. 103–11.

37. Work with aliens was assigned almost exclusively to the NLCSSW by the Wartime Commission of the Federal Council of Churches.

Lutheran servicemen whose addresses were provided; pastors were appointed to serve the Student Army Training Corps at church colleges; and women were enlisted for volunteer work through a women's committee.

The NLCSSW had considerable success in raising money, in coordinating Lutheran services in the war emergency, and in establishing a "lobby" (the first director found the term offensive and hotly denied that he was a lobbyist) to represent Lutheran interests before the federal government. Representing the commission at Washington was Lauritz Larsen, a pastor in the NLCA who had been serving a Brooklyn parish. He was to become the first full-time executive director of the National Lutheran Council and another leading figure in the movement toward establishing the Lutheran World Convention.

Of equal importance for our purposes was the decision of the NLCSSW to send representatives to Paris to explore ways of providing relief for the French church and creating an American ministry to servicemen on leave. It took several months to overcome the delaying tactics of the U.S. government in issuing passports (despite the lobbying of Larsen), but finally Charles J. Smith (a clergyman) and Frank M. Riter (a lawyer) sailed for Europe. Later on, Michael J. Stolee, a professor at Luther Seminary in St. Paul, Minnesota, and fluent in French, was also asked to represent the commission in this work. This action of the NLCSSW and the continuation of its program by the European Commission of the National Lutheran Council, to which we will return shortly, led to expressions of hope for the calling of a world conference of Lutherans.

The National Lutheran Council

As important as the Commission for Soldiers' and Sailors' Welfare was for giving Lutherans a way of doing together what they could not do separately, it had been in existence for only a short time when some of its inadequacies became obvious. A ministry to service personnel, which was the boundary of the commission's authorization, was not the only need that had to be met cooperatively. The first problem rose out of the attacks on Lutherans because of the American hysteria over foreign languages; this made imperative a continuing official and representative Lutheran presence in Washington. The hysteria was most evident in the Midwest, where Lutherans were scrutinized by "100 percent Americans" who were determined to rid society of everything German. State and local councils of defense took legal and illegal action against suspected Germanophiles. Governors issued proclamations and state legislatures passed laws forbidding the use of German and other foreign languages in public worship. Lauritz Larsen requested permission to appear before the Council of National Defense in Washington to plead the cause of foreign-language churches. Writing to the director, Grosvenor B. Clarkson, he said:

> You are no doubt aware of Governor Harding's proclamation for Iowa, and that he still insists that it should be enforced. In many of the western states . . . the Councils of Defense have been very unreasonable . . . with reference to the use of the German language. I know, for instance, of a case in South Dakota where the pastor was forbidden to speak a few words of comfort [in German] to a couple of late arrivals from Germany who had lost their little child by death, and of another instance where the pastor was refused [permission] to administer communion to an old dying woman in the German language, which was the only medium of bringing a little comfort to her. I know of counties in Texas where the use of German . . . is absolutely forbidden in public worship. . . . In Iowa it does not only apply to German but to all foreign languages.[38]

A voice in Washington was unquestionably required.

In addition to the pressing problem of protesting linguistic injustices, two other needs cried out for concerted, organized action, both of which the ad hoc commission was not intended to address. There was the need for a home mission ministry in communities where defense industries were mushrooming. Lutheran cooperation in this area was particularly vulnerable to accusations from Missouri and other "orthodox" Lutherans that churches would be practicing "sinful unionism," since cooperation went beyond "externals" and involved a spiritual ministry of Word and Sacrament to all Lutherans, even to those from churches that were not in pulpit and altar fellowship. Despite this anxiety the majority of Lutherans felt the need to do something.

The third problem involved Lutheran cooperation in providing aid for Europe's war-stricken churches. The physical destruction and

---

38. Larsen to Clarkson, December 30, 1918, in the Archives of Cooperative Lutheranism, Lutheran Council/U.S.A., New York City (hereafter referred to as ArCL).

spiritual chaos left countless European Lutherans in need and their
mission work in Asia, Africa, and Oceania without support. Joint fund-
raising and publicity for services on a much broader scale than that of
the NLCSSW would be imperative. To the pioneers in cooperation a
new and more comprehensively authorized Lutheran agency was the
logical answer. From several quarters came proposals in mid-1918 for
such an agency. The National Lutheran Editors Association, one of the
first pan-Lutheran cooperative groups, suggested that the presidents
move to bring about such "concerted action." Frederick H. Knubel
saw the need clearly and urged presidents Theodore E. Schmauk
(General Council), Morris G. G. Scherer (United Synod, South), Victor
G. A. Tressler (General Synod), and Hans G. Stub (NLCA) to take the
lead in promoting a new agency.

In July and August 1918, preliminary meetings of presidents and
others in Harrisburg and Pittsburgh laid plans for the organization of
a "Lutheran Federal Council" in Chicago on September 6. Once
again, church-body presidents were willing to take immediate action
without waiting for church bodies to approve. In addition to the four
named above, Augustana, the Danish Lutheran Church, Iowa,
the Lutheran Free Church, and Ohio attended the Chicago meeting and approved of the agency, which was named the National
Lutheran Council (NLC). The United Danish Lutheran Church,
Buffalo Synod, and Icelandic Synod gave their support before the
year's end. The Missouri Synod, although represented at the
two preliminary meetings, again declined to take part. Its traditional
criticism of other Lutherans on doctrinal and practical grounds, plus
frictions between its Army and Navy Board and the NLCSSW, and
unrestrained criticism of the coming United Lutheran Church
made continued isolation inevitable.[39]

Awareness of the long-range possibilities for an agency such as the
National Lutheran Council is clear from the statement of purpose the
founders adopted: statistical information for all American Lutherans,

---

39. All materials on NLC origins and activities are in ArCL. A good history is Went.
Lutherans in Concert. Also useful is Osborne Hauge's *Lutherans Working Together: A
History of the National Lutheran Council, 1918–1943* (New York: NLC, 1945). The
above summary is largely from Fred W. Meuser in Nelson, ed., *Lutherans in North
America,* pp. 403–14.

Fifth Avenue, New York, 1918-1927: Headquarters of the National Lutheran Council, ninth floor, Knabe Piano Building. Notables from the early years were photographed on the roof in 1919.

Standing, F. H. Knubel, L. Larsen, E. F. Eilert.

Seated, S. G. Youngert, J. A. Morehead, G. A. Fandrey.

publicity on matters affecting all Lutherans, representation of Lutherans to all other entities, joint action on problems arising out of the war, coordination of activities related to social, economic, and intellectual conditions affecting Christianity, fostering of loyalty to the nation, and maintaining proper relations between church and state.[40] Headquarters were to be in New York. Representation was 1 for every 100,000 confirmed members or one-third fraction thereof. Hans G. Stub (NLCA) was elected president; John L. Zimmerman (General Synod layman), vice-president; Lauritz Larsen (NLCA), secretary. In view of later developments toward a world Lutheran community, one must bear in mind that besides such persons as Knubel, Stub, and Larsen there were other men, also active in the formation of the National Lutheran Council, who emerged as leaders of the Lutheran World Convention, notably Charles M. Jacobs, professor at the Philadelphia Seminary; Lars W. Boe, president of St. Olaf College; and Gustav A. Brandelle, president of the Augustana Synod.

The striking contrast between the specific purpose of the Commission for Soldiers' and Sailors' Welfare and the more general mandate of the National Lutheran Council explains in part why some member bodies and some presidents were not convinced of the need for the new council. In committing their churches to membership, some had exceeded their actual authority, and their second thoughts had to be put to the test during the council's early years. Frederick K. Wentz, however, is correct in saying that "the Council came into being because of a sense of urgency shared by many Lutherans," that it "sprang into existence" and was "born running" with a full agenda from the start, and that it reflected a "real pioneering spirit" which was to become a trend in twentieth-century Lutheranism.[41]

CRISIS IN THE COUNCIL

Two developments in the National Lutheran Council caused difficulty for Europeans who found American Lutheranism puzzling and disturbing. The first was the aggressive leadership of the Americans. Their compassion for their brethren and their generous imple-

---

40. Wentz, *Lutherans in Concert*, p. 19.
41. Ibid.

mentation of this compassion by the expenditure of energy, time, money, and personnel were viewed with ambivalence in Europe. German Lutherans especially, while deeply grateful for the gestures of mercy, suffered under the double burden of war-guilt (which they were reluctant to admit) and the feeling that leadership in things Lutheran was slipping from their hands to those of the Americans. The National Lutheran Council in 1919 established a European Commission consisting of John A. Morehead (ULCA), Gustav A. Fandrey (Iowa), Sven G. Youngert (Augustana), George Taylor Rygh (NLCA), and Henry J. Schuh (Ohio). Michael J. Stolee (NLCA), who, it will be remembered, had represented the NLCSSW, was asked to return to Europe under the auspices of the National Lutheran Council as an additional commissioner. All these men embarked on their common task with a sense of dedication and a desire to be instruments of reconstruction and reconciliation. The commissioners had been instructed by the NLC to investigate and report the situation of each Lutheran group in the war-involved countries; they were to offer American assistance in solving the ecclesiastical problems of their brethren; and they were empowered to spend up to $50,000. Private instructions came from the Iowa Synod, which said that American Lutheran aid should go only to "orthodox" Lutherans. This was a hint of trouble to come, but it did not dampen the eagerness of the group to carry out its commission.[42]

The second cause for uneasiness among the Europeans was theological in nature. Although they conceded that Americans were excellent administrators and tireless religious "activists," many Germans and Scandinavians looked with jaundiced eye at the theological stance and scholarly endeavor of American Lutherans. Their scholarship was judged minimal and their theology seemed archaic, uncertain, even naive. These opinions were given substance when it was learned that the continued existence of the National Lutheran Council was threatened by a theological rift that came during the first two years of its life. Although the rift did not destroy the agency, the council was weakened, its trumpet giving a quavering, uncertain sound. The story needs a brief rehearsal.

In 1918 there were two main groupings of Lutherans, the Synodical

42. Ibid., pp. 41–44.

Conference (1872) and the new National Lutheran Council. The largest body in the former was the Missouri Synod; the largest body in the latter was the United Lutheran Church. These two represented opposite views regarding church unity. The ULC was committed to unity on the basis of the generally received confessions of Lutheranism; the Missouri Synod went beyond this to require agreement in extraconfessional theses covering doctrine and practice.

To understand developments in the 1920s, one must be aware that non-Missourian Midwestern Lutherans were uneasy between these two ecclesiastical colossi. On the one hand, they cooperated with the United Lutheran Church, as witnessed by the formation of the National Lutheran Council, but at the same time they were suspicious of the doctrinal and ecumenical stance of their "big sister." Their feelings about Missouri and the Synodical Conference were likewise mixed. They were unhappy about Missourian exclusivism, but in large measure they judged this body to be "more Lutheran" than the United Church. Although the division in the National Lutheran Council was not articulated in 1918 and therefore did not immediately hinder the cooperative efforts of the NLC, it was now clear that two potentially divisive points of view regarding confessional Lutheranism lay alongside each other in the council.

The occasion that brought out the differences was the definition and implementation of the NLC's policy of "cooperation in externals." Fearing "unionism" (i.e., fellowship without doctrinal agreement), some Midwestern Lutherans insisted that cooperation be limited to *res externae* in contrast to *res internae.* But where was the boundary between "external" and "internal"? What could be done cooperatively without complete doctrinal agreement?[43] One of the most critical problems after World War I, as already noted, was that of ministering to people who had moved into wartime industrial centers. Clearly this ought to be a cooperative enterprise, because the home mission boards of individual church bodies were unable to cope with the situation. Therefore, a meeting of the NLC's executive committee and home mission representatives was held at Columbus, Ohio, on

43. Lauritz Larsen, "Unity," *Lutheran Church Herald,* April 1, 1919, p. 194. Cf. Hauge, *Lutherans Working Together,* pp. 39–40.

December 18, 1918. It produced agreement that the work should be undertaken. However, at the insistence of Hans G. Stub a resolution was passed requesting the presidents of member churches to constitute a "Joint Committee to confer on questions of doctrine and practice, with a view to the coordination of their home mission and other work." Behind this resolution lay Stub's fear of unionism, because joint home mission work was hardly cooperation "in externals."[44]

The Joint Conference on Doctrine and Practice met March 11–13, 1919, in Chicago.[45] It had been previously agreed that four papers reflecting the viewpoints of their respective churches should be presented by Henry Eyster Jacobs (ULCA), Conrad H. L. Schuette (Ohio Synod), Friedrich Richter (Iowa Synod), and Hans G. Stub (NLCA). A special NLC resolution had requested Knubel "to prepare a statement which shall define the essentials of a catholic spirit as viewed by the Lutheran Church."

After the reading of Knubel's paper on the general principles of catholicity, the particular synodical viewpoints were presented. Jacobs moved that Stub's paper be made the basis of the preliminary discussion before turning to the question of catholicity. Therewith the remaining sessions were devoted to Stub's presentation. After considerable discussion and amendment, the paper was referred by the group to the churches. The articles contained in it were subsequently known as the Chicago Theses. The other main paper, Knubel's "The Essentials of a Catholic Spirit," could not be discussed for lack of time. Therefore a subcommittee consisting of Knubel, Stub, and

44. NLC, *Annual Report . . . 1919,* pp. 13–15; cf. Hauge, *Lutherans Working Together,* pp. 41–42. Stub admits his part in this. See his "Representatives from Eight Lutheran Church Bodies . . . ," *Lutheran Church Herald,* March 21, 1919, p. 180. In a letter to Knubel, Stub reported that certain elements in the NLCA were attacking the NLC. Moreover, the Church Council of the NLCA, having endorsed the organization of the NLC, refused to approve cooperation with other Lutherans in home mission work. Stub wrote: "I hope, my dear Dr. Knubel, that you will now better understand . . . my specific reasons for having advocated strongly the meeting in Chicago on doctrine and practice. If I had not insisted so strongly on this meeting which so many regarded as entirely superfluous, I would have made myself subject to the charge of unionism." Stub to Knubel, February 20, 1919, microfilm, Gullixson Library, Luther-Northwestern Seminaries, St. Paul.

45. See the microfilm copy of the minutes in Knubel-Stub Correspondence, Gullixson Library, Luther-Northwestern Seminaries. Besides Stub, NLCA representatives were J. N. Kildahl and C. J. Eastvold.

Theodore E. Schmauk was appointed to consider the paper and report to a later meeting of the same group. Moreover, the conference voted to publish it as well as Jacobs' paper entitled "Constructive Lutheranism." [46]

Knubel's, Jacobs's, and Stub's papers proved to be of profound significance in the shaping of American Lutheranism, setting forth two points of view: "Ecumenical confessionalism" (Knubel and Jacobs) and "exclusive confessionalism" (Stub). Later developments among churches of the National Lutheran Council revolved about the positions expressed and implied in these documents. The Knubel-Jacobs position insisted that there is an organic union among all parts of God's truth, but a necessary difference of order and importance. When it is recognized that the gospel alone is central and constitutive of the church, there is the foundation for a true catholic spirit in the church. The second point of view ("exclusive confessionalism") can safely be said to have represented Midwestern Lutheranism, including the Missouri Synod, which had not been involved in the discussion. [47]

Two things were now clear: (1) Although the National Lutheran Council had called the meeting, the joint conference action was not an action of the NLC. All enactments would have to be referred to the member churches; (2) The joint conference had not completed its task, because the council request for a statement "which shall define the essentials of a catholic spirit as viewed by the Lutheran Church" had not been discussed.

When Knubel returned home, he sent a letter to Stub seeking to arrange a time for the subcommittee to consider "the essentials of a catholic spirit." He also wrote out a précis of the Chicago meeting, stating his own view that a policy statement on the "essentials of a catholic spirit" was urgently needed because of the pressing problems facing the church in the postwar world. The issues of Bolshevism and other anti-Christian forces, in addition to the ecumenical discussion of

46. NLC Joint Conference on Doctrine and Practice, *Minutes . . . March 11–13, 1919,* p. 18. The papers by Knubel and Jacobs were published in *Lutheran Church Review* 38 (April 1919): 187–97, 198–212.

47. Stub later reported Missouri enthusiasm over the Chicago Theses. NLC Joint Conference on Doctrine and Practice, *Minutes . . . January 27–28, 1920,* microfilm, Gullixson Library, Luther-Northwestern Seminaries, p. 19.

"Faith and Order," demanded that Lutherans think through the problem of catholicity.[48]

In November, Knubel, Stub, and Charles M. Jacobs, who replaced the ailing Schmauk, met to carry out their assignment. It was already apparent by the fall of 1919 that Stub was not eager to pursue the problem of catholicity. His own theological position (the Chicago paper) was, he felt, the proper point of departure for an approach to other Lutherans. Moreover, certain elements in his own church body, notably pastors of the former Norwegian Synod, were extremely critical of the National Lutheran Council.[49] Lars W. Boe wrote confidentially to Knubel that Stub had become nervous because of the opposition. Therefore, said Boe, "he will insist strongly on the Chicago Theses. . . . As I understand it you people feel that the Lutheran Church cannot get together on a negative declaration, and *I agree with you*. Dr. Stub, however, is liable to look at the question from the standpoint of a settlement of . . . old difficulties . . . rather than . . . making a common declaration over against the outside world [italics added]." Boe went on to assure Knubel that he himself supported the ULCA standpoint and hoped the Chicago Theses would not be the cause of the NLC's dissolution.[50]

A subsequent meeting, January 27–28, 1920, finally centered on "The Essentials of a Catholic Spirit," a recasting by Jacobs of Knubel's earlier paper. Stub refused to affix his signature to the document because he judged it to be beyond the perimeters of "orthodox" Lutheranism. Moreover, he said, it was too voluminous; his own Chicago Theses were more to the point. In addition, his theses had

48. This statement is in the Knubel-Stub Correspondence, microfilm, Gullixson Library, Luther-Northwestern Seminaries. Knubel was far from satisfied with the Chicago conference. He felt that the Midwestern Lutherans were unfair to the ULCA in questioning its Lutheranism. Writing to Stub following the conference, Knubel said, "We are not on trial as Lutherans and do not propose that we shall be on trial." (Knubel to Stub, August 26, 1919, Knubel-Stub Correspondence.) Writing to Schmauk, whose illness kept him from the conference, he remarked that the representatives of the Joint Synod of Ohio were especially discourteous. Knubel reported that R. C. H. Lenski (Ohio) had made an outright attack on the ULCA; this provoked Knubel's quiet but firm rejoinder. (Knubel to Schmauk, March 18, 1919, Knubel-Stub Correspondence.)

49. See Jacobs to Knubel, November 29, 1919, Knubel-Stub Correspondence. Jacobs says that to heed Stub's objections would be to remove the heart from "catholicity."

50. Boe to Knubel, October 17, 1919, Knubel-Stub Correspondence.

won the accolade of the Missouri Synod's official organ, *Lehre und Wehre*. To adopt the Knubel-Jacobs statement would serve only to alienate Missouri. The "catholicity" statement's sad omission of the affirmation that the Bible is "the inerrant Word of God," and the failure to reaffirm the doctrine of the Real Presence in the sacrament of the Lord's Supper, could only confirm true Lutherans in their judgment of the ULCA as theologically "liberal." Certainly his own church (NLCA), whose Articles of Union forbade churchly cooperation with non-Lutherans, would see this document as a legitimation of "unionism."[51]

Although another abortive meeting of the committee was held (March 11–12, 1920 in Chicago), the National Lutheran Council never again dealt with the doctrinal problem raised by "The Essentials of a Catholic Spirit." Its authors, discouraged by the intransigence represented by Stub, were rewarded by the action of the 1920 ULCA convention in Washington, D.C., which made the statement its own. Henceforth, American Lutheran history has referred to it as the Washington Declaration.[52]

As a consequence of these events and the attitudes reflected by them, Lutheranism within the National Lutheran Council came to a parting of the ways. The United Lutherans moved ahead on the basis of the Washington Declaration on catholicity; the Midwestern Lu-

---

51. NLC Joint Conference, *Minutes . . . January 27–28, 1920*, pp. 18–27. Stub did not mention that two-thirds of the NLCA (the United Church and the Hauge Synod) had unanimously accepted an "Interpretation" of Article Three, which allowed participation in the ecumenical movement. However, his former church, the Norwegian Synod, had accepted the "Interpretation" with the stipulation that it reserved the right to "witness against" cooperative practices. Obviously Stub was now speaking not as president of the NLCA but as one who had been a member of the old Norwegian Synod.

52. The paper, fully recorded in the minutes, was again reworked by Jacobs for presentation to the 1920 convention of the ULCA in Washington, D.C., where it was adopted as an official policy of the church. ULCA, *Minutes . . . 1920*, pp. 85, 92–101, 449–55. The spirit and purpose of the report, said Jacobs, grew out of the problem in the history of American Lutheranism. The old General Synod had habitually taken an attitude of tolerance toward other churches; the General Council, together with most of the rest of American Lutheranism, kept aloof from others. Therefore, in dealing with the problem of catholicity in the church, it was necessary to disregard both these historical traditions and "endeavor to get down to bed-rock of what is always right and true; to determine, and then to define the principles." Charles M. Jacobs, "The Washington Declaration: An Interpretation," *Lutheran Church Review* 40 (January 1921): 1–21. There was an evident connection between this "Declaration" and the American Lutheran resolution to seek "confessional representation" (see Chapter 11) in the World Council of Churches.

therans picked up Stub's Chicago Theses as a banner. Instead of a single-voiced and full-orbed Lutheran testimony within the National Lutheran Council, there emerged two distinct parties, each waving its own flag. Ironically, the initial cause—mission and cooperation in industrial areas—was forgotten.

In this way the situation came to an uneasy rest in 1920. The National Lutheran Council had been established, two theological and ecclesiastical points of view had emerged within the council, and cooperation was theoretically limited to "external affairs." Meanwhile, the churches cooperated in overseas relief for European Lutheran churches, an activity that was judged to fall under the rubric of "external affairs." Despite both overseas and domestic cooperation, the next few years witnessed a pulling away from the United Lutheran Church and a drawing together of the Joint Synod of Ohio, the Iowa Synod, and the Norwegian Lutheran Church. One of the contributing factors, in addition to those evident from the previous discussion, was the modernist-fundamentalist controversy of the 1920s, in which the Lutherans actually took no part. The Midwestern Lutherans, however, felt that the United Lutheran Church was equivocal on the question of the inerrancy of the Bible. Stub, Richard C. H. Lenski (Joint Synod of Ohio), and others were especially insistent that a statement on the verbal inspiration and consequent inerrancy of Scripture, in the context of modernism, ought to be promulgated. In this setting, the non–Synodical Conference Lutherans of the Mississippi Valley, especially the Norwegians and the Germans, were moving closer together. By 1925 a new alignment within the National Lutheran Council was in process and threatened the continued existence of the NLC. All subsequent intra-Lutheran tensions and efforts toward further unity— the formation of The American Lutheran Church (1960) and the Lutheran Church in America (1962), and the Missouri Synod conflict (1959–77)—can be understood only against the background of these fateful events of 1919 and 1920.

Meanwhile, however, some individuals within the National Lutheran Council worked tirelessly to keep alive the sense of a common Lutheran identity both in America and in Europe. Knubel, Larsen, Jacobs, Morehead, and Boe refused to let the fires of unity die out. For the moment, they had achieved about as much as possible on the domestic scene. They refused, however, to be deterred or silenced in their vigorous advocacy of cooperation overseas. Largely as a result of their vision of ultimate unity and their conviction that Christians, especially those of the same household of faith, must bear one another's burdens, interest in world Lutheranism remained alive. As a result of the council's overseas relief work and its subsequent over-tures to the General Evangelical Lutheran Conference (AELK) and the Lutheran League (*Lutherischer Bund*) of Germany, the stage was set for the establishment of the Lutheran World Convention.

In the next chapter we shall see how prewar contacts between American Lutherans and the mother churches of Europe were reestab-lished, how new contacts were made, and how, after four hundred years of "invisible unity," Lutheranism began to express visibly its internal catholicity and oneness on the global level.

4

On Converging Paths

The idea of a world fellowship of Lutherans was hardly a burning issue among the denomination's leaders in America. A similar attitude prevailed among German and Scandinavian churchmen. The pressure of immediate problems left most Lutherans with little energy and less time to give thoughtful consideration to establishing a Lutheran world organization. In America, for example, parochial and sectional demands seemed to exhaust all available resources. The task of missions to the immigrants, the erection of church buildings, the founding of schools and institutions of mercy, the establishing of a Lutheran presence in a predominantly Anglo-American Protestant milieu—all these matters seemed to require immediate attention and large sums of money, of which there was never enough. Had it not been for the high degree of dedication and Christian commitment of both laity and clergy, the planting of Lutheranism in North America would no doubt have been an unimpressive and less-than-fruitful enterprise. Although the European church circumstances differed from the American, the lassitude toward global Lutheranism was identical. To assume, however, that Lutherans did virtually nothing to foster their international relationships prior to the distressing postwar circumstances that prodded them to engage in united action would be an injustice to history. John A. Morehead, who was to become known as "Mr. World Lutheran," wrote in 1928: "Considerable progress had been made before 1914 both in Europe and America toward conscious inner unity and its expression in free associations or practical agencies."[1] What Morehead reported was indeed true; there were evidences of a continuity between prewar and postwar international contacts. Some of these relationships need identification and brief elucidation.

1. ULCA, *Minutes . . . 1928*, p. 597.

TRANSATLANTIC CONTACTS

Basically, the reason for continuing contacts between European and American Lutherans was immigration. The immigrant churches needed ministers, financial help, books, and spiritual guidance from the mother churches. In some instances "the old country" paid little if any attention to those who had departed for America. In fact, some civil and church authorities warned that emigration was a traitorous desertion of the fatherland. For example, Bishop Jacob Neumann of Bergen, Norway, felt impelled in 1837 to send an episcopal letter to the "emigration-smitten" farmers of his diocese in which he pictured the unhappy consequences of succumbing to the "America fever."[2] However, although many of the Scandinavian and German authorities took a dark view of the flight from the homeland, once it had become an irreversible stream leaders realized that the church must not break off all relations with its wandering and vagrant children.

An outstanding example of eighteenth-century transatlantic contact was the relationship between the famous pietistic foundation at Halle and the German immigrants in colonial America. It was to the latter that the "Halle fathers" in 1742 sent Henry Melchior Muhlenberg, who was to establish himself as the "patriarch" of American Lutherans by an astonishing ministry of both the spoken and written Word. Muhlenberg's headquarters were in southeastern Pennsylvania, but his ministry and counsel were sought from Maine to Georgia. He sent detailed reports of his work to Halle, where "the fathers" successfully kept the mission in America before the German people by publishing "News from the United German Ev. Lutheran Congregations in North America." These serial publications, popularly known as *Hallesche Nachrichten* ("Halle Reports"), were instrumental in bringing ministers, lay catechists, and money to the American colony.[3]

The increase in contacts during the nineteenth century followed

---

2. See "Bishop Jacob Neumann's Word of Admonition to the Peasants," in *Studies and Records,* trans. and ed. Gunnar J. Malmin (Minneapolis: Norwegian-American Historical Association, 1926), 1:95–109.

3. See Theodore G. Tappert in E. Clifford Nelson, ed., *The Lutherans in North America* (Philadelphia: Fortress Press, 1975), pp. 22 n. 4, 26–31, 44–46. Cf. Abdel Ross Wentz, *A Basic History of Lutheranism in America,* rev. ed. (Philadelphia: Fortress Press, 1964), pp. 38–39.

upon the developing concerns on both sides of the Atlantic to minister to the spiritual needs of the immigrants. Friedrich C. D. Wyneken (1810–76), a young pastor from Hannover, arrived in the Midwest in 1838 to serve congregations in Indiana. Extensive trips soon convinced him that the frontier missionary task demanded reinforcement. This prompted him to send an "emergency appeal" to the church in Germany. In it he said: "What will become of our brethren in 10 or 20 years if help does not come? To the disgrace of the German name, to the shame of the church, and to eternal reproach before the Lord a German population that knows nothing of its God and Savior will inhabit the West."[4] The vivid descriptions and the urgent tone of Wyneken's "Macedonian cry" caused Wilhelm Loehe (1808–72) of Neuendettelsau (Bavaria) to enlist young men for pastoral service in America. These "Loehe men" provided a bridge between Germany and Midwestern Lutherans in the Missouri, the Ohio, and especially the Iowa synods.

Although the number of men trained under Loehe at Neuendettelsau was impressive, the needs were never fully met. Special arrangements, therefore, were initiated with other theological centers in order to increase the flow of ministerial candidates to America. For example, two "practical" seminaries in Schleswig-Holstein provided the General Council and the General Synod—whose seminaries at Philadelphia and Gettysburg were not preparing German-speaking pastors—with seminary graduates ready to serve the German diaspora in America. The schools at Kropp and Brecklum provided the General Council and the General Synod, respectively, with approximately 350 pastors over a span of four or five decades.[5]

A third point of contact between European and American churches in the nineteenth century was made through the deaconess work established by William A. Passavant (1821–94). With the assistance of the German "father" of the deaconess movement, Theodore Fliedner,

4. Friedrich Wyneken, *Die Not der deutschen Lutheraner in Nordamerika*, American edition (Pittsburgh: Druckerei der Lutherischen Kirchenzeitung, 1844), p. 33. English translation in Carl Meyer, ed., *Moving Frontiers* (St. Louis: Concordia Publishing House, 1964), p. 97.

5. Theodore G. Tappert, *History of the Lutheran Theological Seminary at Philadelphia 1864–1964* (Philadelphia: Lutheran Theological Seminary, 1964), pp. 64–65; and Willard D. Allbeck, "Christian Jensen and the Germans of the General Synod," *Lutheran Church Quarterly* 13 (1940): 268–78.

and four deaconesses whom he brought to America in 1849, Passavant succeeded in organizing and fostering a diaconal sisterhood whose activities extended from Pittsburgh to Philadelphia, to Chicago and Milwaukee, to Minneapolis and Omaha.[6]

One of the most fruitful inter-Lutheran relationships was in the area of world missionary work. Common problems of mission strategy, translations of the Bible, religious literature, and liturgies existed in each field. As Lutheran missionaries became acquainted with one another they welcomed cooperative efforts. Missionaries from Leipzig, Hermannsburg, Brecklum, and Neuendettelsau—to mention but a few examples—encountered American, Norwegian, Danish, Swedish, and Finnish missionaries in Asia and Africa. As a result of their endeavors in facing common tasks, these missionaries saw clearly the desirability of cooperative ventures that could lead eventually to an organized Lutheran world community.

Numerous other contacts in the nineteenth century helped prepare the way for the realization of this goal. One of these was the literary exchange represented by letters, books, and periodicals. Official correspondence between church leaders and institutions on both sides of the Atlantic dealt not only with the pressing problems associated with the religious life of the immigrants, but also with theological issues. When rationalism threatened American Lutherans during the first decades of the nineteenth century, Samuel S. Schmucker, president of Gettysburg Seminary, translated and published a German theological textbook that was calculated to combat rationalism and to preserve an evangelical witness in America.[7] Two colleagues of Schmucker, Henry Eyster Jacobs and Clifford A. Hay, translated and edited Heinrich Schmid's anthology of seventeenth-century Lutheran dogmaticians as a contribution to the confessional revival in America.[8]

---

6. George H. Gerberding, *Life and Letters of W. A. Passavant* (Greenville, Pa.: Young Lutheran Co., 1906), pp. 195–96. Cf. Frederick S. Weiser, *Love's Response* (Philadelphia: ULCA Board of Publication, 1962), p. 54.

7. See the preface of Samuel S. Schmucker's *An Elementary Course of Biblical Theology Translated from the Work of Professors Storr and Flatt*, 2 vols. (Andover, Mass.: Flagg & Gould, 1826).

8. Heinrich Schmid, *Die Dogmatik der ev.-luth. Kirche, dargestellt und aus den Quellen belegt* (Erlangen: Carl Heyder, 1847). English translation: *Doctrinal Theology of the Evangelical Lutheran Church*, 2d ed. (Philadelphia: Lutheran Publication Society, 1889).

Among the Norwegian-Americans, several official communications on theological matters were sent overseas for clarification. Best known were the unsuccessful attempts of the Norwegian Synod to obtain support for its (and Missouri's) views on slavery from the theological faculty at the University of Christiania (Oslo) and from Adolph G. von Harless, the founder of the Erlangen school and the first president of the Allgemeine Evangelisch-Lutherische Konferenz (AELK).[9]

Church periodicals and theological journals were exchanged between both sides. The flow of ideas and information provided, perhaps unconsciously, a sense of pan-Lutheranism. The American periodicals most frequently read in Europe were naturally those published in the German and Scandinavian languages. Some of the better known were *Das Evangelische Magazin* (Pennsylvania Ministerium), *Lutherische Kirchenzeitung* (Ohio Synod), *Kirchliches Informatorium* (Buffalo Synod), *Kirchenblatt und Kirchliche Zeitschrift* (Iowa Synod), *Der Lutheraner* and *Lehre und Wehre* (Missouri Synod), *Kirkelige Maanedstidende, Ev. Luthersk Kirketidende,* and *Lutheraneren* (Norwegian), *Augustana, Tidskrift för Teologi,* and *Hemlandet* (Swedish). American Lutherans would look for information about European Lutherans in such periodicals as *Evangelische Kirchenzeitung* (ed. Hengstenberg), *Kirchliche Mitteilungen* (ed. Loehe), *Allgemeine Evangelisch-Lutherische Kirchenzeitung* (organ of the AELK), and *Zeitschrift für Protestantismus und Kirche* (ed. Adolph von Harless).

Although distance, time, and money limited the overseas pleasure-travel of American Lutherans, there were nevertheless a few whose churchly and academic interests brought them into personal contact with Europeans. Some young men, for example, did graduate work in theology, philosophy, and history in European universities and returned to America with broadened vision and deepened insights. One such person was John Nicholas Lenker (1858–1929), whose experiences in Germany and Scandinavia led him to devote his life to cultivating pan-Lutheran interests. In addition to his concern with making Luther's writings known to English-reading Americans (the Lenker edition of Luther's works), he set himself the task of alleviating

---

9. *Beretning . . . for den norsk-ev. luth. Kirke i Amerika . . . 1866*, pp. 40–66; and ibid., *1867*, pp. 86–103.

the widespread ignorance that Lutherans had of one another's life and activity. By travel and correspondence, he assembled data on Lutheranism around the world. The result was the publication of his widely circulated book, *Lutherans in All Lands* (Milwaukee: Lutherans in All Lands Co., 1893), in which he argued that there was a catholicity to Lutheran church life as well as to theological confession. As evidence of the book's influence, Willard D. Allbeck points out that it was referred to by Nathan Söderblom at Eisenach in 1923 as a factor to be reckoned with in assessing the Lutheran World Convention.[10]

In the same year that Lenker's book appeared (1893), the Augustana Synod celebrated the 200th anniversary of the establishment of evangelical Lutheranism as the confession of the Church of Sweden. A prominent Swedish bishop, Knut H. G. von Scheele, represented the king and the Church of Sweden at the jubilee in Rock Island, Illinois. Von Scheele, the first Lutheran bishop to visit America and the first prominent Scandinavian churchman to associate himself with the AELK, became a visible expression in America of pan-Lutheranism.[11]

TENTATIVE PROPOSALS FOR WORLD LUTHERANISM

In the light of and in response to the contacts between European and American Lutherans prior to World War I, it was natural to expect proposals from time to time that Lutherans should organize themselves as a worldwide community. All parties were jealous of their own national or territorial churchliness and therefore cautious, if not nervous, about proposing a "world church." Nonetheless, they felt the need for some kind of organization to express the Lutheran fellowship that transcended national boundaries. The Anglicans, Baptists, Con-

---

10. Willard D. Allbeck, "A Study of American Participation in Inter-Lutheran Cooperation Prior to the Formation of the Lutheran World Federation," prepared for the Department of Theology of the LWF, 1962, p. 7 (in the Archives of Cooperative Lutheranism, Lutheran Council/U.S.A., New York City [hereafter referred to as ArCL]). Cf. LWC, *Minutes . . . Eisenach . . . August 19–26, 1923* (Philadelphia: United Lutheran Publication House, 1925), p. 25.

11. An interesting account of von Scheele's visit is related in Herman Fritschel, *Biography of Sigmund and Gottfried Fritschel* (Milwaukee, 1951), p. 108. Sigmund Fritschel, who had represented the General Council at the Leipzig meeting (1870) of the AELK, was on the program with von Scheele at Rock Island and evoked a public display of affection from the bishop.

gregationalists, Methodists, and Presbyterians had already established worldwide organizations.[12] Shouldn't the Lutherans do the same? We have noted that official correspondence and personal representations had occurred between the AELK in Germany and Lutherans in America. In fact, the hope had been expressed in 1909 in America that the AELK might be expanded beyond Germany and Scandinavia to become the framework of a world congress of all Lutherans who "accept *ex animo* the Confessions of our church."[13] This was followed up six years later by the proposal that Lutherans in the United States organize an American Lutheran Federation and then unite in an appeal to the AELK to lead the way in forming a "world federation . . . of Lutheranism." This world federation would be divided into "an American branch . . . perhaps a Scandinavian branch . . . and an Oriental branch . . . in addition to . . . the parent German branch."[14]

American Lutheran preoccupation with local problems caused disinterest in worldwide expression of Lutheranism until World War I intruded. Common catastrophe, not common confession, seemed to provide the only sufficient motive to transcend contentment with provinciality and parochialism. Thus, as World War I ended, "the calamity theory" of Lutheran unity was born.[15]

REPAIRING BROKEN RELATIONSHIPS

When the war ended, some American churchmen saw that pre-1914 transatlantic inter-Lutheran relationships, fragile as they may have been and broken as they now were, desperately needed rehabilitation. Two organizations, the National Lutheran Commission for Soldiers' and Sailors' Welfare and the National Lutheran Council were at hand to reestablish the overseas links. The former agency, as we have noted, was an emergency arrangement to minister to Lutheran servicemen and women. Its success was beyond expectations. The churches, however, realized that the NLCSSW had been a trailblazer for fruitful

12. Ruth Rouse and Stephen C. Neill, eds., *A History of the Ecumenical Movement, 1517–1948,* 2d ed. (Philadelphia: Westminster Press, 1967), pp. 613–15.
13. General Council, *Minutes . . . 1909,* p. 241.
14. Ibid., *1915,* pp. 281–82.
15. E. Theodore Bachmann, *The Epic of Faith* (New York: NLC, 1952), p. 11.

cooperative effort, but that its ad hoc character did not qualify it to be the continuing agency for admittedly necessary Lutheran cooperation. Therefore, as described in the previous chapter, the National Lutheran Council came into being (1918) to serve as a permanent organization for united Lutheran action.

As regards overseas contacts, the NLC found it unnecessary to begin *de novo*. They recalled that the NLCSSW had sent two emissaries (Charles J. Smith and ,Frank M. Riter) to Paris with careful instructions that they seek ways in which French and American Lutherans could cooperate. The instructions included a caveat to the effect that the commission could in no way bind American Lutherans to provide funds for reconstruction.[16] Having left New York on September 18, 1918, Smith and Riter quickly established contact with Henri Bach, chairman of the War Commission of the French Lutheran Church, and were soon immersed in their duties. Smith returned to his New York parish at the end of two months, but Riter extended his stay until mid-January 1919. At the annual meeting of the commission the two men submitted an extensive report in which they incorporated a series of recommendations entitled "How America Can Help."[17] Included was the suggestion that a "permanent" representative be sent to France. He should be a pastor who could speak French, and "a cultured gentleman" who could interpret American Lutheranism "to our French brethren."[18] The "permanent" representative was Michael J. Stolee of Luther Seminary, St. Paul, who arrived in Paris on March 17, 1919, and worked with energy and success until his return in early September. Stolee's report to the commission dealt almost exclusively with the condition of Lutheranism in France, which in his opinion had suffered not only from the ravages of war but from its minority status and its theological insecurity.[19]

Before the NLCSSW ceased to exist, and before its representative in Paris returned to the United States, the National Lutheran Council had been organized (September 6, 1918). One of its declared purposes was to "deal with problems arising out of war and other emergen-

16. NLCSSW, *Reports . . . October 16, 1918*, p. 38.
17. Ibid., *November 4, 1919*, pp. 38–57.
18. Ibid., p. 54.
19. Ibid., pp. 57–62.

cies."[20] This objective opened the way for a continuation and extension of the overseas contacts made by the NLCSSW. Frederick H. Knubel, president of the United Lutheran Church and chairman of the NLCSSW, proposed that the new National Lutheran Council, of which he was a chief architect, establish a European Commission to represent the council in overseas relief and reconstruction. The executive committee, authorized to name and send a commission to Europe, appointed the following: John A. Morehead (ULCA), chairman; Sven G. Youngert (Augustana); Gustav A. Fandrey (Iowa Synod); George Taylor Rygh (Norwegian); Charles M. Jacobs (ULCA), who declined the appointment; and Henry J. Schuh (1854–1934) (Ohio Synod). Originally, the U.S. Department of State granted passports only to Morehead, Fandrey, and Youngert. A short time later (July 1919), Rygh and Schuh were able to join their colleagues.[21] The instructions to the members of the commission took the following form:

> As representatives of the National Lutheran Council in America you are charged to learn definitely the present ecclesiastical situation and problems of each group of Lutherans in European lands which were involved in war; their plans for the solution of their own ecclesiastical problems, and how far they will require the aid and counsel of other groups; ever mindful, in the fulfillment of your mission, of the cardinal purposes of the National Lutheran Council, among which is the fostering of true Christian loyalty.
>
> Your appointment imposes upon you the following specific duties:
>
> I. You will convey to the Lutherans there the sincere and cordial greetings of the Lutheran Church in America, with assurances of its deep interest and ready willingness to participate in the solution of their ecclesiastical problems.
>
> II. You will ascertain the conditions confronting each Lutheran group, with a view to enable the National Lutheran Council intelligently to afford such counsel and succor as will contribute to strengthen, hearten, and encourage them in establishing the Church of the Unaltered Augsburg Confession in harmonious relationship to our whole household of faith.
>
> In all these premises you are charged to report back to the National Lutheran Council at the earliest opportunity.

20. NLC, *Annual Report . . . November 8, 1919*, p. 52.
21. Ibid., pp. 19–20. John Alfred Morehead (1867–1936), president of Roanoke (Virginia) College, became the foremost American leader in world Lutheranism. Charles M. Jacobs (1875–1938), who declined appointment in the hope of devoting himself exclusively to academic life at the Philadelphia seminary, found himself drawn into a dual role as American Lutheranism's leading theological spokesman and as a churchman of national and international repute.

For the purpose set forth in your instructions your Commission will have all the powers that the National Lutheran Council itself possesses; and you are authorized to make, at your discretion, preliminary expenditures to the maximum amount of $50,000. Any expenditures to be made in excess of $50,000 shall first receive the approval of the Executive Committee of the National Lutheran Council.[22]

Appended to these instructions was a statement by Friedrich Richter, president of the Iowa Synod, insisting that American aid be limited to loyally confessional Lutherans; moreover, he urged the commission members to petition the American representatives at the Paris Peace Conference to transfer orphaned German missions to the Lutherans of America.

The instructions, both official and unofficial, were to have long-term results. For Americans they reflected not only a deep-flowing love and compassion for all suffering humanity but also a particular concern to strengthen the Lutheran churches of Europe. The limited money and the desperate needs forced the Americans to walk a tightrope between broadcasting their resources thinly among all needy peoples without regard for creed or confession, or husbanding the aid for careful distribution among needy Lutherans in weakened churches that required both physical and spiritual assistance if they were to resume a vital place in the Lutheran ecclesiastical household. There was no easy solution to the problem; the realities of the historical situation invariably complicated the implementation of principles. For example, when American Lutheran members of the commission in Europe faced the unmitigated suffering of all kinds of persons, a measured and consistent application of relief along confessional lines was hardly possible or even desirable. Morehead's first report to the National Lutheran Council on December 18, 1919, put the problem this way: "Doctrinal discussion with the suffering is not entirely apropos."[23]

As a matter of fact, nobody could foresee the nature of the problems to be confronted; the implications of American Lutheran involvement in postwar Europe were almost totally unpredictable. One member of the executive committee, Victor G. A. Tressler, recognized the ambiguities of this venture of faith. Said he, "The question really is,

22. Ibid.
23. Ibid., p. 62.

whether or not American [Lutherans are] ready and able to [assume a role in] world leadership."[24] In the light of subsequent developments, this opinion proved to be valid. With the benefit of hindsight, about the only safe and unquestioned conclusion we can draw is that, by the NLC's appointment of a European Commission, Americans were taking the initial steps in reestablishing contacts with their overseas brethren, and that is all.

AMERICANS DISCOVER POSTWAR EUROPE

The emissaries of the National Lutheran Council arrived in France in the summer of 1919 and then, summoned by cablegram, were back in New York on December 18, 1919.[25] This preliminary phase of exploration, it was soon learned, required a headquarters from which operations could be directed. The first center quite naturally was Paris, where Michael J. Stolee was completing his duties under the NLCSSW. Stolee welcomed the NLC ambassadors (Morehead, Youngert, Fandrey), helped them establish an address, and made arrangements for the transfer of funds from America. He had already made contact with the delegations (United States and other nations) at the Paris Peace Conference and had obtained information about orphaned German missions in Asia and Africa. He reported that delegates of the Baltic States were eager to meet the Americans.[26]

Morehead and his colleagues promptly made Stolee an unofficial member of the commission and looked to him for guidance in establishing contact with French Lutherans. From the time of his arrival in March, Stolee had followed a policy of reconstruction rather than relief, the rationale being ecclesiastical rather than humanitarian. American Lutheran churches, he argued, had determined to funnel aid to those churches that were unequivocally Lutheran in their confession. Morehead and his fellow commission members quickly learned that French Lutheranism was an odd mix of theological

---

24. NLC, "Proceedings . . . 1918," p. 33.
25. John A. Morehead, "General Report of the Chairman . . . ," supplement to NLC, *Annual Report . . . November 6, 1919*, pp. 55–67.
26. Stolee to NLC, June 28, 1919; cited by Allbeck, "Study of American Participation."

liberals, ecclesiastical "unionists" (cooperating closely with the French Reformed Church), and a small minority of "confessional Lutherans." It was with the latter that general, but not exclusive, relations were established. After a short time the Americans turned their attention to other areas of concern. It was decided that Rygh (Norwegian background) and Youngert (Swedish background) should go to the Baltic States via Scandinavia. Schuh and Fandrey (German background) should visit Hungary and Austria. Morehead and Stolee should go to Poland.

The circumstances of the visit to Poland require some explanation because of later developments. The 900,000 Lutherans in Poland were primarily German-speaking. These were to be found in two Lutheran churches and three "Union" churches, after the pattern of the Prussian Union. The ecclesiastical divisions were partially transcended by the common language and customs. Two points of view as to relations with Germany were evident at the war's end. One element, led by Superintendent Paul Blau, considered all Germans in Poland a part of Germany, even though they lived under Polish political administration. According to this group, the German Poles, though politically Polish, should continue ecclesiastically as an integral part of the Prussian territorial church in Germany even after the signing of the peace treaty. A second point of view was represented by the general superintendent of the Evangelical Augsburg Church, Julius Bursche, a German-Pole who was committed to Polish nationalism and independence from German influences, having labored for parity between the Polish Lutheran minority and the German-speaking majority. This show of loyalty to Polish nationalism was rewarded by an appointment to be one of his country's delegates to the Paris Peace Conference, where he was to act as spokesman for Poland's religious minorities. As a fairly prominent Pole (he was a personal acquaintance of Poland's first prime minister, the famous musician Ignace Jan Paderewski), Bursche was asked to publish the story of Polish church life in French periodicals. Bursche's account came to Morehead's attention; characteristically, he sought out the author and quickly established a friendly relationship. In a short time Bursche introduced him to Paderewski, who in turn urged Morehead to come to Poland to survey the situation. In fact, Paderewski invited Morehead and Stolee to travel to Warsaw

Swiss-Austrian border, 1919: American commissioner Professor Michael J. Stolee with Polish Premier Ignace Jan Paderewski, about to board the premier's special relief train to Poland.

with him and Madame Paderewski on the premier's private train.[27] Journeying through Switzerland to avoid Germany, they arrived in Warsaw on July 22, 1919, remained there a little over a fortnight, and returned to Paris on August 9.

The Warsaw stay had two major results. The first was the realization by the Americans that if Polish Lutherans were to survive as a church, American assistance was imperative. The second, not apparent to Morehead and Stolee, grew out of their selection of Bursche as the person through whom relief funds and material aid would be dispensed. Unknown to the Americans was the fact that Bursche's role in Poland was deeply resented in Germany, and by their decision to work through Bursche the Americans were caught in the middle between the bitterly anti-German Poles and the anti-Polish Germans. The latter looked upon Bursche, whose ethnic origin was German, as a traitor to

27. For brief accounts of these events see Samuel Trexler, *John A. Morehead* (New York: G. P. Putnam's Sons, 1938), pp. 65–73. Cf. Bengt Wadensjö, *Toward a World Lutheran Communion: Developments in Lutheran Cooperation up to 1929* (Uppsala: Verbum, 1970), pp. 102–3, 125.

German interests. One of the prominent Lutherans in Germany called him "one of the bitterest and most hatefilled enemies of the German people."[28]

The American connection with Bursche explains in large measure the suspicion and ill will that German Lutherans felt toward the Americans during the summer of 1919. Unable to understand why American Lutherans of German extraction had given support to the Allies during the war, deeply resentful of American concurrence in placing "war guilt" on Germany, and smolderingly bitter over the hunger blockade that threatened mass extermination of the population, the German Lutherans looked with jaundiced eye on the presence of an American delegation. It was a case of "beware of Greeks bearing gifts."[29] Although this attitude softened by autumn (1919), a fairly well-concealed but lingering chill was occasionally manifested in German relationships with the American churchmen.[30]

Meanwhile the members of the European Commission had arranged to rendezvous at Copenhagen on August 16 for reports and an assessment of their mission.[31] By this time, permission had been obtained to enter Germany (Morehead traveled to Copenhagen via Cologne and Berlin; Fandrey attended a meeting in Hermannsburg) and to see at first hand the terrible effects of the hunger blockade. It was clear to Morehead that he and his colleagues must use every opportunity to obtain direct personal information about the German situation. An occasion soon presented itself at the first postwar meeting of the AELK, September 9 – 11, 1919, in Leipzig. Morehead, who had

28. The quotation is attributed to Baron Wilhelm von Pechmann, a German nationalist and a well-known Lutheran layman who was active in both Lutheran and pan-Protestant circles in Germany. Cited by Wadensjö, *Toward a World Lutheran Communion*, p. 222.

29. The editor of a German periodical wrote a plea for a more sympathetic understanding of the American gesture. See W[ilhelm] L[aible], "Von unseren amerikanischen Brüdern," in *Allgemeine Evangelisch-Lutherische Kirchenzeitung* 53 (1920): 385–88.

30. Even after Eisenach (1923) and until the 1930s, the Americans found it expedient to handle this touchy relationship with kid gloves. Letters between the two American members (Morehead and Boe) of the LWC executive committee refer to the problem, especially as it centered in Wilhelm von Pechmann of Munich.

31. Trexler, *Morehead*, p. 71. Accounts of the initial investigations were sent back to America. These were published most consistently in *The Lutheran*, the official organ of the ULCA; see issues of September 4, 1919, pp. 373–74; September 18, 1919, p. 413; September 25, 1919, pp. 433, 442; and October 2, 1919, p. 453 (a condensed report on the Copenhagen meeting).

returned to Poland after the Copenhagen meeting, joined Fandrey and Schuh in Leipzig. The presence of the Americans did much to remove German suspicions and to reestablish and cement ties that had been broken by the war.

In a letter published in *The Lutheran* (October 23, 1919), Morehead gave an account of the conference and summarized the discussion of the major issues. One question was related to the impending separation of church and state. Should the church in Germany be a confessional church or a German national church? The advocates of the latter suggested the need to make confessional concessions to other Protestants in order to unite all Protestants to preserve a united German people. The opponents argued that nothing would be gained by compromises and that the church of postwar Germany should be reorganized on an unequivocally confessional basis. Morehead observed that a true *Volkskirche*, a church of the entire people, was a dream that could not be realized. The supporters of this "people's church" were vainly seeking to hold on to the prestige and prominence now lost by the dissolution of the state church. Moreover, the proponents of the *Volkskirche* failed to take into consideration the fact that already 25 million social democrats and the postwar Spartacists (Communists) were estranged from the church. Although the AELK made its aims clear at Leipzig, no decision was reached. However, subsequent developments through the Nazi era and World War II led to the transformation of the AELK into the United Lutheran Church in Germany (VELKD) in 1948, thus indicating that the AELK eventually opted for the confessional principle.[32]

Two additional matters of major importance at Leipzig should be noted. One was the warm but unexpected reception given to the Americans present. Morehead reported: "Profound gratitude was expressed [to] the National Lutheran Council in caring for Lutheran missions in German colonies during . . . the Great War."[33] The sincerity of the German welcome was unquestioned, and it contrib-

---

32. See "Meeting of the Lutheran Allgemeine Konferenz in Germany," *The Lutheran*, October 16, 1919, p. 499. For the AELK's aim to be both a confessional church and a people's church see Theodore E. Schmauk, "The Call of the Allgemeine Konferenz," *Lutheran Church Review* 38 (October 1919): 331.
33. *The Lutheran*, October 23, 1919, p. 513.

uted to a partial dissipation of German uneasiness about the Americans and created a new atmosphere of openness.

The final observation from Leipzig dealt with the postwar political and economic condition in Germany. The great fear was always of Bolshevism, whose fortunes could only be enhanced by a long delay in the ratification of a peace treaty, by neglecting the desperate economic conditions, and by the lack of food and coal for the coming winter. In the light of the overwhelming concern with "the Red menace," Morehead's comment is highly significant. He observed, "No party in Germany at present seems strong enough to maintain a government that can meet the requirements of the situation." Within a decade—by 1929—the church and all Germans saw such a party rising to power, the National Socialists, who promised to crush Bolshevism and to provide a program of "positive Christianity" for Germany. Only after another decade had passed was Hitlerism seen as a reminder of the biblical contention that the devil disguises himself "as an angel of light" (2 Cor. 11:14). Morehead continued, "Is the blood of another revolution to be shed to stabilize Germany and stem the tide of Bolshevism?" Even if Morehead had lived to experience World War II, he could not have received a complete answer to his question.

Following the Leipzig meeting, the entire NLC European Commission met in Berlin, October 6 – 7, 1919, and adopted "principles of action" regarding distribution of funds for relief and reconstruction. It was evident to the members of the commission that the churchly and spiritual character of their mission in Europe must be made clear to "the people of every nation" and that their overall aim was to strengthen the "Evangelical Lutheran Church in each country." The concluding statement asserted that the "fraternal and helpful relations established" should be "judiciously utilized by the Commission to further . . . federation among the Lutheran Churches of all countries of the world."[34]

The conviction of the commission members that a world Lutheran organization was imperative was the basis for the recommendation the commissioners made to an adjourned meeting of the National Lutheran Council on December 18, 1919, in New York. Chairman Morehead spoke at length and with feeling about the challenge to the

34. NLC, *Annual Report . . . November 6, 1919*, pp. 27–28.

church for continued and united action to meet the spiritual and physical needs of European brethren.[35] In fact, the political and social unrest, the corrosive nationalisms, the human exhaustion by war and revolutions, and the need for radical reorganization in both state and church governments all led him to say that the problem was "so great that mere human understanding cannot now fully comprehend or picture it."[36] The discussion of the report provided the commission members with the opportunity to emphasize not only that there was a challenge to American Lutherans but also that great and irreparable losses to Lutheranism everywhere would be sustained unless solidarity could be given expression by some international organization.

The discussion between the members of the commission and the members of the NLC led to two resolutions, one urging the union of American Lutheran churches, the second recommending "that the thought of taking steps toward the formation of a Lutheran world federation be proposed for the consideration of the National Lutheran Council." The word "federation" was later changed to "conference," whereupon the whole matter of a world conference was referred to a subcommittee consisting of Frederick H. Knubel, Hans G. Stub, J. Michael Reu, and Charles M. Jacobs.[37]

The inclusion of Stub and Reu in this important committee calls for special attention. As president of the National Lutheran Council, Stub naturally belonged on such a committee, but he was also president of the Norwegian Lutheran Church, which included Missourian elements. His own cautious views about Lutheran unity at home and abroad were supported by conservative elements in the church, and as a result he was less than enthusiastic about both the NLC resolutions (concerning union of American Lutherans and federation of world Lutherans).[38] Meanwhile his own church body was questioning its continued membership in the National Lutheran Council. Most of the

35. Morehead, "General Report of the Chairman of the European Commission . . . ," Adjourned Meeting, NLC, December 18, 1919, supplement in NLC, *Annual Report . . . November 6, 1919*, pp. 55–67.
36. Ibid., p. 66.
37. NLC, "Proceedings . . . 1919," p. 8; mimeographed minutes of the Adjourned Meeting are in ArCL.
38. For Stub's attitude see Knubel-Stub Correspondence, microfilm, Gullixson Library, Luther-Northwestern Seminaries, St. Paul; see esp. Stub to Knubel, February 20, 1919, and Boe to Knubel, October 17, 1919. See also Boe to Larsen, August 2, 1919, and Larsen to Boe, August 6, 1919; and Boe to G. L. Kieffer, August 16, 1919, Lars W. Boe Papers, box 4, folder 3, St. Olaf College Archives, Northfield, Minnesota.

opposition was eventually overcome, and finally in June 1920 it adopted a resolution favorable to the NLC.[39]

Reu's appointment must be interpreted as a gesture to neutralize his outbursts of criticism against the National Lutheran Council and to enlist his support of its work on both the domestic front and the overseas front. Reu's opposition threatened to cut off Iowa Synod support of the NLC (Iowa did in fact withdraw from the council from 1920 to 1930), and he was already appealing to dissident elements in the Ohio Synod and the Norwegian Lutheran Church to endorse his views.[40]

As could be expected, the subcommittee on a Lutheran world conference continued in name only. Stub retired from the NLC presidency in 1920, and Reu remained an active critic of the council and its overseas involvements. It was not until after the annual meeting of the National Lutheran Council (1920) that a new commmittee, with Charles M. Jacobs as chairman, vigorously addressed the idea of a world Lutheran conference.[41]

Meanwhile, following the 1919 meeting of the NLC, Morehead had been asked to be the permanent chairman of the council's European Commission. This necessitated his resignation from the presidency of Roanoke College, which had given him a leave for his first term in Europe, June–December 1919. He embarked on his second trip on

39. E. Clifford Nelson, *The Lutheran Church among Norwegian-Americans* (Minneapolis: Augsburg Publishing House, 1960), 2:299–302. Cf. NLC, *Annual Report . . . 1920*, pp. 7–8.

40. The crisis was touched off by Reu's article "Unmissverständliche Klarstellung in Sachen des National Luth. Councils zur Notwendigkeit geworden," *Kirchliche Zeitschrift* 43 (November/December 1919): 578–85. The article was reprinted in the Ohio Synod's organ *Lutherische Kirchenzeitung*, November 22, 1919, pp. 738–40, with a laudatory introduction by its editor, Richard C. H. Lenski. This criticism was compounded by editor Theodore Graebner's writing in the Missouri Synod's *Lutheran Witness*, November 25, 1919, pp. 376–79. Reu referred to the Polish-Lutheran Julius Bursche as a "mean, ungrateful fellow," a "common liar," and "the agent of his master, Paderewski." The executive secretary of the NLC, Lauritz Larsen, after corresponding with Charles M. Jacobs and others (Larsen described Reu's article as "one of the nastiest and meanest articles I have ever read"; Larsen to Jacobs, November 28, 1919), prepared a detailed and lucid reply to Reu. He concluded it with a question: "Has [Reu] not opened the way for strife and civil war within the Church just when it needs to conserve all strength and all resources to meet the attacks from without and to cope with the great problems before it?" See Larsen and other papers in "NLC, Series: Early," box 1, folder 12, in ArCL.

41. Frederick K. Wentz, *Lutherans in Concert* (Minneapolis: Augsburg Publishing House, 1968), p. 57. Cf. Charles M. Jacobs, "National Lutheran Council in Annual Convention," *The Lutheran*, December 30, 1920, pp. 12–13.

January 16, 1920.[42] In April he was joined by Michael J. Stolee as a second member of the European Commission; and in July, when Morehead's health began to give way because of excessive work and travel, the council's executive secretary, Lauritz Larsen, found it necessary to spend four months in Europe assisting him. Prior to Larsen's arrival at the end of July, Morehead and Stolee had set themselves an exhausting schedule that brought them from Poland to the Baltic States, through Scandinavia, Germany, Austria, and Switzerland. Stolee's reports between May and mid-August 1920 made frequent reference to Morehead's illness. In one letter (from Geneva) to Larsen, Stolee had written:

This is a personal letter, but Dr. Morehead knows I am writing it. Sounds serious and is serious. *Dr. Morehead has been poorly for some time,* and I need not tell you how anxious I have been about it. He appears to be feeling better today, and so I am going to let you have the whole story.

He was a man in the best of health, apparently, when I came to join him in Berlin this spring and I remember that I said so in a letter to you. I revised my opinion the very next week on our trip to Hamburg. Then I *noticed how nervous he was,* and you may well imagine how I felt when he was to sign his name to a paper and *was too shaky to do it!* The spell passed away though, and his palpitation of the heart ceased sufficiently to permit the signature. He told me then that he felt overworked and that a serious breakdown which he suffered 20 years ago seemed to be asserting itself again. But he was still hoping for the best and of course was glad to have me with him.

Then we had to go to the long neglected Baltic provinces. It would have seemed most prudent for me to go alone, but he felt that it was a two man's job, and so did I. It was a very strenuous trip. No letting up or relaxation for a whole month or more; no, not even time enough for a single report, something that caused us very much worry too, because we knew how you felt about not getting any publicity matter, nor news of any kind. His nervousness, you may be sure, did not get any chance to improve under such circumstances. But he is wonderfully plucky and has will power enough for half a dozen! And it is by sheer will power that he kept at it. As we left Finland he began getting a moderate attack of Influenza; at Copenhagen he was sick but we hurried on to Berlin where he was very sick, but he still insisted on traveling on to Vienna where our Headquarters are. . . . We stayed three days in Vienna and he seemed to feel somewhat better, [so] we decided to travel together as far as to Geneva, where he could rest a while and I "make" France in the meantime. So we

42. Trexler, *Morehead,* pp. 77–78. Cf. NLC, *Annual Report . . . 1920,* p. 35.

came here, but it was a trying trip for poor Morehead. He had to lean on me as we left the train here and of course he was put to bed as soon as we came to our hotel. The doctor tells us he is suffering from over work, exhaustion, that his nerves are in a serious condition, and that the Influenza has left him a bad case of Sciatic-nerve trouble, making it extremely painful to walk or move about.

We have both hoped that the trouble would be a matter of only a short duration, so of course he did not want to write about it, and I felt I had no right to do so unless he wished me to. But it has been a serious time for both of us. Today he is feeling very much better and is able to be up. He intends to return to Vienna in a few days though the doctor tells him, and I second the doctor, that he ought to stay here and rest for two weeks at least. But he is rather hard to persuade. He must work, work, work, until his nerves give way, and another but much more serious collapse will result.[43]

On boarding the train at Vienna en route to Geneva, Stolee and Morehead discovered that Premier and Madame Paderewski ("and her pet dog") were also traveling to Geneva on their way to Oxford University, where the Polish statesman was to receive an honorary doctorate. They enjoyed recalling their trip together to Warsaw the previous summer. Stolee's letter also mentioned meeting the famous John R. Mott, who, like Stolee and Morehead, was going to an international missionary conference in Geneva. Morehead rested in Geneva and then accompanied Stolee to France. There they parted, Morehead to Vienna to recuperate and Stolee to Germany and Italy. Morehead recovered sufficiently to meet Larsen at Rotterdam at the end of July, and Stolee left Berlin in mid-August to return to the seminary in St. Paul in time for the new academic year.

After Stolee's departure, Morehead welcomed the presence and assistance of Lauritz Larsen, who assumed much of the burden during the next few months. Larsen returned to the United States in time to attend the annual meeting of the National Lutheran Council (Chicago, December 7, 1920). As the council's executive secretary, he presented an account of the work of the European Commission. The three-hour

---

43. Stolee to Larsen, June 24, 1920, in ArCL. A portion of Stolee's European diary (May [19?]–August 11, 1920), which is a valuable source concerning the travels and relief work undertaken by Morehead, Larsen, and Stolee, includes frequent references to Morehead's poor health. The diary was made available to the writer by the Stolee family.

report, during which "the delegates sat spellbound,"[44] was signed by Morehead, Stolee, and Larsen and covered the current state of church affairs in Europe and included proposals for immediate and future action. In addition to its vivid description of material destruction, economic erosion, and human distress, the report revealed that the Lutheran church faced serious moral and religious threats, chief of which were overt communism, liberal Protestant theology, and subtle Roman Catholicism.

The recommendations with which the report concluded ought to be read in the light of the above-expressed fears. First, it was proposed that the work of the European Commission be continued and increased (Morehead was the only member of the commission remaining in Europe); second, the American churches must prepare to care for a large-scale immigration from Europe (this turned out to be an exaggerated expectation); third, relief and reconstruction should be expanded to include Russia (that is, to support organized Christianity in the face of atheistic communism); and finally, the earlier proposal for a Lutheran world conference was now to be seen as even more imperative.[45]

Opposition to the last point was voiced by Hans G. Stub, the retiring president of the NLC, and by a delegate from the Ohio Synod. Both men objected because they feared that the ecumenical views of Swedish archbishop Nathan Söderblom would dominate the world conference and thus lead Americans into a situation of theological compromise. In reply, Larsen argued against such a negative approach and urged that "for the sake of Lutheran unity in America, Lutheran unity in the world" the council approve the recommendation. This was done.[46]

---

44. Jacobs, "National Lutheran Council," p. 12.
45. The report is in NLC, *Annual Report . . . 1920,* pp. 34–77. The recommendations are found on pp. 73–74.
46. See Larsen to Morehead, December 13, 1920, in ArCL, LWC unit, box 2, Pre-Eisenach General 1920. Larsen's supporters in his own church body (NLCA) were few. Many thought he was "too much influenced by Eastern Lutheranism." A discouraged Larsen almost accepted a call to be president of Thiel College (Pa.), but he was dissuaded by Boe, who argued that the NLC needed him more than Thiel did. Larsen to Boe, December 14, 1921; and Boe to Larsen, December 21, 1921, Boe Papers, box 10, folder 10. In 1920 an attempt had been made to lure Larsen away from the "Eastern influence" by offering him the presidency of Augustana (NLCA) College, Sioux Falls, South Dakota. Larsen to Boe, June 24, 1920, Boe Papers, box 7, folder 6.

AMERICANS PLAN FOR A WORLD CONVENTION

Before the National Lutheran Council adjourned its annual meeting in 1920, it authorized the executive commmittee to make "preliminary arrangements" for a world conference. Lauritz Larsen (elected council president in 1920 to replace Stub) soon named a planning committee with Charles M. Jacobs as chairman.[47] Even prior to the NLC's decision, Larsen was aware of Jacobs's positive views about an international conference. After an exchange of correspondence, it was agreed that they would prepare a proposal for consideration and adoption by the council.[48] A "Memorandum . . . on General Lutheran Conference," dated December 27, 1920, proposed that the National Lutheran Council take the initiative in bringing the conference to the attention of the European churches, with whom Morehead should act as a liaison. The earliest possible date would be the summer of 1922, and the best place would be in a neutral country, Switzerland being the most acceptable.[49] The memorandum underwent subsequent revision and refinement by the authors and others. Knubel, for example, suggested that some name other than "conference" be used, lest the Germans of the AELK say, "We are the General Lutheran Conference."

The revised Jacobs/Larsen document was adopted by the executive committee of the NLC "as a guide to the committee," to whom Jacobs presented it on April 20, 1921.[50] Although the proposal was not

47. The committee members, besides Jacobs, were C. C. Kloth, Fred H. Meyer, Mauritz Stolpe, and Abdel Ross Wentz. Morehead and Larsen were to be ex officio members. The naming of Jacobs as chairman grew out of Larsen's high regard for him as a churchman and theologian. The mutual trust had ripened over the years, and Larsen found himself increasingly seeking his friend's advice. See Larsen to Jacobs, 1920 correspondence, in ArCL, LWC unit, box 2, folder 2.

48. Jacobs was a member of the earlier (1919) committee and was quite aware that Stub, and especially Reu, would oppose a Lutheran world convention. Therefore he proposed that a plan including the ideas of Larsen, Knubel, and himself should be placed before the NLC. Moreover, it should be prepared with an eye to acceptance by Ihmels (and other Germans), whom Jacobs judged to be "at sea on the whole matter of Church organization." To support this judgment, he urged Larsen to read Ihmels's article "The Present State of the Church in Germany," *Lutheran Church Review* 39 (October 1920): 387 – 409. See Jacobs to Larsen, November 16, 1920, In ArCL. LWC unit, box 2, folder 2.

49. A typescript copy of Jacob's initial proposal is in ibid.

50. See NLC, "Executive Committee Minutes, January 17 – 18, 1921" and "Minutes of the Committee of the National Lutheran Council on a Lutheran World Convention." April 20, 1921, New York, in ArCL, LWC unit, box 1, folder 2.

adopted as presented, the document is reproduced here because its authors had anticipated several problems that actually arose later; moreover, they suggested possible solutions. The committee apparently felt that to anticipate problems might needlessly create problems, and so they eliminated much of the proposal in its final report, which is also reproduced here.

The Jacobs/Larsen Proposal

In considering the subject of an International Lutheran Conference there are six questions which require preliminary settlement. They are:

    I. The Name
   II. The Purpose
  III. The Program
   IV. The Membership
    V. The Manner of Calling
   VI. The Time and Place of Meeting

I. As regards the name it is suggested that it be simply "International Lutheran Convention." This avoids any conflict in names with the "Allgemeine Konferenz." It does not imply the existence of the proposal of a permanent organization. At the same time it does suggest the character of the assembly as an emergency measure. Under conditions which do now exist, it is a counsel of prudence and wisdom that those who claim the name of Lutheran should come together to discuss the emergency, the measure of common action that has been taken in view of the emergency, and the measure of common action that may be possible and expedient in the future.

II. The purpose of the meeting should be *to promote clearer understanding within and among the groups represented.*

III. The program should grow out of the purpose of the meeting. It is manifestly impossible to adopt a program without previous consultation of all the groups, or at least of the more important groups. Nevertheless, it is needful that that group which takes the initiative in the calling of such a Convention should have some definite ideas concerning the things it desires to see discussed.

It is suggested that in negotiations with the other Lutheran groups the National Lutheran Council shall insist that a place be given to the following topics.

    I. "The Confessions in the Church"
   II. "Methods and Principles of Church Organization"
  III. "The Relation of the Lutheran Churches to Programs of Church Unity"

It is also suggested that in the discussion of each of these topics the Lutheran Church of America shall insist that it have a place on the program, so that its testimony on all these points may be clear and ample.

These two suggestions may be considered fundamental to the whole plan of American participation in the Convention. There is little doubt that the other groups will assent to them, but refusal so to assent would be sufficient reason for the Lutheran Church of America to refuse to participate. Additional subjects might be suggested, such as Financial Methods in Free Churches, the Problems of Religious Education (dealing less with the content of such education than with its machinery and methods). No doubt there are other practical points which the European groups would suggest. But the convention would go far toward fulfilling its purpose if the three main subjects here suggested were adequately discussed. With these features incorporated in the program there would be no reason to fear that the Lutherans of America would be prevented from bearing testimony to their faith.

IV. The problem of membership is the most serious that has to be faced. There are three possible ways in which the question can be decided. The first is to have the membership composed of *official representatives* of regularly organized and established Lutheran Church bodies. These representatives would speak not as individuals, but as representatives of their churches. Such a plan would commend itself, if the Lutheran Churches of Europe were organized along the same lines as those of America, but this is not the case. The most of them are, or have been until recently, State Churches. Those that are not now State Churches are most of them National Churches. They do not even assume responsibility as churches for such work as Foreign or Inner Missions. It may be doubted whether their ecclesiastical limitations would permit the heads of these churches to assume the responsibility of appointing delegates.

The second solution of the problem is to have the membership *personal*. In this plan the Convention would have the precedent of the two most important general Lutheran organizations in Europe, the Allgemeine Konferenz and the Lutherische [*sic*] Bund. Both are organized societies which enlist their membership from among interested individuals. No member has a voice because of his official position, nor is anyone deprived of a voice because he holds no official position. They are, in this sense, "free" conferences, though they maintain a regular organization, and at least one of them maintains a periodical that is used for propaganda.

To this plan of membership there are two serious objections. The first is that the convention might become no more than a gathering of unimportant individuals whose participation would carry no weight in their own Church bodies. Such personal assemblages usually attract the extremists, and repel the more solid membership of the Churches. The second objection is that it would prevent the American members from going as delegates, which would practically exclude the Americans from participation. The mere matter of finance would become prohibitive.

A third possibility is that the membership should be "mixed," i.e., in part official and in part unofficial. Those churches which are so organized that they can appoint delegates could be asked to make such appointments. The churches which are not so organized could be represented by unofficial delegates, who might be chosen by groups within the churches. Practically all the older churches of Europe contain such organized groups. By coming in contact with the groups it would be possible to secure the attendance of men who are recognized leaders in their own churches.

It is suggested that the plan of mixed membership be adopted tentatively, with the understanding that official representation shall be secured wherever possible, and where that is not possible, that the members be chosen by the most important groups within the church concerned.

V. The method of calling the Convention presents some difficulties akin to those of membership. It is suggested that, as a first step, the representatives of the National Council in Europe—at present Dr. Morehead only—approach the heads of the Allgemeine Konferenz and the Lutherische [sic] Bund and discuss with them the best method of getting together such a Convention as is here projected. It should be made clear that in the call for such a Convention the Church bodies of America must act as an independent unit. We shall be in better position to determine the exact method of the call after hearing reports from Europe.

VI. The time of the meeting should be the earliest for which it is possible to arrange, but inasmuch as negotiations have to be carried on at long range and the whole project is as yet entirely new, it is suggested that it be fixed for the summer of 1922.

The place should be one of the countries of Europe which were neutral during the War. Because of its greater accessibility to the parts of Europe from which the delegates would come, it is suggested that Switzerland be chosen.

In order that all of these matters may receive careful consideration, and that the negotiations for the Convention may be got underway as early as possible it is suggested:

FIRST, that a committee be appointed to have the matter of preliminary arrangements in charge, with instructions to report regularly to this Executive Committee.

SECOND, that all of these suggestions be conveyed through this committee to the Chairman of the European Commission, with the request that he will consult the representatives of the European churches and give the committee the benefit of his advice and experience in regard to the matters in question.[51]

The committee's revision of the Jacobs/Larsen document was pre-

---

51. NLC, "Proceedings . . . 1921," pp. 7ff.

sented to the National Lutheran Council on May 3, 1921, and adopted in the following form:

I. The *name* given to the gathering should be "An International Lutheran Convention."

II. The *purpose* of the Convention should be to promote clearer understandings within and among the groups represented, with a view to the possible strengthening of present co-operation in the countries concerned and in the foreign mission field, and to the preservation and strengthening of Lutheranism throughout the world.

III. As subjects of discussion the National Lutheran Council should propose the inclusion of the following topics:

1. The Confessions in the Church
2. Methods and Principles of Church Organization
3. The Attitude of the Lutheran Church to Proposed Programmes of Union with other Churches
4. Foreign Mission Problems

Other topics, suggested by other participants in the Convention, would also have a place in the programme.

IV. The *call* for the holding of the Convention should be issued by the National Lutheran Council, acting jointly with the Allgemeine Lutherische Konferenz and the Lutherische [*sic*] Bund.

V. The personnel of the membership should be determined through the bodies signing the call. Each of these bodies should endeavor to secure the presence of representatives from all of its own groups. There should then be appointed a joint committee on Programme and Membership, which should invite to the Convention additional members, not connected with any of the three bodies.

(NOTE: The National Lutheran Council has no jurisdiction over the personnel of the membership from its constituent bodies. Each of the general bodies co-operating in the National Lutheran Council will name its own representatives and bear their necessary expenses.)

The membership of the Convention should not exceed one hundred and fifty.

VI. The *time* of the meeting should be the latter part of the summer of 1922, if possible in the month of August.

VII. The *place* should be in a country which was neutral during the war, and The Hague should be suggested as probably best suited for this purpose.[52]

Numerous questions had to be resolved before an official call and invitation to a Lutheran World Convention (as it soon came to be called) could be extended. One was the relationship between the American planning committee and its European counterpart. The proposal indicated that the call for the convention should be issued by

52. NLC, *Annual Report . . . November 3, 1921*, p. 42.

the National Lutheran Council for the Americans and the General Evangelical Lutheran Conference (AELK) and the Lutheran League (*Lutherischer Bund*) for the Germans. Three circumstances should be noted here. First, the Lutheran League was a small but strongly confessional group that had separated from the AELK in 1908 over the question of granting voting rights to Lutherans who were members of the Prussian Union. It drew its members from the Lutheran *Landeskirchen* and the Free Churches. Second, although the AELK included Scandinavians, its membership was largely German. The proposed Lutheran World Convention was therefore seen in a large measure as a joint venture by Americans and Germans. Third, neither of the German groups could speak for the official German churches because membership in the AELK and the Lutheran League, as noted above, was by individuals, not by churches. What then should be the nature of membership in the Lutheran World Convention?

From the outset, therefore, the National Lutheran Council recognized that a great responsibility rested upon the person or persons chosen to be the liaison. The natural choice was John A. Morehead, who was asked by the NLC executive committee to approach the leaders of the AELK and the Lutheran League to discuss the nature of membership and the best method of calling such a convention together.[53] After meeting with Ludwig Ihmels, president of the AELK, Morehead reported Ihmels's eagerness for a Lutheran World Convention and his gratitude to the Americans for teaching the Europeans to think "not simply of the German Lutheran Church and the Polish Lutheran Church and the Swedish Lutheran Church, but of the Lutheran Church of the world."[54]

Before returning to the United States for meetings in September 1921, Morehead was successful in obtaining statements of support from both the AELK and the Lutheran League. The former adopted a resolution indicating its basic agreement with the American plan for a Lutheran World Convention ("*grundsätzlich mit dem von Amerika ausgehenden Plan eines lutherischen Weltkonvents einverstanden*") and its willingness to sign a joint invitation. Details of arrangements were to be worked out by a Joint Committee on Arrangements, on

53. NLC, "Minutes . . . Executive Committee . . . January 17–18, 1921," in ArCL.
54. NLC, "Proceedings . . . 1921," p. 57 (cited in Allbeck, "Study of American Participation, p. 37), in ArCL.

which the AELK would be represented by its executive committee. The Lutheran League expressed its appreciation for the American Lutheran initiative and its continuing interest in international Lutheran solidarity, but it felt that its numerical and financial weaknesses did not allow it to assume any responsibilities and that therefore it must regretfully decline the invitation to join the NLC and the AELK in issuing the call to the convention. However, as if to demonstrate its desire to be a partner in the venture, it appointed a five-man group to represent the Lutheran League in the Joint Committee on Arrangements. In light of these developments, Morehead urged that the NLC be represented by an equal number on the joint committee. The NLC's Committee for a Lutheran World Convention adopted a resolution stating that the European Commission (at the moment only Morehead) represent it on the joint committee. In case the joint committee should meet at a time when Morehead was the sole commissioner in Europe, one other person should be sent by the NLC to serve with him. The committee also asked Jacobs and Larsen "to draft a tentative form of the invitation to the World Convention."[55]

The draft, like the original American proposal for a Lutheran World Convention, was largely the work of Charles M. Jacobs.[56] It stated that there are good reasons for a world gathering of Lutherans: The war-impoverished churches need the help of brethren, and world Lutheranism must be "a bulwark of evangelical truth" against aggressive Roman Catholic error and the "complete godlessness" of a secular society (communism and humanistic secularism were not mentioned but implied). Moreover, Lutherans need to recognize the bond of faith that makes them one. "This bond has always existed, but we have been too little conscious of it to give it adequate expression." The purpose of the convention is "to promote clearer understanding" and the extension of cooperation among all "who adhere to the Lutheran Confessions." The "Call" closed with the hope that the convention

55. NLC, "Minutes of the Committee . . . for a Lutheran World Convention, September 28, 1921," pp. 3–5, in ArCL, LWC unit, box 1, folder 2.
56. Although Larsen no doubt made editorial suggestions here and there, the words and style are characteristic of Jacobs. A comparative reading of the "Proposal" and the "Call," together with other documents known to have been written largely by Jacobs (the Washington Declaration [1920], the Savannah Declaration [1934], the Baltimore Declaration [1938]), reveals a single authorship.

would preserve and strengthen "confessional Lutheranism throughout the world."[57]

One feature of the "Call" not found in the May 3 revision of Jacobs's earlier "proposal" was the difficult question of membership. Jacobs had addressed the problem in the original "proposal" by recognizing the fact that membership in the convention would have to be "mixed." By that he meant that American Lutherans would be represented by delegates officially appointed by their church bodies. The European churches, however, as "folk churches" and nominally Lutheran, might readily appoint representatives who were not "consciously Lutheran." Therefore, the AELK, whose membership (unlike the NLC) was made up not of churches but of confessionally conscious individuals, would naturally issue the invitation to confessionally concerned persons within the territorial folk churches. With this in mind, Jacobs had provided alternate forms of invitation: "The Allgemeine evangelisch-lutherische Konferenz and the National Lutheran Council of America invite you" (1) to be present at . . . (individual membership), or (2) to send representatives . . . (ecclesiastical representation).[58]

The first meeting of the Joint (American-European) Committee for a Lutheran World Convention was held in Leipzig on January 12, 1922. The American representatives, in addition to Morehead, were Gustav A. Brandelle, president of the Augustana Synod, and A. C. Ernst of the Joint Synod of Ohio, both of whom had been appointed by the National Lutheran Council. Although the Leipzig meeting revealed unanimity about the proposed convention, some issues received close scrutiny and produced sharp discussion, notably that of representation. Could one avoid offending state (territorial) churches by not sending them invitations? Could the confessional character of the LWC be

---

57. The confessional role of the LWC (and later the LWF) has been both criticized and defended. Bengt Wadensjö, *Toward a Lutheran World Communion: Developments in Lutheran Cooperation up to 1929* (Uppsala: Verbum, 1970), writing out of the background of "openness" in the Church of Sweden and minimal appreciation of the Lutheran struggle for an identity in pluralistic America, tends to see the LWC as a product of American hyperconfessionalism totally committed to self-preservation and closed to the "pan-Protestantism" found among the more "advanced" Lutherans in Scandinavia and Germany. This of course was a misreading of men like Jacobs, Larsen, Knubel, Morehead, and Boe.

58. The full text of "the Call" is to be found in NLC, "Minutes of the Committee . . . for a Lutheran World Convention, December 30, 1921," pp. 1–2, in ArCL, LWC unit, box 1, folder 2.

assured in any other way than by the sending of invitations to selected, confessionally conscious individuals? This question was left open for the time being. It was clear, however, that elimination of nationalism must remain a primary aim of the planners. Confessionally sound churches not associated with the AELK (e.g., Czechoslovakia, Hungary, Austria) should be invited *as churches*. American churches outside the National Lutheran Council, namely, the Iowa Synod and the Synodical Conference bodies, should receive invitations.

The question of place of meeting produced the sharpest exchange. The American proposal had suggested a site in a neutral country (Switzerland and Holland had been proposed). At Leipzig the Americans shifted ground and proposed Budapest, where the Lutheran minority, it was argued, would be strengthened by a world meeting. The Germans rejected that idea as completely unacceptable. Now that the Americans were no longer insisting that the convention meet in a neutral country, the Germans seized a tactical advantage and urged strongly that Eisenach be the site. The Americans reported that they were "staggered by the force of this unexpected attack." Fearing that selection of Eisenach would be a yielding to German nationalism and a danger to the international and global dimension of Lutheranism, the Americans quickly pointed out that the Joint Committee on Arrangements lacked power to act in this matter. It was clear that committee members would have to discuss the thorny question of place and invitations with their respective agencies, thus requiring additional meetings of the joint committee. This also meant that a world conference in 1922 was out of the question; it would have to be postponed to 1923.[59]

The American response to the report of its representatives was a mixture of hope and dismay. The dismay grew out of the assessment by Morehead and Ernst that the Germans had "no strong enthusiasm" for the convention, partly for economic and political reasons and partly for the emotional reasons associated with being the defeated enemy in the recent war. Nevertheless there was some hope; the Germans demonstrated a clear intellectual conviction that a "great hour in the history

59. See the letter report ("Lutheran World Convention") to Lauritz Larsen, dated January 23, 1922, Moscow, Russia, and signed by Morehead and Ernst, in the Abdel Ross Wentz Papers, in ArCL. Cf. Larsen to Jacobs, February 6, 1922, in ArCL.

of Lutheranism has struck" and that a Lutheran world convention would hold up this fact for everyone to see.[60] Jacobs, the chairman of the American Committee, was upset, even angered, by the German attitude. "If we go to Eisenach," he wrote to Larsen, "it will seem that the Lutheran church of the world is . . . making [the church in Germany] the center of Lutheran work. . . . We will appear again as branches and twigs of the great vine whose roots are in the soil of Saxony. At the present time, I would vote to give up the project rather than to go to Eisenach, a place which I love and will surely visit if I ever go to Europe again."[61]

Jacobs's emotion-charged attitude underwent a reluctant change when it was learned that, if a Lutheran world convention were to be held at all, it would of economic necessity have to be held in Germany.[62] Recognizing this fact, the Joint Committee on Arrangements held meetings on June 8, 1922 (in Leipzig) and September 21, 1922 (in Frankfurt am Main). The committee dealt with problems of who should receive the invitations to Eisenach and what should be the nature of the program and agenda for the convention.[63] Although the decisions were to be referred back to the authorizing agencies (the NLC and the AELK) for ratification, they were on the whole definitive for the shape of the Eisenach meeting. Regarding the invitations, it was agreed that American Lutherans and European "free churches" should be invited to send official ecclesiastical representatives but that AELK-related Germans and Scandinavians should be invited as individuals, with a view to including officials of the territorial folk churches and groups such as "the large conferences, the union of Free Churches . . . the ministry to the diaspora, the foreign mission societies, the diaconic union, and international committees." Since these distinctions had now been made, a common invitation, without the alternate forms, could be sent to all. In order to emphasize the

60. Letter report to Larsen, January 23, 1922, p. 2.
61. Jacobs to Larsen, February 10, 1922, in ArCL.
62. The depreciation of the German mark by runaway inflation dictated this decision. Charles M. Jacobs, "Memorandum for Delegates to the World Convention," p. 2, Wentz Papers, in ArCL. The American representatives concurred, having been given power to act. NLC, "Proceedings . . . 1922," p. 18.
63. "Vorstandssitzung, am 8. Juni 1922"; "Sitzung der engeren Konferenz, am 8. Juni, 1922 in Leipzig"; and "Weltkonvent für das Luthertum: Vorbereitungssitzung in Frankfurt am Main am 21. September 1922," in ArCL.

difference between American voluntary confessionality and the European territorial confessionality, it was agreed that American delegates should be apportioned on a ratio of 1 to every 100,000 *communicants* or fraction thereof. The ratio for European territorial folk churches should be 1 to every 500,000 *baptized* members in a given church.[64] The number of delegates should not exceed two hundred.

The second matter on which the joint committee reached a consensus was the selection of general topics for the Eisenach program. The American proposal (May 3, 1921) had included a section entitled "Methods and Principles of Church Organization." It was felt that the long American experience in free-church organization would be helpful, especially in postwar Germany where the old state-church system had ceased to exist. The Germans, however, asked that this topic be eliminated, not because it was distasteful but because it was too big for adequate treatment and because the formation of new territorial church constitutions was already so far advanced that there was no point in using time at Eisenach for discussion of the topic.[65]

The other topics suggested in the American proposal were welcomed and supplemented by the joint committee. Topics for the main lectures were to be "The Ecumenical Character of Lutheranism," "The Confessions, the Indispensable Basis of the Lutheran Church," and "That They All May Be One! What Can the Lutheran Church Contribute to This End?" Other addresses would be prepared on interchurch aid, ministry to the diaspora, and foreign missions. Daily devotional services with sermons were also projected. Nominations for lecturers, preachers, and other participants were discussed and largely agreed upon. The official languages would be German and English, the temporary presiding officer would be Ludwig Ihmels, and the dates would be August 19–25.[66]

Before the end of 1922 the plans for the convention were fairly well in hand, and on November 15 the official call, signed by Ludwig Ihmels as president of the AELK and Lauritz Larsen as president of the National Lutheran Council, was sent out. The document, published on a letterhead, follows.

---

64. Jacobs, "Memorandum for Delegates to the World Convention," p. 2.
65. Morehead and Ernst to Larsen, January 23, 1922, p. 2, Wentz Papers, in ArCL.
66. "Weltkonvent . . . Vorbereitungssitzung . . . am 21. September 1922," in ArCL.

LUTHERISCHER WELTKONVENT 1923

National Lutheran Council   Allgemeine Evangelisch-Lutherische Konferenz
437 Fifth Avenue, New York, N.Y.   Leipzig, Carolinenstrasse 19

In the name of the Father and of the Son and of the Holy Ghost. Amen.

Our Lord Jesus Christ has committed to His Church on earth the work of preaching the Gospel to all the world. The form and manner of that preaching he has left to the determination of the Church itself, amid the conditions of time and place in which it lives, and under the guidance of the Holy Spirit, whom he has promised and sent. For this reason it lies within the power of the Church to adopt such measures, from time to time, as may seem best adapted for the performance of its divinely given task and for the preservation of the purity of the Gospel.

The Church is now passing through one of the critical moments of its history. The events of the past few years have wrought far-reaching changes throughout the world. In many lands the conditions under which the Church must labor have completely altered. New conditions have raised new problems and created new difficulties. Forces of evil and unbelief are seeking to destroy the Church, and want and poverty are hindering it, in many lands, in the fulfillment of its mission. But the Church still remains, and its task continues unchanged. It still must preach the Gospel and administer the Sacraments and minister to men in works of serving love. Among the churches that have suffered through the events of recent years none has suffered more than the Lutheran Church. With organizations weakened in many parts of the world, and with members impoverished, it stands, in many lands, as the chief bulwark of evangelical truth against Roman error, on the one hand, and complete godlessness on the other. As members of the Lutheran Church we believe that the Reformation was a divinely ordered movement and that the Lutheran Confessions are genuine testimonies to the truth of Scripture. Holding this to be true, we believe it to be our solemn and God-given duty to maintain and to proclaim this truth everywhere and under all conditions.

And inasmuch as we know the Lutheran Church to be distributed through many organizations, in many parts of the world, we believe that the time has come when adherents of the Lutheran Confessions throughout the world should meet in conference to discuss with one another matters of present and future moment. We also recognize that the time has come when such a meeting for conference is possible. However sad and bitter the experiences through which it has come to us, we believe that the Lutherans of the world recognize today more fully than ever in their history the strength of the bond of faith which stretches across all lines of race and nation and makes them one. This bond has always existed, but we have been too little conscious of it to give it adequate expression, even through conference.

For these reasons, the Allgemeine Evangelisch-Lutherische Konferenz and the National Lutheran Council of America invite you to send representatives to a World Convention of Lutherans, to be held at Eisenach, beginning the 19th day of August 1923. The purpose of this Convention is not to create any new international organization, or to effect any changes in organizations now existing, but rather to promote clearer understandings, in their home lands and in the Foreign Mission fields, among those who adhere to the Lutheran Confessions, with a view to the possible strengthening and extension of such co-operations as now exist among them. It is the earnest expectation and the hearty desire of those who have planned this Convention that it may help toward the preservation and strengthening of confessional Lutheranism throughout the world.

President,
Allgemeine Evangelisch-Lutherische Konferenz

[Signature: Ihmels]

President,
National Lutheran Council
[Signature: Larsen]

With the issuance of this official call, the National Lutheran Council's role in making arrangements for the convention came to an end. The NLC had seen its task as merely that of an agent for the church bodies; therefore, to go beyond its role as the catalyst or initiator would be to exceed its authority. Henceforth its Committee for the Lutheran World Convention would need to be replaced by a new Committee on Arrangements, the members of which would be chosen from those churches that responded affirmatively to the official call to name delegates to Eisenach.

At the end of 1922, only three bodies had declared their intentions to be represented: the Augustana Synod, the United Lutheran Church in America, and the Joint Synod of Ohio. It was especially embarrassing to Larsen, who with Ihmels had signed the official call, that his own church body (the NLCA) was reluctant to commit itself. A couple of years earlier, elements within that church had almost prevented membership in the NLC. Now some of the same caution was being manifested toward the Lutheran World Convention. When the negative attitudes of other churches, notably the Iowa Synod, were revealed, and when questions about the American role continued to emanate from European Lutherans, it was obvious that the new Committee on Arrangements would have a full agenda of problems to address between January and August 1923. The flurry of last-minute preparations for the Eisenach assembly is the subject for the next chapter.

5

The Final Planning Stage for Eisenach

For almost four hundred years Lutheran churches throughout the world had maintained relatively independent existences. Each church seemed quite satisfied that it could manage its own affairs without the advice and consent of others. But sounds of change during the last fifty years of the quadricentennium alerted churchmen in both Europe and America to the need for a manifested unity that would transcend nationalism, political, geographical, and cultural boundaries, and theological and ecclesiastical differences. By 1920 it was clear to several leaders that Lutheran unity was a necessary response not only to external needs—such as those growing out of advancing secularism and destructive warfare—but also to the ecumenical thrust inherent in Lutheran confessional theology.

The road leading to a recognition of the need for unity was an obstacle course that was negotiated only with the exercise of patience, spontaneous and calculated goodwill, political skill, and theological integrity. The willingness to make judicious compromises on peripheral matters while remaining intransigent on central issues, and the sagacity to know the difference, characterized the most adroit among the negotiators.

Thus, when the official call and invitation to a Lutheran world convention was issued in 1922 there seemed to be reason for optimism.[1] The goal appeared to be in sight, the prospects were bright,

1. The official "Call" and invitation as reproduced in the previous chapter was undated. However, it appears to have been sent on November 15, 1922. See Bengt Wadensjö, *Toward a World Lutheran Communion: Developments in Lutheran Cooperation up to 1929* (Uppsala: Verbum, 1970), p. 146. Lauritz Larsen, a co-signer with Ludwig Ihmels, was in Germany at the time; the letterhead was printed in German, and the signatures were personally inscribed. It is logical to assume that it was mailed when Larsen and Ihmels conferred at Leipzig.

and hopes were high. It looked as if the committee had only to tie up the loose ends and count the days to Eisenach. The probability of a slip twixt the cup and the lip seemed small. The momentum built up over the last three or four years would carry the process to its anticipated conclusion.

But if the modest optimism of the planning committees gave their expectations a roseate hue, the circumstances of the moment and the vagaries of history brought people back to the realities of the world of 1923. The horizon on both sides of the Atlantic was clouded by the rise of new problems and the persistence of some old ones. A few issues were peculiar to the American situation, others were common to both sides.

This chapter will show how the final planning stage was bedeviled with thorny questions that threatened the movement. Fortunately most of them were solved or eliminated by August 1923, but a few lingered on to color the assembly itself and to shape the subsequent course of the Lutheran World Convention.

PROBLEMS ON THE AMERICAN SIDE

The executive committee of the National Lutheran Council met on October 11, 1922, and adopted a resolution that effectively removed the NLC from its role as the American representative in planning the Lutheran World Convention. Since the council considered itself an "agency" without ecclesiastical authority, it must now make way for the American churches which would be officially represented at Eisenach and whose task it would be to carry forward the plans for the convention. Anticipating the issuance of the formal call and invitation of all Lutheran churches in America, including the Missouri Synod and other bodies that did not belong to the National Lutheran Council (e.g., the Iowa Synod), the executive committee adopted a resolution which stated that "as soon as three general bodies have appointed members of the American Committee on General Arrangements . . . this [new] Committee on Arrangements be called together by the Executive Secretary [Lauritz Larsen] of the Council." By early January 1923, three churches had taken action to be represented at Eisenach: the United Lutheran Church, the Joint Synod of Ohio, and the Augustana Synod. Each had appointed its representative to the new Committee on Arrangements, which had its initial meeting in New York City on January 12, 1923.[2] As convener of the meeting, Lauritz Larsen reported that the Joint American-European Committee had met three times in 1922, twice at Leipzig (January 12 and June 8) and the third time at Frankfurt am Main (September 21, 1922).[3] John A. Morehead had represented the National Lutheran Council at all these meetings. Present at Leipzig in January, in addition to Morehead, were Gustav A. Brandelle and A. C. Ernst. In June, Morehead was accompanied only by Ernst, in September at Frankfurt only by Larsen. As noted in the preceding chapter, it was at the latter meeting that the Eisenach program began to take shape. Its details were now reported to the American Committee, which promptly approved the Frankfurt decisions and thus gave support to the actions of the American representatives, Morehead and Larsen.

This initial meeting of the new American Committee was significant for a number of reasons. First, of course, was the fact that the transition from NLC leadership to official ecclesiastical sponsorship of the Lutheran World Convention had been successfully accomplished. This was no doubt due in large part to the contributions made by Morehead and Larsen and to the happy fact that the personnel of the new committee was only slightly altered from the earlier one.

Second, the minutes of the meeting reveal some consternation that as of January 1923 only three church bodies were officially and actively engaged in promoting a Lutheran World Convention. What, for example, could be done to mitigate the hesitation of the strong Norwegian Lutheran Church and to transform the Iowa Synod from its

2. American Committee on Arrangements, "Minutes . . . January 12, 1923," in the Archives of Cooperative Lutheranism, Lutheran Council/U.S.A., New York City (hereafter referred to as ArCL). Members: For ULCA, Charles M. Jacobs, chairman, and Abdel Ross Wentz; Ohio Synod, Conrad H. L. Schuette (represented by Fred H. Meyer); Augustana, Gustav A. Brandelle. John A. Morehead and Lauritz Larsen were elected "advisory" members, Larsen being asked to serve as secretary pro tem. Although the NLCA had not officially accepted the invitation to Eisenach by May 1923, Hans G. Stub had appointed Helmer Halvorson to sit as an "advisory" member on the American Committee.

3. The European Committee members were Ludwig Ihmels, soon to be chosen bishop of Saxony (see *Allgemeine Evangelisch-Lutherische Kirchenzeitung* [AELKZ], 1922, col. 287, for notice of Ihmels's election to the Saxon bishopric); Carl Paul, director of the Leipzig Mission Society; and Wilhelm Laible, editor of the *AELKZ*.

role as a critic to that of a supporter of the convention? Moreover, apathy was perhaps as much of an obstacle as outright antagonism toward the Lutheran World Convention. How could this be alleviated?

Third, undetectable in the minutes but starkly present as another major problem were the illnesses of Morehead and Larsen, both of whom were eventually to sacrifice their lives in the cause of Lutheran unity in America and abroad. Therefore, in describing the problems faced by the American Committee on Arrangements in the last twelve months prior to Eisenach, the health of these two men must be seen as an important factor.

Morehead had allowed himself to be assigned tasks that were beyond the strength of his body and nervous system. As noted earlier, his 1920 colleague and traveling companion, Michael J. Stolee, often confided to friends that he was concerned about Morehead's relentless schedule and its effects upon his health. In fact, said Stolee, Morehead broke down completely under the strain of overwork and anxiety. News of this led the National Lutheran Council to send Lauritz Larsen to Europe at the end of the summer (1920) for a few months to relieve Morehead of some burdens and to give him opportunity to recover his health. In 1921, Morehead was joined by his wife and daughter, who sought with some success to confine him to the perimeters of his strength. Nevertheless, he could not close his eyes to the famine in Russia, the continuing need for food and clothing in other parts of Europe, the allocation of money to the well-organized German churches, whose splendid institutions and publications had been paralyzed when the war wiped out their considerable financial resources. The disastrous postwar inflation had only added to their woes. In the face of such conditions, Morehead sent urgent pleas back to America. Despite the fact that the churches were feeling the effects of the mild economic recession of the early 1920s, the overwhelming needs only made him more importunate and led him to seek funds also from such humanitarian organizations as the Red Cross and the American Relief Association, whose director was Herbert Hoover. Incidentally, Morehead enjoyed a cordial and helpful relationship with Hoover. In July 1921, Morehead was recalled to America to rekindle the generosity and flagging zeal of church people who had become "weary in well-doing." A heavy schedule brought him from city to city, where he addressed thousands of persons and impressed on them the needs of fellow Christians in Europe.

When the National Lutheran Council's annual meeting was held (November 3, 1921), it was clear that the scope and intensity of Morehead's mission had exerted an extraordinary drain on his energies. He reported that he had personally ministered to churches in Austria, Bulgaria, Constantinople, Czechoslovakia, Danzig, Estonia, Latvia, Lithuania, Finland, Hungary, Romania, Poland, Italy, Yugoslavia, France, Germany, the Ukraine, and through refugee pastors to churches in Russia and the Republic of Georgia.[4] Thus, both in America and in Europe, Morehead had become a minister-at-large for the world Lutheran family. Like the apostle Paul he could say, "And, apart from other things, there is the daily pressure upon me of my anxiety for all the churches" (2 Cor. 11:28).

Before the year was out, Morehead was back in Europe, this time rejoicing that the Russian government had finally given permission— under the threat of plague and starvation—to the American Relief Association, and with it the National Lutheran Council, to enter Soviet territory. Once again Morehead gave himself unstintingly to the immense task of relief, seeking to reach those in most dire circumstances and to reestablish contact with Russian Lutherans who, prior to the Bolshevik Revolution, numbered four million, including Baltic Lutherans. Despite the fact that he now had the temporary assistance of an American pastor, A. C. Ernst from Stillwater, Minnesota, the pace of his ministry soon exacted its toll. Word was received at the NLC office in New York that Morehead, suffering from a duodenal ulcer and nervous exhaustion, was on the verge of collapse. During the previous five months, he had traveled ten thousand miles in severe Russian cold and under the most primitive conditions. The horrors of the famine were never far from his sensitive soul. Finally, in mid-July, he entered a sanitarium at Baden-Baden for treatment and recupera-

4. For an account of Morehead's life and work see Samuel Trexler, *John A. Morehead* (New York: G. P. Putnam's Sons, 1938). In addition, the Morehead correspondence and reports in ArCL provide details of his mission. Cf. also Willard D. Allbeck, "A Study of American Participation in Inter-Lutheran Cooperation Prior to the Formation of the Lutheran World Federation," unpublished manuscript, prepared for the Department of Theology, LWF-American Branch, New York, 1962.

tion. Meanwhile, Ernst was completing his tour of duty and had returned to his Minnesota parish and synodical responsibilities. This meant, of course, that the great work begun by Morehead and the other NLC commissioners who had given temporary service was in danger of falling apart. Moreover, the American participation in the Joint Committee on Arrangements for the Eisenach convention was in jeopardy.

Lauritz Larsen now found it necessary once again, as in 1920, to go to the aid of his friend Morehead and to assume the tasks that both of them realized had to be carried on if the American Lutheran stewardship to its European fellow believers was to be fulfilled. Larsen's correspondence reveals that he had considered going to Europe even before he heard of Morehead's breakdown. In a letter to Hans G. Stub (NLCA) he said that he had given up the earlier plans to go to Copenhagen to attend meetings on European relief work, but that now in the new emergency surrounding Morehead (and with the urging of Knubel and Jacobs) he was making arrangements to depart as soon as possible.[5]

Larsen negotiated with Oscar C. Mees, a clergyman from the Joint Synod of Ohio, to take over as acting executive director of the National Lutheran Council during his absence and then on July 29, 1922, sailed for Copenhagen. There he met and conferred with sundry churchmen and obtained firsthand reports on conditions in Lutheran churches in Europe—from France on the west to Russia on the east, from Scandinavia in the north to Yugoslavia in the south.[6] Then Larsen

5. Larsen to Stub, July 20, 1922, Lars W. Boe Papers, box 14, folder 7, St. Olaf College Archives, Northfield, Minnesota. Although Larsen does not identify the Copenhagen conference, it is clear from other sources that he was referring to a meeting of the World Alliance for Promoting International Friendship Through the Churches and the Konferenz zur Prüfung der Lage des europäischen Protestantismus (Conference for Investigating the State of European Protestantism), the latter held in Copenhagen's large Inner Mission meeting hall in Bethesda (the meeting was sometimes referred to as "the Bethesda Conference"), August 10–12, 1922. The initiative for the latter had come from the Federal Council of Churches of Christ in America and was being held to determine relief needs in European Protestantism. Cf. Wadensjö, *Toward a World Lutheran Communion*, pp. 111–13; and Ruth Rouse and Stephen C. Neill, eds., *A History of the Ecumenical Movement 1517–1948*, 2d ed. (Philadelphia: Westminster Press, 1967), p. 558. Alfred Th. Jørgensen of Copenhagen had been commissioned by Harald Ostenfeld to represent the Danish Church. Much of the leadership of the Bethesda Conference fell to Jørgensen, thus involving him in ecumenical affairs as well as in the LWC.

6. See Larsen to Mees, August 8, 1922 (from Copenhagen), Lauritz Larsen Papers, in ArCL.

journeyed to Baden-Baden to visit the convalescing Morehead, whom he found cheerful but "indescribably tired and exceedingly nervous." Nevertheless, Morehead outlined for Larsen the most pressing matters and sent him on his way. Larsen plunged into a whirlwind tour of Russia and other European countries, consulted with church leaders at every stop, and met with committees that were supervising distribution of money and goods.

During August and September, Morehead's health improved enough that he could make plans to sail for New York on September 27, 1922. Six days before, on September 21, he arranged to meet Larsen at Frankfurt am Main, where the two of them attended the meeting of the Joint Committee on Arrangements for the Lutheran World Convention. Following the meeting Morehead returned to the United States, and Larsen resumed his vigorous program of visitation and counsel. Finally, weary and exhausted from his heavy exertions, he too sailed for New York, arriving on December 9, 1922.

Although Larsen had picked up an infection in Russia and was suffering from a severe cold, he had to prepare agendas for two important meetings. The first meeting was that of the new American Committee on Arrangements, January 12, 1923, a summary of which is found at the beginning of this section. The second was the annual meeting of the National Lutheran Council, January 18, 1923, in Cleveland, following which Larsen had a number of speaking engagements in the interest of the Lutheran World Service Appeal. Prior to all these matters he had to find time to prepare his own report for the annual meeting and to address the desk work that had accumulated during his four months of absence from the office.

Both Larsen and Morehead made detailed reports to the annual meeting of the NLC, whose decisions were made largely as responses to these presentations.[7] Significant was the resolution to press the need to continue financial appeals by the cooperating churches for relief in Central Europe and especially in Russia. It was reiterated that the original goal of $5,000,000 over several years was urgently needed, not only for relief in Europe but also for war-orphaned mission fields.[8] The

7. NLC, "Minutes, Fifth Annual Meeting . . . 1923," pp. 2, 3, 8, in ArCL.
8. Ibid., p. 5.

American Committee on Arrangements requested that it be represented on the Joint Committee on Arrangements by the NLC's European Commission. For all practical purposes this meant Morehead, because other commissioners had come and gone, giving only limited time and help to the cause.[9]

Of latter-day interest was Morehead's recommendation that the National Lutheran Council "take under earnest advisement" the many opportunities for ecumenical cooperation in Europe and in mission fields. Morehead, who had struggled to maintain a responsible confessionality within American religious pluralism, has been unjustly criticized as an opponent of ecumenism and as one of the leading American Lutherans seeking with almost conspiratorial ambition to use world Lutheranism to advance a sort of confessional imperialism.[10]

The future of the National Lutheran Council's administrative structure was also apparently discussed at this meeting. There was the question whether the office of president should be "passed around" among the cooperating churches and a new office of executive secretary be established. Although the minutes do not reveal any discussion or decision on this matter, other sources indicate that the subcommittee on Larsen's report (Carl C. Hein, Morris G. G. Scherer, and Lars W. Boe) must have discussed the issue.[11] As we will note shortly, the NLC would make this change in the near future.

Meanwhile, the National Lutheran Council adjourned, and Larsen, its weary and feverish president, traveled to Erie, Pennsylvania, on Saturday, January 20, to carry out a full schedule of services in Erie churches on Sunday January 21. His energies, now almost exhausted,

---

9. Ibid. The NLC expressed appreciation to Morehead as chairman of the European Commission and to commission members A. C. Ernst and W. L. Scheding. Ernst had recently returned to the States; Scheding continued his work in Russia (1922–23). Cf. Trexler, *Morehead*, p. 103. The NLC minutes reported that C. Theodore Benze, a professor at Philadelphia Seminary, had been appointed to work with Morehead and was now in Europe (NLC, "Minutes, Fifth Annual Meeting . . . 1923," p. 5). Benze remained in Europe into 1924, returning in September to resume his duties at the seminary.

10. A notable example of inability to see Morehead's ecumenical interests alongside his confessionality is Wadensjö's *Toward a World Lutheran Communion*.

11. Boe to Oscar C. Mees, February 8, 1923, Boe Papers, box 16, folder 5. Boe writes, "In the reorganization, which undoubtedly will become necessary, I hope they will adopt the recommendation made by *our Committee,* that the Secretary be made the executive officer, and [the] presidency be passed about the presidents of the synods. . . ." (italics added).

were insufficient to ward off disease, and he was forced to enter the local hospital, where his illness was diagnosed as pneumonia. Without the benefit of modern miracle drugs, his weakened body was unable to offer resistance to the virulent infection, and a week later on Sunday, January 28, 1923, he died. Larsen was only forty years old.[12]

The whole church recognized that it had sustained a major loss. Larsen's death in the prime of life and in the midst of a turbulent era that demanded the qualities of leadership he had demonstrated made the church's sorrow even more acute. Tributes to his ministry came from church leaders in America, France, Germany, Austria, Poland, Russia, Alsace, and Czechoslovakia. Frederick H. Knubel spoke for many:

> From an intimate knowledge of Dr. Larsen I would say that to human eyes there was no life of greater promise than his in our Lutheran Church of this country. . . . One is inclined to say, "an enemy hath done this." By God's grace that which has happened may, however, be a blessing to every wounded heart and to the church. It is ours to turn more positively than ever to that grace. Thus shall . . . we be enabled to trust Him who enriched us with that promising life and who will ever give.[13]

Larsen's close friend Lars W. Boe, president of St. Olaf College and one of the councillors at the January 18 meeting of the NLC, expressed his personal sense of loss in Larsen's death to one of its officers. Then in characteristic fashion he concluded by saying that there was but one thing to do, and that was to get on with the work.[14]

That is exactly what was done. A special meeting of the National Lutheran Council was held in Chicago on February 16, 1923, to fill the vacancy caused by Larsen's death. Conrad H. L. Schuette, president of the Joint Synod of Ohio and vice-president of the NLC, was elected council president. Since he could not devote full time to the position, the council decided that the time was propitious to implement the earlier suggestion—which apparently had been discussed on January 18 at Cleveland—to create the office of executive director. Larsen, as

---

12. Larsen was born November 28, 1882, in Decorah, Iowa, into a distinguished family of clergymen and educators. His father, also Lauritz Larsen, was president of Luther College in Decorah. Larsen's obituary is in *The Lutheran*, February 8, 1923, p. 14.

13. Ibid., p. 15.

14. Boe to E. F. Eilert, February 1, 1923, Boe Papers, box 15, folder 9.

the NLC's full-time president, had actually served as its chief executive as well. The office of president would now be largely honorary, with the administrative duties falling to the executive director. But who should he be? The one person who knew more about Lutheran problems worldwide than anyone else was of course John A. Morehead. The council promptly recognized this and proceeded to elect him.[15]

The assumption of the new office meant that Morehead now occupied a dual role. Already director of the NLC's European Commission, he now was given the added duties of directing the council's North American program. Like Larsen before him, the fifty-six-year-old Morehead had magnificent gifts of leadership and a compassionate spirit that thrust him selflessly into the servant role. Fortunately the European relief work of the American Lutheran churches was showing signs of becoming less demanding. Moreover, the American churches were feeling the pinch of the economic recession, and voices were being raised questioning the council's role as an agency for relief work.[16] At least it seemed legitimate to ask whether the era of emergency relief was drawing to an end. Perhaps the new era of Lutheran world cooperation, presaged by Eisenach, would reduce the domestic burdens and relax the internal tensions normally faced by the NLC, thus freeing Morehead in part from his tasks as a fund-raiser and allowing him to concentrate on arrangements for Eisenach. The churches of the NLC were hardly guilty of thoughtless exploitation in asking Morehead to direct the council.

In any case, Morehead set out almost immediately for Europe—he left New York on March 3—and spent five busy weeks in Bremen, Riga, Moscow, Leipzig, and Paris. In Moscow he and one of the two other NLC European Commission members, C. Theodore Benze, met with Soviet authorities in order to facilitate distribution of relief to Russian Lutherans. In Leipzig he represented the American Committee on Arrangements for Eisenach at a meeting on March 26 of the joint committee and helped put the finishing touches on

15. *The Lutheran,* March 1, 1923, p. 3.
16. Ibid.

the Eisenach program. By April 6 he was back in New York, where a collection of problems tangled into a Gordian knot awaited his attention.[17]

Chief among these problems was the somewhat less than enthusiastic response of the churches to the Eisenach invitation. Naturally this was of grave concern to Morehead and his co-workers, Jacobs, Knubel, Boe, Brandelle, and the NLC's president, Schuette. It was not unexpected that the small linguistic synods would find it financially difficult to be represented at Eisenach, and it was hardly a surprise that the Missouri Synod and its partners in the Synodical Conference would reject participation on the grounds of what they regarded as "sinful unionism." It was, however, a matter of deep distress when two of the major Midwestern Lutheran bodies, the Iowa Synod and the Norwegian Lutheran Church, remained reluctant to commit themselves to the Lutheran World Convention.

In 1920 the Iowa Synod had withdrawn from the council because it judged the latter's activities to be in violation of what had come to be called "cooperation in *res externae*" (external matters). Originally a principle advanced to delimit Lutheran cooperative efforts in America, it had been extended more recently to the European scene. Iowa's leaders, Friedrich Richter and Gustav A. Fandrey, gave support to the synod's chief critic of the National Lutheran Council, Iowa's well-known theologian, J. Michael Reu, a Germanophile whose ethnic loyalties, though deeply rooted, were not strong enough to overcome his distrust of "German liberal theology." It was the council's alleged disregard of "liberalism" that made it suspect to Reu and the Iowa Synod.[18]

Nevertheless, when the idea of a Lutheran World Convention was proposed and the first planning committee was elected in 1919, Reu, it

17. The European trip in the spring of 1923 is dealt with briefly in Trexler, *Morehead,* pp. 102–3. For an account of the Leipzig meeting see "Sitzung des Vorbereitungsausschusses für den Luth. Weltkonvent . . . 26. Maerz 1923, Leipzig," appended to American Committee on Arrangements, "Minutes . . . April 20, 1923," in ArCL.

18. Frederick K. Wentz, *Lutherans in Concert* (Minneapolis: Augsburg Publishing House, 1968), p. 55. It is interesting to learn that leaders of the German AELK, some of whom were considered "liberal" by Iowa, were eager to have Iowa and Missouri participate in the LWC because they saw them as *Germans* in America who were "very favorable to Germany." Wadensjö, *Toward a World Lutheran Communion,* p. 151.

will be recalled, was one of those named to the committee.[19] The gesture of appointing Reu, perhaps intended to soften his attitude, was not successful. Reu continued his criticism, and the next year (1920) Iowa withdrew from the National Lutheran Council. A new planning committee, without Reu, was then appointed, and, as we have seen, worked successfully with the German AELK to issue the invitation to the Lutheran World Convention. All Lutheran bodies in America, including Iowa, had received the invitation. It was at this juncture (1922) that Iowa's leaders exhibited a renewed interest in being represented at Eisenach.[20] Its leaders made much of the fact that Morehead and others had stated that Eisenach would be a "free conference." By definition, a free conference, in contrast to a synod or convention, was an unofficial forum for theological discussion rather than a convention of official delegates speaking officially for their respective churches. In this context, the suggestion was made that the Iowa Synod be granted the privilege of providing one of two speakers on the second main theme ("The Confessions, the Indispensable Basis of the Lutheran Church"). The logical Iowa choice, of course, would have been Reu.

When the proposal came to the attention of the American Committee on Arrangements on April 20, 1923, it met with flat rejection. The following statement was made:

> The American Committee believes first, that the naming of Americans for places on the program should be entirely in its hands; second, that no member of the Iowa Synod should be given such a place unless the Iowa Synod shall decide to send official representatives, inasmuch as the other American church bodies will be officially represented.[21]

As if to lock in this decision, the American Committee proceeded to name Sven J. Sebelius, of Augustana Seminary, Rock Island, to deliver

---

19. See above, Chapter 4, n. 40.

20. American Committee on Arrangements, "Minutes . . . January 12, 1923," p. 1, in ArCL.

21. American Committee on Arrangements, "Minutes . . . April 20, 1923," p. 1, in ArCL. There was some inconsistency in this decision. Hans G. Stub had been accorded a place on the Eisenach program without action by his own church (NLCA) to be officially represented at Eisenach. See "Sitzung des Vorbereitungsausschusses für den Luth. Weltkonvent . . . 26. Maerz 1923," p. 1. The minutes say that Stub was to deliver the opening sermon at Eisenach. Stub was a member of the American Committee that took the action of April 20.

the official response to the main lecture on the topic that had been assigned earlier to Alfred Th. Jørgensen of Copenhagen. The committee added that should the Iowa Synod send official representatives one of them would be allowed to participate in the discussion. As it turned out, two members of the Iowa Synod, Reu and a Pastor E. Moehl, did make the trip to Eisenach, and Reu was accorded opportunity to speak during the discussion period.[22] In this way the problem of Iowa resolved itself.

More important than the Iowa Synod problem was the question concerning the participation of the Norwegian Lutheran Church of America. The NLC's president, Larsen, writing to NLCA president Hans G. Stub in midsummer 1922, mentioned his distress that the NLCA did not seem to be enthusiastic about the proposed Lutheran World Convention. He listed his reasons for "the absolute necessity of such a convention" and then asked Stub to urge the NLCA Church Council to take action in favor of sending delegates to Eisenach. If the Church Council should plead lack of authorization for this step, said Larsen, it should at least name a temporary appointee (to the planning committee) to act on behalf of the Norwegian Lutheran Church until its 1923 convention could properly elect delegates.[23]

Meanwhile, Larsen had gone to Europe, and Oscar C. Mees, as acting director of the NLC, wrote Boe wondering if Stub was genuinely opposed to participation in the Lutheran World Convention. Boe replied that Stub was not antagonistic to the idea. In fact, he had presented it to the Church Council of the NLCA, which "decided to refer the matter without any recommendation" to the June convention of the church body. Boe went on to urge the acting director to make it

22. See the official report, *The Lutheran World Convention . . . Eisenach . . . August 19th to 26th, 1923* (Philadelphia: United Lutheran Publication House, 1925), pp. 18 and 87–90. The publication *AELKZ* carried a detailed account of the Eisenach proceedings. The editor reported that the two Iowa Synod men arrived three days late, Wednesday August 22, in time to hear Jørgensen's lecture. When Chairman Ihmels announced their arrival, the reporter wrote, "A happy murmur went through the hall at this announcement." Wadensjö claims the late arrival was calculated to emphasize the Iowa Synod's "independence of the NLC." Wadensjö, *Toward a World Lutheran Communion*, p. 144.

23. Larsen to Stub, July 20, 1922, Boe Papers, box 14, folder 7. Apparently Stub himself named Helmer Halvorson as an "advisory" member to sit on the American Committee when he (Stub) could not be present. Halvorson, whose name appears on the letterhead of the committee, had succeeded Lauritz Larsen in 1919 as pastor of Zion Church, Brooklyn, New York. Cf. *Who's Who . . . Pastors . . . Norwegian Lutheran Synods . . . 1843–1927* (Minneapolis: Augsburg Publishing House, 1928), p. 210.

plain to all churches fearful of "unionism" that this Lutheran world gathering would be a "free conference." He himself was planning to appear before the next meeting of the NLCA Church Council (in February 1923) to push participation at Eisenach.[24]

The American leaders of the Lutheran world movement were acutely aware that a negative response from the NLCA would deal a telling blow to their hopes. This church was the third largest body (behind the ULCA and the Missouri Synod) in American Lutheranism. Should it refuse to act favorably, it would mean that only 45 percent of Lutherans in America would be represented at Eisenach. In light of this, a chronicle of some events between January and June 1923 may be revealing.

1. On January 18, 1923, as noted earlier, the National Lutheran Council met. For some unexplained reason, Hans G. Stub was absent but was represented at this important meeting by Lars W. Boe. When Stub was nominated (among others) to membership on the powerful executive committee, it was Boe who made the motion for election.[25]

2. On March 26, 1923, the Joint Committee on Arrangements for the Lutheran World Convention met in Leipzig. Without any explanation or record of discussion, the minutes register the following: "Es soll der Eroeffnungsgottesdienst shon [sic] am Sonntag, den 19. August abends stattfinden und dabei D. Stub die Predigt halten."[26] This announcement that Stub would be delivering the opening sermon at Eisenach should be seen in the light of (a) the American eagerness to bring the hesitant NLCA into the LWC; (b) the fact that the NLCA would not be making a decision to be officially represented until June 1923; (c) and the earlier action of the American Committee on Arrangements denying the Iowa Synod a place on the convention program because it had not yet decided to send official representatives to Eisenach. That the NLCA could be assigned a place on the program before it had decided to send delegates to Eisenach seems to say that

24. Boe to Mees, November 27, 1922, Boe Papers, box 13, folder 13. Stub wrote to Larsen on December 19, 1922, reiterating what Boe had said (cited by Willard D. Allbeck, "A Study of American Participation in Inter-Lutheran Cooperation Prior to the Formation of the Lutheran World Federation," prepared for the Department of Theology of the LWF, 1962, p. 30, in ArCL).

25. NLC, "Minutes . . . January 18, 1923," pp. 1, 7, in ArCL.

26. "Sitzung des Vorbereitungsausschusses . . . 26. Maerz 1923," p. 1.

established principles could be set aside when they threatened to thwart the hopes of the planners.[27]

3. On April 20, 1923, the American Committee on Arrangements met in New York, and this time NLCA president Stub was present. After the January 12 meeting, the invitation to preach at Eisenach had become public information (also, the Leipzig minutes, carrying the announcement, were attached to the minutes of this meeting in New York).

4. Some time after April 20 and prior to June, Charles M. Jacobs, chairman of the American Committee on Arrangements, sent out a carefully written "Memorandum for Delegates to the World Convention." He pointed out that the "Norwegian Lutheran Church holds advisory membership" in the committee, pending the June action of the church. Moreover, he too pointed out that the NLCA's president had been asked to deliver the opening sermon.

In view of these items and their testimony to the orchestrated character of events, the NLCA was hardly in a position to take any other than favorable action. This it did, and voted to send its president to Eisenach.[28]

PROBLEMS COMMON TO BOTH SIDES

While Morehead and the American Committee on Arrangements dealt with the specifically American issues, a parallel set of exigencies engaged the attention of both Europeans and Americans. Each requires mention.

First, there was the persistent question, Should the Lutheran World Convention be considered a "free conference," a "nonrecurring" event? Or should it be thought of as the first step toward a permanent world organization? In 1919, when the Americans first advanced the

27. The agenda for the Leipzig meeting indicated that two world famous choirs, the Thomanerchor of Leipzig and the St. Olaf Lutheran Choir, St. Olaf College, Northfield, Minnesota, were being invited to present concerts at Eisenach. Although both choirs surely could be invited on merit alone, the participation of the St. Olaf Choir could only enhance the chances of a favorable vote by the NLCA in June, because St. Olaf College belonged to the NLCA. As it turned out, neither choir was able to be present at Eisenach.

28. NLCA, *Report . . . 1923*, pp. 17, 115. The invisible director of the "orchestra" was no doubt Boe.

need for a Lutheran world conference, they were motivated by their experiences in postwar relief work. It appeared to Morehead and others that a Lutheran world conference was needed in order to increase mutual understanding and strengthen the Lutheran witness. Initially, although no organizational plan for the future was in mind, the Americans may have had vague notions of some kind of permanent organization. If so, this conception was quickly dismissed by the hard reality that the churches on both sides of the Atlantic took a jaundiced view of such an idea. When Morehead discussed the matter with the Germans, he quickly detected their defensive attitudes; they feared that Lutheran world leadership could very well be slipping from them to the Americans. In order to disabuse them of fear, Morehead repeatedly assured them that the proposed world conference would be "a one-time, nonrecurring event," which would not threaten to replace the AELK as the permanent organization for international cooperation.[29]

Morehead and the Committee on Arrangements soon discovered that some Americans were likewise opposed to the creation of a global organization for Lutherans. The reasons, however, were different from those ascribed to the Germans. The Iowa Synod and individuals in other bodies had theological objections to participation in anything more than a theological open forum, "a free conference," which had no implications for ecclesial fellowship. Such a conference would give American theologians—like Reu—an opportunity to witness against the "liberalism" of both European and American Lutherans.

Although this problem of a permanent organization for world Lutheranism remained unresolved prior to Eisenach, the LWC was to find it necessary to deal with the issue.

The second problem arose out of the largely bilateral conversations between the Americans and the Germans. What role did the Scandinavians play in world Lutheranism? Morehead and the NLC European Commission members had had relatively minimal contact with Scandinavians, and the latter had demonstrated minimal interest in affairs

---

29. Wadensjö, *Toward a World Lutheran Communion*, pp. 148–49. Cf. Kurt Schmidt-Clausen, *Vom Lutherischen Weltkonvent zum Lutherischen Weltbund* (Gütersloh: Gerd Mohn, 1976), pp. 38–40. Schmidt-Clausen thinks that Wadensjö has misrepresented the Americans. They were certainly not engaging in a card game in which they had not laid all their cards on the table. Rather, the Americans were honestly seeking a way to bring world Lutherans together.

beyond their national borders. Ever since the days of Bismarckian aggression, when Denmark lost its southern territory to Prussia, the Danes were understandably defensive over against Germans. With the recovery of Slesvig after the defeat of Germany in 1918, the Danes were reintegrating the Slesvig churches into Danish church life. Meanwhile, the Norwegians were preoccupied with internecine theological conflict that split the church into a liberal party, which associated itself with the theological faculty at the University of Christiania (Oslo, 1924), and a conservative party that gave support to a newly established "independent faculty" (*Menighetsfakulteten*). Thus Norwegian churchmen found little time and less interest in American-German plans for a world conference.

The one Scandinavian exception was Sweden, whose great ecclesiastical spokesman and theologian, Archbishop Nathan Söderblom, was giving leadership to the infant ecumenical movement.[30] Söderblom's relentless advocacy of the church's role in the secular world and his broad-ranging theological views (his capacious mind sought to integrate biblical criticism, church history, history of religions, Ritschlianism, pietism, and Lutheranism into what he might prefer to call "evangelical catholicism") produced enthusiastic disciples and outspoken critics. Criticism, though not always justified, spread as quickly as his reputation. This occurred in Scandinavia (including his own Swedish church) as well as in Germany and America. In these circumstances it was understandable that the movement to unite the Lutheran family would be ill-served by giving prominence to one whose views were divisive. Söderblom, of course, was fully conscious of the critical opinions, but he also saw the significance and potential strength of the emerging pan-Lutheran movement and sought earnestly to solidify his contacts with its leadership, especially with Ludwig Ihmels, whose friendship he had cherished since 1912, when the two had been colleagues on the theological faculty at the University of Leipzig.[31] Quite openly, the Swedish archbishop endeavored to sweep the pan-Lutheran movement into his own ecumenical plans.[32] Although he was unsuccessful in this, his activity resulted eventually

---

30. Perhaps the best work in English about Söderblom is Bengt Sundkler, *Nathan Söderblom: His Life and Work* (Lund: Gleerups, 1968).
31. Ibid., p. 294. Cf. Wadensjö, *Toward a World Lutheran Communion*, p. 109.
32. Wadensjö, *Toward a World Lutheran Communion*, pp. 100–110, 152–61.

in the realization that the Lutheran World Convention must be seen as much more than the enterprise of two groups of Lutherans, the Germans and the Americans; an American-German axis would ultimately be self-defeating. A third group, the Scandinavian, must be accorded its rightful place.[33] From 1923 to the 1960s, global Lutheranism recognized itself as possessing three "groups" or "centers of strength" (Germany, Scandinavia, and North America). This "polycentric" character remained until the present, when a fourth "center"—the Lutherans of the Third World—has been recognized.[34]

A third problem, intrinsically related to the concerns over Söderblom, was the question of maintaining a Lutheran identity in the emerging ecumenical movement. The opponents of ecumenism equated it with "unionism." But those like Ihmels in Germany and Knubel and Jacobs in America, who were convinced that Lutherans must recognize and participate in the ecumenical movement, wrestled with the problem of confessional particularity and evangelical catholicity. German Lutherans, who had experienced the "unionism" or the ecumenism represented by the Prussian Union, were reluctant to rush headlong into ecumenical alliances. The Americans who were ecumenically sympathetic, if not enthusiastic, said to themselves, "If the effort to unite Lutherans is beset with so much difficulty, think what turmoil would occur if we moved too hastily into the ecumenical world; Lutheran solidarity must have priority." This explains in part the irritation that the National Lutheran Council and Morehead exhibited in response to the ecumenical pressures of Söderblom, whom Morehead described (to Larsen) as "our agile friend" who was seeking to drive a wedge between the council and the AELK. It should be remembered that the latter's president, Ihmels, was a close friend of Söderblom.[35]

The restraint of the Lutherans was not without justification. The American leaders in the ecumenical movement were chiefly non-

---

33. Ibid., pp. 155–56.
34. Kurt Schmidt-Clausen refers to this principle as "Polyzentrismus"; see his *Vom Lutherischen Weltkonvent*, p. 41. The fourth "center" was active in the LWF after World War II. In 1977, at the LWF assembly in Dar es Salaam, the assembly elected for the first time a representative of this "fourth center," Tanzanian bishop Josiah Mutabuuzi Kibira, to the office of president. Cf. "Persons," *Lutheran World* 24, no. 4 (1977): 475–79.
35. See Morehead to Larsen, and Morehead to Jordan, January 4, 1922; and Morehead to Söderblom, January 3, 1922; in ArCL.

Lutheran Protestants who had minimal contact with the Reformation theological tradition and were often advocates of a Ritschlian "kingdom of God" theology that found expression during the 1920s and 1930s in slogans like "Deeds not creeds." At the same time, the German Protestant churches, constitutionally separated from the state after World War I, had formed in 1922 the Federation of German Evangelical Churches (Deutscher Evangelischer Kirchenbund [DEK]). From the very first, the DEK was actively represented in the plans for Söderblom's Life and Work Conference (Stockholm, 1925). The chief German participant was H. Kapler, president of the DEK and a member of the Prussian Union church. Kapler was enchanted by Söderblom,[36] critical of German Lutherans, and not a little influenced himself by Ritschlianism. His words "Doctrine divides, but service unites," quoted by the planning committee for Stockholm,[37] quickly became catchwords for ecumenical enthusiasts. German Lutherans looked upon this and all ecumenical appeals "to build the kingdom of God on earth" as theological superficiality.[38]

The lack of ecumenical enthusiasm consequently arose not merely out of exclusivist arrogance or narrow-minded Lutheran self-satisfaction buttressed by synthetic arguments, but also out of theological and practical convictions, none of which would deny the catholic *una sancta*.

A fourth problem that needed to be settled prior to the Lutheran World Convention was the selection of program participants. As early as September 1922 the Joint Committee on Arrangements had reached the unanimous decision that its chairman, Ludwig Ihmels (he became Bishop of Saxony in 1922) should be appointed to act as chairman of the opening session of the convention, at which time the convention itself would elect its regular chairman.[39] Most of the program partici-

---

36. Sundkler, *Söderblom*, pp. 346–47.
37. Rouse and Neill, eds., *History of the Ecumenical Movement*, pp. 540–41. Kapler, it should be noted, was the 1933 chairman of the committee to reorganize the German church under Hitler.
38. Ihmels, who, at Söderblom's invitation, was to deliver one of the main lectures at Stockholm, said, "Nothing could be more mistaken or more disastrous than to suppose that we mortal men have to build up God's Kingdom in the world." Ibid., p. 547.
39. "Weltkonvent . . . Vorbereitungssitzung . . . am 21. September 1922"; cf. American Committee on Arrangements, "Minutes . . . January 12, 1923," p. 3. As was to be expected, the convention elected Ihmels to be its permanent presiding officer.

pants were selected without the serious clash of nationalistic or theological interests. We have noted the political circumstances that led the joint committee to appoint Hans G. Stub to deliver the opening sermon, and the action that foreclosed the Iowa Synod's attempt to have its leading theologian, J. Michael Reu, on the program. There was wholehearted concurrence that Ihmels should be asked to deliver one of the main lectures, "The Ecumenical Character of Lutheranism."

No explanatory comments appear in the records about the appointment of Alfred Th. Jørgensen (Copenhagen) to deliver the main lecture, "The Confessions, the Indispensable Basis of the Lutheran Church." Jørgensen had been one of the few Scandinavian members of the AELK prior to World War I. He was known to the Germans as a confessionally oriented theologian of the Inner Mission (pietistic) wing of the Danish Church who had won the confidence not only of the Germans (this was notable because of Jørgensen's strong stand on the Slesvig border conflict with Germany) but of other Scandinavians.[40] Moreover, in contrast to Sweden's Nathan Söderblom, his theological and church views commended themselves to the Americans. Along with two other Scandinavians, Edvard Sverdrup of Norway and Adolf Wallerius of Sweden, Jørgensen had been chosen by the AELK to name "confessionally oriented" delegates for Eisenach.[41] Therefore Jørgensen was deemed a wise choice both theologically and politically (he would be the sole Scandinavian representative on the list of main lecturers) to deal with the role of the confessions in world Lutheranism.[42]

The American Committee had been given the responsibility of choosing the American program participants. Thus there could be no debate when the Americans nominated Frederick H. Knubel to discuss the topic "That They May All Be One! What Can the Lutheran Church Contribute to This End?" This was indeed an assignment for which Knubel was eminently qualified by temperament and by

40. Wadensjö, *Toward a World Lutheran Communion*, pp. 114–15. Jørgensen's reputation among Norway's conservatives was high. In 1924 he was offered a professorship at *Menighetsfakultetet*.

41. Ibid., pp. 141–43.

42. This is the topic that the Iowa Synod had hoped would be assigned to Reu. See above, pp. 124–25.

theological conviction. In retrospect, however, the question was raised whether the best-known advocate of Christian unity, Nathan Söderblom, ought not to have been given this honor. As it was, conservative Lutheran voices in Germany, Scandinavia, and America felt that Söderblom had not yet demonstrated that he was a true blue Lutheran. Hence they did not find it "convenient to allow his name to appear on the programme," although Ihmels secured an ad hoc opportunity for his friend to deliver a greeting to the Eisenach assembly.[43]

A fifth and final problem to be resolved prior to Eisenach was a whole network of social and political questions that centered in Germany but had international repercussions. The problem posed was, Should the church speak to the socio-political issues? While churchmen on both sides of the Atlantic were struggling to develop a modus operandi to bring Lutherans of the world together, the homeland of the Reformation was trying to work out a postwar national and international existence. The years of the ill-fated Weimar Republic saw Germans struggling arduously but unsuccessfully to introduce democratic principles into their political structures. The special postwar problems were, of course, immense. There was the hunger blockade imposed by the Allies and continued after the armistice in order to hasten the German signing of the peace treaty. Whether the blockade actually increased desire to accept the peace terms may be questionable, but Germans were sure it increased the death rate among children and the elderly and consequently magnified the bitterness and animosity toward the victors. Moreover, the Treaty of Versailles was soon referred to as "the *Diktat* of Versailles" and "a shameful and murderous peace," whose aim was to reduce Germany to economic slavery and political impotence. Especially abhorrent was the malevolent Article 231, the infamous clause placing "war guilt" on Germany and demanding acceptance of responsibility for military aggression.

The bitterness created by the treaty was quickly compounded by the economic woes of inflation. In 1914 the U.S. dollar bought 4.2

---

43. Sundkler, *Söderblom*, p. 294. Cf. Schmidt-Clausen (*Vom Lutherischen Weltkonvent*, pp. 49–50), who has raised the question whether Söderblom was not the logical person for this assignment but was denied it because of misunderstanding, mistrust, and narrow viewpoints.

German marks. By 1919 the ratio was 14 marks to the dollar; by 1922 it had jumped to 493.2 marks. During the summer of 1923, just before the Eisenach convention, the escalation reached 353,412 marks to the dollar. By December of the same year, the inconceivable sum of 4,200,000 million [*sic*] marks were needed to purchase a dollar.[44]

The incalculable damage to the German psyche and body economic provided fertile soil for political extremists, especially those of the left wing. Liberal intellectuals, not a few of whom were Jews, had long given vocal support to Marxist socialism. Now the workers, driven by unemployment and inflation, saw revolutionary communism as their only hope, and large numbers turned to the Spartacists (German Communists), whose organ *Die Rote Fahne* ("The Red Flag") was demanding that all power be given to the workers and soldiers. The growth of the left made it possible for Communists briefly to take over some provincial governments.[45] How serious this was for the churches is made clear by the situation in Thuringia and Saxony, where the Communists had taken power in 1923. The Lutheran World Convention was scheduled to be held in Thuringia (Eisenach), and Saxon bishop Ludwig Ihmels, the presiding officer, came to Eisenach knowing that the Communists had issued an edict seeking to remove him from office. Only the intervention of the German army under General Hans von Seeckt and the resulting breakup of the Communist control removed the threat of civil war and restored a semblance of political stability just as the Eisenach assembly was getting under way.

All these German problems—Versailles, inflation, communism—involved not only international political leaders but also international church leaders in Europe and America, Lutherans as well as other Protestants and Catholics. What should be the position of the churches on these great public issues? This was the burning question.

44. Much has been written about the effects of the inflation on ordinary German people. An especially vivid account, based on letters written by wives of pastors in Leipzig, describes the sad attempts to secure food and clothing. One example: "And how is it with milk which is a necessity . . . for the children? At the price of *240 billion marks* per quart, milk is no longer obtainable. Alas, the poor children and the mothers are broken down by anxiety for daily bread! [italics added]." "Spending the Week's Wage," *The Lutheran*, December 20, 1923, p. 7.
45. One of the better historical interpretations of the period is Erich Eyck, *A History of the Weimar Republic*, 2 vols., trans. Harlan P. Hanson and Robert G. L. Waite (Cambridge: Harvard University Press, 1962).

The decisive event for the Lutherans in this regard had occurred as a result of the Franco-Belgian occupation of the Ruhr on January 11, 1923. The French, heavily burdened by war debts to England and America, demanded that Germany pay its reparations. The French premier, Raymond Poincaré, suspected the Germans of causing their own inflation to avoid reparations. They "had intentionally devalued the mark and were going bankrupt on purpose"; this would make German payment of reparations impossible. To avoid this eventuality, the French reasoned, the only way left open to them was to secure physical control of Germany's great industrial area. Thus they justified the occupation of the Ruhr, and in so doing overrode the strong opposition of both England and America.

In less than a month the bishops of the Church of Sweden, under the leadership of Nathan Söderblom, published a protest in which they said, "The course now being sown will bear fruit in new and more frightful wars." They then appealed to Christians in all lands for united prayer and action, and then urged all responsible statesmen, and especially, "you, Mr. President of the United States," to call a conference to deal with the crisis.[46] The Swedish action naturally received an enthusiastic welcome in Germany, not least among Lutheran churchmen. At the same time, however, the latter expressed distress that fellow Lutherans in other churches were silent.[47] The French, of course, took umbrage at the Swedish reprimand, not least at the mention of U.S. President Harding. Why should the American president be singled out for special address when the other addressees included Premier Poincaré, French Protestant leader Wilfred Monod, the British prime minister, and the archbishop of Canterbury?[48] Söderblom was distressed that the French, whom he genuinely loved and admired and among whom he had many friends, had misunderstood him. He insisted, with the "Appeal" itself, that his intentions were honorable: "We judge nobody, because man sees in part." He added, "With politics, I as a churchman have nothing to do."[49] But in

---

46. The Swedish bishops' appeal is printed in full in *The Lutheran*, April 5, 1923, p. 2.
47. An article appeared in the *AELKZ* entitled "Warum schweigen die Anderen?" (*AELKZ* [1923], cols. 121–22).
48. Sundkler, *Söderblom*, p. 334.
49. Cited in ibid., p. 335.

the midst of the postwar tensions, no ex post facto declaration such as this would prevent a political interpretation of the document.

In America, the Söderblom action, no matter how well-intentioned and peace-oriented it might have been, was seen by the Lutherans as an exacerbation of the already serious nationalisms in the world Lutheran family, and if allowed to go unchecked could set back or even destroy the plans for a Lutheran world convention. Correspondence between Morehead and Ihmels resulted in the latter's assurance that he would try to keep the Söderblom affair from becoming a threat to the Eisenach assembly.[50] But Morehead was also worried that Söderblom, who would be present at Eisenach in August, might feel constrained to ask the convention to discuss the Ruhr occupation. To forestall this, Morehead asked Jørgensen in Copenhagen, who had already written of his worry over the Swedish action, to serve as an intermediary between him (Morehead) and Söderblom. The message to be delivered was simple: The introduction of this political issue at Eisenach would be potentially disastrous to the whole movement for Lutheran unity. Jørgensen's arguments were apparently persuasive, and Söderblom promised he would keep the Ruhr question out of the Eisenach deliberations.[51]

In the light of *l'affaire* Söderblom, and its threat to undo everything that had been achieved so far to neutralize potentially divisive nationalism at Eisenach, the decisions of both the Joint Committee and the American Committee on Arrangements became intelligible and even praiseworthy. When the joint committee met in Leipzig on March 23, 1923 (Ihmels, of course, was present), Morehead had pointed out the potential danger should the Eisenach convention take a political stance on the Ruhr question. The "Appeal" by the Swedish bishops was hardly a wise move. Surely Eisenach must confine itself to "purely Christian and ecclesiastical matters," otherwise the convention would be torn apart by dissension and all the efforts to unite the Lutheran family would become a mockery. The joint committee declared itself to be of the same mind and authorized Morehead to communicate these sentiments to any and all who had been upset by

50. Morehead to Ihmels, April 16, 1923; Ihmels to Morehead, May 1, 1923, in ArCL.
51. Morehead to Jørgensen, July 3, 1923; Jørgensen to Morehead, August 10, 1923, in ArCL.

this issue. Less than a month later the American Committee expressed its "complete agreement" with the decision of the joint committee "that the Convention must bear an entirely churchly and by no means political character."[52]

Modern-day critics of the Lutheran World Convention have pointed pejoratively to the convention's statement "National and international politics do not belong in the World Convention's platform," charging that it is another example of alleged Lutheran "quietism" and subservience to the powers that be.[53] This opinion must be judged hasty and questionable, at least after one has established the motives and purposes of the Lutheran World Convention and glimpsed the complexities of uniting a multinational ecclesiastical family that four hundred years earlier had renounced the unitive powers of a papal presence. As a matter of fact, the miracle of Eisenach was that it happened at all.

52. "Sitzung des Vorbereitungsausschusses für den Luth. Weltkonvent . . . 26. Maerz 1923."
53. See Armin Boyens, "Lutheranism in the Time of Dictators: The Lutheran World Convention 1923–1929," *Lutheran World* 23, no. 3 (1976): 230.

6

The Lutheran World Convention:
Eisenach 1923

At first glance the city of Eisenach hardly commended itself as a convention center. In 1923 its population was about 40,000. The city lay in a picturesque landscape on the northwestern slopes of the Thuringian Forest approximately twenty-five kilometers east of the present-day border between the German Federal Republic and the Soviet German Democratic Republic. If not remote, it was at least provincial and ill-equipped to entertain the first international convention on German soil since the end of World War I. Despite its evident drawbacks, Eisenach was rich in Reformation lore. Specifically, the town's *Lutherhaus* commemorated the fact that a portion of the Reformer's youth was spent at a school in Eisenach. Far more significant, however, was the prominence of the famed Wartburg Castle, which looked over the city from its hilltop site. Here it was that the "Obedient Rebel" had been kept in protective custody by order of the benevolent elector of Saxony, Frederick the Wise. Outlawed by the Edict of Worms (1521), Luther had lived in the safety of the Wartburg and prepared his monumental German translation of the New Testament. The opulence of tradition in Eisenach and its beloved Wartburg extended back beyond the Reformation era to the days of the medieval minnesingers, whose music tournament on the Wartburg is romantically recalled in Richard Wagner's *Tannhäuser*. But more important in the history of music was the fact that Eisenach was also Johann Sebastian Bach's birthplace (1685).

Although the official records of world Lutheranism do not reveal why the German members of the Committee on Arrangements recommended Eisenach over apparently more suitable cities such as Leip-

Eisenach, Saxony, Germany, 1923: First Lutheran World Convention delegates visit the historic Wartburg Castle.

zig, Hannover, or Hamburg, it is reasonable to assume that some romanticism dictated the choice. The Wartburg did indeed call to mind the sturdy Reformer. Its walls secured his life for the cause of the gospel and gave him the leisure to translate into the vernacular the written record of that gospel. And to sing "Ein' feste Burg" in the shadow of the Wartburg would surely remind Lutherans that the Reformation pointed not to Luther but to Jesus Christ, the Man of God's own choosing, who "holds the field victorious."

With some such expectations, about 150 officially appointed delegates and 50 registered observers, plus hundreds of visitors, came to Eisenach in August 1923.[1] About 20 nations and more than 60 million Lutherans were represented at the Lutheran World Convention, which the German editor Wilhelm Laible was soon describing as "a unique church council." It was unique for a number of reasons: It was brought about not by doctrinal strife (as were the Council of Nicaea and others) but by a love-motivated program of relief; unlike many efforts to unite the churches externally without the inner unity of faith, Eisenach was already one in faith and "the confession of the Fathers," and it was and wished to be both a *Lutheran* convention and a *global* convention. Laible found another reason for enthusiasm: The Lutheran church, long despised and ignored by the public, was now seen for what it was, a mighty and vigorous world church. To this unabashed ecclesiastical triumphalism, the reporter added a form of *linguistic* triumphalism. He boasted, "Historians will note that when

---

1. There are two chief sources for this chapter, the official report in English and the detailed German narrative account by Wilhelm Laible. The first is the report of the American Committee on Arrangements, *The Lutheran World Convention: The Minutes, Addresses and Discussions of the Conference . . . Eisenach August . . . 1923* (Philadelphia: United Lutheran Publication House, 1925) (hereafter referred to as *LWC . . . 1923*). The German account by Laible is "Der lutherische Weltkonvent in Eisenach, 19.–24. August 1923," published in Leipzig in *Allgemeine Evangelisch-Lutherische Kirchenzeitung* (hereafter referred to as *AELKZ*). The *AELKZ* account, beginning September 7, 1923, and ending January 11, 1924, would be published as the official German protocol of the meeting. See Jürgen L. Neve, "The Lutheran Convention at Eisenach," *Lutheran Quarterly* 54 (July 1924): 305. Four valuable additional accounts of the Eisenach convention are Bengt Wadensjö, *Toward a World Lutheran Communion: Developments in Lutheran Cooperation up to 1929* (Uppsala: Verbum, 1970); Kurt Schmidt-Clausen, *Vom Lutherischen Weltkonvent zum Lutherischen Weltbund* (Gütersloh: Gerd Mohn, 1976); Charles M. Jacobs, "The Lutheran World Convention: A Retrospect," *Lutheran Church Review* 42 (October 1923): 285–97; and the report by Neve, already cited in this note.

Lutherans convened it was the language of Luther that was the world language."[2]

Superficial enthusiasms aside, one can imagine the excitement and genuine pleasure that was present when delegates, most of whom were unknown to each other, rose to let themselves be identified at the opening roll call. It must have been, in Laible's words, "a memorable moment." In order to understand this and other "memorable moments," this chapter will consist mainly of a narrative report, which will be followed by two short sections, one dealing with the significant issues and the other dealing with varied reactions to or evaluations of Eisenach with special reference to the American response.

THE CHRONICLE OF EISENACH
AUGUST 19-24, 1923

In view of the current political and economic exigencies, many people had wondered whether the convention would actually take place. The difficulties were somehow surmounted, and by the end of the second full week in August the delegates and visitors were arriving at their Eisenach quarters and preparing for what promised to be a new and historic experience in Lutheranism.[3] The Joint Committee on Arrangements had requested that all Lutheran congregations throughout the world set aside Sunday, August 19, as World Convention Sunday and offer special prayers that "the Holy Spirit may guide the deliberations" of the assembly.[4] Thus, in an atmosphere of restrained excitement and religious devotion the Lutheran World Convention began.

---

2. *AELKZ*, 1923, cols. 573–74. Not all delegates understood German. In fact, when the ULCA chose its delegates it made a point of selecting at least one who was entirely monolingual (English), for the express purpose of showing the Lutheran world that people can be true Lutherans without understanding German.

3. Laible reports that delegates were housed in private homes, many rent-free, as well as in hotels (ibid.).

4. *The Lutheran*, June 14, 1923, pp. 1–2. The Missouri Synod, which did not accept the invitation to Eisenach, nevertheless urged its members to make the convention a subject of prayer, so that it would "redound to the honor and prosperity of true Lutheranism." The editor of *The Lutheran* remarked that prayer should seek not only God's protection against heresy but also God's power to guide and energize the church to move out from its protective walls to attack secularism and unbelief. *The Lutheran* July 19, 1923, p. 3.

Sunday, August 19. The first event of the day was the ceremonial opening of the literature exhibit in the Fürstenhof Hotel at noon. Quite in keeping with the fact that Luther had translated the New Testament in Eisenach, the exhibit was a biblical display in two sections: "The Illustrating of the Bible in Luther's Day" and "The Circulating of the Bible as the Book of Mankind." Ludwig Ihmels and Carl Paul, director of the Leipzig Mission Society and, like Ihmels, a member of the German Committee on Arrangements for the convention, spoke briefly about the appropriateness of the exhibit, pointing out that just as Luther and the Bible belong together, so also the Lutheran World Convention and the Bible belong together. The exhibit was more than just another display of Bibles. Its materials had been carefully gathered from the Kultur Museum in Leipzig, the state libraries at Gotha, Stuttgart, and Wolfenbüttel, and the official libraries of the Thuringian provincial church. Under the expertise of its directors, the exhibit became a remarkable display of valuable items belonging both to the history of biblical literature and to the history of art.

At six o'clock in the evening the bells of Eisenach rang out the call for worship at the opening service in the great St. George's Church, where Luther had preached on his way to Worms in 1521. With a seating capacity of 2,500, the Gothic edifice was filled to the last pew, and hundreds had to be turned away. The service, with its traditional Lutheran liturgy and festive choirs, began with Luther's hymn of invocation, "Come, Holy Spirit, God and Lord." The official German reporter observed that this was indeed the Lutheran church as it ought to be, a congregation of believers standing in the presence of God, calling upon the Holy Spirit. The sermon was preached by Hans G. Stub, president of the Norwegian Lutheran Church of America. Speaking in German,[5] he based his sermon on 1 Kings 21:1–3, Naboth's answer to Ahab's demand for his vineyard: "The Lord forbid that I should give you the inheritance of my fathers." He applied this

---

5. The two official languages of the assembly were German and English. All the main lectures but one were in German. Five addresses were given in English: Gustav A. Brandelle's speech on the opening day, Charles M. Jacobs's Wartburg locution, the "main lecture" by Frederick H. Knubel, a brief speech by John A. Morehead, and the closing address in St. George's Church by Abdel Ross Wentz.

directly to the Lutheran church as gathered in this convention, saying that under no circumstances, even if life itself were endangered, would Lutherans surrender the inheritance they had received from their fathers. He developed this theme by describing the inheritance in keeping with the familiar formulations of Reformation "truths" as articulated by nineteenth-century confessionalism: the authority of Scripture ("the Word of God") and the doctrine of justification. From these two "truths" a third emerges, the priesthood of believers, in which the whole of life is a thank-offering to God.[6]

Monday, August 20. Like the opening service of the previous evening, the Monday sessions were open to the public. The remainder of the convention, except for the closing service in St. George's Church, was to be "closed." A word of explanation is in order. According to Jürgen L. Neve, who was one of three secretaries of the convention, the Germans had insisted that the official sessions be closed to all but regularly appointed, ticket-carrying delegates (who numbered 150) and to 50 additional "friendly visitors" who could be trusted to treat "the matters of the conference with proper discretion."[7] It was felt that these restrictions were necessary to keep the convention from becoming "a mass meeting" and to allow the cultivation of personal friendships, thus promoting "inner union" among world Lutherans. Moreover, the "closed" sessions were needed to prevent "opponents of historic Lutheranism" from exposing the weaknesses of Lutherans to public gaze. Since a world conference of Lutherans had never been held, one could not know in advance what to expect. If heated discussions occurred, it was better that differences be settled *en famille;* Lutheranism's dirty linen should not be aired in public.

But Monday was a "public day," when sessions were open to everybody. The purpose of this, according to the official English and

---

6. Stub's use of German is noted in Neve, "Lutheran Convention," p. 317. The full English text of the sermon is included in the appendix of *LWC . . . 1923,* pp. 181–85. Stub's unconscious assumption of the validity of the nineteenth-century interpretation of the Lutheran heritage as expressed scholastically in "truth" principles (called the "formal"and "material" principles of the Reformation by August von Twesten, Friedrich Schleiermacher's successor at the University of Berlin) must have been jarring to some of the theologians in the congregation, such as Ihmels, Philipp Bachmann (Erlangen), Jacobs (United States), and surely Söderblom. We will return to this matter in our examination of the issues at Eisenach.

7. Neve, "Lutheran Convention," p. 302. Cf. Laible in *AELKZ,* 1923, col. 574.

German reports, was to permit the throng of nondelegate visitors to get "some taste of the Convention."[8] Had this action not been taken, there would no doubt have been scores of dedicated church people unhappy and disgruntled at being summarily excluded from even a small part in this historic event. Accordingly, after morning prayer services in the chapel of the deaconess motherhouse, the grand salon of the Hotel Fürstenhof was filled to capacity with an attentive audience, which heard Ludwig Ihmels deliver the "Address of Welcome."[9]

Ihmels chose his words carefully, saying that his thoughts went back to a somewhat similar convention in 1911, when the AELK met at Uppsala. It was the contrasts rather than the similarities, however, that now stirred his mind as he recalled, somewhat nostalgically, Uppsala and the peace and glory of prewar days.[10] Although he assured his listeners he would make no political references ("we are concerned here with purely religious purposes"), he asked rhetorically, "Where today is the peace of the nations?" and answered his own question by saying, "Mankind is riven with strife and hate." But in spite of the magnitude of contemporary tensions and animosities, God has drawn people from the east and the west to Eisenach, where Lutherans were now demonstrating that a common faith and a unity of spirit could lift people above the warfare of the past and the disjunctions of the present. The vision and labors of noble men like the lamented American Lutheran leader Lauritz Larsen were now being realized.[11]

Ihmels closed his address with prayer and then officially declared the Lutheran World Convention open. He quickly moved to the program for the remainder of the session, a series of welcomes from

8. *LWC . . . 1923*, pp. 20–21. Cf. *AELKZ*, 1923, col. 576.

9. *AELKZ*, 1923, col. 576. The daily sessions began at 10:00 A.M. and concluded at 2:45 P.M. At 3:00 P.M. a common meal was served at one of the Eisenach hotels. Evening sessions began at 6:00 P.M. *Lutheran Church Herald*, September 25, 1923, p. 1124; *The Lutheran Companion*, October 6, 1923, pp. 633–35.

10. For the moment, Ihmels had forgotten the tensions that characterized Uppsala: Danes versus Germans, Norwegians versus Swedes, and Americans versus Germans— the two former arising out of political problems, the latter out of ecclesiastical and theological differences over the role of "Prussian Union Lutherans." For example, Alfred Th. Jørgensen, one of the main lecturers at Eisenach, had been asked prior to 1911 to serve on the executive committee of the AELK. He accepted, on the condition he would not be expected to promote the cause of this predominantly German organization among Danes. On Uppsala (1911) see Wadensjö, *Toward a World Lutheran Communion*, pp. 25, 27, 33–34, 43–46.

11. This reference to Larsen was one of several during the course of the convention.

local church and civic leaders to which Nathan Söderblom responded. Official greetings from American Lutherans were spoken by Gustav A. Brandelle, president of the Augustana Synod. The last greeting came from Hans Fliedner of Madrid, who spoke on behalf of the German Evangelical Mission in Spain. With these amenities concluded, John A. Morehead delivered the main lecture of the morning. Short addresses by Theophil Meyer, general superintendent (bishop) of Moscow, and Oberkirchenrat Heinrich Cordes of Leipzig, brought the session to a close.

From among these many speeches, those of Söderblom, Morehead, and Meyer require brief comments. Each in its own way illuminates some of the inner dynamics of the convention itself and adumbrates issues and activities that were to engage world Lutheranism. We have already noted the towering significance of Nathan Söderblom. He was without question the best-known Lutheran in the world, but at the same time he was a highly controversial figure in Lutheran circles. To have assigned him a main lecture would surely have caused disruption, perhaps even a serious threat to the Lutheran world unity movement; to have ignored him, however, would have been stupid and boorish. How then to solve the dilemma? This seems to have been accomplished by asking Söderblom,[12] whose name was not on the official program of speakers, to give the above-mentioned "Address of Response"[13] to the ceremonial German welcome. This was, of course, a minor assignment, but Söderblom graciously acquiesced, and he delivered a short speech which, from one point of view, was a brilliant tour de force. Speaking with great eloquence, he testified to the overriding significance of Luther in his own personal religious life and theological understanding, a statement that could but warm the hearts of even his most suspicious and critical listeners. He deplored the misinterpretation of the faith by Roman Catholics, liberals (he consciously excluded himself from the very group to which his opponents consigned him), and even some "evangelical Christians." He said: "Luther's special mission lay in the fact that he revealed again, as no

---

12. Söderblom's biographer says, "It was Ihmels . . . who secured for Söderblom the opportunity to speak at Eisenach." Bengt Sundkler, *Nathan Söderblom: His Life and Work* (Lund: Gleerups, 1968), p. 294.

13. *LWC . . . 1923*, pp. 23–26.

other since the days of St. Paul had done, the boundless depths of the love of God in the Crucified One. And this evangelical doctrine of salvation alone through the grace of God is *our mission to keep forever pure and whole* [italics added]." No "confessionalist" Lutheran could have spoken more clearly and unambiguously about the evangelical heart of the Scriptures and the Lutheran faith. There may have been some, perhaps many, who sat on their hands, unwilling to believe what they heard. But Söderblom's sincerity was transparent, and he saw no inconsistency between evangelical Lutheranism and evangelical catholicism.[14]

Finally, Söderblom addressed the question of world Lutheranism itself. He saw Eisenach as a splendid testimony to the way in which "unity of faith" transcended "every political and physical boundary." That is, he was saying that the convention was wise in refusing to allow political and nationalistic questions to intrude themselves and thus thwart the expression of unity. He then thanked the American Lutherans for being the first to come with help for their European brethren after the war. They and the Germans had indeed been mainly responsible for this Eisenach congress; in the future, however, one must see world Lutheranism as a polycentric phenomenon consisting of three geographic areas: Germany, North America, and the Balto-Scandinavian North. Although organization was indeed a secondary matter, he said, "I trust that we shall not leave Eisenach without giving form to our sense of fellowship."[15]

The main address of this session was delivered by John A. Morehead on the theme "Let Us Help One Another."[16] When the chairman

14. Söderblom was a recognized Luther scholar in his own right. His great work *Humor och melankoli och andra Lutherstudier* (Humor and Melancholy and Other Luther Studies), published in 1919, had placed him in the front ranks of the Luther renaissance. Although his interpretation of Luther differed in some major respects from that of other great scholars (for example, Karl Holl), he insisted that Luther research led not to Luther but to the gospel that Luther proclaimed. Cf. Sundkler, *Söderblom*, pp. 292–95, 298.

15. The organizational "form" that eventually emerged recognized the Söderblomian polycentric profile of world Lutheranism. For example, it became a matter of principle that a balanced representation of the three "centers" should characterize committees, elected officials, and so on. By the time the Lutheran World Convention became the Lutheran World Federation, the official languages of assemblies and other meetings were German, English, and Scandinavian (Swedish). After World War II, the "polycentric" principle was expanded from three to four centers, the fourth being the Third World.

16. See *LWC . . . 1923*, pp. 29–39.

introduced him, the audience burst into spontaneous applause.[17] As the writer of the German protocol observed, this was only natural. After all, Morehead was the best-known and most popular American personality among European Lutherans. Furthermore, he had given not only his time and energy to the work of mercy, but almost his life as well. His address, given in German, was significant for two reasons. It provided a concise review of the motives and the extent of the vast relief work in Europe carried on by American churches through the National Lutheran Council. Up to July 1923 the NLC had provided $2,243,351 for food, reconstruction, and aid to orphaned missions. In addition, 2.5 million pounds of clothing had been distributed.[18] The pattern established by the National Lutheran Council under Morehead was to shape in large measure the American Lutheran relief work during and after World War II.

Morehead's address is also noteworthy because of its vigorous and persuasive arguments for the continuation of the Lutheran World Convention as a central agency for carrying out the common concerns of international Lutheranism. Assurances had been made, it will be remembered, that Eisenach would have the nature of a "nonrecurring event." Skittish Lutherans on both sides of the Atlantic had been promised that this would be "a free conference," a forum for discussing current problems and searching out Lutheran self-identity. In no way was Eisenach to be thought of as possessing an ecclesial or theological character; its resolutions or decisions would have no binding power.

Although Morehead had generally shared these concerns, he was now clearly stating that if the Lutheran World Convention ceased to exist some other international Lutheran agency would have to be created to replace it. He did not say it, and he may not have understood it, but the issue was simply, What is the Lutheran doctrine of the church? If it is proper to call a local parish "church," and by extension a regional or national synod of congregations (the United Lutheran *Church* in America, the *Church* of Sweden), why does an international synod of Lutherans not possess ecclesial character? This

17. *AELKZ*, 1923, col. 588.
18. Not included in Morehead's report were the sums raised by the Iowa Synod ($650,000) and the Missouri Synod ($700,000). Figures cited in Neve, "Lutheran Convention," p. 306.

question, unspoken at Eisenach, would lie hidden in the proposals of the Committee on Organization. In fact, it persisted as a gnawing and unresolved concern in the 1980s.

The address of Theophil Meyer (Moscow) focused Lutheran attention on the "Russian problem."[19] The work of Americans like John A. Morehead, Lauritz Larsen, C. Theodore Benze, and W. L. Scheding had resulted in firsthand reports of conditions among Lutherans in the famine-stricken Soviet Union after the Communist revolution. The Americans shared the German, and indeed the whole Western, fear of Marxism, so relief as a weapon against ideology was a central concern. How could Lutherans promote the survival of more than a million co-religionists under avowedly atheistic Bolshevism? Meyer's eloquent and emotional address galvanized the attention of Lutherans on the plight of their Russian brethren for years to come. In fact, even the rise of Nazism in the 1930s did not deflect the abortive efforts to save Lutheranism in Russia. When the demise of institutional Lutheranism in Russia occurred, it was due not so much to lack of outside support as to the hostile attitude of Soviet authorities.[20] In any case, the words and activity of Meyer at Eisenach in large measure accounted for world Lutheran attention to the Russian problem. Who could but be moved by his closing peroration, "In the name of a million Lutheran Christians, I once more ask: *Panem propter Deum* [Bread for God's sake]"?

A gathering of Lutherans at Eisenach would hardly be complete without a pilgrimage to the Wartburg. With this in mind, the program committee had planned a celebration in the courtyard of the castle. Despite a pouring rain, two thousand pilgrims struggled up the mountain to participate in the 4:00 P.M. festivities that featured brief addresses by Ludwig Ihmels and Charles M. Jacobs.[21] Standing on a balcony above the courtyard, Ihmels asked his hearers to see the church of the Reformation as contending "for the faith" and "in the

19. *LWC . . . 1923*, pp. 40–47.
20. A Swedish view of the situation laid much of the failure at the door of American Lutheranism's "narrow confessionalism." Wadensjö, *Toward a World Lutheran Communion*, pp. 187–201.
21. Morehead had suggested to Carl Paul of Leipzig that Jacobs, chairman of the American Committee on Arrangements, join Ihmels in addressing the Wartburg celebration. See Morehead to Paul, June 22, 1923, in Archives of Cooperative Lutheranism, Lutheran Council/U.S.A., New York City (hereafter referred to as ArCL).

Eisenach, 1923: Lutheran World Convention Steering Committee. C. Paul, L. Ihmels, J. A. Morehead, C. M. Jacobs.

faith." Employing the syllables of "Wartburg," he reminded the audience that the struggle "for" and "in the faith" not infrequently created circumstances when people must wait (*warten*) in the confidence that the Word of God is a secure fortress (*Burg*). Ihmels was implying, of course, that the church was now in such a situation. Jacobs's speech was a clear statement of the interlocking relationships of the major themes in Luther's theology: liberty of conscience under the Word; freedom from the guilt of sin and the despotism of earthly securities through Christ's redemptive work; the connection between the preached Word (*verbum dei vocale*) and Holy Scripture; and the relation between the Gospel and tradition.

The Wartburg celebration, which some enthusiastic observers judged to be the high point of the convention, naturally included the hymn "A Mighty Fortress." In addition, antiphonal singing by youth choirs, the common confession of faith using the words of the Apostles' Creed, and a hymn concluded the program.[22]

Although no formal evening session of the convention was held, the "Church Conference" of Thuringia sponsored a lecture by a young Erlangen professor, Werner Elert, on the topic "The Future of Lutheranism."[23] Thus ended the first full day of the convention.

Tuesday, August 21. Unlike Monday's sessions, which had been open to the public, admittance to the remainder of the convention, except for the final service, was by ticket only. The first of the closed sessions, held in the assembly room of a community social building, was called to order by the temporary chairman, Ludwig Ihmels, who since the death of Lauritz Larsen was the only surviving signer of the official "Call" to the convention. The agenda had three main parts: business meeting, formal lectures, and discussion of the theme.

Ludwig Ihmels requested Carl Paul, a member of the German Committee on Arrangements and unofficial "director" of the assembly,[24] to call the roll of delegates, who were asked to stand at their places in order that names and faces might be associated.[25] After

22. *LWC . . . 1923*, pp. 8–9, 50–55. Cf. Paul Fleisch, *Für Kirche und Bekenntnis: Geschichte der Allgemeinen Evangelisch-Lutherischen Konferenz* (Berlin: Lutherisches Verlagshaus, 1956), p. 94. One of the enthusiastic evaluations was by Söderblom. See Wadensjö, *Toward a World Lutheran Communion*, p. 325, n. 4.

23. Elert, who was to become a distinguished figure in theological circles by mid-century, was described by one observer as follows: "He is still a young man, but a real theologian who does not merely copy the past, but reproduces its truth in harmony with Scripture and Confession . . . reviewing the systems of the past." Neve, "Lutheran Convention," p. 308. Elert's best-known work is *Morphologie des Luthertums* (Munich: Beck'sche Verlagsbuchhandlung, 1931–32; English translation: *The Structure of Lutheranism*, trans. Walter Hansen [St. Louis: Concordia Publishing House, 1962]). It should be noted that evening programs, with the exception of the "Fourth Closed Session" on Thursday, August 23, were not a part of the official agenda for the convention. Nevertheless, the German account in *AELKZ* includes a full report of these ancillary meetings.

24. After the LWF was formed in 1947 at Lund, subsequent assemblies were usually under the direction of a local "assembly director" and a Committee on Arrangements working under the executive committee and the specific national committee of the LWF.

25. The delegates listed in the official English report number 157. Representatives of American churches were as follows: *ULCA:* Frederick H. Knubel, John A. Morehead, Charles M. Jacobs, Abdel Ross Wentz, Andrew G. Voigt, C. Theodore Benze, E. Hoffmann (Canada), Franklin F. Fry, E. Clarence Miller, Jürgen L. Neve; *Augustana:* Gustav A. Brandelle, Sven J. Sebelius; *Ohio:* Carl C. Hein, W. von Fischer; *Iowa:* J. Michael Reu, E. Moehl; *Norwegian:* Hans G. Stub; *Undesignated:* Mauritz Stolpe. *LWC*

calling the convention to order, Ihmels was elected permanent chairman on a motion by Charles M. Jacobs, chairman of the American Committee on Arrangements. Four secretaries (Wilhelm Laible of Leipzig; Jürgen L. Neve of Springfield, Ohio; Per Pehrsson of Gothenburg; and Carl Paul of Leipzig) and two recorders (both of whom were Germans) were elected.

Ihmels explained that the Joint Committee on Arrangements had recommended that the convention elect three committees: (1) a Business Committee, to serve as the executive group of the assembly concerned with the program, the credentials of delegates, and the seating of visitors; (2) a Committee on Resolutions, to prepare resolutions arising out of the lectures and discussion; and (3) a Committee on Organization, to make "proposals for possible establishment of a business office, or bureau, for the carrying on of relationships established through the Convention." The first was largely honorary and consisted of bishops (including church "superintendents" and "presidents"). Among those named were Ihmels (*ex officio*), Söderblom, Knubel, and Stub, who with other bishops were seated on the platform. The leading members of the Committee on Resolutions were Charles M. Jacobs and Carl C. Hein (United States), Theodor Kaftan (Germany), and Per Pehrsson (Sweden). The third committee included Wilhelm von Pechmann, an active German layman, Bishop Hjalmar Danell (Sweden), Wilhelm Laible (Germany), Theophil Meyer (Moscow), and Gustav A. Brandelle and Andrew G. Voigt (United States). The reports of these last two committees were to have long-term significance for world Lutheranism.

. . . *1923*, pp. 16–19; cf. Jürgen L. Neve, *Betrachtungen zum Ersten Lutherischen Weltkonvent in Eisenach* (Burlington, Iowa: Lutheran Literary Board, 1924), p. 17. For an American's comments on some of the various delegates from around the world see Jacobs, "Lutheran World Convention," pp. 291–92. The following are some examples. Morehead: "The most important figure in world Lutheranism today"; Ihmels: "Always forceful, always spiritual, going straight as an arrow to the heart of the subject"; Söderblom: "Rather quiet here, speaking only once, but . . . taking his audience to him"; another American on Söderblom: "The star attraction of several groups" (Sven J. Sebelius, "Observations . . . ," *The Lutheran Companion*, October 6, 1923); J. A. Asirvadam (Madras): "Dark in color but with snow-white hair . . . speaking polished English"; Jørgensen: "Short of stature, master of a half dozen languages, clear of thought and fearless in expression"; Paul: "The 'wheelhorse' . . . in whose mind were all the details of the convention."

With the business completed, the convention was ready to turn to the main topic of the day, "The Ecumenical Character of the Lutheran Church."[26] Since Ihmels was scheduled to make this first formal presentation, he asked Hans G. Stub to take the chair. Ludwig Ihmels was a felicitous choice to deliver a lecture on the ecumenical nature of Lutheranism. His reputation as a theologian and scholar in the Erlangen tradition commanded the attention not only of Lutherans but also of theologians in other communions as well. His churchmanship had been exercised in the complex German scene and was recognized abroad through his presidency of the General Evangelical Lutheran Conference (AELK). With the end of the church-state system following the war, he had been chosen bishop of the church in Saxony, where "just in the days when the convention met, the decree of enforced retirement [had been] issued by the Red government."[27]

The first part of Ihmels's address dealt with the universal experience of sin and the need to live by faith in Christ, "who is our righteousness." This starting point in religious experience was characteristic of Erlangen theology and was seen by Ihmels as an essential ingredient of Lutheranism. He said: "We may therefore nurture the paradox that the thing which proves the ecumenical character of Lutheranism is its one-sidedness. [Lutheranism] thinks of man only in his relation to God, therefore it has a word to say to everyone who is human." That ecumenical word is Christ, from whom arises "the strong consciousness of *unity with all believers in Christ, of all times and in all communions.*"

Ihmels then moved in the second part of his lecture to the Christology of the church catholic, as expressed in the ecumenical creeds. Against the Ritschlian theologians who rejected the creedal Christology as metaphysics ("the hellenization of the gospel"), Ihmels insisted that the ancient dogma about Christ was soteriological, not metaphysical. Christ the Word was not a philosophical abstraction but God's Word by which God justifies sinners. Therefore, when people say that Luther accepted uncritically the ancient Christology and then added something entirely new (justification by grace through faith), making it

---

26. Ihmels's address, the response by Jaakko Gummerus, bishop of Finland, and the record of the discussion are found in the official report, *LWC . . . 1923*, pp. 56–72.
27. Jacobs, "Lutheran World Convention," p. 291.

the hermeneutical center of Christianity, they are falsifying Luther. To draw a sharp distinction between the Christ of the ecumenical creeds and justification is impossible. The content of the ecumenical dogma of Christ the Word and the message of justification is one and the same. This one message, Ihmels said, was "the Word of reconciliation" committed to the church (2 Cor. 5:19). Lutherans have no thought of supplementing this universal message in any way. Where contemporary churches do not take this Word seriously, Lutherans have an ecumenical responsibility to insist on an earnest confession of "Christ alone." In the conflict of ecclesiastical communions, Lutherans are not concerned at all "with the obstinate defense" of something that they cling to as the private possession of Lutherans. Rather, their concern is "the ecumenical confession concerning Christ." He concluded, "With this as our center, we are in a position to recognize the truth that other communions have, and to learn from it." After all, the purpose of the church is not self-glorification; the Lutheran church, "just because she is a Church of faith, must also be a Church of repentance, or she will cease to exist." Jesus Christ is "the same yesterday, today, and forever." In his name "we become one with all who believe on him."

For those with eyes to see and ears to hear, Ihmels's argument was but an exposition of Article VII of the Augsburg Confession, which stipulated agreement in the *doctrina* (teaching and proclamation) of the gospel as sufficient for the unity of the church. Article VII was the ecumenical center of evangelical catholicity. The Lutheran confessions were intended not as a wall between churches but as a safeguard for the proclamation of the church catholic. The interest was not in going "into all the world to make Lutherans of all nations," but rather in making sure that the catholic gospel of salvation by grace through faith in Christ would continue to be the heart and center of the ecumenical church.

The discussion of the topic was introduced by a second but briefer discourse by Jaakko Gummerus, who saw the geographic spread of Lutheranism as a witness to its supernational and thus ecumenical character. It is worthwhile to note that some of the delegates best qualified to speak on the ecumenical question—namely, Söderblom, Jacobs, and Knubel—were conspicuously silent in the discussion that followed. The only American to participate in the debate was Hans G.

Stub, who said that Lutherans readily admit that true believers are to be found in other churches, but that the Lutheran church is "the true visible church" whose ecumenical character lies "in the ecumenical character of her doctrine." This was, of course, the "orthodox Lutheran" solution to the ecumenical problem. Stub and other participants failed to see the ecumenical thrust of Article VII and therefore shaped their remarks to justifying the existence of Lutheranism as an independent and particularist entity in Christendom. This was without a doubt a laudable and necessary endeavor, but none of the remarks penetrated to the core of the ecumenical problem in the manner of Ihmels's profound analysis of the issue. The comments, sincere and earnest as they were, might better have been reserved for the next day, when the theme dealt with the confessional identity of the Lutheran church.

Wednesday, August 22. It was natural that a discussion of confessional particularity should follow upon the previous day's concern with catholicity. Assigned to deliver the address on the theme "The Confessions as Indispensable Foundation of the Lutheran Church" was Alfred Th. Jørgensen of Copenhagen.

It will be recalled that the Iowa Synod had hoped to have its best-known theologian, J. Michael Reu, participate as one of the officially designated lecturers on this topic. The American program committee had decided that lecturers must belong to churches formally represented at Eisenach and had therefore invited Sven J. Sebelius of the Augustana Synod to share the platform with Jørgensen. Nevertheless, Reu had come to Eisenach and was no doubt present at the "open sessions." By Wednesday morning a cablegram from the Iowa Synod, which was holding its annual convention in August, reported that it had elected two delegates to the Eisenach congress, Reu and E. Moehl.[28] Thus armed with proper credentials, Reu could at least participate in the discussion, and this he was prepared to do.

----

28. Ibid., p. 289. Cf. *LWC . . . 1923*, p. 11. The German protocol has a somewhat euphoric account of Reu's arrival: The convention would have missed the presence of this famous German-American whose deeds of love for the German people after the war, though given little publicity, were known to God; a happy ripple of sound spread through the assembly hall when Ihmels announced the arrival. See *AELKZ*, 1923, col. 653.

The wording of the topic assigned to Jørgensen provided Lutherans with a genuine difficulty. The words "indispensable foundation" were, from one point of view, inconsistent with Luther's theology. Luther had insisted that the church is "the creature of the Word of God" (*creatura verbum dei*). That is to say, it is the Word of God which is indispensable to the foundation of the church, and Christ is that Word of God. Thus, where the Word is, there is the catholic church, and that Word is present in sermon (evangelical proclamation) and sacrament.

Jørgensen dealt with this problem by reference to Matthew 16:18 ("You are Peter, and on this rock I will build my church"), which he interpreted as being Christ's affirmation and promise to those who like Peter confess Jesus as "the Messiah, the Son of the living God." It is this confession that is indispensable to the foundation of the church.[29] The fact remains that a variety of *churches* have come into existence, that there are several confessional communities. What then are the factors in a churchly confession? (1) The great and common factor, the divine power that creates a confessing faith, namely, the salvatory work that centers in Jesus; (2) the factor of personal faith, whereby the godly appropriate salvation; and (3) "the social or confessional factor which distinguishes the particular Church from all other churches." The Lutheran confessions are therefore the *doctrina publica* that characterize this communion as an identifiable, distinguishable, historical community within Christendom.

At this point Jørgensen turned to the all-important question of the authority of the confessions and introduced a novel principle of interpretation. He distinguished between what he called *immobilia* and *mobilia*. The former referred to those confessional writings that arise directly from the revelatory, salvatory events witnessed to in Holy Scripture. These are changeless (*immobilia*). But alongside the *immobilia* are many explanatory, clarifying statements, theological elucidations "presented in the current literary tongue," problems that are historically conditioned. These are *mobilia*, which require reformulation in every age in order that they may bear clear contemporary testimony to the changeless confession of Christ. That is, the *mobilia*

---

29. Jørgensen's lecture and the discussion of it are in *LWC . . . 1923,* pp. 73–93.

show the need for reinterpretation in the context of the contemporary historical situation. This does not result in the elimination of confessions or the creation of new creeds; instead, it means movement in the direction established by the *immobilia,* the application of the Word which is confessed to the current scene. Illustrative of his meaning, said Jørgensen, was the Washington Declaration adopted by the United Lutheran Church in America at its 1920 convention. This document did not alter or amend the confessions in any way; instead, it explained the ULCA's attitude toward other churches in the context of American pluralistic denominationalism, an attitude that grew out of its conviction that the confessional principle must be "the living and indispensable foundation of our Church." Such a confessional hermeneutic would enable the church to navigate the treacherous theological waters between the Scylla of "an old-fashioned" theology (*die blosze Repristinations-theologie*) that is incapable of application to present circumstances, and the Charybdis of the "new theology with its leveling tendency" (*Nivellierungstheologie*), which blots out all confessional distinction by substituting "history of religions for the facts of salvation and a system of morals for the Christian experience of sin and grace."

It was the discovery or rediscovery of the confessional principle of Lutheranism that made Eisenach such a significant event. Here, continued Jørgensen, on a common confessional basis, former enemies, national and personal, had learned they could and should unite. Said Jørgensen, "We have met together for the first time; it dare not be the last." It was quite clear that Jørgensen, as well as others, was moving away from the notion of Eisenach as a nonrecurring event. Indeed, his enthusiasm led him to propose "an international theological faculty, true to the confessions, where students from all lands could assemble. . . . Of what inestimable worth one semester under such a faculty would be for the students. . . . Then, truly, the ideal of an international Church would be approached."

The discussion period was opened by a brief address by Sven J. Sebelius of Augustana Seminary at Rock Island, Illinois. He apparently did not fully understand Jørgensen's argument, from which he (Sebelius) concluded that the Formula of Concord would have to be counted among the *mobilia.* The Formula of Concord had served the

American Lutherans very well in their two-front war with the Romanists and the Reformed. Therefore, he would have to reject the
distinction between *immobilia* and *mobilia* and see the Lutheran
confessions in their totality as valid.

Several interventions were made from the floor, but only two were
of significance for our purposes here: a fairly lengthy locution by
Iowa's Reu and a briefer statement by Philipp Bachmann of Erlangen.
Reu's prepared statement declared that the confessional position of a
church body must include three essential teachings: the absolute
recognition of original sin, the substitutionary satisfaction and atonement of Jesus Christ, and the a priori (Reu: "it is presupposed") of
biblical inspiration, including the *suggestio verbi* (verbal inspiration).
Avoiding the term "inerrancy," he gave this explanation: "The Holy
Scriptures are for me in their totality the authoritative, sufficient,
absolutely dependable, sure and vital presentation of the revelation of
God once given for our salvation, as they were formed through a
peculiar operation of the Holy Spirit upon the writers. And this fact, I
repeat it, belongs to the content of the confessions." Reu concluded by
asserting that liberal theology was "a great lie born of hell"; apparently, however, he would say that despite its birth *in* Germany it was
not of Germany, a fact that was attested by the continued presence of a
vital, positive Lutheran theology among some Germans.[30]

Philipp Bachmann felt that some "response from the German
teachers of theology" was in order. Without addressing Reu directly,
he reminded the assembly of the significance of the "Erlangen
theology," which had appropriated Johann C. K. von Hofmann's
phrase *"Neue Weise alte Wahrheit zu lehren"* ("To teach the old truth
in a new way"). The knowledgeable listeners would immediately
catch the allusion to von Hofmann's work in biblical hermeneutics
which attacked the position upheld by Reu.[31] Bachmann agreed with
Jørgensen that the distinction between *immobilia* and *mobilia* must
be drawn. The difficulty lay in determining the boundaries of each. In
such a situation, the Lutheran theologian especially must learn to

---

30. Ibid., pp. 87–90.
31. See Johann C. K. von Hofmann, *Biblische Hermeneutik*, ed. W. Volk (Nördlingen:
C. H. Beck, 1880). English translation: *Interpreting the Bible*, trans. Christian Preus
(Minneapolis: Augsburg Publishing House, 1959).

speak with great responsibility, lest the vital union between church
and the confessions cease to exist.

There was no further formal debate about biblical inspiration at
Eisenach. The German theologians felt that the subject as such had not
been under discussion in Jørgensen's paper and was only "dragged in"
by Reu. Moreover, it was much too important a matter to be dealt with
in a superficial way. One reporter noted that between sessions there
was considerable informal discussion and that following the convention several post-Eisenach articles in German referred to the Reu
incident as potentially divisive.[32]

The session concluded with summary statements by Jørgensen and
Ihmels. The former remarked that, despite the diversity of views,
there was an unmistakable agreement that the confessional principle
belonged unambiguously to the matter of church unity. Ihmels
underscored what Jørgensen had said in his lecture and declared, "For
us the Scripture is *norma normans* ['the norming norm'] and its heart
and center is Jesus Christ. Our task remains to hold firmly to the Word
in Scripture and in the confession of our Lord."[33]

Thursday, August 23. The theme for the third closed session was
church unity, and the topic assigned to Frederick H. Knubel, president
of the United Lutheran Church in America, was "That They All May
Be One—What Can the Lutheran Church Contribute to This End?"
Knubel's paper was the only main lecture presented in English, not
because the author could not speak German but because he wished to
emphasize the convention's bilingual principle and to avoid giving
support to a tendency toward linguistic imperialism. As to the method
employed by Knubel, a mild surprise was expressed in the German
protocol that the lecture was an exegetical overview of the Epistle to
the Ephesians rather than a development of the topic along the lines of
systematic theology.

---

32. See Neve, "Lutheran Convention," p. 312.
33. *AELKZ*, 1923, cols. 673, 674. Schmidt-Clausen observes that Jørgensen's ability
to relate the confessional theology of Lutheranism to the problems of church unity,
the nature of the church (the Lutheran church as "an international church"), relief
work, and other social and human needs was remarkable. In fact, his Eisenach
presentation was no doubt one reason that he was to be elected to the LWC's executive
committee. Schmidt-Clausen, *Vom Lutherischen Weltkonvent*, p. 64.

Although no new ground was broken, the lecturer expounded the Epistle in a noncontroversial manner that would win general approval. The central theme of the apostolic witness was Christian unity, which all Christians favored theoretically but found difficult to demonstrate in the everyday world. After discussing the power, the source, and the development of unity, Knubel listed six principles on which and from which every plan of union must proceed:

1. The unity of the church already exists. It is a "given" in Christ. The task of Christians is to manifest this unity to the world.

2. Unity is a mystery. Like the mystery of Christ's person and the Word of God, the mystery of the church is open only to faith. A united church, as a visible manifestation of the given unity of the church, can never penetrate and thus demonstrate the full scope of the mystery.

3. The unity of the church is related intimately to the reconciling death of Christ. The gospel creates the church; the cross is at the center of the gospel. Therefore, unity is cruciform.

4. The power of unity is divine; it resides in the Head of the church. This power must not be compromised or confused with the shallow display of strength before the world associated with "increased efficiency" of a "united front."

5. The manifestation of unity is a process or growth characteristic of the church as a living organism. Hasty external union of all Christians might check that process and stunt the growth, thus hardening the form at too low a level.

6. Full realization of unity will come about only by a common faith in the gospel and "a common confession of the same."

Knubel did not forget the question that was a major part of the assigned topic: "What can the Lutheran church contribute to this end [unity]?" His answer was largely confined to the traditional categories of nineteenth-century theologizing, with its emphasis on the "material" and "formal" principles as identifying marks of the Lutheran church. Like Stub in his opening sermon, Knubel reflected on the captivity of American Lutheran theology to what was alleged to be the "Reformation principles" which, as a matter of historical fact, arose neither in the sixteenth century nor in the seventeenth (when "form" and "matter" were reintroduced into theological discourse) but in the nineteenth century.

Fortunately, Knubel broke out of his traditionalism with a genuinely Lutheran statement on the unity of the church which was a model of theological clarity and evangelical witness: "The Church exists and exists unitedly in the full confession of Jesus Christ who died for all, who is testified to in all the Scriptures, and who lives and works with power in and through His Word and Sacraments."[34] From this definition and the affirmation that unity already exists where Christ is confessed as the author and center of unity, Knubel drew the conclusion that it is imperative for Christians to manifest in visible form what they already possess, and that this is "a word which this Lutheran World Convention may well take to heart. There is necessity that we as Lutherans from all parts of the world realize our unity, promoting under our Lord both the fundamental principles thereof and also the practical manifestation before the world."[35]

In the general discussion that followed Knubel's lecture, there was frequent and approving reference to the affirmation of the givenness of Christian unity. There was, however, a variety of opinion on how this given unity could best be manifested. Some expressed distaste for organizational unity and applauded those statements in the lecture which warned against overhasty external union. For example, Hans G. Stub, who was the only American making a substantive contribution to the discussion, urged caution, lest basic differences in doctrine be overlooked. One German delegate maintained that Lutherans were not playacting when they announced a concern for the unity of the church. There were those, he said, who criticized Lutherans for their insistence on confessional integrity and caricatured them as a sectarian group that "delights in the disruption of Christendom." This, he retorted, was a specious charge born of rancor and a failure to appreciate the Lutheran evangelical concern. On the other hand, two Danish theologians—one a bishop—were grateful for Knubel's emphasis on visible unity, that for which Christ has prayed (John 17). Lutherans, he said, dare not remain aloof from the modern ecumenical movement.

In summing up the discussion, Ludwig Ihmels asserted that there

34. *LWC* . . . , *1923*, p. 105.
35. Ibid., p. 108.

seemed to be fundamental agreement but that very little progress had been made toward answering the question "What can we do?" Jürgen L. Neve, the American secretary of the convention, called attention to the Washington Declaration (1920), of which Knubel and Jacobs were the authors. He recommended it for study.[36] The session could finally be characterized as enthusiastic about spiritual unity but vague about visible unity.

The fourth closed session took place on the evening of the same day, Thursday, August 23. Two papers on Lutheran missions were read. Carl Paul dealt with the historical development and special character of the Lutheran participation in the missionary enterprise. He recognized the danger of shaping missions in the image of European and American churches, but asserted that Lutheranism's innate regard for local ethnic characteristics was a safeguard against combining an alien Western culture with the proclamation of the gospel. Although World War I imposed severe trials on orphaned German missions, non-Germans who came to the rescue were impressed with the thoroughness of the work done and with the "strong love for the Church" which had been engendered.[37]

The second paper, prepared by C. Theodore Benze of Philadelphia but read by Carl Paul (Benze was ill), picked up the theme of war-orphaned missions, with which the previous lecture had closed. Benze pointed out that Scandinavian and American churches sought to continue the mission work that had been threatened with collapse when the war necessitated the departure of German missionaries. The large work of the Leipzig Missionary Society was cared for by Swedes. American Lutherans, despite considerable anti-German sentiment and domestic economic inflation, were able to give support to former German missions in India, East Africa, New Guinea, and China.

Benze's paper must therefore be seen in relation to the American initiative for a Lutheran world conference. The cause of war-orphaned missions, alongside postwar relief and reconstruction, was uppermost in the life and work of the National Lutheran Council during the early

36. Ibid., pp. 12–13.
37. Ibid., p. 130.

years prior to the calling of the Eisenach convention. The patterns established in those years were to prove helpful when similar problems and needs arising out of Nazism and World War II led the Lutherans of America into programs such as Lutheran World Action and Lutheran World Relief.

Friday, August 24. The fifth closed session heard three papers on "The Lutheran Dispersion," as well as reports from the resolutions and organization committees. The Lutheran dispersion, likened to the Septuagint description of the Jews of the Diaspora living outside Judaea, consisted of emigrants, refugees, businessmen, and even embassies, for whom the mother churches of Germany and Scandinavia had spiritual responsibility. Max Ahner of Leipzig addressed the topic from the perspective of the German churches and suggested that eventually a center must be created "for the common activity of all the churches and all the countries. In that way, the unity of the Lutheran Church would come to the clearest expression." [38]

Carl C. Hein, vice-president of the Joint Synod of Ohio, described the American perception of this ministry in the second paper. The work in the United States and Canada was at one time wholly a ministry to the diaspora. In fact, it was in some measure a continuing characteristic of the church's ministry in North America. Special features of this work were the problems associated with language transition, the American principle of religious voluntarism, unity in doctrine and practice, and the building of schools (colleges and seminaries) to educate pastors and to maintain a Lutheran identity in the New World. One of the chief obstacles to the mission in America was the deplorable disunity within the church that bears Luther's name. American Lutheranism's great need was to overcome its lamentable divisions, and until that was accomplished the work would be seriously handicapped.[39]

The third paper, given by Per Pehrsson of Gothenburg, Sweden, reflected the perspective of the Nordic lands and perhaps unconsciously supported Söderblom's proposal that world Lutheranism

---

38. Ibid., p. 151.
39. Ibid., pp. 152–58.

must be seen as polycentric (German, American, Scandinavian). Pehrsson reviewed historically the Scandinavian ministry to the diaspora. He gave qualified support to Ahner's proposal for a central agency that might serve as a clearinghouse of information and a central office to which petitions might be submitted by diaspora congregations, Lutheran and even non-Lutheran. The problem, he contended, was a "delicate" one.[40]

The discussion that followed the three papers was interrupted by the reports of two important committees, the Committee on Organization and the Committee on Resolutions. The convention finally summarized the reports in "five resolutions," which were adopted after thorough discussion. The resolutions, described by a post–World War II historian of the Lutheran World Federation as the "enduring results of Eisenach,"[41] provide a helpful transition to this chapter's concluding section, "The Significant Issues at Eisenach."

Resolution One. The first resolution, whose chief author was Charles M. Jacobs, chairman of the committee, dealt with the role and significance of the church's confession. The statement, adopted at Eisenach, remains virtually unaltered today as the confessional basis of the Lutheran World Federation. It reads:

> The Lutheran World Convention acknowledges the Holy Scriptures of the Old and New Testaments as the only source and the infallible norm of all church doctrine and practice, and sees in the Confessions of the Lutheran Church, especially in the Unaltered Augsburg Confession and Luther's Small Catechism, a [German: *the*] pure exposition of the Word of God.[42]

40. Ibid., pp. 158–67.
41. Siegfried Grundmann, *Der Lutherische Weltbund* (Cologne: Böhlau, 1957), p. 338. There is a discrepancy between the official English and German minutes of the Eisenach convention. Most of our references have been to the English edition (*LWC . . . 1923*). In this instance, however, it seems preferable to follow the more complete German minutes (*Lutherischer Weltkonvent zu Eisenach* [Leipzig: Dörffling & Franke, 1925]) The English edition has no mention of the "five resolutions," and especially conspicuous by its absence is the fourth resolution; which dealt with ecumenically oriented relief work. The report in the columns of *AELKZ* (cols. 788–91) corresponds to the German minutes. Schmidt-Clausen's *Vom Lutherischen Weltkonvent zum Lutherischen Weltbund* (1976), Grundmann's *Der Lutherische Weltbund* (1957), and Wadensjö's *Toward a World Lutheran Communion* (1970) likewise use the German rather than the English source.
42. The English version of the text is according to the American minutes, *LWC . . . 1923*, p. 15. The divergence between the English ("a") and the German ("the") texts prompted a brief debate in the LWF later on. Cf. Grundmann, *Lutherische Weltbund*, pp. 367ff., 396ff.

Resolution Two. The second resolution dealt with Christian nurture of the young in a secular world:

> In view of the present movements against the Christian education and confessional instruction of our baptized young people, the Lutheran World Convention calls upon all Lutheran Christians to strive with all earnestness in behalf of the Christian instruction and education of our young people, and especially to labor that Luther's Small Catechism may be preserved to them.

Resolution Three. The third resolution sought to identify the *whole* Lutheran World Convention with the relief work that had been begun and carried on almost exclusively by the Americans and the Scandinavians. Hence the resolution said:

> The Lutheran World Convention calls upon all Lutheran Christians not to grow weary in brotherly love until the Lord shall put an end to distress.

These first three resolutions, presented by the Committee on Resolutions as its report, were understandably the three "fundamental" resolutions basic to the continuing work of the Lutheran World Convention. The remaining resolutions were practical outgrowths and applications of principles enunciated in the prior statements.

Resolution Four. The fourth resolution, for example, was directed to the issue of ecumenical relations in relief work. It established the possibility of contact and consultation with the non-Lutheran agency "The European Central Office for Evangelical Relief Work" at Zurich. At the same time, however, it called attention to the recently created Lutheran relief agency (*Lutherische Hilfsaktion*). Although the new agency was to be the one official channel for Lutheran relief and was to exhibit its own character or profile, its program was not to be conducted in isolation from the other Protestant relief agency. The resolution read:

> The Lutheran World Convention takes cognizance of the existence of a European central office (*Zentralstelle*) for Protestant relief work in Zurich and recommends to the *Lutheran Relief Agency* that in its work it maintain informational contact with this Central Office [italics added].[43]

---

43. *Lutherischer Weltkonvent zu Eisenach*, p. 244. Cf. *AELKZ*, 1923, col. 788; Wadensjö, *Toward a World Lutheran Communion*, pp. 170–71; and Schmidt-Clausen, *Lutherischen Weltkonvent*, p. 88.

Resolution Five. The fifth resolution was the longest and certainly the most far-reaching in its effect on the future role of the Lutheran World Convention. It should be recalled that one of the pre-Eisenach arguments to persuade reluctant churches to participate in the convention was that it was to be a nonrecurring, "free conference," a Lutheran world forum to discuss common problems. Now, however, the Committee on Organization, whose report constituted this resolution, had obviously obtained "the sense of the meeting" and brought in a recommendation that spelled the end of the convention's "one-time character." It had been generally agreed that it was neither advisable nor necessary for a world organization of Lutherans formally to adopt a constitution. Nevertheless, by placing the confessional paragraph (Resolution One) together with the structural paragraph (Resolution Five), the convention would be in possession of at least a quasi-constitution, an instrument (as subsequent years were to show) that would provide the means to hold Lutheranism together until after World War II. The resolution, presented by the committee's chairman Wilhelm von Pechmann, an active member of the AELK, urged the creation of an organization that was strikingly similar to the AELK. Consisting of seven parts (according to the German protocol), the resolution made the following provisions:[44]

(a) Two committees should be established, a small "executive committee" and a "larger standing committee."

(b) Administrative duties should belong to the executive committee, which should be responsible for arranging the next assembly of the Lutheran World Convention. In addition, it should concern itself with cooperative efforts in the areas of works of mercy, ministry to the Lutheran diaspora, and world missions, in accordance with resources at hand. Likewise, it should address such tasks as were referred to in Morehead's lecture. Finally, it was to speak or act in the interest of the whole of Lutheranism and in its name when emergency situations or other serious reasons made it desirable.

(c) The executive committee members were to be Ludwig Ihmels

---

44. *Lutherischer Weltkonvent zu Eisenach*, pp. 244–45. Cf. *AELKZ*, 1923, cols. 788–89. The abbreviated English version is in *LWC . . . 1923*, pp. 14–15.

(Germany), Alfred Th. Jørgensen (Denmark), John A. Morehead (United States), Lars W. Boe (United States), Wilhelm von Pechmann (Germany), and Viktor Rundgren (Sweden).[45]

(d) The executive committee should organize itself as soon as possible, because all administrative details would be turned over to it.

(e) The larger standing committee should act as the representative of all churches participating in the world convention. Its membership should consist of not less than seven or more than ten from Germany and the United States,[46] three from Sweden, two each from Denmark, Norway, Finland, and one each from other countries. In countries where there is more than one established church or where within one church there exist nationalistic groups, each group should be entitled to representation (Poland's Lutherans were divided, one Polish group, one German). Ihmels and Morehead were authorized to establish a firm numerical membership and to call the committee together.

(f) Both committees should choose members to fill vacancies.

(g) The two proposals, (1) that the membership of the next assembly of the Lutheran World Convention should be in proportion to the number of ordained clergymen, including theological professors, in each church, and (2) that a general student help fund should be established, were referred to the executive committee.

After the assembly adopted the five resolutions (the reports of the resolutions and organization committees), the convention hastened to its conclusion. Not unlike other conferences, impatient delegates were showing eagerness to leave for their homes. With a general word of thanks to all who had participated, and a special word to the "convention manager," Ludwig Ihmels terminated this last "closed session" with prayer and the benediction.

The concluding service, like the opening service, was held in St.

45. The official English minutes (*LWC . . . 1923*, p. 14) insert after Morehead and Boe the words "provided the approval of the American church-bodies participating shall be secured." Rundgren was unable to accept; named in his place was Per Pehrsson. Schmidt-Clausen points out that the best-known Lutheran in the world, Nathan Söderblom, was consciously excluded. See *Vom Lutherischen Weltkonvent,* p. 96.

46. A later agreement divided the American representation as follows: four from the ULCA, one each from the Joint Synod of Ohio, the NLCA, the Augustana Synod, and the Iowa Synod. Two additional places were reserved for churches that might decide later to participate even though they were not represented at Eisenach. See Neve, "Lutheran Convention," p. 314.

George's Church, where a capacity congregation had gathered. Two brief addresses (by Bishop Danell of Sweden and J. D. Asirvadam, secretary of the Tamil Church in India) were followed by the main address by Abdel Ross Wentz, who spoke on "The Impressions Made by the Convention." He mentioned four: (1) By God's grace, Eisenach had been a distinct success, beyond the expectations of its planners; (2) The convention demonstrated dramatically the manifold character (ecclesiastical, national, racial) of world Lutheranism; (3) Despite its great diversity, Lutheranism possessed an essential unity: common faith in Christ, common adherence to the Word of God in the Scriptures, and common acceptance of the Lutheran confessions; (4) The future looked bright. The resolutions adopted indicated that the first Lutheran World Convention would not be the last one, and the world Lutheran church could now speak with one voice.

The service concluded appropriately with a word of farewell by Chairman Ihmels.

Charles M. Jacobs, recollecting this service after his return to America, wrote: "The writer . . . was seated beside a pastor from Hannover whose name he did not know. This pastor turned to him and said, 'All of this would have been impossible, if Germany had won the war; would it not?' When the reply was in the affirmative, he remarked, 'Then, even in our defeat, there is something to be thankful for.' "[47]

THE SIGNIFICANT ISSUES AT EISENACH

The overarching issue at Eisenach was clearly the problem of Lutheran identity in the twentieth century. Was or is Lutheranism simply a "confessional movement" within Christendom? Is it but a "sect" or a "denomination" in the Christian world? Or is Lutheranism an identifiable, visible, ecclesial entity bearing the marks of the church of the Nicene Creed's "one holy catholic and apostolic church"? If so, in what does its oneness, holiness, catholicity, and apostolicity consist? The Eisenach convention struggled with this question, and although it did not address directly and comprehensively the Nicene marks, or

47. Charles M. Jacobs, "The Lutheran World Convention: A Retrospect," p. 297.

Lauritz Larsen

John A. Morehead

Ludwig Ihmels

Hans G. Stub

Frederick H. Knubel

Lars W. Boe

Alfred Th. Jørgensen

Wilhelm von Pechmann

Charles M. Jacobs

even the traditional Lutheran marks (Word and Sacraments), its topics were vigorous attestations to its ecclesiological concern. One American observer commented that other Christians refused to permit Lutherans to be a church. In a sense this had been true. The Reformed (Calvinists) and Union people perceived Lutherans as simply a part (indigestible?) of the larger Protestant church. Romanism saw them as "the Lutheran virus," a sectarian poison (Rome in 1923 had not yet moved to the "generous" pre–Vatican II attitude toward other Christians as "separated brethren").[48] But now Eisenach gave expression to the determination of Lutherans to be a church. This determination, however, was inadequate by itself to carry Lutherans beyond their traditional ecclesiastical ideas, their national idiosyncrasies and prejudices, and their theological differences to a full-orbed and comprehensive Lutheran ecclesiology. Eisenach was a cautious and timid beginning, a modest breakthrough toward a Lutheran self-understanding on a global and ecumenical scale. Its development and achievement were to be delayed by diverse factors for many years, well toward the twenty-first century.

Nevertheless, Eisenach raised the basic issue under which, as we now recognize, the other issues—confessionality, ecumenism, unity, service, and organization—were all subsumed. These important sub-issues were intertwined. None of them could be effectively addressed in isolation from the others, and when troublesome questions arose in the discussion of the various theological and organizational matters, one could usually see that differences were rooted in the diverse understandings of what it meant to be a Lutheran church.

Much of the difficulty lay in the very novelty of the Eisenach experience. Except for a few leaders, the Lutherans were unacquainted with one another; the history, traditions, customs, and manners of the churches and nations were largely unknown.[49] The

48. Neve, "Lutheran Convention," p. 319. The Catholic attitude had been expressed by Pope Leo XIII in his 1879 encyclical "Aeternis patris," in which he said that the antidote to Lutheran and other heresies was to require Catholic schools to teach the theology of Thomas Aquinas.

49. The "culture shock" was illustrated in European uneasiness with American parliamentary procedures or in American uneasiness in the presence of European theological sophistication and personal habits. Even after World War II, it was reported that Danish Lutheran deaconesses were astounded to hear that American Lutheran pastors' wives used lipstick and other cosmetics—so shocked, in fact, that they dropped their cigars.

deep fissures created by World War I, and the subsequent international politics and economic dislocations, only compounded the problems. For example, it was thought that French Lutherans would not set foot on German soil because of lingering postwar bitterness. However, John A. Morehead and Frederick H. Knubel, enroute to Eisenach, paid a fraternal visit to French Lutherans in Paris. This resulted in the presence at Eisenach of two Frenchmen, Henri Bach of Paris and E. Stricker of Strasbourg. As far as is known, Eisenach 1923 was the first international assembly of any kind where Germans and Frenchmen met after World War I.

Last, but certainly not least, were the theological differences. Although everybody at Eisenach was excessively polite, for fear that the fragile community might break up, a potential conflict between "old Lutheranism" (nineteenth-century style) and "neo-Lutheranism" (twentieth-century style) was ever present. This was not merely a difference between naive American theologians and learned European theologians, as Wadensjö's oversimplified account has it, but a division that was present to varying degrees within most of the churches and groups represented at the convention. When Eisenach demonstrated that all were committed to the Lutheran confessions, this did not mean theological uniformity, in fact, not even that all were agreed on the meaning of confessionality. Some regarded confession of the gospel primarily as an activity past and present, the confessions themselves being the continuing safeguard to assure the evangelical character of the church's proclamation. Others viewed the confessions as quantitative legal (church law) doctrinal standards. The irony of the Eisenach theological statement is that the English version describes the confessions for the American churches—who, according to Wadensjö, were hopelessly "orthodox" and hyperconfessional—as "a pure exposition of the Word of God." The German version prepared for the AELK and Scandinavian churches—who, according to Wadensjö, were confessionally less legalistic and ecumenically more "open"— describes the confessions as *"die lautere Wiedergabe des Wortes Gottes* [the pure repetition of God's Word]." Here was a "theology of articles"—the indefinite article had become a definite article with all the implications resident in each.

Moreover, there were those who, like J. Michael Reu, declared that the Lutheran church must include in its confessional position the doctrine of the verbal inspiration of the Scriptures; he quoted in Latin the "old Lutheran" formula that the Holy Spirit provided the New Testament writers with *impulsus ad scribendum, suggestio rerum, suggestio verbi* (the impulse to write, the suggestion of the facts and the words). Had Reu's opinion prevailed, it is clear that there would have been no confessional agreement at Eisenach. Alfred Th. Jørgensen, who had delivered the main lecture on the role of the confessions, was no doubt expressing the convention's sentiment when he said that it was a "gratifying circumstance that, despite the variety of opinions expressed, there was evident a unanimous desire to recognize the confessions as the foundation of our union."[50]

The cleft between nineteenth-century Lutheranism and the theology emerging from the Luther renaissance was evident in the categories used by Stub and Knubel on the one hand, and those used by Ihmels, Jacobs, Jørgensen, Söderblom, Carl Stange of Göttingen, and Philipp Bachmann of Erlangen on the other hand. Stub and Knubel, ironically at opposite ends of the American Lutheran spectrum, nevertheless used the distinction, drawn by nineteenth-century scholasticism, between the so-called "formal" and "material" principles of the Reformation.[51] This distinction had been largely discarded by Luther scholars who saw in it an intrusion of the Aristotelian categories of "form" and "matter" which were totally alien to Luther and eventually destructive of evangelical theology. Albert Hauck, the Leipzig University church historian, had pointed out that for Luther there was only one hermeneutical principle, namely, the Word of God, the gospel concerning justification by grace through faith in Christ. This was the central and unitive principle of the Scripture, "the article of a standing church." There were others, of course, who like Hauck were asking the church to see Luther's theology of the gracious justification of the sinner as the one Word of God for the church to the world, but it is especially significant for an understanding of what was occurring at Eisenach to know that Hauck's influence was present in several persons. Jacobs, for example, had studied under Hauck at Leipzig;

50. *LWC . . . 1923*, p. 93.
51. See especially Knubel's address on unity in *LWC . . . 1923*, p. 104.

Ihmels and Söderblom had been colleagues of Hauck at Leipzig and shared his theological insights.[52]

The confessional issue at Eisenach was more complicated and more subtle than a superficial reading of the record might reveal. A few leaders recognized that there could be confessional unity without theological uniformity. To have pressed, in Missourian style, for an agreement on all matters of doctrine and practice would have aborted the whole enterprise of establishing a Lutheran identity in the world ecclesiastical community.

In a similar way the ecumenical issue—which surfaced not so much in the discussions of lectures of Ihmels, Jørgensen, and Knubel as in the practical implementation of Lutheranism's concern for its diaspora—was interwoven with maintaining a Lutheran identity and presence in service to emigrants, refugees, and other dislocated Lutherans. To have this work absorbed by the ecumenical *Zentralstelle* in Zurich, it was reasoned, would have shut off American Lutheran support for the Lutheran World Convention (American Lutherans saw the *Zentralstelle* as the brainchild and manipulative handiwork of the "liberalistic" Federal Council of Churches). Eisenach's Resolution Four provided for ecumenical consultation and contact but no surrender of its diaspora ministry to a bland and indiscriminate ecumenical Protestantism.

Perhaps the most far-reaching decision of the assembly was the provision for a continuation of the Lutheran World Convention (Resolution Five). Although without constitutionally sharp focus or clear-cut delineations, a significant advance in churchliness was demonstrated by the fact that membership in future assemblies would be by

---

52. The originator of the "formal and material" principles of the Reformation was Schleiermacher's successor at the University of Berlin, August D. C. Twesten (1789–1876). See his *Vorlesungen über die Dogmatik der ev. luth. Kirche nach dem Kompendium des Herren Dr. W. M. L. De Wette*, 4th ed. (Hamburg: Friedrich Perthe, 1837), 1:257–61. For a report on Hauck's view, see John O. Evjen, "Some Aspects of the Work and Requirements of a Graduate School of Theology," *The Wittenberg Bulletin* 23 (January 4, 1926): 47 (document in Lars W. Boe Papers, box 81, folder 9, St. Olaf College Archives, Northfield, Minnesota). Cf. also Hans-Dietrich Loock, *Offenbarung und Geschichte: Untersuchungen am Werke Albert Haucks* (Hamburg: Herbert Reich Evangelischer Verlag, 1964), pp. 69–74, where the author discusses Hauck's emphasis on justification (including redemption and reconciliation) as God's one word to a sinful world (see esp. pp. 72–73). On Söderblom and Hauck see Sundkler, *Söderblom*, pp. 85–86. On Jacobs and Hauck see Jacobs's obituary in *The Lutheran*, April 13, 1938, pp. 2, 22; April 20, 1938, pp. 22, 23, 30.

churches, not by individuals (as was true of European representatives at Eisenach). The standing committee should act as the representative "of all churches participating in the World Convention." This, of course, had nothing to say about the churchly character of the convention itself.

Despite the fact that lectures and formal discussions had made several references to "the Lutheran church" and to its existence as an identifiable world community, nobody at Eisenach advanced the thought that this particular assembly of Lutherans was in fact a visible church. There were indeed "churches" back home in Sweden, in Schleswig-Holstein, in the United States, and in Canada, but Eisenach was merely a world conference of selected individuals from countries in Europe and of delegates from American "churches." Although the ecclesiological nature of the Eisenach event was not raised in any serious fashion, it was never far away. For example, with all the fervent declarations of loyalty to the confessions, nobody stopped to think what Article VII of the Augsburg Confession (the church is the assembly of believers where the gospel is proclaimed and the sacraments are administered according to the gospel) signified for the assembly of believers congregated at Eisenach. Indeed, the gospel was proclaimed and taught in sermons and lectures, but the worshiping community had foregone the celebration of Holy Communion.[53] In retrospect this may seem astonishing and even inexcusable, but given the circumstances it is understandable. Traditionally, Lutherans had limited the Augsburg Confession's description of the assembly of believers to the local parish congregation, which was the "essential church." All other "churches" were churches not in a theological sense but in an administrative or constitutional sense, as, for example, "the Church of Norway" or "the Evangelical Lutheran Church of Hannover." Moreover, if a convention (synod) of a regional or national church were to celebrate the Holy Communion, the service must be sponsored by a local parish, which (it was thought) alone had the "right" to conduct such a service. At Eisenach, there was no Lutheran parish to sponsor the Communion service (Eisenach's congregations were members of the "Evangelical

53. Neve, "Lutheran Convention," p. 320.

Church of Thuringia," constitutionally not Lutheran until 1924); therefore, Holy Communion was omitted.[54] The convention remained but a religious "conference," which could not function as a "church," that is, it could not celebrate the Lord's Supper.

Moreover, there was another consideration. Some Lutherans argued that Holy Communion presupposed complete agreement in doctrine and practice. Not a few delegates would have been unable to participate because they were convinced there was no agreement in "the doctrine of the gospel." Whether they were right or wrong was academic at Eisenach. The practical consequence of holding a Communion service would have assuredly been divisive rather than unitive. In America and in some European circles, the critics would charge that Eisenach was an act of "sinful unionism," a consorting with heretics who denied the verbal inspiration of the Bible and other touchstones of "true Lutheranism."

Although the chief issues at Eisenach can be subsumed under the ecclesiological question, one must not forget the critical political, nationalistic, and economic circumstances that provided the atmosphere in which the first Lutheran World Convention was held. Charles M. Jacobs gives a vivid description of the historical context and hints at the reason the burning issues of the everyday world were deliberately avoided at Eisenach:

> Among the striking features of the convention was the seriousness which marked all of its deliberations. The delegates clearly recognized the fact that they were assembled at a critical moment in the history of the Lutheran Church. Many of them came from countries in which the Church has been passing through years of fiery trial. Most of them came from lands where it is even now experiencing, or just emerging from, the sorest poverty and economic distress. To these men there was no temptation to indulge in boasting about the state of the Church. The delegates from more favored lands, especially those who were forming their first acquaintance with Europe since the war, were sobered and oppressed by the things which they saw and heard around them. The crushing poverty of pastors and professors, the grim specter of starvation hovering along the border of the coming Winter, the violent hostility of the powerful

---

54. For information on the Thuringian church see Wolfgang Schanze, "Der kirchliche Zusammenschluss in Thüringen nach 1918," *Ev. Lutherische Kirchenzeitung: Festausgabe zum 60. Geburtstag von Präsident D. Heinz Brunotte* 10 (June 11, 1956): 243–45. Cf. *Evangelisches Kirchen Lexikon* 3:1439–41; and *Religion in Geschichte und Gegenwart*, 3d ed. (Tübingen, 1957–65), 6:878–79.

communistic party to the Church and all it stands for, the influence of Rome, steadily growing and directed toward the extirpation of Protestantism, the keen political tension, the dangers lurking in the international hatreds which the Treaty of Versailles has only sharpened, the complete prostration of the German nation, with the heel of France upon its neck— all these things were in evidence, and all of them forboded, as they still forbode, times of bitter trial yet to come. And yet these things did not come upon the floor of the convention. The Germans had passed their word that nothing should be said which could be construed as politics or propaganda, and their word was kept loyally and to the letter. . . . The chairman of the American committee, which insisted upon this condition from the start, cannot refrain from paying this tribute to the good faith of the German delegates, with a full sense of how difficult their situation was.[55]

Quite clearly the postwar feelings, if given a chance, might well have flared up and the convention could have ended in disarray and dissension, destroying all hopes for bringing long-separated Lutherans into a visible world community. As it was, a genuine spirit of unity and a remarkable longing for continuing fellowship grew and prevailed at Eisenach.

Although the "secular" issues, such as nationalism, were carefully avoided, they were not thus permanently set aside. As a matter of fact, persisting nationalistic hostilities would surface in the post-Eisenach years. Germans, for example, felt that they were being discriminated against, excluded from places of leadership in world Lutheranism, and forced to bear the onus of war guilt and the other injustices of the Versailles Treaty. Whether true or false, the sentiment lasted for years and no doubt contributed to the ease with which so many Germans believed the promises of Hitler to restore national pride and dignity. At least, in retrospect, one can understand why the world political issues were consciously suppressed lest they tear apart the community of faith so visible at Eisenach.

RESPONSE TO EISENACH

Although our study of the Lutheran World Convention has been and will continue to be consciously approached from the American perspective, it is helpful to note briefly some of the assessments voiced in

55. Jacobs, "Lutheran World Convention," pp. 292–93.

Germany as well as in America. The editor of the widely read and
influential German periodical *Allgemeine Evangelisch-Lutherische
Kirchenzeitung (AELKZ)*, Wilhelm Laible, gave voice to what some
might call "the Lutheran reaction." Writing a few days after the
convention's close, he said:

> People left Eisenach deeply moved emotionally. Everyone had the strong
> impression that something significant had occurred and would continue to
> occur. Moreover, there was no doubt that an inner unity, which had not
> previously existed, had been forged. The Lutheran World Convention had
> been a bright sign in a darkened world. Though but an infant now, pray
> God that it may grow into the adulthood of Christ.[56]

At the end of August, Wilhelm von Pechmann, a layman active in
both Lutheran and ecumenical circles, felt constrained to reply to
charges written in a Munich newspaper by one Hans Bauer. The latter
claimed that Eisenach possessed no significance for the people as a
whole. It was a gathering of clergymen who refused to recognize that
Lutheranism no longer possessed inner strength. There were communists, socialists, and monarchists who would die for their causes, but
where was the Lutheran who would go to his death for his faith? Von
Pechmann's response was vigorous and well argued. He said that had
Bauer personally experienced Eisenach he would not have been so
cavalier and insipid in his attack. Lutherans had found one another at
Eisenach and were determined to remain together, not in the interests
of sectarian protectionism but for the strengthening of the whole of
Protestantism, in fact, the whole of Christendom.[57]

Other Germans attacked the Lutherans not out of sneering contempt
for their weakness but out of fear of their strength and solidarity. They
saw Eisenach as a threat to the ecumenical movement and a step
toward confessional triumphalism.[58] This attitude, born in response to
Eisenach, was to "darken the horizons and disturb the sleep of
ecumenical leadership" for the next half-century as non-Lutheran
churchmen watched with fascination and alarm the inner solidarity
and global outreach of Eisenach's grandchild, the Lutheran World
Federation.[59]

---

56. *AELKZ*, 1923, col. 791.
57. Ibid., cols. 643–44. Cf. *The Lutheran*, October 25, 1923, p. 2.
58. Wadensjö, *Toward a World Lutheran Communion*, p. 179.
59. Warren A. Quanbeck, "The Ecumenical Role of the LWF," *Lutheran World* 24,
no. 4 (1977): 400.

The American Lutheran reaction to Eisenach moved from enthusiastic hope to sharp criticism to virtual indifference. Abdel Ross Wentz,
Charles M. Jacobs, and Jürgen L. Neve, all of whom were ULCA
delegates, gave favorable evaluations. Even before the assembly
ended, Wentz, as we have noted, had been asked to give on-the-spot
impressions. He concluded these by saying that Eisenach was a sign
betokening *"a glorious future . . .* before our Lutheran Church."[60]
Jacobs's review, somewhat less sanguine, stated that Eisenach's full
significance was not yet apparent, but that the assembly had "placed
the Church, for the first time in its four hundred years of history, in a
position where common action along many lines is possible. It now
remains a question how far the desire for common action, based on
common confession of faith, and in the face of a widespread and
distressing need, will avail to overcome the forces that have been
divisive of the Lutheran Church in the past and kept [it] in complete,
though not splendid, isolation."[61] Neve concluded a lengthy account of
Eisenach by stating the hope that "out of the organization as it now has
taken shape there will develop something which is not yet: a larger
real union of the Lutheran Church—in all parts of the world, a union in
which the principles of the unaltered Augsburg Confession are consciously recognized and are functioning in the Church life."[62]

The editorial comment in Lutheran periodicals generally reflected
the position of the church body to which the editor belonged. Nathan
R. Melhorn, editor of *The Lutheran* (ULCA) and the officially appointed press officer at Eisenach, wrote: "It was freely prophesied that
Eisenach would be another talk-fest. . . . Naturally even the delegates were surprised when real unity emerged. . . ."[63] A writer in an
official Missouri Synod journal pointed out that his church required
complete doctrinal agreement for fellowship and worship. Since this
was obviously lacking at Eisenach, the assembly was but a gathering of
"unionists." The prevalence of doctrinal indifferentism at Eisenach
was the very thing that Missouri had fought from the earliest
beginnings.[64]

60. *LWC . . . 1923*, p. 177.
61. *Lutheran Church Review* 42 (October 1923): 297.
62. Neve, "Lutheran Convention," p. 322.
63. *The Lutheran*, September 27, 1923, pp. 3–4.
64. *Lehre und Wehre* 70 (May 1924): 138.

J. Michael Reu, besides being a professor at Wartburg Seminary of the Iowa Synod, was editor of the synod's German-language journal. He wrote that he was pleased that there were numerous conservatives present, and that this fact assured him that a Lutheran church based on the Reformation and the confessions would continue to exist. There were, however, some ominous signs. Although Resolution One affirmed the revelatory character of Scripture, it was equivocal on inspiration. He was convinced that most of the delegates were "liberals" who believed that the Bible "contains" rather than "is" the Word of God. Moreover, the confessional article was weak in that it did not specify the requirements for pulpit and altar fellowship. Reu added that he would have liked to see the executive committee elected by the churches rather than by the convention.[65] The Iowa Synod continued to be a thorny problem for the executive committee between Eisenach and the Copenhagen assembly in 1929. It is noteworthy that Reu's critical voice was softened after he had been asked to deliver one of the main lectures at Copenhagen.

Another American Lutheran, Carl C. Hein of the Joint Synod of Ohio, who had delivered one of the main lectures at Eisenach, judged the convention successful, especially in view of German secularism, theological liberalism, and church "unionism." Moreover, the convention avoided the temptations to speak on political issues and to become a "superchurch." On the debit side, however, was the inability to affirm the verbal inspiration of the Bible, and it was questionable that there was agreement on original sin and conversion.[66]

Of special interest to the student of American Lutheran history was the silence of the Norwegian Lutheran Church of America. Its president, Hans G. Stub, had been prominent at Eisenach, but the church's chief organ, *The Lutheran Church Herald*, carried no report or comment by him. In reporting to the Church Council the signal honor conferred on Lars W. Boe, president of St. Olaf College, he pointed out

---

65. *Kirchliche Zeitschrift* 48 (January 1924): 9ff.
66. *Pastors' Monthly*, December 1923, pp. 795ff. Cited in Willard D. Allbeck, "A Study of American Participation in Inter-Lutheran Cooperation Prior to the Formation of the Lutheran World Federation," prepared for the Department of Theology of the LWF, 1962, p. 43, in ArCL.

that the appointment awaited approval by the church. Although charged with ratifying Boe's new role and thus committing the church to participation in the Lutheran World Convention, with one exception the district conventions in 1924 failed—either by lack of interest or by disapproval—to provide the ratification requested by Eisenach Resolution Three. Boe overlooked this less-than-enthusiastic support, accepted the appointment (without Stub's veto), and joined Morehead in giving dynamic and influential leadership to the movement for Lutheran unity in America and abroad.[67]

The executive committee organized itself before departure from Eisenach by choosing John A. Morehead (United States) as chairman, Ludwig Ihmels (Germany) as vice-chairman; Wilhelm von Pechmann (Germany) as recording secretary; and Alfred Th. Jørgensen (Denmark) as treasurer.[68] Later, after Lars W. Boe accepted membership on the committee, he was asked to be assistant treasurer. The considerable financial support expected from the U.S. churches made it expedient to have an American officer through whom funds could be channeled to Jørgensen. Thus established, the executive committee was set to face the tasks assigned to it at Eisenach and to shape in large measure the future course of world Lutheranism. The story of the next six years to the Copenhagen convention of 1929 will be the subject of the next chapter.

Our detailed report and extended analysis of the Eisenach assembly have been deemed necessary in order to evaluate properly its significance. No church "family" was so distressed and divided by World War I as was the Lutheran church. None of the other major denominations—the Reformed, the Anglicans, the Methodists, the Baptists, yes, even the Roman Catholics—was so deeply wounded and broken asunder as was the Lutheran. Eisenach, with all its weaknesses, was a superlative occurrence. It was a religious expression, a reconciling experience, and a churchly event. That it happened at all was a miracle of grace.

Moreover, the coming into existence of the Lutheran World Convention was a significant manifestation of Lutheranism as an international

67. NLCA, *Report . . . 1924*, pp. 16, 113.
68. See the German minutes: "Engerer Ausschuss, I. Sitzung, II. Sitzung, 24. VIII. 23," Boe Papers, box 98, folder 2.

religious reality in the atmosphere of rising ecumenical interests. It fashioned a global confessional body alongside other global confessional groups such as the Anglican Lambeth Conference (1867), the Calvinist Alliance of Reformed Churches Throughout the World Holding the Presbyterian System (1875), the Methodist Ecumenical Conference (1881), the Union of Old Catholic Churches (1889), the International Congregational Council (1891), and the Baptist World Congress (1905). Eisenach was noteworthy in that, while consciously seeking a Lutheran world identity, it sought quite as consciously to determine how Lutherans might contribute to the ecumenical movement. Finally, its strong program of relief and assistance to orphaned missions prepared the Lutheran World Convention for the unforeseen responsibilities that Hitlerism and World War II were to place upon it. To repeat the words of Laible, "something significant had occurred and would continue to occur." This was Eisenach 1923.

7

The Executive Committee, 1923–29

The issues that surfaced in the pre-Eisenach deliberations and at Eisenach itself led to decisions that were to give shape to global Lutheranism and to determine its direction until 1947, when the Lutheran World Federation was formed. During the years immediately following Eisenach and prior to the events associated with the assembly at Copenhagen (1929), the story of the Lutheran World Convention was largely the story of its executive committee. We shall attempt, therefore, to describe the role of the executive committee and to summarize and evaluate its activities in preparation for the second assembly at Copenhagen.

THE ROLE OF THE EXECUTIVE COMMITTEE

Delegates at Eisenach had found it inadvisable to draft and adopt a constitution. Nevertheless, in order to provide some structure and continuity to the Lutheran world movement, the convention established two committees. The first, consisting of six members, was responsible for administrative duties. The second, with perhaps as many as fifty persons from the churches and groups participating in the Lutheran World Convention, had only vaguely defined tasks. The intention seemed to be to provide a broad representative group that would serve as a "continuation" committee to function between assemblies. This did not occur, however, and the six-member committee became the continuation committee as well as the executive committee. The six were John A. Morehead, Lars W. Boe, Ludwig Ihmels, Wilhelm von Pechmann, Alfred Th. Jørgensen, and Viktor Rundgren.

This action, as Kurt Schmidt-Clausen points out, was the signal that one of the chief premises of those who planned the Eisenach assembly (that it should be a nonrecurring "free conference") had been forsaken. Several of the speakers (Ludwig Ihmels, Nathan Söderblom, John A. Morehead, Alfred Th. Jørgensen, and others) had simply taken it for granted that Eisenach would be only the first of subsequent Lutheran world conferences. The resolution to name the two committees was but Exhibit A of this change. The five resolutions adopted at the final business session at Eisenach became the guidelines for the elected officers as they entered upon the constitutionless future of world Lutheranism.[1]

The Germans identified the committee simply as *der engere Ausschuss* (the smaller committee). The Americans referred to it sometimes as the Committee of Six, sometimes as the Continuation Committee, sometimes as the Executive Committee for Continuation Work. Finally, "The Executive Committee" became the usual designation. Between 1923 and 1929 seven meetings of the group were held (Eisenach, August 1923, following the assembly; Copenhagen, December 8–10, 1923; Gothenburg and Hindas [Sweden], November 15–19, 1924; The Hague, November 9–15, 1925; Dresden, June 30–July 7, 1926; Prague and Budapest, October 24–November 8, 1927; Copenhagen, June 19–29, 1928).

Despite the fact that Resolution Five at Eisenach had set forth the duties of the executive committee,[2] questions were frequently asked in America concerning the committee's tasks. Especially noteworthy was the persisting anxiety of the Iowa Synod, the Joint Synod of Ohio, and the Norwegian Lutheran Church of America.[3] Under these circumstances John A. Morehead felt it necessary to correspond with his American colleague Lars W. Boe about the matter. While conceding that there may have been some ambiguity in the Eisenach resolutions, it was Morehead's opinion that the difficulty lay in the conflicting interpretations given them by the American church press. Of course

1. Kurt Schmidt-Clausen, *Vom Lutherischen Weltkonvent zum Lutherischen Weltbund* (Gütersloh: Gerd Mohn, 1976), pp. 85–86.
2. See above, Chapter 6.
3. See Friedrich Richter to Morehead, March 11, 1924; and Boe to Morehead, January 8, 1924, Lars W. Boe Papers, box 98, folder 2, St. Olaf College Archives, Northfield, Minnesota.

this did not imply that the executive committee could define its role unilaterally; its definition must be congruent with the action taken at Eisenach. Moreover, the committee must be clear about its role in order to facilitate the decisions of those American Lutheran church bodies that were considering whether to participate in the Lutheran World Convention.[4] The church bodies that exhibited anxiety about joining the Lutheran World Convention—notably the Iowa Synod, whose president in 1928 was Gustav A. Fandrey—led Morehead to describe the duties of the executive committee as follows:

> Starting with the simple but positive doctrinal statement adopted at Eisenach, the Executive Committee for Continuation Work has endeavored faithfully to rally the forces of the Lutheran Churches throughout the world to a re-examination of the Faith of the Fathers to the end of the discovery and increase of true inner unity in the positive faith of the Gospel as confessed by the Church of the Reformation. We have also endeavored to encourage by giving information and by recommendations the voluntary cooperation of Lutherans everywhere in vital Lutheran relief tasks, particularly in Russia. When the account of its stewardship is rendered in a full report at Copenhagen next year, the work of the Executive Committee will be ended. The future of the movement will then be in the Hands of God and of the Second Lutheran World Convention, subject entirely to the approval of the home Churches. In the present formative stage of the Lutheran World Convention movement, the Executive Committee for Continuation Work finds it necessary to move slowly with patience and discretion. But it is the strategic moment for the friends of conservative Lutheranism everywhere, in our judgment, to appoint *official delegates* to the Copenhagen Convention so that from within they may bear witness to the truth and aid in determining the accepted principles and form of the Lutheran World Convention movement [italics added].[5]

This statement, together with agenda items at the Hindas-Gothenburg (1924) meeting, showed that the executive committee interpreted its role under the Eisenach resolution to be somewhat broader than the Iowa Synod could allow.[6]

Despite the uncertain corporate and legal status of the Lutheran

---

4. Morehead to Boe, March 13, 1924, Boe Papers, box 98, folder 2.
5. Morehead to Fandrey, October 24, 1928, Boe Papers, box 99, folder 4.
6. "Agenda . . . Executive Committee, Gothenburg, Sweden, Nov. 15–19, 1924," p. 2, in the Archives of Cooperative Lutheranism, Lutheran Council/U.S.A., New York City (hereafter referred to as ArCL). The agenda items and the minutes no doubt intensified the anxiety in the Iowa Synod.

Gothenburg, Sweden, 1926: Executive Committee of the Lutheran World Convention. *Standing*, Alfred Th. Jørgensen, Per Pehrsson, Lars W. Boe. *Seated*, Wilhelm von Pechmann, John A. Morehead, Ludwig Ihmels.

World Convention (no evidence as to incorporation of the convention has been uncovered), the executive committee went about its tasks, interpreting Eisenach's five resolutions according to its best understanding. This led to the kinds of activity proposed at Eisenach itself (including the postassembly organizational meeting of the committee at Eisenach) and the first "official" meeting of the committee at Copenhagen (1923).

THE ACTIVITIES OF THE EXECUTIVE COMMITTEE

More than a dozen major items engaged the executive committee in the years prior to the second assembly in 1929. We shall look at seven of these, giving varying degrees of attention to details.

1. Membership of the Committee

The Lutheran World Convention had named six churchmen representing the three "centers" of world Lutheranism: Germany, Scandinavia, and North America.[7] Two of those named, Viktor Rundgren of Sweden and Lars W. Boe of the United States, had not been in attendance at Eisenach. Consequently, the newly elected chairman of the committee, Morehead, was instructed to send each of them a formal notice of election.[8] Rundgren replied that it was impossible for him to serve. The committee, having been given authority to fill vacancies, replaced him with Per Pehrsson of Gothenburg, who had delivered one of the lectures at the Eisenach assembly.[9]

When Morehead informed Boe of his election, he reported that Eisenach had named the committee members with the understanding that the "appointments should stand subject to any different action by the participating bodies in America."[10] Boe was hesitant about accepting the appointment for several reasons. As president of St. Olaf College, he was reluctant to assume duties that would oblige him to be absent from his office for at least a month each year in order to attend committee meetings in Europe. This problem was compounded when the college chapel was destroyed by fire on September 22, 1923. This loss would necessitate his heavy engagement in emergency fund-raising for rebuilding. Although Boe was honored by the appointment and regarded it as "a wonderful opportunity," he thought that the convention had "made a mistake" in selecting him and said he would gladly step aside in favor of a better qualified person. Boe seldom showed a lack of confidence in his competence to handle assign-

7. This action grew out of Söderblom's urgent proposal that world Lutheranism must be seen as polycentric. The LWC was not to be viewed as being primarily German or American. Cf. Schmidt-Clausen, *Vom Lutherischen Weltkonvent*, p. 41.

8. "Engerer Ausschuss, II Sitzung 24. VIII. 23," Boe Papers, box 98, folder 2.

9. "Lutherischer Weltkonvent. Ständiger Ausschuss . . . Kopenhagen 8.–10. Dezember 1923," in ArCL. Morehead had asked Ihmels prior to the Copenhagen meeting to report to him about the qualifications of Pehrsson as a replacement for Rundgren. He pointed out that the Scandinavian members of the committee must represent all three countries. The Swedes, known for their sensitivity, needed careful consideration, although (Morehead continued) they do not "yield anything in sensitiveness to the Norwegians." Pehrsson was also a public figure in Sweden, a member of the parliament. See Morehead to Ihmels, November 9, 1923(?), in ArCL.

10. Morehead to Boe, September 12, 1923, Boe Papers, box 98, folder 1.

ments, but in this case he was genuinely disturbed. He mentioned his inadequacy in speaking German and his possible unacceptability to Hans G. Stub and certain powerful conservative elements in the Norwegian Lutheran Church.[11] Morehead sought to reassure him and finally persuaded him to accept. The following excerpt from the voluminous correspondence between Morehead and Boe illustrates Morehead's persuasiveness:

> As I understand it, all the members of the American delegations, including Dr. Stub and Dr. Reu of Iowa, voted in favor of the nomination of yourself and myself as the two American representatives on the Committee of Six. Of course, I should feel unable to attempt to interpret all of Dr. Stub's views and I should not feel it right to undertake to do so even if I had the ability. However, I believe you can rely upon the statement of fact as to his voting for you and myself for membership in the Executive Committee. Please note that you were not elected by the Lutheran World Convention as a representative of the Norwegian Lutheran Church of America no more than I was elected as the representative of the United Lutheran Church in America. We were both elected to represent all the Lutherans of America who participated in the Lutheran World Convention. If you should decline election, the Norwegian Lutheran Church would not have the right to name anyone else in your stead, but someone else would be appointed by the other members of the Committee of Six to represent all participating American Lutherans. If the United Lutheran Church should fail to approve the action of the Lutheran World Convention in appointing an Executive Committee, my name would be automatically dropped from the Committee and the second American member would be appointed from a body which did approve. The consequences of the non-approval of the action of the World Convention by the Norwegian Lutheran Church of America would, of course, be similar in your case. Hence you see that this Executive Committee of the Lutheran World Convention is an established fact. It does exist and will exist and has authority to function. It is for the bodies who have participated in the Convention to say whether or not they will share in the international Lutheran movement or not. But the movement itself has by the grace of God been begun and will by the grace of God go forward. You have been honored with this great election, my dear Doctor, and I earnestly desire that you shall be my colleague in this wonderful opportunity of service. I

---

11. Boe to Morehead, September 17, 1923. Boe was fully aware of his low standing among some members of the former Norwegian Synod who objected to his work for Lutheran unity, especially his interest in the NLC. Johan C. K. Preus, for example, sought unsuccessfully to prevent "fellowship and cooperation" in the NLC. See *Lutheran Church Herald*, June 24, 1919, p. 392. In light of this history, Boe correctly anticipated guarded objections to the LWC and the less than enthusiastic ratification of his appointment to the executive committee. See E. Clifford Nelson, *The Lutheran Church among Norwegian-Americans* (Minneapolis: Augsburg Publishing House, 1960), 2:326.

am satisfied that the United Lutheran Church will approve the action of the Eisenach Convention.[12]

Boe served on the executive committee with Morehead until the latter's retirement in 1935. For the next seven years, until his death in 1942, Boe remained an alternate member of the committee but played a less active role.

2. The Larger Committee

The Eisenach assembly had authorized Morehead and Ihmels to form the "Larger Committee." These two felt this was beyond their competence and requested the executive committee to act with them. At its meeting in Copenhagen, December 8–10, 1923, the executive committee recommended that American church bodies choose eight members (four places were assigned to the ULCA, and one each to the Joint Synod, NLCA, Augustana, and Iowa). In addition, two places would be reserved for other American Lutheran bodies that might in the future decide to participate in the convention. As for members from Lutheran groups in Europe, the committee deferred action until the next meeting.[13]

Considerable time and effort were devoted to the question of the Larger Committee by the executive committee at its 1924, 1925, and 1926 meetings. Finally a list of more than fifty names was approved.[14]

12. Morehead to Boe, September 21, 1923, Boe Papers, box 98, folder 1. After Boe accepted the office, he found it impossible to attend the first meeting of the committee at Copenhagen, December 8–10, 1923. In this situation he suggested that he resign and proposed that Jacob A. O. Stub, son of Hans G. Stub, be named in his place. Morehead replied: "I am not in favor of your resigning. If you resign, then the Joint Synod, the Swedish Augustana, Iowa, or any other Lutheran bodies in America that approve the action at Eisenach, will have the right to a voice in naming your successor. There you are! I really believe it is better to have no representative in your place than to set a wrong precedent right at the beginning—a precedent that will influence actions on both sides of the water. . . . I should be delighted to have Dr. J. A. O. Stub as a traveling companion, but it is not a personal question. It is not even a question of . . . keeping the peace [among American Lutherans]. . . . I wish I could solve [your] difficulties . . . by imparting to you a sort of radio . . . omnipresence so that you could be at St. Olaf and Copenhagen both." Morehead to Boe, November 7, 1923, Boe Papers, box 98, folder 1.
13. "An Abridged Report of the Minutes . . . Executive Committee . . . , Copenhagen, Dec. 8–10, 1923," p. 1, in ArCL.
14. See "Protokoll des ständigen Ausschusses des Lutherischen Weltkonvents, Gothenburg/Hindas, 15.–19. November 1924," pp. 7–10, in ArCL. "Sitzung des Executivkomitees des lutherischen Weltkonvents in Haag . . . 9.–12. November, 1925," p. 1, Boe Papers, box 101, folder 10; "Report of the Executive Committee . . . to Members of the Large Committee . . . , Dresden, July 8, 1926," p. 2, in LWF Archives, Geneva, Switzerland, "Luth. Weltkonvent." Cf. "From Report . . . of Lutheran World Convention," *Lutheran Church Herald*, July 15, 1925, pp. 878–79.

The Larger Committee, however, never became a functioning organ of the Lutheran World Convention. As named, it did indeed carry out the resolution of the Eisenach assembly to create a body that would be "representative of all the churches participating in the Lutheran World Convention." Nevertheless, the hope that such a committee might serve as "an interim parliament" between assemblies (something achieved later by the LWF executive committee and the Central Committee of the World Council of Churches) was never realized; it existed only on paper without ever having been convened. Schmidt-Clausen suggests two reasons for this: (1) The Eisenach resolution that authorized the formation of the Larger Committee made no provision for financing such a committee, nor did it delineate its responsibilities; (2) circumstances led the executive committee to assume duties not anticipated by Eisenach. Moreover, this whole development must be seen in relationship to the fact that no central bureau or secretariat in Europe had been established.[15]

3. The Central Bureau

The agenda for the 1923 (Copenhagen) meeting of the executive committee listed the question of establishing a "Central Bureau," or secretariat, for the Lutheran World Convention.[16] This is surprising, because neither the English nor the German reports of the Eisenach proceedings contain a reference to a central bureau or secretariat. Nevertheless, the official minutes of the executive committee meeting in Copenhagen, December 8–10, 1923, record an extended discussion of the matter. Per Pehrsson, the Swedish member, objected to estab-

---

15. Schmidt-Clausen, *Vom Lutherischen Weltkonvent*, p. 99. Bengt Wadensjö sees the history of the Larger Committee and the secretariat as linked to a grand American Lutheran scheme to control the world movement on the basis of a smug and unreflective confessionalism. It was, he charges, for this reason that Morehead was elected chairman of the executive committee. Ihmels had been elected chairman of the LWC on nomination by the American Charles M. Jacobs. Now, when the executive committee was to be organized, Ihmels was placed in the uncomfortable position of *quid pro quo*, whereby he felt he had to nominate Morehead. See Bengt Wadensjö, *Toward a World Lutheran Communion: Developments in Lutheran Cooperation up to 1929* (Uppsala: Verbum, 1970), pp. 175–78. Schmidt-Clausen has replied that this is an untenable and undocumented conclusion. Far from being a grand "American maneuver," the selection of Morehead was quite in keeping with the prevailing international postwar political and economic circumstances. Moreover, the fact was that Morehead was the only member of the executive committee who had an office (in New York) from which the affairs of the budgetless LWC could be administered! See Schmidt-Clausen, *Vom Lutherischen Weltkonvent*, pp. 92–93, n. 401.
16. "Meeting of the Executive Committee . . . Dec. 8–10, 1923," p. 1, in ArCL.

lishing a secretariat because it would be a move toward centralization; Alfred Th. Jørgensen (Copenhagen) thought that Morehead's office should be the "provisional" bureau; Morehead himself was reluctant because he was already burdened with Lutheran world relief matters and feared that additional duties might jeopardize this good work. The Germans argued that at least a beginning must be made to move beyond mere relief work. Ludwig Ihmels said that when the idea of a central bureau was broached in committee at Eisenach, it had not been intended that a secretariat be merely an office for the administration of relief. No agreement could be reached, so Pehrsson's motion "to lay it on the table" was adopted.[17]

This discussion reveals quite clearly that something must have been said at Eisenach about a general secretariat. That this was the case is evident from Ihmels's comment mentioned above and from a later letter from Baron Wilhelm von Pechmann to Morehead, in which the baron sadly admitted that indeed no official decision had been reached at Eisenach regarding a central bureau and its location in Germany (the lack of funds foreclosed this possibility). Von Pechmann did say that the Committee on Organization, of which he was chairman, had understood that a central secretariat located in Germany would eventually be established.[18] Uncertain as to the actual state of this affair, Morehead wrote the following letter to one of the American members of the Eisenach Committee on Organization:

October 22nd, 1925

Prof. Andrew G. Voigt, D.D., LL.D.
Columbia, South Carolina

Dear Dr. Voigt:

Dr. Boe and I go aboard the *S/S Columbus* Wednesday night, October 28th, for she sails at 1:30 A.M. on the following morning. Before that time, I am very anxious to have a letter from you.

The German members of the Executive Committee of the Lutheran World Convention claim that there was a private understanding within the Committee on Organization at Eisenach that the Central Bureau proposed to be established in the interest of world Lutheranism would be located in

17. "Lutherischer Weltkonvent. Ständiger Ausschuss . . . Kopenhagen 8.–10. Dezember 1923," pp. 7 – 8, in ArCL.
18. Von Pechmann to Morehead, January 10, 1925, in ArCL. This was substantiated in a letter from Carl Paul (Leipzig) to Morehead, October 2, 1925, in ArCL.

Germany. Other members of the Committee, including Dr. Boe and myself, have taken the position that we are bound only by the public report of the Committee on Organization as approved by the Lutheran World Convention itself at Eisenach. In other words, we believe that we are free to consider the matter on its merits when the proper time comes for the establishment of a Central Bureau with the approval of participating Lutheran Church Bodies and groups throughout the world. But the German members of the Committee are very uncompromising in their contention. We wish to know the facts.

Did the Committee on Organization actually have a "private agreement" on this subject of the location of the Central Bureau? Or, was this view merely discussed and favored by some individuals? I shall appreciate your full and frank statement of the facts about the matter at your earliest convenience. I am making the same request of Dr. Brandelle. I have seen Dr. E. Clarence Miller personally and he has promised to give me his recollections in writing.

Personally, I knew nothing about this alleged private understanding until my return to America after the Eisenach Convention. Of course, you understand that we only desire to arm ourselves with the facts in view of the probable consideration of this question at our coming meeting at The Hague.

Hoping you are well and with cordial personal greeting, I remain,

Faithfully yours,

John A. Morehead, Chairman,
Executive Committee

JAM:SW

Morehead received the following reply:

Lutheran Seminary
Columbia, S.C.,
Oct. 24, 1925

J. A. Morehead, D.D.
New York, N.Y.

Dear Doctor:

Your letter of the 22nd in reference to the location of the Central Bureau came to my hands this morning. I am happy to be able to give a definite reply to your inquiry, because I have a vivid recollection of what occurred at the meeting of the Committee on Organization at Eisenach.

The German members of the Executive Committee are right in their claim, which you say they make, that there was a private understanding within the Committee that the Central Bureau would be established in Germany.

This is what happened, as I very well recall, in that first meeting of the Committee. Freiherr von Pechmann as president proposed for consideration a scheme which he had in writing. A section of this he would read and then ask the members individually for their opinions. The first important section was one describing the organization of the World Conference as a continuation of the Allgemeine Lutherische Konferenz. There was opposition to this and it fell to me to speak a good deal to get this idea of the Allgemeine Konferenz out of our plan of organization. We finally succeeded. When we came to the subject of a Central Bureau there was again a difference of view. The opposition to a location in Germany was not near as strong as to the Allgemeine Konferenz proposal. Moreover the Germans under the lead of Freiherr von Pechmann implored us not to locate outside of Germany, as that would add to the humiliation Germany as a nation was suffering under at the time. I did not press the point further nor did anybody else. My impression always has been if that item had been forced to a vote, we who favored a non-German location would have been in the minority. So that left this detail to be worked out by the Executive Committee that was to be and was created; but the understanding of the Germans was that the location was to be in Germany and nobody urged any opposing view.

Immediately after this meeting I told Dr. Knubel that I had felt constrained to yield on this point of location. He was not satisfied and said in effect that this would have to be settled afterwards. I do not know whether he will recall this conversation in the hotel in Eisenach.

You are at liberty to make any proper use of this letter you deem advisable.

Wishing you a pleasant voyage and a successful meeting,

Yours very sincerely,

/A. G. Voigt[19]

The question of a central bureau continued to agitate the executive committee for the next decade, during which time the issue threatened to produce a major split between the Germans and the Americans on the executive committee. Although the Danish member of the committee, Jørgensen, sought to be a mediator, he gave his private support to the Americans. This was no doubt known to the Germans, who were still smarting from attitudes created by World War I and the Versailles Treaty. They saw Germany surrounded by hostile neighbors from France on the west to the Slavs on the east. Now, they judged, the Americans were adding their power and influence to perpetuate Germany's humiliation and working to remove the numerically overwhelming German Lutherans from their "rightful" place of leadership in world Lutheranism. Von Pechmann was especially incensed, and he wrote passionately to Morehead that Germany's enemies had waged "a

19. The Morehead-Voigt correspondence is in ArCL.

war of extermination" against the fatherland. Although Germans would never cease to be grateful to American Lutherans for their magnanimous relief work, which had been directed not only to needs in Germany but also to needs in Russia and other places, nevertheless, he said, "We cannot cease pointing out the injustice which puts our freedom into chains, and tramples our honor into the dust." He continued by insisting that Germany must be accorded its proper place among the nations, because "every people is a special creation of God." This did not mean that Germans considered themselves better than other people—that would be sinful egoism—but that, under God, Germans also had a serious responsibility in the world. This was now being denied, and he could only conclude that Germany was *machtlos* and *friedlos* ("powerless" and "peaceless").[20]

Morehead, however, insisted that the Lutheran World Convention must not become involved in the politics of Germany or any other nation. The supranationalism of the Lutheran World Convention and a common Christian faith made it possible for Germans, Americans, Frenchmen, and many others to work together on a purely churchly basis.[21] Despite what Morehead called "this high basis," the Germans continued to assess the issue of a central bureau in the light of alleged postwar hostility to Germany. Even though Morehead was quite sure that something had been said privately at Eisenach about a future central bureau, he wrote a German friend that his and Boe's position— in fact, the position of the whole executive committee—on the issue had to be based on the public decision reached at Eisenach:

> As to the question of a private understanding at Eisenach to the effect that the Central Bureau of the Lutheran World Convention, when located, would be established in Germany, I must positively state to you that I was not consulted at Eisenach about it until I returned to America. The Committee on Organization presented a report to the Eisenach Convention, which contained no reference to the establishment of a Central Bureau nor to its location, which was adopted. Our Executive Committee is bound by the action of the Eisenach Convention. We are not bound by

20. Von Pechmann said that on his return trip from Eisenach in 1923 his map showed that he would pass near three villages, two of which had the name *Machtlos* and the other *Friedlos*. These names symbolized postwar Germany. Von Pechmann's long letter to Morehead was written over a period of time; the dates were January 10, 1925, January 22, 1925, and February 5, 1925; see ArCL.

21. Morehead to von Pechmann, December 26, 1924, in ArCL.

any private agreement of individuals. To my certain knowledge, the combined American delegations were not consulted upon any private understanding about the location of the Central Bureau and certainly what one or more individuals may have said privately cannot bind even the American delegation. This matter touches my own personal honor very nearly. I should never have accepted the Chairmanship of the Executive Committee on the basis of private agreements or understandings. In the interest of the peace and progress of our movement and above all in the interest of the Evangelical Lutheran Church and its service of Christ's Kingdom, I beseech our German brethren not to be so untactful and unwise as to press the unjustifiable claim that there was a private understanding. Such a claim would discredit the Lutheran World Convention in many quarters of the world because of the strong public feeling against diplomacy by private agreements in the political realm.

The questions of having a Central Bureau and of its location ought to be entirely open questions to be considered on their merits by the Executive Committee. If it is best for the cause of world Lutheranism for the location to be in any particular country, whether Germany or others, our Executive Committee ought to be free to reach its conclusions for sound reasons with which it can support its action and recommendations. Any other course would be unworthy of the Church we represent.[22]

As far as the Americans were concerned, the time was not ripe to move in the direction of centralization. The formation of a secretariat would most surely be interpreted by some American Lutherans (notably the Ohio and Iowa synods) as a concentration of power. Boe wrote shortly after he accepted membership on the executive committee that it would be necessary "to insist upon [the LWC's] being a 'free conference.' " Otherwise Iowa and Ohio would lose interest in world Lutheranism.[23] Morehead concurred, and a few years later he expressed the same views to Ihmels:

At the present moment . . . we are . . . engaged in endeavoring to enlist the Joint Synod of Ohio and the Iowa Synod for participation in the Lutheran World Convention. . . . [They] would be frightened away if we advance so far beyond the conception of a free conference . . . as to establish a Central Bureau.[24]

22. Morehead to Carl Paul, Leipzig, October 16, 1925, p. 2, in ArCL. Paul, it will be recalled, had been a member of the German Committee on Arrangements and was virtual convention "manager" at Eisenach.
23. Boe to Morehead, January 8, 1924, in ArCL.
24. Morehead to Ihmels, April 27, 1927, Boe Papers, box 98, folder 12.

Although definitions differed among the Americans,[25] it was the concept of the Lutheran World Convention as "a free conference" and the absence of any Eisenach directive to the executive committee—as well as the persistence of ill feeling between Germany and her wartime enemies on the Continent—that caused the Americans to delay action on the issue of a central bureau.

Thus it came about that the meetings of the executive committee prior to the second assembly of the convention at Copenhagen (1929) repeatedly postponed action on this sensitive issue. Immediately prior to the assembly, the executive committee met at Skodsborg, a town on the Danish "Gold Coast" about ten miles north of Copenhagen, in order to complete last-minute details. Both Morehead and Boe were eager that their views about a central bureau be understood (Boe was a member of the committee to deal with the future organization of the LWC). Therefore, Morehead asked the executive committee to spend some time discussing the issue. He said that in the interval since Eisenach the Lutheran World Convention had grown in solidarity and that perhaps the time had come to move toward a stronger organization, such as would be implied by the establishment of a central bureau. He pointed out, however, that highly vocal opposition to centralization continued in certain quarters. In the light of this, should the report of the executive committee to the assembly recommend a central bureau or not? The discussion surprisingly revealed that von Pechmann, who had been named chairman of the Committee on Organization, was no longer urging the German position. In fact, he wrote out a proposal that was quite in line with the American views on the matter. It was unanimously approved and incorporated into Morehead's report.[26]

---

25. The Midwestern German synods, including Missouri, thought of a "free conference" as a gathering of individuals, not representatives of church bodies, for the purpose of doctrinal discussion. Morehead and Boe, and very likely Ihmels, looked upon a "free conference" as an assembly whose decisions or resolutions were not binding on the churches or groups represented by the delegates or participants. Morehead wrote Boe that the Iowa Synod and others in America would prefer the LWC to be a "free conference *talkfest*" (October 27, 1928, Boe Papers, box 99, folder 4).

26. "Protokoll des Exekutivkomitees zu Skodsborg, 21.–24. Juni, 1929," p. 2, in ArCL. The report of the executive committee presented to the assembly by Morehead includes a section entitled "Preparations for the Second Lutheran World Convention," where von Pechmann's portion is included. See LWC Executive Committee, *The Second Lutheran World Convention . . . Copenhagen . . . 1929* (Philadelphia: United Lutheran Publication House, 1930), pp. 166–68.

During the years between the Copenhagen (1929) and Paris (1935) assemblies, the issue remained largely quiescent, but an informal meeting in early 1935 between the American members of the executive committee and presidents of NLC church bodies and others produced proposals for a reorganization of the Lutheran World Convention.[27] Subsequent suggestions by Frederick H. Knubel (ULCA) and Lars W. Boe were submitted to the executive committee for presentation to the Paris assembly. Included in the final report was the recommendation that the executive committee appoint an "executive secretary" whose office would be "at the place of residence of the president."[28] Following the approval of the report at Paris, Hanns Lilje, secretary of the Christian Student Movement in Germany, was selected as executive (general) secretary by the executive committee in 1936 and began his duties January 1, 1937, with headquarters in Berlin.[29]

By way of recapitulation a few summary observations about a central bureau may be helpful:

A. The American members of the executive committee had been reluctant to move rapidly on the question of a central bureau for several reasons. One was the obvious lack of a formal directive from the Eisenach assembly. Another was their concern lest some Midwestern Lutheran bodies, who were prospective members of the Lutheran World Convention, might be frightened away by the bugaboo of a "superchurch." Moreover, the insistence of the Germans that the proposed central bureau be located in Germany would no doubt be viewed with jaundiced eyes by non-German churches on the Continent, as well as by Lutherans in America, because of lingering postwar feelings toward Germany.

B. The Scandinavians, especially the Danes and the Swedes (the

27. "Proceedings: Informal Meeting . . . at Request of American Members of the Executive Committee of the Lutheran World Convention . . . New York, January 18, 1935," in ArCL.

28. *The Lutheran World Almanac and Encyclopedia 1934 –1937* (New York: NLC, 1937), p. 32. Boe's proposals, many of which were incorporated in the report, made no mention of a secretariat. See Boe to Members of the Executive Committee, September 9, 1935, Lilje A/I, in Archiv des Lutherischen Kirchenamtes, Hannover, Germany. However, Knubel specifically proposed that an executive secretary (not older than age forty-five or fifty; it was said that Jørgensen, age sixty-one, had been desirous of the office), not a member of the executive committee, be named. Knubel to Boe, September 30, 1935, p. 2, in ArCL.

29. *Lutheran World Almanac . . . 1934 –1937*, pp. 35–36.

Norwegians and the Finns were hardly involved), were generally sympathetic with the Americans. The Swedes were hesitant, notably because they felt the move would be financially burdensome and ecclesiastically threatening. They thought that a central bureau would jeopardize the independence of the Church of Sweden.

C. The Germans, after a long and unsuccessful struggle to actualize what they considered to have been an oral promise made at Eisenach, finally withdrew their pressure at Copenhagen in 1929, only to see their hopes rekindled by an American proposal adopted by the Paris convention in 1935.

D. The establishment of a central bureau and the appointment of a German as executive secretary were fateful events. As it turned out, the location of the bureau in Berlin gave the Lutheran World Convention a significant listening post within Nazi Germany for a time and a point of contact for resumption of worldwide Lutheran relationships after World War II.

E. Finally, the decision to establish a central bureau for the Lutheran World Convention provided a model for the creation of a general secretariat for the Lutheran World Federation after World War II in Geneva, Switzerland, an institution that has existed alongside the secretariat of the World Council of Churches to the present day.

4. Help for the Church in Russia

The ringing words (*"Panem propter Deum"*) of Theophil Meyer, general superintendent of Moscow, at the Eisenach assembly were not soon forgotten by the Lutheran World Convention and its executive committee. In fact, the attention given to the Lutherans in Russia during the 1920s and early 1930s is in itself a book-length topic. In czarist days the Lutherans numbered an estimated four to five million living under the church (Lutheran) constitution of 1832. The provisional Russian government abolished this constitution in 1917. The next year, the Baltic States and other heavily Lutheran territories were separated from Russia, with the result that not more than one million Lutherans remained in the new Soviet state.[30] Under the Soviet

---

30. "Lutheranism in Russia," in *The Encyclopedia of the Lutheran Church*, ed. Julius Bodensieck (Minneapolis: Augsburg Publishing House, 1965), 3:2079ff. Since most Lutherans in Russia were found among German colonies, they had been natural targets for Russian hostility even prior to the Bolshevik Revolution.

regime a law declaring separation of church and state was enacted in 1918. Operating under this law, the Lutherans held a general synod in 1924, adopted a new ecclesiastical constitution, and elected Theophil Meyer of Moscow as bishop and chairman of the consistory (church council). Arthur Malmgren of Petrograd (Leningrad) and one or two others were also given the episcopal title.

The adversities faced by Russian Lutherans were seen at first hand by the members of the NLC European Commission in the early 1920s. In the beginning Morehead had worked tirelessly and alone. Later he had received much needed assistance from A. C. Ernst, W. L. Scheding, and C. Theodore Benze. All these men reported the pitiful conditions of the church: excessive Soviet taxes were levied on pastors and congregations; the 1920–22 famine had debilitating and demoralizing effects, especially in the large colony of Volga Lutherans; and the churches were suffering from a ministerial shortage. Prior to 1918 most Russian Lutheran pastors had received their theological education at the University of Dorpat. With the separation of the Baltic States in 1918, Dorpat ceased to be accessible. In this situation, Arthur Malmgren founded a seminary in Leningrad in 1924–25. Partly because of the Soviet "New Economic Policy" of 1921 and financial help from the Lutheran World Convention, the Leningrad seminary was able to prepare a sizable number of candidates for the ministry. This lasted only until the mid-1930s, when the Soviets under Stalin abolished the seminary. Malmgren had been sent into exile on an island in the White Sea in 1929. He remained in the concentration camp until his release in 1936. A very sick man, he was granted permission to emigrate to Germany, where he died in 1947.

In one way the year 1929, the year of the second assembly of the Lutheran World Convention, marked the turning point for the Lutheran church in Russia. Overt persecution, exile of pastors, forcible collectivization of agriculture (the landowning farmers, the Kulaks, were often Lutherans), and another famine brought church life to a virtual standstill. By 1937, organized Lutheran work was forced to cease. One can readily understand the executive committee's concern for the future of Lutheranism in Russia, an issue on which the American and European committee members were solidly united. Although the German members had a natural ethnic affinity for their brethren in Russia, Morehead frequently complained that they were ineffective in awakening the compassion of the masses of German Lutherans to the suffering in the east. Nevertheless, every meeting of the committee between 1923 and 1929 heard reports and passed resolutions about the problem, issuing urgent pleas to the churches to send money and goods for Russian relief. In keeping with the policy of the Lutheran World Convention to avoid involvement in the internal politics of all countries, no public statements were issued regarding the relations of Lutherans to the Soviet regime. The task as seen by the executive committee was churchly.[31] How much Morehead, Boe, and their European colleagues actually knew about the internal Russian problem is not clear. What is transparent was their single-minded drive to relieve suffering and their devotion to preserve the church and its evangelical witness in a communist country. The official reports of the committee provide ample evidence of these high motives and the unremitting dedication of the committee.[32]

A brief summary of the Russian-related activities of the committee must begin with its first formal meeting at Copenhagen in late 1923. A letter from Theophil Meyer, bishop of Moscow, requested money for sending a pastor on a two-year ministry to 80,000 pastorless Lutherans in Siberia and to support the proposed seminary in Leningrad. A subcommittee was appointed to investigate ways and means for the accomplishment of these tasks.[33] In anticipation of the next meeting of the executive committee (Gothenburg-Hindas, 1924), Morehead wrote to Ihmels that although the situation in Russia looked bleak, he was encouraged that Russian pastors and people were taking the initiative "in working out for themselves as Russian citizens a modus vivendi for

31. One of the inconsistencies of post–World War II attacks on Lutherans' relations to the state occurred in ecumenical circles. The shrill criticism that they did not make public attacks on Nazism was most vocal among Barthians. The same critical voices were strangely silent when Lutherans, by the same rationale, did not issue public condemnation of the Soviet regime.

32. Regrettably, Wadensjö ascribes less than honorable motives to the committee, especially its American members. He wrote that when the German proposal for a central bureau was not implemented in the 1920s, the executive committee cast around for a project to justify its continued existence. Therefore, he alleged, something must be found to stimulate and hold the interest of world Lutheranism: "The only comparable object for an activity similar to NLC's European aid was afforded by the [Lutherans in the] Soviet Union." *Toward a World Lutheran Communion*, p. 186.

33. See "Lutherischer Weltkonvent. Ständiger Ausschuss, Kopenhagen 8.–10. Dezember 1923," p. 9, in ArCL; and "An Abridged Report of the Minutes . . . Executive Committee . . . Copenhagen, Dec. 8–10, 1923," p. 2, in ArCL.

the Lutheran Church in relation to the Soviet government. . . . I feel deeply that this is their task, [but] . . . we ought to give them all the moral support in our power."[34]

Very little would be known about the committee's discussion and actions at Gothenburg-Hindas in 1924 if one were to depend on the official minutes. The secretary, Wilhelm von Pechmann, mentioned a communication from the bishop of Moscow, to which the committee responded with a carefully worded statement about Lutheran desires to help the brethren in the Soviet Union. Von Pechmann concluded: *"Auf Einzelheiten soll auch hier im Protokoll nicht eingegangen werden"* (Details cannot be entered into the minutes).[35] The details, however, were fully reported by Morehead on his return to New York. The report reproduced the extensive correspondence between Morehead and the Russian church leaders.[36] From these documents it becomes clear that the committee moved with both determination and caution to respond most effectively to the unmistakable need. First, the committee urged all churches participating in the Lutheran World Convention to receive offerings for the Lutherans in Russia, but that care be taken to avoid imprudent publicity or agitation that might stir up the wrath of the Communists. Next the committee accepted the offer of the National Lutheran Council to send a member to Russia to secure firsthand information and to establish channels for the transfer of funds. Oscar C. Mees spent three months in Europe in a fruitless effort to obtain an entry permit from Soviet authorities. This meant that only driblets of money would find their way, perhaps through private channels, to Russia. However, quite suddenly, the door was opened by three changes: (1) Remittances not exceeding one hundred dollars could be sent through banking channels to relatives. It would be unwise, however, to send gifts to pastors and church officials, because they would immediately be placed under surveillance by the Soviet police; (2) Theophil Meyer had received official permission to travel to famine-stricken Asiatic Russia and to distribute three thou-

---

34. Morehead to Ihmels, May 9, 1924, in ArCL.
35. "Protokoll des ständigen Ausschusses . . . Gothenburg/Hindas, 15.–19. November 1924," p. 12, in ArCL.
36. See "Substance of Conclusive Discussions and Recommendations of the Executive Committee . . . Gothenburg and Hindas, November 15–19, 1924," pp. 6–8, in ArCL.

sand dollars for the relief of those in desperate need; (3) The frustrating negotiations of Arthur Malmgren to establish a seminary in Leningrad were rewarded by assurances on December 10, 1924, that the official permit would soon be in hand. This arrived on April 15, 1925, but with the conditions that the new institution be called a "School of the Prophets" or "Bible School" (*Biblische Erziehungsschule für Pastoren*) rather than a theological seminary. "Theological" would not be allowed by a state in which "God" was not recognized, and the word "seminary" was too reminiscent of Russia's prerevolution era.[37]

Morehead's report continued with the good news that Alfred Th. Jørgensen, the LWC treasurer, acting in cooperation with Carl Paul, was already in receipt of funds earmarked for Russia and that larger sums were now anticipated. Morehead concluded with an additional word of caution that Lutherans in the West must go about the task of raising and transmitting money in a most discreet manner. Unusual attention from the West would endanger the work and even the lives of pastors and other Christians who were under suspicion as subversives and potential counterrevolutionaries.

The following year (1925), the executive committee met at The Hague in Holland (despite the objection of Germans who interpreted the choice of meeting place as just another slap in the face). Once again the Russian problem was a part of the agenda. The minutes report the following: (1) Although both Meyer and Malmgren had been invited to The Hague, neither was granted a travel visa; (2) Morehead, however, was able to report that (a) the Siberian famine continued unabated; (b) only seventy-nine pastors remained in service, leaving two-thirds of the parishes with pulpit vacancies; and (c) the "seminary," now located in the manor house of a Russian nobleman, had opened its doors in September 1925 to twenty-four seminarians, who in due course would be prepared to take up the ministerial slack in the church. In light of these developments, Morehead was happy to announce that the National Lutheran Council had provided $5,000 for the seminary and that German church sources had supplied another $1,100. In addition, an American layman had given $5,000 to

37. Ibid., Exhibit VI, Malmgren to Morehead, April 17, 1925.

the cause. This, of course, was not enough; at least $50,000 was required annually for Russian relief. Therefore, the story needed to be told to all churches participating in the Lutheran World Convention. Morehead's continuing caveat was: Send money through Soviet-approved channels (e.g., *die deutsche Bank*), not directly to Malmgren or Meyer, lest they be judged as having ties to the West. So the task must be undertaken "with great care."[38]

The executive committee's activity regarding the Russian question remained relatively unchanged through the Copenhagen assembly (1929). As noted earlier, Stalin was able to exercise sole dictatorial power by 1929, and that meant increased distress for the churches. Nevertheless, the Lutheran World Convention had sent $133,237 to Russia, almost $128,000 of which had come from American Lutherans.[39] A discernible plateau in the "Russian story" occurred between 1929 and 1931, but the early 1930s witnessed some dramatic events in connection with the colony of Harbin refugees en route from Manchuria to South America. We shall return to this episode in the post-Copenhagen narrative that will engage our attention in the next chapter.

5. Publicity and Information

In the 1920s, Madison Avenue had not yet become the synonym for sophisticated public-relations techniques, both blatant and subtle. Despite the relative naiveté of the churches, the experience of the Americans, especially those who, like Otto H. Pannkoke, had been actively engaged in the former Lutheran Bureau (1917), brought about an awareness of the need for effective publicity in promoting church-wide causes.[40] This was not lost on those who were now seeking to raise the churches' consciousness of their far-flung opportunities and

38. "An die Mitglieder des Exekutivkomitees . . . Den Haag, Holland, 9.–13. November 1925" (sent out by acting secretary Jørgensen [von Pechmann was ill] November 21, 1925), pp. 1, 3–4, Boe Papers, box 101, folder 10.

39. Wadensjö, *Toward a World Lutheran Communion*, p. 190. The author points out that Swedish contributions were funneled through the Gustavus Adolphus Union rather than through the LWC. According to Wadensjö, the former was more "ecumenical" and as such resented by the Americans (Morehead and Boe), who wanted the Russian Lutherans to know that help was coming from their "confessional" brethren in the West.

40. Frederick K. Wentz, *Lutherans in Concert* (Minneapolis: Augsburg Publishing House, 1968), pp. 9–10. Cf. Otto H. Pannkoke, *A Great Church Finds Itself* (published by the author, 1966), pp. 63–77.

responsibilities through the Lutheran World Convention. Throughout its short history the executive committee had enjoyed some promotional success by the use of news releases, articles in church papers, and extensive correspondence.[41] At The Hague meeting (1925) of the executive committee, consideration was given to the publication of a Lutheran world journal, but estimated costs in money and personnel placed this project out of reach. The proposal, however, was reactivated following World War II in the establishment of the *Lutheran World/Lutherische Rundschau* as the official organ of world Lutheranism.[42]

The need for information and publicity about world Lutheranism was faced at the Dresden (1926) meeting of the executive committee, at which it was decided to publish a handbook on global Lutheranism. The intention was twofold: to provide accurate data on Lutheran churches around the world and to reflect the growing solidarity of global Lutheranism. The handbook was to be ready for distribution at the next assembly of the convention and was to be printed in German and English.[43] An editorial committee, reflecting the three "centers" of world Lutheranism, was appointed. Included in the troika were Alfred Th. Jørgensen of Copenhagen as the general editor, Abdel Ross Wentz of Gettysburg, and Werner Elert of Erlangen. When Elert declined, Paul Fleisch, Oberkirchenrat from Hannover, replaced him. Almost one hundred churchmen in Europe and America assisted the board of editors in providing data and articles for the handbook. Wentz's American committee consisted of Carl A. Mellby, St. Olaf College, Northfield, Minnesota; A. T. Lundholm, Augustana College and Seminary, Rock Island, Illinois; and P. H. Buehring, Capital University, Columbus, Ohio. Other Americans were added

---

41. Morehead, for example, wrote to President Herbert Hoover, inviting him to send greetings to the LWC (Morehead to Herbert Hoover, May 13, 1929, in ArCL). Morehead had become acquainted with Hoover in 1921 when the latter was chief of the American Relief Association, through whose good offices Morehead had first gained entry to Russia. The White House replied that the President sent greetings only to international groups in which the government was officially represented. See also Samuel Trexler, *John A. Morehead* (New York: G. P. Putnam's Sons, 1938), pp. 81, 88–89.

42. The journal continued until 1977, when rising costs and other considerations brought about its demise.

43. "Protokoll . . . Sitzung des Fortsetzungskomitees des luth. Weltkomitees in Dresden 1.–7. Juli, 1926," p. 9, Boe Papers, box 101, folder 10.

as the project developed. The book that emerged, the first in a series from 1929 to 1977, bore the title *The Lutheran Churches of the World*.[44]

6. The Ecumenical Issue

From the very first, the Lutheran World Convention was occupied with the ecumenical question vis-à-vis Roman Catholicism on the one hand and non-Lutheran Protestantism on the other. Two of the main lecturers (Ihmels and Knubel) at Eisenach had argued that Lutheranism at its heart was ecumenical and that it was under obligation to manifest its given unity before the world. From that time to the present, world Lutheranism has struggled with the question of evangelical identity within the church catholic.

With regard to Roman Catholicism, the Lutheran church and other Protestants feared the political power of institutional Romanism. Moreover, Lutherans clung tenaciously to their conviction that Luther had placed his finger on the great heresy of Rome: the pope and the hierarchy had suppressed the evangel. The events of the nineteenth and early twentieth centuries served only to undergird the suspicions of Rome's political machinations and theological arrogance implicit in the promulgation of papal infallibility. It is no surprise, therefore, that in the pre–Vatican II years of the 1920s and 1930s Lutherans feared the effects of the aggressive publicity that issued from the Vatican, and warned leaders to be alert to the activity of the papal diplomats. The best strategy in these circumstances, it was reasoned, was to tell Lutherans around the world that "the Roman menace" was genuine. At The Hague meeting of the executive committee (1925), for example, reports were requested as to what measures the churches were employing to combat Catholic aggression.[45] The frequent references in

44. See "The Origin and Purpose of This Book," *The Lutheran Churches of the World*, ed. Alfred Th. Jørgensen, Paul Fleisch, and Abdel Ross Wentz (Minneapolis: Augsburg Publishing House 1929[?]), pp. 11–15. Cf. *The Lutheran World Almanac and Encyclopedia 1927–1928* (New York: NLC, 1927), p. 22. Cf. also Morehead to Werner Elert, August 12, 1926; and Morehead to Wentz, January 8, 1927, in ArCL.

45. "Sitzung des Exekutivkomitees . . . in Haag, 9.–12. November, 1925," p. 5, Boe Papers, box 101, folder 10.

correspondence and minutes to the Catholic problem indicated that there was very little thought given to cultivation of better relations with the Vatican. To the contrary, Roman Catholicism, like communism and humanism, was reckoned to be the enemy of true Christian faith. Therefore, ecumenism could not include Rome.[46]

The sharp anti-ecumenical stance was only slightly attenuated when it came to cooperation and fellowship with non-Lutheran Protestants. A number of circumstances forced Lutherans to face the ecumenical question and to define a posture that was faithful to the gospel. The world missionary movement, for example, revealed perhaps more than anything else the scandal of Protestant disunity, a situation that was vigorously deplored at the famous World Missionary Conference at Edinburgh in 1910.

Out of the deliberations at Edinburgh grew the International Missionary Council and the Faith and Order movement, both of which pointed to the clear connection between the mission of the church and the reunion of the churches. World War I effectively stopped this ecumenical thrust, but by 1919 the movement received a fresh impetus from the World Alliance for Promoting International Friendship Through the Churches meeting in Oud Wassenaar, Holland. One of the leading personages there was the youthful Nathan Söderblom, later the Lutheran archbishop of Uppsala. It was he who became the most conspicuous champion of a world conference on moral and social questions. Under his guidance the Universal Christian Conference on Life and Work (as distinguished from "Faith and Order") was held in Stockholm during August 1925. Two years later, while the Life and Work movement was gaining strength, a parallel ecumenical group, represented by the World Conference on Faith and Order, met at Lausanne, Switzerland. It should be noted that the Life and Work movement had arisen directly out of a moral revulsion to the passions of World War I and a yearning for peace and social justice.

---

46. World Lutherans were no different from "Protestant" Americans, whose anti-Romanism flourished during the nineteenth century. Although Catholics did achieve public offices on the municipal and state levels in many areas of the United States, Catholic Alfred E. Smith was roundly defeated for the presidency in 1928. More than thirty years were to intervene before a Catholic was elected to the nation's highest office.

Faith and Order, on the other hand, devoted its attentions to problems of doctrine and polity that separated the churches. These two movements ultimately flowed into the World Council of Churches in 1948.[47]

These developments on the ecumenical scene compelled Lutherans to reassess their traditional position on involvement with non-Lutherans. There were some Lutheran ecumenists who frowned on the "confessional isolation" of Lutherans and saw the Lutheran World Convention as an obstacle to Christian unity; others were committed to participation in the ecumenical movement while simultaneously cultivating a Lutheran consciousness; still others interpreted ecumenism in the light of "unionism" on the order of the Prussian Union and therefore saw it as a weakening of the witness to the gospel and consequently as an enemy of Christian unity. World Lutheranism, therefore, was serious about the Protestant ecumenical movement. American Lutherans by and large had very little contact with "pan-Protestantism." The only group prior to 1918 which had formal relations with the Federal Council of Churches of Christ (U.S.A.) was the General Synod, a body that ceased to exist when it merged into the United Lutheran Church in America (1918).[48]

In Germany both the General Evangelical Lutheran Conference (AELK) and the Lutheran League (*Lutherischer Bund*) were advocates of Lutheran confessionality, in contrast to the kind of ecumenism represented by the Prussian Union churches. The AELK was more "ecumenically minded" than the Lutheran League. Some of the leading figures (Ihmels and von Pechmann) of the AELK participated in interchurch conferences, for example, Söderblom's Life and Work Conference in Stockholm in 1925. Unlike the members of the Lutheran League, they favored admission of Lutherans who were members of the Prussian Union (*Vereinslutheraner*) into the AELK and the

47. For details see Ruth Rouse and Stephen C. Neill, eds., *A History of the Ecumenical Movement 1517–1948*, 2d ed. (Philadelphia: Westminster Press, 1967). Cf. G. K. A. Bell, *The Kingship of Christ: The Story of the World Council of Churches* (Harmondsworth, Middlesex: Penguin Books, 1954).

48. See Fred W. Meuser, "Facing the Twentieth Century, 1900–1930," in E. Clifford Nelson, ed., *The Lutherans in North America* (Philadelphia: Fortress Press, 1975), p. 387. The ULCA in 1922 rejected membership in the Federal Council of Churches but voted a "consultative affiliation" that permitted voice but no vote. Ibid., p. 440.

Lutheran World Convention. As a matter of fact, this attitude had caused the withdrawal of many participants to form the Lutheran League in 1908.[49]

In Scandinavia, particularly in Sweden and Denmark, the threshold of Lutheran confessional consciousness was not as high as in Germany and America. For one thing, there were state churches (they preferred to call themselves "folk churches") which, unlike German Lutheran churches, had not faced an internal problem such as that posed by the Prussian Union. Unlike the American Lutherans, they were spared the difficulty of maintaining a Lutheran identity within a religious pluralism. Moreover, the relative homogeneous national and cultural character of Scandinavian Lutheranism made the internal theological and ethnic struggle of American Lutherans virtually incomprehensible to them. It was not strange that the Lutheran World Convention had a major task in reconciling the disparate attitudes toward the ecumenical movement and in adopting a posture that would be both Lutheran and ecumenical.[50]

At least two major events focused attention on the issue. In 1922 the Federal Council of the Churches of Christ in America and the Swiss Evangelical Church Federation had sponsored a conference on European relief at Copenhagen, the so-called Bethesda Conference.[51] The participants formed the European Central Bureau for Inter-Church Aid (*Die Europäische Zentralstelle für kirchliche Hilfsaktionen*), with offices in Zurich. As already noted, the Eisenach assembly (1923) took cognizance of the *Zentralstelle*, but urged its participating churches to funnel their contributions through the recently created Lutheran relief agency. However, efforts were made to coordinate their actions with the Zurich Central Bureau.[52]

More significant for Lutherans was the Universal Christian Conference on Life and Work (Stockholm, 1925). The intention of Stockholm, according to Söderblom and other leaders, was not to denigrate Faith

49. Paul Fleisch, *Für Kirche und Bekenntnis. Geschichte der Allgemeinen Evangelisch-Lutherischen Konferenz* (Berlin: Lutherisches Verlagshaus, 1956), pp. 55–59.
50. It was not until 1936 that the executive committee adopted a well-worked-out statement on ecumenism prepared by Abdel Ross Wentz and the executive secretary, Hanns Lilje. "Lutherans and Ecumenical Movements," *Lutheran World Almanac . . . 1934–1937*, pp. 36–38.
51. See above, Chapter 5.
52. See above, Chapter 6.

and Order, whose goal of theological and ecclesiastical unity, though praiseworthy, was admittedly distant. The aim of Stockholm would be "to apply Christian principles to burning social and international problems." It was felt that Christian churches of divergent theological traditions could cooperate in the arena of social ethics and international issues. To this end the official invitation said: "We hope . . . to be able to formulate programmes and devise means for making them effective, whereby the *fatherhood of God and the brotherhood of all peoples* will become more completely realized."[53] It was precisely the wording of the invitation and the intention to avoid theological discussion that raised a warning flag to many Lutherans. Adolf von Harnack, the son of conservative Lutheran Theodosius Harnack but a disciple of Albrecht Ritschl, had left classical Lutheranism to become the leader of a magisterial liberalism that reigned in Berlin at the turn of the century. His famous book, *Das Wesen des Christentums* (1900), had reduced the New Testament "gospel" to a message about the religion Jesus believed and practiced. Its tenets were the fatherhood of God, the divine sonship of man, and the infinite value of the human soul.[54]

To have the familiar phrases of liberalism incorporated into the Stockholm invitation, whether its authors were liberals or not, was deeply disturbing to some members of the Lutheran World Convention and its executive committee. Söderblom's assurances—that the absence of theological questions did not imply that they were of secondary importance—could not persuade Morehead to accept an invitation to represent the Lutheran World Convention at Stockholm. Nevertheless, individual committee members—Ihmels, von Pechmann, and Jørgensen—were in attendance.[55] Other Scandinavians and Germans were of course also present, as were a few American Lutherans. Prominent among the Germans was jurist Hermann Kapler, one of the lay leaders of the Prussian Union church. The ecumenical movement ascribes the phrase "Doctrine divides, but

53. Rouse and Neill, *History of the Ecumenical Movement*, pp. 540–42.
54. Adolf von Harnack, *What Is Christianity?* (New York: Harper & Brothers, 1957), p. 68. Cf. Anders Nygren, *Agape and Eros* (London: SPCK, 1953), p. 135. Nygren says that Harnack interpreted the New Testament word *agape* as "love of neighbor," thus reducing religion to "plain, unvarnished morality."
55. Wadensjö, *Toward a World Lutheran Communion*, p. 252.

service unites" to Kapler. If accurate, this reflected his rather superficial theological outlook and his allegiance to the Ritschl-Harnack school. When this aphorism was picked up by American as well as European liberals ("deeds not creeds"), it hardly endeared him to Lutherans who tended to equate the ecumenical movement with theological irresponsibility.[56]

Among the Germans at Stockholm, Söderblom considered Ihmels his "greatest prize." Despite the ecumenical hesitation of Lutherans, Ihmels had been persuaded by his friend Söderblom's disarming argument that "the Stockholm Conference must [have] a consciously Lutheran voice." Söderblom rewarded Ihmels by asking him to deliver one of the two keynote addresses.

Despite Söderblom's assurances that Stockholm would avoid theological debate by concentrating on social ethics, the divergences were quickly apparent. Bishop F. T. Woods (England) sounded the Ritschlian-Harnackian affirmation of the kingdom of God as ethical rather than eschatological, a prominent theme among both English and American liberal Protestants. Its utterance in the 1920s lay at the root of much of the American Lutheran objection to the ecumenical movement. Ihmels challenged the presuppositions of the previous speaker by saying, "Nothing could be more mistaken or more disastrous than to suppose that we mortal men have to build up God's kingdom in the world."[57] Ever since Ritschl, liberals had subordinated the doctrine of justification to the motif of an ethical kingdom of God,

---

56. Rouse and Neill, *History of the Ecumenical Movement*, p. 540. Kapler's later role in the Nazi era was something less than impressive. Wilhelm Brandt, *Friedrich von Bodelschwingh, 1877–1946. Nachfolger und Gestalter* (Bethel bei Bielefeld: Verlagshandlung der Anstalt Bethel, 1967), p. 123. The famous von Bodelschwingh described Kapler in 1933 as an "old and tired man . . . a simple man who was unable to stand up to the Nazis; he was no church leader." Cf. Friedrich von Bodelschwingh, "Dreissig Tage an einer Wegwende deutscher Kirchengeschichte," pp. 7–8, in Bethel Archiv, Bethel bei Bielefeld, Germany.

57. Rouse and Neill, *History of the Ecumenical Movement*, p. 547. Von Bodelschwingh, who was also present at Stockholm, maintained that Söderblom himself was confused about the nature of the kingdom of God, a mistake that was rooted in failure to make Luther's distinction between the "two realms" of God's activity on earth. See Brandt, "Stockholmer Konferenz," in *Von Bodelschwingh*, pp. 88–90. Ihmels, incidentally, absented himself for theological reasons from the Holy Communion service to which all conference participants were invited. See Bengt Sundkler, *Nathan Söderblom: His Life and Work* (Lund: Gleerups, 1968), p. 371, n. 1.

which they declared was the central teaching of the New Testament. The tension between the two views, ethical and eschatological, came to dominate much of the discussion at Stockholm, and because the theological issue was allegedly avoided, much misunderstanding ensued and colored post-Stockholm evaluations.

One of the hopes for Stockholm had been expressed by the Swedish king in his formal welcome. He referred to it as "The Nicaea of Ethics," calling attention to the first ecumenical council of Nicaea (A.D. 325), from which the Nicene Creed emerged.[58] This was a goal which was more extravagant and pretentious than that of the conference's leadership. Nevertheless, later when opponents evaluated Stockholm, they quoted the phrase scornfully and pejoratively. For example, John O. Evjen, professor in a ULCA college, wrote that although Söderblom was inoffensively ostentatious, "his Stockholm Conference was too ambitious, that *ethical Nice* [*sic*] *of the North*, in its aims and principles [was] closer to Zwingli than to Luther [italics added]."[59]

What was the reaction of the American members of the executive committee to the Stockholm conference? In the first place, Morehead wrote that participation by the executive committee *qua* executive committee would be unwise because it would bring about division among Lutherans and thus provide one more obstacle to the realization of Lutheran unity. Moreover, any officially authorized statement for presentation of "the Lutheran position" by the executive committee would understandably be resented by the leaders of the conference.[60] However, there could be no objection to individual participation in the conference by members of the executive committee. Neither these nor other Lutheran participants would represent the Lutheran World Convention.

As a result of Ihmels's participation in the Stockholm conference, one thorny issue emerged. Conservatives in Europe and America ascribed to him "guilt by association." They could hardly criticize the content of his address, because it had been a strong Lutheran state-

---

58. Rouse and Neill, *History of the Ecumenical Movement*, p. 550.
59. Evjen to Boe, November 27, 1940, Boe Papers, box 81, folder 9.
60. Morehead to Erich Stange, April 30, 1924, in ArCL.

ment. Nevertheless, in this situation Ihmels was asked by the executive committee to make a personal evaluation of the conference for presentation to The Hague meeting (1925). This he did orally, informally, and disappointingly, resulting in the committee's request that he prepare and publish a report as his personal assessment of Stockholm. Ihmels agreed to do this.[61]

The following month, both Morehead and Boe received copies of Ihmels's written evaluation, which he wished to publish as soon as possible under the title "Unsere Stellung zum Stockholmer Weltkonvent" (Our Position Regarding the Stockholm World Conference), along with the explanatory note that it was authorized for publication by the executive committee.[62] Morehead conferred with Boe; the two agreed that Ihmels's report was a personal statement and therefore must not be published as if authorized by the executive committee. That would make the "Committee officially responsible for what the Bishop says . . . and will mean taking a definite position with reference to the Stockholm Conference." There was no objection to Ihmels's publishing his own views—in fact, the committee at The Hague had urged this—but the imprimatur of the executive committee would invite attacks from all quarters, not least from those who were already critical of the Lutheran World Convention. A radiogram was sent to Ihmels requesting him to withhold publication until he received a follow-up letter.[63] Ihmels cabled back that he too would be sending a letter explaining why he had gone ahead and published the article. By December 22 the letter had not yet arrived, so Morehead, in order to protect the executive committee, sent a second cable: "Hope you did not publish article as being authorized by Executive Committee."[64] But the damage had been done; the article appeared in the official organ of the AELK.[65] Why Ihmels acted in haste is not known, but apparently his decision was precipitated by rising criticism from within his own circles in Germany. It was not surprising that Morehead and Boe were upset and considered a public refutation of Ihmels.

61. "Sitzung des Exekutivkomittees . . . in Haag . . . 9.–12. November, 1925," p. 6, Boe Papers, box 101, folder 10.
62. Ihmels to Morehead, December 1, 1925, Boe Papers, box 98, folder 7.
63. Morehead to Boe, December 16, 1925, Boe Papers, box 98, folder 7.
64. Morehead to Boe, December 22, 1925, Boe Papers, box 98, folder 7.
65. *Allgemeine Evangelisch-Lutherische Kirchenzeitung,* 1925, col. 977–981.

Fortunately, this became unnecessary when Ihmels's statement went unnoticed in the American Lutheran press.[66]

Was the nervous American reaction to the Ihmels-Stockholm affair merely a tempest in a teapot? In view of how it turned out, the answer is yes. Nonetheless, the Stockholm conference evoked a wide-ranging controversy, even beyond Lutheranism, on both sides of the Atlantic and in Asia. Stockholm was especially awkward for Lutherans. For one thing, Söderblom, the founding father and guiding spirit of Life and Work, was perhaps the best-known Lutheran in the world. It was difficult to turn against him, not least because he had urged Lutherans to be present so that Stockholm would not be deprived of hearing a strong Lutheran voice on the critical political and social issues of the day.

It was just at this point—"the Lutheran voice"—that the difficulties arose. Instead of one voice, there seemed to be at least three, two of which gave "an uncertain sound" with regard to the basic theological issue: Luther's teaching regarding the "two realms" of God's gracious action in the world. At Stockholm the problem surfaced not in traditionally Lutheran terminology ("the two kingdoms") but in two quite different interpretations of the New Testament phrase "the kingdom of God." As pointed out above, liberal English and American Protestants tended to think of the kingdom of God in Ritschlian terms. Nathan Söderblom, the hospitable host, had a capacious theological mind in which he sought to embrace and blend Lutheranism, pietism, history of religions (*Religionsgeschichte*), and Ritschlianism. At Stockholm he seemed to view "the kingdom of God" in ethical, this-worldly terms (the Americans' phrase was "Social Gospel").[67] Thus, it seemed

66. Morehead to Boe, March 4, 1926, Boe Papers, box 98, folder 8. On March 3, 1926, Morehead wrote to Ihmels a step-by-step account of the whole "Ihmels-Stockholm" matter, with special reference to unfavorable reactions to Stockholm from Johan C. K. Preus (NLCA), Friedrich Richter, and J. Michael Reu (Iowa Synod). Since the Ohio, Iowa, and Buffalo synods were planning a merger, it was important that nothing be done to deter the new body (the American Lutheran Church, 1930) from affiliating with the LWC.

67. One of the Germans, Friedrich von Bodelschwingh of Bethel, whose life was immersed in a ministry of social welfare, remarked that Söderblom's opening sermon ended with a quotation from a well-known Swedish hymn, the text of which was in the hands of the worshipers. In Söderblom's impulsive way, said von Bodelschwingh, he changed the last line, the original of which was an address to the Lord as the only "way out of the disquiet of this poor world," so that it read, "Make our world new!" Brandt, *Friedrich von Bodelschwingh*, pp. 89–90.

to some in the audience that he was lending his voice to a "kingdom of God" theology bereft of eschatological dimensions.

The second "voice" in the Lutheran reaction to Stockholm was that of traditional and conventional Lutheran theology, which understood the "kingdom of God" solely in eschatological, otherworldly terms. The objections of many pietistically oriented and orthodox German, Scandinavian, and American Lutherans were centered on this misconception. The weakness of their view was that they did not know or failed to understand Luther's theologically undergirded social ethics, his teaching of "God's kingdom of the left hand," focusing on law, justice, peace—what he called "civil righteousness"—in contrast to the "spiritual righteousness" wrought by faith in the gospel of gracious forgiveness. The latter was God's "proper work" to bring humankind into fellowship with God. His other work ("civil righteousness") was certainly not "improper"; in fact, it was absolutely necessary if the world was to stand. But Luther called it God's *opus alienum*, "strange work," an activity strangely different from the justification of the ungodly by grace through faith. Though "strange," it was still a witness to God's loving kingly rule of the world.

The third "voice" was that of Ihmels, who seemed to stand alone at Stockholm in his understanding and articulation of this locus of Luther's theology. In the debate that occurred in America, the reaction of conservatives like Friedrich Richter and J. Michael Reu (Iowa), Johan C. K. Preus (Norwegian), and Carl C. Hein (Ohio) was to be expected. Somewhat surprising was the attitude of Morehead and Boe, who likewise were critical of Stockholm. Whether they failed to grasp the theological issue at stake ("the kingdom on the left") cannot be readily determined, but what is clear is that both men feared that were they to support the Stockholm conference the movement toward American Lutheran unity would be hindered and the already fragile allegiance to the Lutheran World Convention would be attenuated.

In some ways, the storm surrounding Stockholm was but an extension of basic differences between Reformed (also Roman Catholic) and Lutheran theology. It was also a harbinger of the conflict between the post–World War II Barthian teaching regarding the "lordship of Christ" and Neo-Lutheranism's fidelity to Luther's dialectic. It was not strange that the Lutheran World Convention had a major task in reconciling the divergent attitudes toward the ecumenical move-ment.[68]

7. Planning the Second Assembly
of the Lutheran World Convention

The executive committee was often referred to as the continuation committee because of the Eisenach mandate to plan for the next Lutheran world gathering. The executive committee's early agendas show that this item quickly became a major priority. At the 1925 meeting in The Hague, the executive committee set 1929 as the year for the second world assembly. Some inconclusive discussion relative to the place occurred. Apparently the suggestion had been made that the United States be the site of the 1929 conclave, but Morehead and Boe were not prepared to extend an invitation. Therefore, the commit-tee postponed the decision of place and exact dates to its next meeting in Dresden in 1926.[69]

When the committee assembled at Dresden, Jørgensen returned to the question of the 1929 meeting place by tactfully asking the Americans if they were planning to extend an invitation to the United States. Boe replied that should the world conference be held in America it would surely exacerbate the tensions and divisions within American Lutheranism. These circumstances dictated that the conven-tion be held in Europe. Morehead added that the economic situation also foreclosed an American invitation, whereupon Jørgensen an-nounced that he was authorized to invite the convention to Copenha-gen. Von Pechmann proposed Vienna or Budapest, but his compatriot Ihmels spoke in favor of Copenhagen. The committee then voted

68. "Liberation theology" in the 1970s would be viewed affirmatively by some liberals, Barthians, and Catholics on the one hand, and Lutherans on the other—but for different theological reasons.

69. "Sitzung des Exekutivkomittees . . . in Haag . . . 9.–12. November, 1925," pp. 9, 11, Boe Papers, box 101, folder 10. The Americans expressed their wish that the executive committee might meet in America prior to the 1929 assembly. For a variety of reasons, this did not occur until 1936. Ihmels reported to von Pechmann, who was unable to be at The Hague because of illness (he was also angry that the committee was meeting in Holland rather than Germany), that it was surprising that the Americans showed no eagerness to be hosts for the next world convention. Ihmels himself preferred Germany, but knowing that that was impossible he suggested Budapest or Stockholm. Jørgensen, he said, had strongly proposed Copenhagen; he (Ihmels) predicted that the committee would agree with Jørgensen. Ihmels to von Pechmann, November 16, 1925, in Archiv der Landeskirche Bayerns in Nuremberg, Germany, Pers. XXIII, no. 20.

unanimously to accept the Danish invitation.[70] The precise dates would be determined later, but preferences were expressed for the last half of June or the end of August and early September 1929.

A tentative program—emphasizing Christian education in light of the quadricentennial of Luther's catechisms (1529), and evangelical faith in light of the Marburg Colloquy (1529) and the Augsburg Confession (1530)—was adopted. Provision was made for a continuation of the Eisenach emphasis on Lutheran unity and the ecumenical movement. Three commissions were to be appointed to make studies of the Lutheran attitude toward social and political issues (no doubt a response to the Stockholm Conference on Life and Work), the role of foreign missions, and the continuing ministry to the Lutheran diaspora. As noted earlier, the Dresden meeting also took steps to prepare a "Handbook on World Lutheranism," which was to be published in time for the Copenhagen assembly.

A noteworthy celebration took place toward the close of the sessions in Dresden. Despite some evidences to the contrary, the Germans wished to show their high regard for the Americans. Consequently, a special service was held on the Fourth of July (a Sunday) to express their affection and to announce that Germany's economic recovery made it unnecessary henceforth to depend on American Lutheran largesse. The work of the National Lutheran Council in Germany could now officially end. In this manner a celebration of America's national "birthday" was combined with a thanksgiving service "for the fellowship that exists between the Lutherans of America and the Lutherans in Germany." Special recognition was voiced by the Germans for the work of the late Lauritz Larsen and the present leadership of John A. Morehead. It was a congenial note on which to end the deliberations at Dresden.

70. "Protokoll für die Sitzung . . . in Dresden 30. Juni–7. Juli, 1926," pp. 6–7, Boe Papers, box 101, folder 10. Boe raised the question of delegates. Should the assembly be open to others than official representatives? No doubt many Americans would plan to tour Scandinavia and Germany before or after the convention. (This observation was prophetic of what actually occurred at Copenhagen in 1929 and after World War II, when the eagerness of Americans to see the "Old Country" grew in leaps and bounds. Hundreds of Americans were present at Lund [1947] and especially at Hannover [1952].) Acting on Boe's proposal, Dresden decided to establish three categories of meetings: (1) for delegates alone, (2) for delegates and convention guests with admission cards, and (3) events open to the public. Ibid., p. 8.

In keeping with a decision reached at The Hague (1925) to conduct "deputations" to minority churches, Dresden commissioned Morehead, Boe, and Jørgensen to visit Lutheran church leaders in Hungary, Yugoslavia, Austria, and France. The purpose of this and other visits was twofold: to give the moral support of world Lutheranism to small and isolated churches, and to obtain accurate ecclesiastical, economic, and political information that could be relayed to the rest of the churches and to the public at large.[71] The "deputation" work was significant not only as a gesture by world Lutheranism to its diaspora minorities but also because it unfortunately provided an occasion for reviving tensions between Americans and Germans. We shall see shortly how this almost got out of hand between 1927 and 1929.

The executive committee met at Prague and Budapest in the autumn of 1927 and at Copenhagen in June 1928.[72] What had previously been agreed on in broad terms soon developed into a discussion of details pertaining to the program. The inevitably related and intertwined problems of nationalistic pride, the fragility of relationships within American Lutheranism, and the persisting tension between confessionalism and ecumenism—all these demanded from the executive committee a high degree of sagacity and patience.

Actually, the decisions regarding the convention's "external" matters were reached without clash. Of the two Dresden suggestions regarding the time of the convention, the June–July period was selected (actual dates were June 26 to July 4, 1929). There was also unanimity about the general topics to be discussed. The presentations were to focus on six areas of concern: Lutheran particularity (including Luther's catechisms, Marburg, Augsburg, and the transmission of the tradition), Lutheran unity and ecumenicity, inner renewal of the church, church and society (three lectures), ministry to the Lutheran diaspora, foreign missions, and the future organization of the Lutheran

71. Ibid., p. 8. Cf. the English summary of minutes, "Fourth Regular Meeting of the Executive Committee . . . Dresden, June 30 to July 6, 1926" and "Report . . . to the Large Committee for the Period from August, 1923, to July, 1926," pp. 2–5, in LWF Archives, Geneva, Switzerland. See also "The Lutheran World Convention," in *Lutheran World Almanac . . . 1927–1928*, pp. 21–22.

72. See especially "Protokoll . . . in Prag und in Budapest, 24. Oktober–1. November, 1927," in ArCL. The Copenhagen meeting (1928) was chiefly devoted to last-minute arrangements; the main decisions for the second assembly were made at Budapest and by the exchange of letters between 1927 and 1929.

World Convention. Although lecturers were not named, the committee adopted a formula that sought an equal distribution of speakers: one-, fourth from the churches of Scandinavia, one-fourth from Germany, one-fourth from America, one-fourth from "others." The latter were eventually drawn from the "minority churches" in Europe and Asia.[73]

The irenic spirit that prevailed at Dresden and Budapest failed to extend into the last eighteen months prior to Copenhagen. The selection of speakers of necessity became a matter of communication between Morehead, as committee chairman, and church leaders in Europe and America. Sharp differences—nationalistic, ecclesiastical, and theological—presented occasions for friction which up to the final weeks threatened to undo the years of labor which had been invested in promoting Lutheran unity at the global level.

The first of several events centered around the sensitivities of Wilhelm von Pechmann, who tended to see an anti-German plot being hatched by Americans on the one hand and Germany's wartime enemies in Europe on the other hand. This feeling had already manifested itself at Eisenach and at meetings of the executive committee. For example, von Pechmann had suspected anti-German sentiments in the decision to meet in Holland (1925) rather than in Germany. Despite Morehead's vigorous disclaimer ("The idea is just as laughable as it is untrue"),[74] the notion died hard, especially in connection with the committee's decision to send "deputations" to minority churches. A case in point was the fact-finding trip to Poland during the days after the Budapest meeting (1927). The entire committee was scheduled to make the journey, but von Pechmann refused to go because he regarded a visit to the Polish bishop Julius Bursche as an act of disloyalty to Germany. Bursche, although of German descent, had cast his lot with the post–World War I nationalism in Poland and hence was regarded by some churchmen in Germany as a "Judas Iscariot" and "the gravedigger" of all things German, including the traditional German connection to Lutheranism in Poland.

Although Ihmels sympathized with von Pechmann, he was willing to accompany the committee to Poland. Morehead's report to Boe

---

73. Ibid., pp. 3–5.
74. Morehead to Ihmels, September 19, 1925, in ArCL.

(who was absent because of illness) described Ihmels at the Warsaw meeting:

> Imagine if you can, Bishop Ihmels sitting between me and General Superintendent [Bishop] Bursche at a conference table with Polish and German-speaking pastors . . . , members of the Lutheran Theological Faculty at Warsaw, and leading laymen of both races. . . ! I feel sure that Bishop Ihmels will have his own troubles about being led into such a situation when he gets back to Germany! But we made a point of giving Bursche an opportunity of presenting his case for Lutheranism in Poland with complete loyalty to the government in the presence of Bishop Ihmels. The latter was much impressed and I do not see how he can ever view Polish church affairs again in the prejudiced German way.[75]

Ihmels did indeed change his mind, but von Pechmann remained intransigent. More and more he perceived the American Lutherans as a threat to German leadership. This notion was given support by what can be called *l'affaire Schneider*. Von Pechmann had been informed that Carl Schneider, a German exchange teacher of theology at Wittenberg University in Springfield, Ohio, had evidence that American Lutherans were convinced that they must "Lutheranize the world" and assume the role of "interpreter to the world of the principles of the Reformation." Schneider, who by one account had "a sharp eye" for the "dark side of American Lutheranism," would be at the Copenhagen assembly in 1929 and would provide von Pechmann with details about "American hyper-Lutheranism" (*Überluthertum*).[76]

The situation became acute in 1928, when von Pechmann learned that Bursche had been proposed as one of the lecturers at Copenhagen. This was more than he could stand. He shot off a letter to

75. Morehead to Boe, November 26, 1927, Boe Papers, box 98, folder 13.
76. Schneider had read an address delivered by Henry Eyster Jacobs on the occasion of the fiftieth anniversary of the Susquehanna Synod in May 1917. Delivered during the height of wartime patriotic fever (America had entered the war in April 1917), this address, read out of context, could indeed be seen by Germans as an exhibition of American chauvinism. See Henry Eyster Jacobs, *The Attitude of the Lutheran Church of America in the Present World Crisis* (Philadelphia: Susquehanna Synod, 1917). Cf. "Proceedings of the . . . Susquehanna Synod . . . May 8–11, 1917," p. 38. The address and the proceedings are available at the Krauth Memorial Library, Lutheran Theological Seminary, Philadelphia, Pennsylvania. Von Pechmann's informants were Hermann Kapler, president of the German Protestant Church Committee, and Franz Rendtorff, head of the Gustavus Adolphus Union. Both men reflected the attitude of the Prussian Union: They were enthusiastic about German Protestantism but cool toward a united Lutheranism. Von Pechmann's correspondence with these men is available at the Archiv der Landeskirche Bayerns, Nuremberg, Germany, Pers. XXIII, No. 22.

Morehead describing Bursche as the most hostile of "the anti-German Poles." Morehead's carefully reasoned reply argued that from the beginning the Lutheran World Convention had sought to exclude political and nationalistic elements from its decisions. Moreover, it would be untenable policy to require that Lutheran speakers from other lands be politically acceptable to the Germans.[77] Morehead relayed this exchange to Boe and said, "I hope you feel as I do that we must stand our ground against nationalism even if it blows up the entire works."[78] The "blowup" very nearly occurred when Morehead's several letters failed to alter von Pechmann's attitude. In a burst of discontent, the baron suggested that Germans should not even participate in the Copenhagen convention. Then, as if to underscore his views, he peremptorily submitted his resignation from the executive committee.[79]

When Morehead's considerable persuasive powers had been seemingly exhausted, Boe took it upon himself to write a long letter to von Pechmann. Without referring to the nationalistic issue per se, he admitted that Americans may have been less than sensitive to what had happened in wartime Europe. Nevertheless, Eisenach had laid upon von Pechmann and the other members of the executive committee a great responsibility to work together for the good of the whole Lutheran church. "I plead with you to think this matter over . . . and give to us the assurance that you will be with us. . . . I am saying this not as a matter of form, but from the bottom of my heart." Von Pechmann replied at once:

> My dear President,
>   Who can resist a letter like yours! I received it here [Berlin] some twenty minutes ago; I have been reading it just now, and you shall have my answer. . . . I withdraw my resignation. It is quite impossible for me to write more. But I think you don't want to read more.[80]

77. Von Pechmann to Morehead, July 26, 1928; Morehead to von Pechmann, September 18, 1928, in ArCL.
78. Morehead to Boe, September 19, 1928, Boe Papers, box 99, folder 3.
79. Von Pechmann to Morehead, December 11, 1928, in ArCL.
80. Boe to von Pechmann, January 22, 1929; von Pechmann to Boe, February 6, 1929, Boe Papers, box 102, folder 15. Von Pechmann customarily wrote in German; this letter was in English. Ordinarily Boe preferred to have Morehead speak for him. He gladly acknowledged his own secondary role. His jocular comment: "I am the *Klokker*. When Morehead chants, I say Amen." In the Dano-Norwegian liturgy the *Klokker* was a lay assistant who read the opening and closing prayers, led the congregational responses and singing, and said the Amens at baptisms. In this case (the von Pechmann resignation), the roles were reversed; Morehead spoke the Amen.

Although the crisis was transcended for the moment, the issue remained unresolved. In fact, it persisted through the summer of 1929 and surfaced again at the executive committee meeting following the Copenhagen convention. It will be necessary to return to this problem in the next chapter.

The remaining pre-Copenhagen items that threatened to be divisive were also connected with the selection of speakers, and not least with the desire of Morehead and Boe to win the Iowa and Ohio synods for the Lutheran World Convention. These two Midwestern German Lutheran bodies, together with the Buffalo Synod, were making plans in the 1920s for a merger (consummated in 1930 and known as the American Lutheran Church). Boe wrote in confidence to Frederick H. Knubel, president of the United Lutheran Church, that he feared this merger would make trouble for the National Lutheran Council and that therefore something should be done to align the new church body with the National Lutheran Council and the Lutheran World Convention.[81] Boe was no doubt thinking of the on-again, off-again relationships of Iowa and Ohio to other Lutherans. Iowa, for example, had abruptly withdrawn from the National Lutheran Council in 1920 and had never affiliated with the Lutheran World Convention. The chief critic in both instances had been J. Michael Reu. The Joint Synod of Ohio's membership did indeed continue through the 1920s, but criticisms of both the National Lutheran Council and the Lutheran World Convention were frequently voiced by its president, Carl C. Hein, and by Richard C. H. Lenski. Morehead wrote to Boe that he was eager to have Iowa and Ohio "strengthen our hands. . . . [But] will they come out to help . . . or remain quiet in their tents while others do the fighting for positive Christianity?"[82]

The executive committee at Budapest (1927) had agreed that one of the main lectures at Copenhagen should deal with "The Origin and Significance of Luther's Large and Small Catechisms." It was generally agreed that the best-qualified person to present this topic was none other than Iowa's J. Michael Reu. Despite his insistence that the Lutheran World Convention be regarded as "an absolutely free conference"—Boe and Morehead rejected this as an unworkable and

81. Boe to Knubel, December 14, 1925, Boe Papers, box 97, folder 6.
82. Morehead to Boe, January 10, 1928, Boe Papers, box 98, folder 13.

irresponsible free-for-all[83]—it was decided to inform him that he had
been tentatively selected to give this lecture at Copenhagen, provided
the Iowa Synod decided to send an official delegation. It was reasoned
that this "carrot on a stick" approach might very well alter his views on
"free conferences" and even influence the Iowa Synod and the
projected American Lutheran Church to join the Lutheran World
Convention. As expected, Reu was honored by the implication of the
inquiry and replied that he had a "positive" attitude toward the
Lutheran World Convention. However, he said that leading men in the
Iowa Synod (George Fritschel and Friedrich Richter) entertained the
Missouri Synod's definition of a free conference as an unofficial gathering of individuals to debate doctrinal issues. Hence they were strongly
opposed to the Lutheran World Convention. Had he argued for Iowa's
participation, it would have been construed as self-serving ("pleading
for myself a . . . trip to Europe").[84]

Meanwhile, during its 1928 convention the Iowa Synod formally
declared its inability to relate itself officially to the Lutheran World
Convention. Unwilling to cut itself off completely, however, it voted
to send its new president, Gustav A. Fandrey, to Copenhagen as "a
friendly visitor." When informed of this action, Morehead wrote
Fandrey that Eisenach had stipulated that only official delegates could
participate in the program at the second convention. Consequently,
Reu was automatically eliminated from consideration. Fandrey replied that he would resign and appoint Reu in his place, but if
Morehead, as the chief executive, would declare officially that the
Lutheran World Convention was "nothing more than a free conference
. . . *as previously defined by me* . . . , I [Fandrey] will lay this
declaration before our Synodical Board, and ask them to authorize Dr.
Reu's appointment as a regular delegate from our Synod [italics
added]." Morehead, nettled by this seemingly picayune mentality,
wrote to Boe that his frank reply to Fandrey reiterated that it was
impossible for the executive committee to accept the Iowa Synod's—or
any other church body's—definition of a free conference. The position
of the Lutheran World Convention was a matter of public record which

---

83. Boe to Morehead, April 17, 1928, Boe Papers, box 99, folder 2.
84. Reu to Morehead, October 24, 1928, in ArCL.

the Iowa Synod was free to accept or reject. He hoped, of course, that Iowa would send its full quota of three official delegates, including Reu as well as Fandrey. Not long thereafter, Morehead was informed that Iowa's executive board had reversed the synod's earlier decision and had appointed Reu as an official delegate, thus making possible his place on the program. This action, coupled with Carl C. Hein's growing interest in Lutheran cooperation, virtually assured that the new American Lutheran Church would join the Lutheran World Convention.[85]

The executive committee faced yet another problem involving American Lutherans at Copenhagen. This time it was the Norwegian Lutheran Church of America, of which Boe was a prominent but sometimes controversial member. His views on Lutheran unity were opposed by a large segment of the Norwegian-American church, notably the Preus family and those whose sympathies lay with the Missouri Synod. In fact, as his biographer notes, he was a prophet who "stood alone"; "few agreed with him." Boe was deeply distressed by his inability to broaden the views of his brethren. His sense of loneliness never made him sour or bitter, but he felt that Morehead alone understood his plight. In one of his letters to his friend he asked poignantly, "Are we wrong [and] are all the others right?"[86] The moments of loneliness would be quickly forgotten as Boe plunged into the task of cementing the tenuous relationship between his own church body and the Lutheran World Convention.

One of the several topics to be presented at Copenhagen was to deal with the church's role in society ("The Lutheran Conception of the Relation between Christianity and the World"). Boe quickly suggested the name of Gustav M. Bruce, professor of New Testament interpretation and Christian social ethics in the theological seminary (St. Paul, Minn.) of the Norwegian Lutheran Church of America. To Boe's mind,

85. The considerable correspondence on the "Iowa problem" is to be found in the Morehead and Boe papers located in New York (ArCL) and in Northfield, Minnesota (St. Olaf College Archives, boxes 98 and 99) covering the period January to November 1928. For details on the attitudes of the merging Midwestern German synods, see Fred W. Meuser, *The Formation of the American Lutheran Church* (Columbus: Wartburg Press, 1958).

86. Erik Hetle, *Lars Wilhelm Boe: A Biography* (Minneapolis: Augsburg Publishing House, 1949), p. 154. See also Boe to Morehead, April 17, 1928, Boe Papers, box 99, folder 2.

the presence of Bruce before a world gathering of Lutheran churchmen and theologians would provide his own church body with a sense
of pride and would serve to meet the criticism of those opposed to the
Lutheran World Convention. Boe's hopes were realized, and his own
church body remained a vigorous and loyal member of the Lutheran
World Convention and its successor, the Lutheran World Federation.[87]

The final pre-Copenhagen dispute that threatened to be internecine
revolved once again around the role of Nathan Söderblom of Sweden.
It was recognized that Söderblom ought to have a place on the program but that his assignment must not provide him a platform to articu-
late his "evangelical catholicity." Therefore, although he was the most
distinguished churchman in Scandinavia, Söderblom would be given
a relatively insignificant place on the program: a short address of welcome. This decision was a political faux pas of the first magnitude. In
the first place, protocol required that the host to the convention,
Harald Ostenfeld, bishop of Copenhagen and primate of Denmark,
welcome the delegates and guests. In the second place, the decision
betrayed a woeful ignorance of Söderblom's theological convictions
and cultured sense of propriety. The Americans, who feared that
Söderblom's presence would have a negative influence on those
churches that were just beginning to overcome their prejudice against
the Lutheran World Convention, would have done well to circulate
widely Söderblom's 1926 article "Why I Am a Lutheran." This personal confession of faith might have laid to rest at least some of the
criticisms and assisted people to recognize that their images of

---

87. Criticism, not of the LWC but of the appointment of Bruce, quickly surfaced.
Bruce had just published a rather superficial and pedantic book, *Luther as an Educator*
(Minneapolis: Augsburg Publishing House, 1928), which provoked an incisive although
intemperate attack by John O. Evjen, a professor at Wittenberg University, Springfield,
Ohio. The latter wrote several articles in the hard-hitting Norwegian language paper
Reform, published by Waldemar Ager, Eau Claire, Wisconsin. See *Reform* 44 (January 3
through February 7, 1929) in the Archives of the Norwegian-American Historical
Association, St. Olaf College, Northfield, Minnesota. The substance of the critique,
peppered with *ad hominem* remarks, was that Bruce was an incompetent scholar. In
addition, a colleague of Bruce at Luther Seminary wrote that the appointment of Bruce
was ridiculous. "What do you suppose the Germans [scholars] will do with [him] at
Copenhagen?" Boe admitted that Bruce's scholarship was not beyond criticism but that
that hardly made his appointment ridiculous. C. M. Weswig to Boe, January 30, 1929;
Boe to Weswig, January 28, 1929, and February 2, 1929. The correspondence on the
Bruce affair is in Boe Papers, box 97, folders 2 and 12.

Söderblom were largely false.[88] Moreover, those Europeans who like the Americans were suspicious of Söderblom could have been informed that, to the distress of most of his Anglo-American ecumenical friends, Söderblom took the lead in the preparation of a Lutheran "intervention" submitted to the Lausanne Faith and Order Conference in 1927. The "intervention" warned against over-hasty publication of statements of doctrine and polity as "finalities." The dignity of this ecumenical conference, said Söderblom and his Lutheran colleagues, demanded a continuing and thorough discussion of such matters in recognition of the Lutheran confession that "unity consists in agreement concerning the doctrine of the gospel and the administration of the sacraments." Although this Lutheran declaration was no doubt "the first embryo of confessional groupings in the ecumenical movement," it was not brought to the attention of the executive committee of the Lutheran World Convention.[89]

Consequently, because Lutherans generally were uninformed as to Söderblom's essential Lutheranism, he was relegated to a minor role, while his episcopal colleague, Sam Stadener, bishop of Strängnäs, was invited to represent Swedish Lutheranism in a lecture on the topic "What Does Lutheranism Offer as Its Distinctive Gift to Christendom?" When Ostenfeld learned of the affront to Söderblom, he wrote to Morehead and the executive committee:

> Two days ago Dr. Jørgensen . . . told me about the program. . . . I was very much surprised that there was not given Archbishop Söderblom a subject of any importance. . . . It is my opinion that we cannot have a Lutheran convention in Scandinavia when the most prominent Lutheran scholar is left out. . . . I am so sorry that I feel compelled to write to you that it is not possible for me to take part in the convention if this decision is not altered.[90]

In fact, it was reported that Ostenfeld had said he would find it

---

88. Henry Goddard Leach, editor of *The Forum*, had invited several churchmen to contribute personal confessions of faith for publication in this highly respected journal. Söderblom's statement, warmly evangelical Lutheran and catholic, is to be found in *The Forum* 75 (April 1926): 510–17.

89. Sundkler, *Söderblom*, pp. 408–10. This action of Söderblom and Anders Nygren led to similar "confessional" statements by other churches, including the Eastern Orthodox.

90. Ostenfeld to Morehead, September 17, 1928, in ArCl.

convenient during the time of the convention to conduct an episcopal visit in the Danish Faroe Islands and Greenland if the insult to Söderblom were not removed.[91]

The executive committee was now in an extremely difficult position. It was impossible to exchange Söderblom for Stadener because the latter had already been invited. Moreover, the Danish primate was not only the official host to the convention, he was also the chairman of the General Danish Committee on Arrangements. In this situation the role of mediator fell to Jørgensen, chairman of the executive committee of the Danish committee,[92] as well as a member of the LWC's executive committee. He now suggested a compromise worked out by himself and Ostenfeld: Söderblom should be invited to lecture on "Luther as a Christian Personality and His Significance for Northern Europe" at the first session. Ostenfeld would give the formal welcome following his opening sermon in the Cathedral of Our Lady. Morehead submitted the proposal to his colleagues on the executive committee, suggesting that they approve this "happy solution" and keep the entire occurrence "strictly confidential."[93] When approval was given, Jørgensen wrote a report to the members of the executive committee in which he said, "The Söderblom affair is completely settled." As a matter of fact, he said, only a very few people in Scandinavia were aware of what had happened. The proposed solution should provide no difficulties for the committee or for Ostenfeld and Söderblom.[94] Morehead, however, was concerned that the "conservative elements in the Norwegian Lutheran Church, the Joint Synod of Ohio, the Iowa, etc.," would be disgruntled, and asked Boe if he thought it necessary to conduct "a little quiet apologetic" for placing Söderblom in such a prominent place. He himself thought it unnecessary.[95] Nevertheless,

91. Sundkler, *Söderblom*, p. 411, n. 4.

92. "Report of the Executive Committee," *Second Lutheran World Convention*, p. 169. The members of both committees are listed by Jørgensen in "An die Mitglieder . . . ," June 7, 1927, Boe Papers, box 101, folder 10.

93. The correspondence occurred in the autumn of 1928. See Ostenfeld to Morehead, September 17, 1928; Morehead to Ostenfeld, October 2, 1928, in ArCL. See also Jørgensen to Morehead, October 17, 1928; Ostenfeld to Morehead, October 16, 1928; Morehead to Ostenfeld, October 31, 1928; and Morehead to Executive Committee Members, October 31, 1928, Boe Papers, box 99, folder 4.

94. Jørgensen, "An die Mitglieder des Exekutivkomitees . . . , 4. December 1928," Boe Papers, box 101, folder 10. Cf. ibid., January 15, 1929, in ArCL.

95. Morehead to Boe, March 20, 1929, Boe Papers, box 99, folder 5.

some weeks later he acknowledged that the Missouri Synod had rejected the invitation to Copenhagen, citing as its excuse the role of Söderblom.[96]

For the most part, the plans for the Second Lutheran World Convention were complete. Some major improvements over the Eisenach arrangements were made. At Eisenach most of the sessions had been closed to the public; at Copenhagen the reverse would be true. Only a few business sessions would be limited to delegates. Moreover, at Eisenach some delegations (primarily the American) were official representatives of their churches, others (primarily German and Scandinavian) were present by invitation. In 1929 the Americans were to continue their practice of sending official church delegations; in Europe some, not all, churches indicated their willingness to do the same. In addition, provision was made for "participants" (approved by delegations) to speak but not to vote in the assembly. The question of "Union Lutherans" (Lutherans who were members of the Prussian or other Union churches) was left to the Germans with the understanding that a Union church itself could not be invited to send de'egates. This was not to deny the Lutheranism of Union church members. Rather, such "true Lutherans" within the Union could be invited as "participants" or given approval by the executive committee when nominated by the German Lutherans.[97]

In these ways, Lutherans from the great churches of Germany, Scandinavia, and America soon were joined by their brethren from the European minority churches and the representatives from India and Japan. Their convergence at Copenhagen was to be significant and colorful.

96. Morehead to Jørgensen, June 17, 1929, in ArCL.
97. Morehead to Ihmels, January 11, 1929, and February 1, 1929, in ArCL.

8

The Copenhagen Congress, 1929

When Lutherans gathered at Copenhagen in 1929, it marked the beginning of the second decade of their cooperative endeavors on a global scale. The initial proposal for an international congress had emanated from the Berlin meeting of the European commissioners of the National Lutheran Council, October 6–7, 1919.[1] The Lutheran World Convention at Eisenach (1923) provided a modest organization for keeping alive the goals of world Lutheranism and for expediting its common work. One of the main tasks of the executive committee, as we have noted, was the planning of the second world congress, this time in Scandinavia.

Little did the delegates at Copenhagen realize that 1929 would be ushering in a decade of events with worldwide reverberations. They could not foresee that the end of the decade would witness the outbreak of the calamitous Second World War which, like World War I, would cause wide and deep chasms within the world Lutheran family. Before examining the main topic of this chapter—the Copenhagen congress—a quick reminder of the situation in the Western world between 1920 and 1935 may help us understand both the successes and the failures of world Lutheranism.

BETWEEN THE WARS

Economics and Politics

The bloodletting of World War I had not only soaked the battlefields in both Western and Eastern Europe but also devastated the economies of the Allies and the Central Powers, especially those of Germany and Russia. The Bolshevik Revolution and the German

1. NLC, *Annual Report . . . November 6, 1919*, pp. 27–28.

exhaustion were at the root of much of the world's malaise for decades. The Allied imposition of 132 billion marks in reparations on Germany, already impoverished, resulted in unimaginable inflation and all but total collapse of Germany's economy by 1923.[2] A surprising recovery followed, however, due largely to the Dawes Plan, which provided an outlet for the United States' excessive gold reserves and an opening of markets for American goods. A credit freeze in 1924, and a loan of 800 million gold marks (chiefly from American banks), produced a dramatic turnaround that the Germans called the *Wirtschaftswunder* of the 1920s.[3] The "economic miracle," which had restored German confidence, was short-lived because the entire system was erected on the narrow and shaky economic base of undercapitalization. This was revealed by the Great Depression, which was so effectively exploited by Hitler and the Nazis.

Interwoven with the postwar turmoil in the economic and social spheres were the vast political developments that were reshaping the face of the entire world. By 1929, Soviet Communism was consolidating its totalitarian rule over the former Russian Empire, reaching from Petrograd in the west to Vladivostok in the east. Mussolini and the Fascists were restoring some of Italy's lost pride ("He made the trains run on time") and encouraging dreams of heightened Roman grandeur under the authority of "the Leader" (*Il Duce*), whose state socialism and state police stood athwart the threat of Marxist international socialism. Meanwhile, to the north, Germany's noble but ineffective experiment under Social Democrats in the Weimar Republic was attacked both from the left by Communists, whose appeals won the allegiance of workers and intellectuals alike, and from the political right: the Catholic Center, the Bavarian People's Party, and the Nationalists, later to be Hitler's allies. The attempt in 1928 at a

2. John Maynard Keynes (1883–1946), a youthful economist and a British member of the Paris peace conference, argued futilely for moderation, but unyielding views prevailed and Germany was saddled with payments to be completed by the late 1980s. The Keynesian economic theories, severely criticized in some quarters today, were employed in Britain and America during the Great Depression and periods of economic recession into the 1970s.

3. By 1930 the Allies began to exercise some common sense and reduced the reparations to 37 billion gold marks, but the Germans stopped their payments during the Great Depression. The de facto situation became de jure when Hitler won the chancellorship in 1933.

coalition government broke apart because the Weimar government in 1929 accepted the Young Plan, which among other things sought to continue reparations to 1982. This reignited and refueled the "war guilt" resentment which Germans had only recently put aside. It was in this milieu that the Nazis, the rising National Socialist German Workers' Party, found their prophet and Führer in Adolf Hitler.

While all this was transpiring in Europe, the U.S. economy rode a crest of prosperity until the stock market crash of 1929 and the Great Depression, which followed soon after. Franklin Delano Roosevelt was elected President in the hope that he would lead America out of the economic wilderness; Hitler became the German leader (*Führer*) for much the same reason; Stalin and Mussolini continued their truculent roles. Economics and politics walked hand in hand into the decade 1929–1939.

Technology

The Western world had long since burst beyond the infancy of the industrial revolution and was now well into the age of technical marvels. In the fields of transportation and communication alone, the 1920s and 1930s witnessed the widening use of the internal combustion engine for land and air travel. America's love affair with the automobile had moved beyond the new pleasures of the first "Volkswagen" (the people's car), namely, Henry Ford's Model T, to more sophisticated models. Farmers saw advantages in replacing horses with tractors. In 1927 a young Swedish-American, Charles Lindbergh, piloted his plane, *The Spirit of St. Louis,* nonstop across the Atlantic. While this was happening, primitive wireless sets and motion picture cameras were refined to become the forerunners of instantaneous audiovisual communications.

American scientists and technicians were not alone in these advances. The British, French, and especially the Germans were also busy. The first television broadcast took place in Berlin on March 8, 1929.[4] The immediate psychological impact of this program was enormous. Germany's wounded spirits revived under the conviction that its industry and technology could cooperate to outproduce the rest

---

4. Walter Laqueur, *Weimar: A Cultural History* (New York: G. P. Putnam's Sons, 1974), p. 34.

of the world. Burghers with nostalgic memories referred to the years between 1925 and 1929 as "The Golden Twenties," while Americans spoke of the same era as "The Roaring Twenties." Native German romanticism was thus fittingly expressed in the word "golden"; "roaring" was not untypical of "bullish" America. In any case, only Huxley-like writers and Orwellian futurists could imagine what these years would bring to coming generations.

The Culture: Life and Manners

As in politics, the posturing intellectuals and the nonposturing masses were often on the same side in questions of life and morals. Thousands of people—intelligentsia as well as the masses—were reading F. Scott Fitzgerald, Sinclair Lewis, H. L. Mencken, Theodore Dreiser, Bertolt Brecht, and Franz Kafka. But, it was argued, it was wasteful merely to read about Marxism and Freudianism; it was silly just to read about the sexual hedonism described by British-American Berlinophile Christopher Isherwood. Theory was one thing and practice another; and when it came to the "new morality" of the current literary genre in Western Europe, people reasoned that reality was to be preferred to fantasy. Sex, like justice, had to be experienced to be genuine. Numerous themes of literature—free love, divorce, marital infidelity, pornography, homosexuality, venereal disease, prostitution, and drug abuse—were more than titillation of imaginations. They shortly became de-stigmatized patterns of behavior for many "emancipated" people. Even the shattering experiences of the Great Depression did little to halt or reverse the trend. Instead, when confronted by the economic woes of 1929–30, large numbers sought to submerge their problems in the narcotic euphoria of *la dolce vita*. What happened on the New York–Hollywood axis was quickly imitated in the capitals of the Western world. Parisians were outstripped by Berliners, whose life-style was aptly summarized by the phrase *"Berlin s'amuse"* ("Berlin amuses itself"). It was a mad dance on the edge of a volcano.

It was hardly surprising that Copenhagen, where the world Lutheran congress was about to convene, would be influenced by nearby Berlin. Unlike Constance in 1415, when the Holy Roman Emperor Sigismund closed the theaters and imprisoned the prostitutes so the ecumenical council could go about its business of executing the heretic John Hus in pious dignity, Copenhagen's happy paganism existed in the shadows of green-spired churches where majestic organs led the liturgical solemnities of worshiping Lutherans.

Religion and the Churches

The theological world of postwar Europe in the 1920s and 1930s was characterized by a revolt against the nineteenth-century Neo-Protestant liberalism regnant prior to World War I. With the publication of Karl Barth's *Romans* (1921) the lines were drawn between the theological "progressives" (or the old liberals) and a new generation of disillusioned liberals who sought to check the erosion of biblical authority and to publish anew the evangelical themes of Reformation theology. This "new theology" was variously characterized: To say it was "dialectical" was to describe its methodological emphasis on the paradoxical nature of revelation; to call it "critical" was to emphasize that both church and world lived constantly under God's "crisis" (*Krisis:* "judgment"); to describe it as "neo-orthodox" was to place it in the historical line of classical catholic and Reformation theology without the trammels of biblicism, repristinationism, and sectarianism. The famous leaders, in addition to Barth, were Emil Brunner, Friedrich Gogarten, and Rudolf Bultmann.

Contemporary with this "new orthodoxy" was the exciting development in historical-theological scholarship known as the Luther renaissance, occurring primarily in Swedish and German universities. Representative Swedes were Einar Billing, Nathan Söderblom, Gustaf Aulén, and Anders Nygren. Most of the Germans counted themselves as heirs of the pioneering research of Karl Holl (Berlin), who inspired scholars to give renewed study to special areas of Luther's thought: revelation, biblical authority, sin and grace (*simul justus et peccator*), law and gospel, and "the two kingdoms." So extensive were these studies that one famous scholar, Wilhelm Pauck (Union Seminary, New York), was led to assert in 1967 that more had been written about Luther in the last fifty years than about any other person. Whether statistically accurate or not, no reputable scholar denied the vigor, the intensity, and the extent of the Luther renaissance. Its fruits, combined with the "realism" of "neo-orthodoxy," struck severe blows against the "idealism" of liberalism and provided new theological alternatives to the calcified, Troeltschian dichotomy between "Old Protestantism" and "New Protestantism."

The revolution in biblical studies was reflected in the British publications *The Riddle of the New Testament* (1934) by Edwyn C. Hoskyns and Francis N. Davey, and *The Apostolic Preaching* (1935) by C. H. Dodd. The Luther renaissance traveled to America by means of such works as Heinrich Boehmer's *Luther in the Light of Recent Research* (1916 and 1930). Later, two British students of Luther, Philip Watson and Gordon Rupp (*Let God Be God!* [1947] and *The Righteousness of God* [1953]) were eagerly read by young American scholars.

What was occurring in European theological circles was slow to cross the Atlantic. Theology in the American 1920s was largely an emotional debate between "fundamentalism" and "liberalism." This state of affairs continued until the results of the German-Scandinavian studies were gradually but reluctantly imported in the late 1920s, obviously too late to have influenced Americans at Copenhagen. The role of delegates at the assembly revealed an astonishing lack of representation from the European Lutheran academic world. Except for Nathan Söderblom, Ludwig Ihmels, and Werner Elert, the intellectual leaders of Lutheranism in Germany and Scandinavia were absent.

On the ecumenical scene, the traditional hostility between papalists and evangelicals showed but miniscule signs of softening, though there were cautious gestures from liberal Catholics, like the editors of *The Commonweal*, a highly respected Roman Catholic journal of opinion published in New York. The journal devoted the lead article in its July 17, 1929, issue to the Lutheran World Convention currently in session. The Lutherans, said the writer, were profoundly conscious of the need for Christian unity and international solidarity in the modern world. "We hope," he said, "that Copenhagen is one little step toward [the] ultimate goal." He observed that the major religious communions, including the Lutherans, were closing ranks.[5] Although traditionally hesitant about ecumenism, Lutherans had not isolated themselves from the pan-Protestant conferences at Edinburgh (1910), Stockholm (1925), Lausanne (1927), and Jerusalem (1928). In fact,

---

5. "One Highway," *The Commonweal*, July 17, 1929. Lutherans were exhibiting an awareness that they constituted one of the four great ecclesiastical groups in Western Christianity. The Catholics, of course, were most numerous, but Lutherans—once united—were the largest Protestant family.

some Lutherans were among the strongest Protestant exponents of the ecumenical spirit.[6]

Despite these involvements, the chief concern for Lutherans gathering in Copenhagen continued to be theological issues rather than world problems, cultural changes, or ecumenism. In this they thought of themselves as true sons of the Reformation. They were convinced that it was a false theology that had prompted the Reformation—Rome's lèse majesté against the sovereignty of the gospel—not the politics of Charles V or the immoralities of the Renaissance papacy. Agreement in these theological matters did not preclude an awareness that their own Lutheran household of faith had only begun to seek ways to overcome domestic disunity. A further weakness was that they were fighting theological liberalism with weapons fashioned in a bygone age, only modestly aware that contemporary evangelical theology had provided new instruments with which to carry on the mission of the church in the world. Claiming that Luther was right in saying that the world cannot be ruled by the gospel, they were nevertheless uncertain about how to be God's servants in the secular realm, "the kingdom of the left."

Like a colossus, the second Lutheran World Convention stood astride two decades of ferment, 1919–29 and 1929–39. What this ferment signified for the Copenhagen congress and the church it represented may be answered by examining what happened at Copenhagen.

THE SECOND LUTHERAN WORLD CONVENTION[7]
JUNE 26–JULY 4, 1929

When the Danes sing their national anthem, they can very well apply its proud phrase "Denmark is a lovely land" to their capital city. Visitors and natives alike are charmed by the city of green copper spires atop churches, castles, the city hall, the stock exchange, and dozens of lesser buildings. Almost one-third of the nation's population (4,500,000) reside in this gracious gateway to Scandinavia. Founded in

---

6. Copenhagen would discuss the problem of Christian unity, and the executive committee in 1936 would adopt a significant statement that would continue to guide Lutheran participation in the ecumenical movement for many decades.

7. The official reports of the Copenhagen assembly were published in German and in English: *Lutherischer Weltkonvent zu Kopenhagen . . . 1929* (Leipzig: Dörffling & Franke, 1929) and *The Second Lutheran World Convention . . . Copenhagen . . . 1929*

A.D. 1167 by Bishop Absalon of Roskilde, the town was named København ("Merchant's Harbor"), and it soon received its own cathedral, the Church of Our Lady (*Vor Frue Kirke*). Destroyed by the British in 1807, the cathedral was rebuilt along bleak and uninteresting lines. One of the German delegates commented that the only thing that saved the building from architectural oblivion was the fact that the famous neoclassic sculptor Bertel Thorvaldsen had adorned its interior with marble statues of Christ and the apostles, but even so the cold beauty of the statues lacked depth and reflected a Greek spirit rather than a biblical spirit. The writer recognized that his views might make the Danes unhappy, so he expressed the hope that his hosts would forgive his heretical opinions![8]

The opening and closing services of the assembly were held in the cathedral located in the Old City across from the Bishop's Palace and near the university (founded A.D. 1479). The convention sessions were held in the large assembly hall of "Bethesda," a building owned by the Danish Inner Mission Society and located at Rømersgade 17, likewise in the Old City. Bethesda also housed the convention headquarters and provided workrooms for committees.

As the proceedings were about to get under way, it was natural that delegates who had been at Eisenach in 1923 noted the changed circumstances. In 1923, Germany was at the depth of its worst monetary inflation. In 1929, the contrasting "Golden Twenties" encouraged hopes that economic woes were past (ironically, the Great Depression was only months away). Eisenach had been a meeting of strangers; only a handful of participants were personally acquainted with one another. At Copenhagen, hearty handshakes and smiling

---

(Philadelphia: United Lutheran Publication House, 1930) (hereafter referred to as *LWC . . . 1929*). A copy of the handwritten but unsigned German minutes is in the LWF Archives, Geneva, Switzerland: "Der lutherische Weltkonvent in Kopenhagen . . . Protokoll." In addition, individual articles in church journals, as well as unpublished letters and narratives, proved valuable in writing this section. The essential documents, of course, are the official proceedings, but like so many such factual records they tend to be dull. Eyewitness accounts by intelligent and involved interpreters are necessary to convey the color and flavor of the event. The best of those used by this writer is Wilhelm Laible, "Der lutherische Weltkonvent in Kopenhagen," serialized in the German Lutheran periodical *Allgemeine Evangelisch-Lutherische Kirchenzeitung* (hereafter referred to as *AELKZ*).

8. Despite Thorvaldsen's neoclassicism, thousands of copies of his *Christus* are to be found in Lutheran churches and homes in Scandinavia, Northern Germany, and America. "The writer" referred to was Laible; cf. *AELKZ*, 1929, col. 682.

Copenhagen, Denmark, 1929: Opening service of the second Lutheran World Convention at the Lutheran Cathedral. King Christian and his party are seated about midway and to the right of the aisle. The Executive Committee is seated opposite on the left just beneath the pulpit.

Copenhagen, 1929: Opening business session of the Lutheran World Convention in Bethesda Hall.

eyes indicated that many delegates were renewing friendships. At Eisenach only the Americans and the German Free Churches were represented by official delegates, whereas Germans and Scandinavians represented organizations or religious institutions, instead of the churches themselves. At Copenhagen virtually all the delegates had been chosen by their respective churches. The German reporter was almost gleeful in recognizing this fact. He said, "At Copenhagen the churches themselves appeared in the persons of the princes of the church." The external expression of this fact was the role played by these princes of the church, whose golden pectoral crosses betokened their episcopal office. Another change was the broader geographic representation of the official delegates. The delegations from the Far East were larger (there were eight delegates from India and Japan), and many of the churches in the newly created postwar nations were likewise well represented. In addition, the 1929 assembly experienced a large influx of nonofficial visitors. The Danes, quite naturally, were the most numerous. The proximity of Germany, Norway, and Sweden encouraged attendance from these lands. Most astonishing— at least to the German reporter—was the arrival of two shiploads of Lutheran pilgrims from America. The gathering of nations had a pentecostal character, except for one detail: Each one did not hear them speaking "in his own language" (Acts 2:6). Although German was still the most commonly understood, English and Scandinavian languages were heard more frequently than at Eisenach. This meant a wider use of oral interpreters and written translations at the sessions. For this exigency and other problems, the efficient local committee had made excellent arrangements. All things were ready for the congress to function.

Wednesday, June 26. At 10:00 A.M. the bells of the Cathedral Church of Our Lady called the world Lutheran congregation to its opening service. Among the worshipers were the Danish king and municipal dignitaries.[9] Harald Ostenfeld, bishop of Sjaelland, the diocese includ-

---

9. King Christian X (1870–1947) was the monarch who became a symbol of Danish resistance to Nazi occupation in World War II. When he started to wear the yellow Star of David, patriotic Danes forgot that he had surrendered Denmark to the German commander with an unnecessary compliment: "You Germans have done the incredible again! One must admit that it is magnificent work." The invasion had been completed between dawn and mid-morning of April 9, 1940. John Toland, *Adolf Hitler*, 2 vols. (Garden City: Doubleday, 1976), 2:696.

ing Copenhagen, preached on Ephesians 2:8–10. The text's stress on grace, faith, and good works lent itself to Lutheran exposition. Ostenfeld explained the traditional teaching of humanity's separation from God in biblical categories: "The thing that separates is not the abyss between the finite and the infinite; [that] abyss is philosophical. The thing that causes the separation is sin, the sin in myself." The graciousness of God (God's offer of forgiveness), he continued, is not mechanical or magical; God addresses people not as lifeless objects but as responsible persons. But even though salvation is by grace alone through faith, these responsible persons are subject to the temptation to pervert grace and to turn faith into a human exercise, a belief in orthodox doctrines. "Let us honor the doctrine for its own use, namely to create clearness of reasoning . . . , but never to replace the personal communion with God."[10]

Despite the sermonic emphasis on the life of grace and faith in the terms of communion or personal fellowship between God and humankind, Copenhagen, like Eisenach, had no celebration of the Holy Communion. Eisenach could explain this by offering several reasons, one of which was that there was no Lutheran congregation in Eisenach to serve as host. Copenhagen could hardly use this excuse; the reason, though not mentioned, must have been the fear that some of the churches represented insisted that communion be reserved for those who had achieved complete theological agreement. As later discussion would reveal, there was considerable diversity between "orthodox" Lutherans (some Americans and German Free Churches) on the one hand, and "evangelical" Lutherans on the other (Ostenfeld himself was in this group, as were Nathan Söderblom, Ludwig Ihmels, Olaf Moe [Norway], and some Americans).

The convention program was resumed in the cathedral at 2:00 P.M. The ceremonial greetings were voiced by Ostenfeld; Ihmels; a physician from India, Samuel John; and Baron Radvansky from Hungary. Appropriately, the Americans were represented by Niels C. Carlsen, president of the United Danish Evangelical Lutheran Church, one of two Danish-American church bodies. It is also worth noting that the kings of Sweden and Norway sent their royal welcomes. The formali-

10. *LWC . . . 1929*, pp. 11–15.

ties completed, the convention heard the first main lecture, an address by Nathan Söderblom on the subject "Luther as a Christian Personality and His Significance for Northern Europe."

As at Eisenach, Söderblom's contribution ranked among the best. Reminding his hearers of his earlier characterization of world Lutheranism as polycentric (Central European, Scandinavian-Baltic, and American), he quickly turned to his favorite theme, church unity. Luther, he said, rejected all sectarianism and declared in the Large Catechism that *una sancta* is one "congregation on earth . . . under one Head, Christ . . . , [called] by the Holy Ghost into one faith; with divers gifts but agreeing in love without sects or schisms." For all his ecumenical concern, Söderblom rejected vigorously the idea that disunity is always the work of Satan [some ecumenists spoke of "the sin and scandal of division"]. "Under the guidance of the Spirit [separation] was necessary in order to save for Christianity spiritual freedom, evangelical truth, and other indispensable gifts which were in danger of being lost or darkened." Therefore, he insisted, the documents of the Reformation, especially the two Luther catechisms, whose 400th anniversaries were being commemorated by the Copenhagen convention, were statements of the catholic faith, unmatched in religious literature as being both evangelical and ecumenical. Not even the Anglican Book of Common Prayer has been so widely and diligently used by the common people. The catechisms' teaching, their doctrinal content devoid of polemics and breathing a great love for the church catholic, was indeed what the great Lutheran dogmatists of the seventeenth century described as *evangelica catholica*.

This concern for catholicity, said Söderblom, was what the Lutheran churches of northern Europe had sought to maintain, but with varying degrees of intensity. By way of illustration, he cited a statement by Eivind Berggrav of Norway, whom he called "the highest priest of Christianity" (his diocese was nearest the North Pole). Berggrav had once described the Scandinavian churches as being one in the evangelical faith but diverse in their emphases. For the Swede, the great ecclesiastical particularity was simply *Kyrkan* (the church); for the Dane it was *Menigheden* (the congregation); for the Norwegian it was *Kristen* (the Christian). All these particularities were vigorously defended without destroying the unity of Scandinavians as faithful witnesses to the evangelically catholic content of Luther's catechisms. Söderblom continued by saying that the great Cathedral of St. John the Divine in New York included side chapels dedicated to different nations and confessions. It might come as a surprise to Germans, who prize Luther so highly, to learn that the Reformer's statue is not in the German chapel. Instead it is to be found in the chapel of Saint Ansgar, the patron saint of Scandinavia, where it stands alongside Saint Knud (Denmark), Saint Olaf (Norway), Saint Eric (Sweden), and Gustavus Adolphus. Scandinavians look upon Luther as belonging not only to Germany and the world but to Scandinavia in particular. It was Luther who spoke so eloquently of the Christ as the Word made flesh dwelling among humankind, among all nations and cultures. Therefore, said Söderblom, it would be appropriate for all convention delegates to stand and, using Luther's explanation of the christological article of the Apostles' Creed, confess the catholic and apostolic faith each in his own language. Paul Fleisch, Oberkirchenrat of Hannover, writing later of this emotional moment, said it was "the high point" alongside the familiar Lutheran liturgy (conducted by clergymen robed in the unfamiliar vestments of the mass) and the familiar Lutheran hymns (including, of course, "Ein' feste Burg").[11]

Following a break, the convention moved to Bethesda and reconvened at 4:30 P.M. John A. Morehead, as chairman of the executive committee, called the convention to order. The roll call showed that the official delegates included 30 from North America, 47 each from Scandinavia and Germany, and 23 from other areas of the world. The German section included two Lutherans who were members of the Prussian Union as official delegates.[12]

The election of officers for the convention's sessions resulted in the

---

11. Paul Fleisch, "Der zweite lutherische Weltkonvent in Kopenhagen," *Evangelische Wahrheit*, July 17, 1929, col. 167, in Archiv des Lutherischen Kirchenamtes, Hannover, Germany, Lilje A/I.

12. The executive committee's planning sessions had given considerable attention to the problem of representation. Morehead had argued that "a Union church" could not be invited to send official delegates. Two options were open: to invite Lutherans in the Union as "participants" or to offer official delegate status to two such persons nominated by the Germans and approved by the whole executive committee. Morehead and Boe favored the first option, but they acquiesced when the Germans preferred "official" to participatory representation. See Morehead to Ihmels, January 11, 1929, and Ihmels to Morehead, February 1, 1929, in the Archives of Cooperative Lutheranism, Lutheran Council/U.S.A., New York City (hereafter referred to as ArCL).

choice of John A. Morehead as president and Ludwig Ihmels as vice-president. Six other vice-presidents were named: Harald Ostenfeld, Denmark; Bishop Danell, Sweden; Arthur Malmgren, Leningrad (in absentia); Frederick H. Knubel, New York; Baron Radvansky, Budapest; and Wilhelm von Pechmann, Munich. Except for Morehead and Ihmels, this committee was without specific functions but acted as the convention's honorary executive council. The other "officials of the convention" were the secretaries, who were to be responsible for the minutes. This group included Alfred Th. Jørgensen—who was named general secretary—two Germans (Erich Stange and Arndt von Kirchbach), two Americans (Emanuel Poppen and Abdel Ross Wentz), and two Scandinavians (Paul Sandegren and Frithiof Frandsen). These six men were Jørgensen's assistants.[13]

When the business matters were disposed of, Morehead introduced J. Michael Reu, who was to give the third formal presentation of the day. The topic was "The Origin and Significance of Luther's Catechisms." The hour was already late, and Reu expressed his irritation ("the day is far spent") at being relegated to the tag end of the day's program, but he proceeded to deliver what the German reporter Laible described as a "masterful lecture" which, despite the lateness of the hour, was heard "with enthusiasm."[14] The lecture, which lasted until 7:00 P.M., was indeed an excellent example of historical research and a closely reasoned statement of the abiding theological and practical significance of Luther's catechetical works. A discussion period was unnecessary, because the program for the following morning would continue the subject of Christian education. Meanwhile, there was an opportunity for weary delegates to rest and refresh themselves before attending the municipal reception at the Copenhagen Town Hall. Borgermester (Mayor) Petersen greeted the guests, who then were entertained by a program of chamber music and a vocal soloist "with incomparable voice." Thus the day ended, a day which

---

13. *LWC . . . 1929*, p. 29. The customary convention committees were Resolutions (chairman: Jaakko Gummerus, Finland), Organization (chairman: Wilhelm von Pechmann), and Nominations (chairman: Frederick H. Knubel, U.S.). The official German proceedings and the handwritten "Protokol" have no record of the appointment of a nominations committee; however, a report from this committee was made in the closing session (ibid., p. 207).

14. *AELKZ*, 1929, col. 704.

prompted the German reporter to comment in retrospect that the assembly's program had left the delegates breathless and surfeited with good things. Wearily he concluded, "Too much of a good thing."

Thursday, June 27. The morning program was to be devoted to a presentation by the bishop of Hannover, August Marahrens, but due to an emergency the bishop was prevented from being present. His paper, a set of theses on the topic "The Duty of the Present Generation to Transmit Its Heritage of Faith by Training the Next Generation" was read by one of his superintendents.

August Marahrens, who was to become a major figure in German and world Lutheranism during the "church struggle" in the Nazi era and World War II, had prepared theses that hinted at the difficulties that would beset the church in its responsibility to preserve and transmit the evangelical tradition. His first thesis asserted the need for "education and authority." Thesis five decried the influence of nineteenth-century developments on the contemporary situation in Germany and asserted that the recent war had led to a denigration of authority and a relativizing of values. Nevertheless, an aroused youth gave him hope that leadership would be forthcoming. If this were to occur, he continued, it was indeed important to recognize the psychology and sociology of youth (thesis six), but the transmission of the heritage was not so much a matter of educational techniques and methods or the setting up of a rigid system of faith as it was the vivification of the evangelical, confessional, and ecumenical character of the catechism witnessed to by the classic chorales of the Reformation. Home, school, and church must be bound together in this task (theses ten and eleven). In the light of later German church history under the Nazis, Marahrens's emphasis on "authority" is worth noting. The discussion of the theses suffered from the absence of their author and evoked little discussion other than predictable comments largely unrelated to one another. However, the discussion period did give Reu an opportunity to make what was actually another address.[15]

The remainder of the day's program was devoted to three lectures, each of which emphasized again the content of the Lutheran theologi-

---

15. Ibid., cols. 708–10. The *AELKZ*, whose editor, Wilhelm Laible, was friendly to Reu, gives a verbatim report. Neither of the official (English or German) proceedings does more than mention that Reu spoke.

cal heritage. Werner Elert was a rising young theologian who, though originally rooted in the German Lutheran free church tradition, had won his spurs in the circle of Luther scholars in the early 1920s. His lecture at Copenhagen, "The Church's Faith and Confession in the Light of Marburg and Augsburg," broke no new ground, but it did give clear and ample evidence that Elert had learned that Luther could not be properly understood within the categories of orthodox interpretations. In fact, his expositions of the meaning of faith, justification, and above all the relation between personal confession of faith and the confession of the church have lost none of their vitality or viability with the passing of years.[16]

Sam Stadener, bishop of Strängnäs, who presented the next lecture, was a reconstructed liberal who now reflected the churchly pietism of a Schartau type of Lutheranism characteristic of much of southwestern Sweden, where the positions of Söderblom were viewed with considerable apprehension.[17] Although his lecture "What Does Lutheranism Offer as Its Distinctive Gift to Christendom?" read out of its intended context might provide fertile ground for a self-congratulatory type of Lutheran triumphalism, it was only the first half of a larger work, the second part of which was "What Can the Other Parts of Christendom Give to Lutheranism?" In it he argued that in ecumenical discussion each tradition must be conscious of its own heritage if it is to be able to appreciate other traditions.[18]

The third lecture devoted to the general topic of Lutheranism's distinctiveness was delivered by the president of the Joint Synod of Ohio, Carl C. Hein. Hein's argument, distilled to its essence, made verbal inspiration of the Scriptures and their consequent inerrancy "marks" of the church. If the church ever surrendered this view of the Scriptures, it would cease to be the church.[19] The discussants refused to pick up Hein's "witness to the truth." This did not mean that the

16. On Elert see *Die Religion in Geschichte und Gegenwart*, 3d ed. (Tübingen, 1957–65), col. 418; and *Twentieth-Century Encyclopedia of Religious Knowledge* (Grand Rapids: Baker, 1955), 1:373. His lecture is in *LWC . . . 1929*, pp. 51–62.

17. Bengt Wadensjö, *Toward a World Lutheran Communion: Developments in Lutheran Cooperation up to 1929* (Uppsala: Verbum, 1970), pp. 265–68.

18. *LWC . . . 1929*, pp. 63–72. Stadener's stature in world Lutheranism and ecumenical circles was recognized when the Church of Sweden considered choosing him to succeed Söderblom as archbishop of Uppsala. However, Erling Eidem was chosen for the post.

19. Ibid., p. 75.

delegates had decided to avoid disagreement; they simply found Hein's approach untenable and left it at that. It was soon apparent, however, that the discussion period had not descended to an exercise in polite generalities and meaningless banalities. The very first respondent was Julius Bursche, bishop of Warsaw, whose strong Polish nationalism was viewed by the Germans as undisguised anti-Germanism. The moment he took the platform, most of the German delegation left the auditorium, and the few who remained were hardly sympathetic listeners. When one German sought to read a prepared reply to Bursche, the chairman ruled that time would not permit.[20] In this way, a potentially strident display of nationalistic sentiments was avoided.

Before the day ended, however, the delegates were privileged to return to the cathedral, where a concert by the Copenhagen Philharmonic Orchestra and the Palestrina Choir, both conducted by Maestro Mogens Wøldike, provided Germans, Poles, and all other potentially antagonistic groups with momentary surcease from the undercurrents of animosity.

The Weekend of June 28 –July 1. An exhausting procession of lectures, services, group meetings, and formal and informal events provided delegates with no sabbath rest. One of the highlights occurred on Friday morning, when Karl Proehle conferred honorary degrees on behalf of the Elizabeth University of Sopron, Hungary, on John A. Morehead, Nathan Söderblom, Franz Rendtorff (head of the Gustavus Adolphus Union), and Ludwig Ihmels.

Following this academic ceremonial, Ludwig Ihmels was introduced to speak on the topic "How Should We Strive for an Inner Awakening of Our Church?" The editor of the *Allgemeine Evangelisch-lutherische Kirchenzeitung (AELKZ)* described it as the high point of the assembly, a fact attested by the almost "breathless silence" that, in contrast to the customary applause, greeted the speaker at the conclusion of his address. When one examines the text, this accolade

---

20. *AELKZ,* 1929, col. 734. The author had requested that his statement, although not read, be included in the minutes. Neither the official English proceedings nor the German include this footnote to German-Polish antipathies. The details of this incident are in Laible's unofficial account of Copenhagen (ibid.).

seems justified. It was no mere repetition of timeworn pious phrases, but piety was profoundly present. The lecture showed the influence of the Erlangen school's emphasis on personal faith and rebirth as the starting point of theology. The lecture stressed orthodox dogma but not orthodoxist dogmatism. It celebrated the Lutheran dialectic of law and gospel without falling into legalistic biblicism or evangelical proclamation apart from the sovereign law of God. As the Reformation knew but one gospel, he argued, so there can be but one church, a church that does not live in isolation from contemporary world problems. Among the latter, he pointed to the challenges presented by the cultured despisers of the church, the alienation of the working classes, the world economic and political situation which Söderblom's Stockholm conference had sought to address, and, even more immediate, the continuing suffering of Germany under the Versailles Treaty, a symbol of which was the nationwide tolling of mourning bells in the fatherland. In all these circumstances the church must be God's eschatological sign, not to preserve Western or any other civilization, but to herald the reign of God.[21]

Following a better-than-average discussion period, the majority of the delegates enjoyed an afternoon sightseeing tour of Copenhagen and a series of evening interest groups (e.g., missions, publications, women's work, diaspora ministry). In itself this was not strange, but no mention, parenthetical or incidental, was made of the German delegation's observance of the day of mourning to which Ihmels had referred in his address. This, of course, had necessitated the absence of the Germans from a working session. So why not, said the agenda, give opportunity to the others to see Copenhagen?

The Germans gathered under the chairmanship of Ihmels to join their countrymen, who at this same moment at home in Germany were assembling in churches to express their grief over the Versailles Treaty. As Ihmels read the official proclamation of Germany's president Paul von Hindenburg, the entire group stood and remained standing through the solemnities of prayer. The short speeches that followed ranged from bitter attacks on the Lutheran World Convention for confining itself to the rarefied stratosphere of theory divorced from

21. *LWC . . . 1929,* pp. 83–92.

the realities of the modern world (Versailles) to defenses of the convention for recognizing that one must first move in the "pure air" of God's Word if one is to deal with worldly realities. Moreover, if there were to be reconciliation and fellowship with non-German churches, practical necessity demanded that the undeniable lie of war guilt must go unmentioned. Bygones must remain bygones, otherwise the wounds of war would only be reopened, and healing among the churches would be postponed. The picture of Germans gathered in prayer on the tenth anniversary of Versailles for their nation's alleged war guilt is so stark that the unprejudiced observers could well have asked themselves if there were things known to the Germans, if not to the Americans and British, that would have made the Allies bear their share of "war guilt" if they had but known. Historical research in recent years has uncovered enough evidence to convince even the most obdurate that there was guilt on both sides. It is well known that Hitler cleverly used what the Germans knew to be true in order to rouse the nation to make reprisal for the enforced post–World War I indignities.[22] A devastating case against the "innocence" of both England and the United States in the matter of bringing the latter into the war has been made by Colin Simpson in *The Truth about the Lusitania*. The political chicanery of the British Admiralty and the U.S. Department of State came to light when the cargo manifest of the *Lusitania* was discovered in 1968 among the private papers of Franklin Delano Roosevelt, who as under secretary of the navy had been privy to the fact that despite official American and British denials, the *Lusitania*'s cargo was almost totally contraband and thus subject to German attack. Until recently it had not been known that Grand Admiral Alfred von Tirpitz and Admiral Lord Fisher of England were in secret communication. The latter wrote to von Tirpitz on March 29, 1916, "I don't blame you for the submarine business. I'd have done exactly the same myself."[23]

The main lecture on Saturday, June 29, "The Lutheran Conception of the Relation between Christianity and the World," was presented by Gustav M. Bruce of Luther Theological Seminary, St. Paul, Minnesota. The topic had been selected as an occasion to address the

22. Cf. Toland, *Adolf Hitler*.
23. Colin Simpson, *The Truth about the Lusitania* (Boston: Little, Brown & Co., 1972), pp. 13–14.

issues raised at Söderblom's Stockholm conference in 1925. Unfortunately, Bruce did not meet the challenge. He bravely asserted that he would deal with "fundamental concepts, such as Authority, Christianity, the Kingdom of God, the Church, Society and State, and the Life of the Christian." The lecturer had obviously given laborious attention to his assignment, but the regrettable result was in many respects but a string of unassimilated quotations from well-known theologians like P. T. Forsyth, Adolf von Harnack, and others. The unofficial German report in the *AELKZ* dismissed the lecture as being of small significance by not printing it; interested readers, it was said, could find it in the convention's official proceedings. In powerful contrast, the editor commented, were the follow-up speeches by Wilhelm von Pechmann (quoted in full) and the insightful analysis made by Wilhelm Zoellner of Münster. An additional statement by Norwegian bishop Maroni and contributions by discussants added little by way of providing a "Lutheran position" in the matter of the church's relation to "the social question."

The day closed on a different kind of social note. The Danish committee on arrangements invited all delegates and the capital's diplomatic corps to a gala banquet in the elegant Hotel d'Angleterre. An indication of the committee's desire to provide its guests with only the best was its selection of Denmark's well-known and highly regarded diplomat, Carl Poul Oscar Moltke (1869–1935), as master of ceremonies. A member of the Danish branch of the von Moltke family of Prussian military fame, he was both a deeply loyal Dane and a committed internationalist, whose broad-gauged views and diplomatic skills had placed him at the center of international affairs.[24] His friendship with Morehead, who gave the banquet address, was of long standing.

Early Monday morning, July 1, 1929, the entire assembly traveled

24. Moltke was a direct descendant of Adam Gottlob Moltke, who was born in Mecklenburg in 1710 and died in Denmark in 1792. The Danish king Frederik V had made him a count (Danish *Greve;* German *Graf*) in 1750. Over the years, the family's international background broadened by marriage to include high-ranking Italians and Americans as well as Germans. Carl Moltke's wife was Cornia Van Rensselaer Thayer of Massachusetts. He had served in numerous diplomatic posts (London, Rome, Berlin, and Washington—as ambassador in the two latter cities). His sensitive understanding of the Danish-German boundary troubles placed him in the leading role to negotiate the treaty that gave Denmark sovereignty over the disputed territory in Slesvig after World War I. He remained active in international affairs until shortly before his death (1935). *Dansk Biografisk Leksikon* 16 (1939): 58.

across the sound to Sweden for a one-day session at Lund. The morning service in Lund's medieval cathedral included the Swedish *Högmässa* (high mass) and a sermon in German by Lund's Edvard M. Rohde.

Moving to the nearby Great Hall of the university's Academic Union, the convention heard one of the more memorable lectures of the 1929 assembly. Delivered by Alfred Th. Jørgensen, the Danish member of the executive committee, the address sought to answer the question "How may the inner unity among the Lutheran churches be furthered?" One observer reported that it touched a central nerve of world Lutheranism, and, although it aroused "a great interest," not all concurred in Jørgensen's optimism, especially as it related to the future structure of the organization.[25]

The address began with a brief historical survey of the movement toward world Lutheran unity. The lecturer then discussed the external hindrances to achieving unity: the language barriers, the ethnic differences, the social disparities. The internal problems of the church included the differences in ecclesiastical polities: Some Lutherans were organized episcopally, some synodically, and still others congregationally. A second problem was the ecumenical issue embracing relationships to Rome as well as to other Protestants. Finally, Jørgensen mentioned "the spiritual differences." It was his contention that the historical background of each church shaped its manner of transmitting the Lutheran doctrinal, liturgical, and homiletical traditions. It was his further contention that when forms stood in the way of evangelical proclamation and inner unity, the church must change its structure. The external husks must go, but "the kernel must remain." The programmatic section of the address contained practical suggestions for reaching out toward the common goals of world Lutheranism. There must be a greater international exchange and association of groups: pastors, professors, missionaries, diaconic and social workers. A joint Lutheran periodical, though presenting linguistic problems, must be kept in mind. At this juncture, Jørgensen reintroduced a proposal he had made at Eisenach, namely, the establishment of an international theological faculty. He was convinced that the future of

25. Laible in *AELKZ*, 1929, col. 820.

world Lutheranism required a systematic, scholarly study of modern Lutheranism. A small core faculty could be supplemented each semester by visiting professors from the various churches.[26]

Although the lecturer and his audience were well aware that world Lutheran unity possessed a paradoxical "already/not yet" character, the most frequently quoted statement from the address indicated the ecclesiological thrust of Jørgensen's argument: "The Lutheran Church of 1929 is not like a motley collection of stones that we are trying to assemble in a mosaic. The modern Lutheran Church, insofar as its members are true to the Confessions, is a unit. It is a Church."[27] How to move from "spiritual" unity to an empirical "union" remained a question for future debate.

The Closed Sessions of July 2–4. In one sense, our consideration of the Jørgensen lecture belongs with the reports and decisions made in the "closed sessions" during the final days of the assembly. The substance of the executive committee's report and the decisions growing out of the recommendations of the various committees (Resolutions, Organization, Nominations) dealt in large measure with the future of the Lutheran World Convention. This too had been a substantial part of Jørgensen's address. Therefore, as we draw the Copenhagen chronicle to an end, it seems appropriate to concentrate on the assembly's actions that dealt most directly with organizational matters and the continuation of churchly work by an agency that by definition disavowed any ecclesiological pretensions. The proper starting point is therefore the report of the executive committee, which Kurt Schmidt-Clausen has described as

26. Neither of Jørgensen's seminal ideas found immediate acceptance. The exigencies of producing a theological journal of world Lutheranism were finally overcome after the Lund assembly in 1947. The LWF implemented the proposal of its first general secretary, Sylvester C. Michelfelder, by publishing briefly a journal in German and English (*Lutherische Welt Rundschau/Lutheran World Review*). Discontinued for two years, the journal (*Lutherische Rundschau/Lutheran World*) was resumed in 1951. It continued until 1977, when financial and other considerations dictated that other media be employed to carry forward the intention of the periodical. With regard to an international faculty, an approximation of Jørgensen's ideal resulted from the suggestion of the German National Committee to the 1957 (Minneapolis) assembly of the LWF for an interconfessional (especially with regard to Roman Catholicism) study. This in turn eventuated in the establishment of the Institute of Ecumenical Research (1965) in Strasbourg.

27. *LWC . . . 1929*, p. 146.

the most important document emerging from the Second Lutheran World Convention.[28]

The report, read by John A. Morehead, began with a survey of Lutheran development leading to the First Lutheran World Convention and its provision for doctrinal and organizational instruments for the continuation of work. The six-man executive committee and the so-called Larger Committee were to build on the foundations laid at Eisenach and to make plans for another global congress. The report included a useful listing of the members of the Larger Committee by countries, and a summary of the executive committee's activities since 1923, especially the preparations for the Copenhagen meeting. Morehead emphasized one of the difficulties:

> Nationalism, in a certain true measure the virtue of all and yet liable in an exaggerated form to become the error of any, has often proven a serious menace to ecumenical Lutheranism. But genuine progress has been made. It becomes increasingly clear that one may be faithful . . . to his own country . . . and yet may become conscious of his unity in the faith with his fellow believers of all races and countries. . . . The committee has constantly emphasized the fact that the movement it represents is purely religious, spiritual and churchly and that its design is to serve freely and impartially all . . . *without involvement in politics, national or international* [italics added].[29]

The financial section of the report showed that the committee had received almost 75,000 Danish crowns for operations; 60,000 had been contributed by American churches. In addition, the committee treasury had been the agency through which over $133,000 had been disbursed for relief work in Russia, the support of minority and diaspora churches, and the utilization of new opportunities for Lutheran work in Switzerland and Galicia, the latter among Polish Ukrainians who

---

28. Kurt Schmidt-Clausen, *Vom Lutherischen Weltkonvent zum Lutherischen Weltbund* (Gütersloh: Gerd Mohn, 1976), p. 113. The English report is in *LWC . . . 1929*, pp. 159–76. The reading of the report was the chief item on the agenda for Tuesday morning, July 2. The afternoon was devoted to an excursion to "the Danish Westminster Abbey," the cathedral at Roskilde. The next afternoon, following the formal session, the delegates were given a tour of North Sjaelland with the compliments of Copenhagen's prestigious newspaper the *Berlingske Tidende*. The convention's social calendar was completed by informal receptions at the Danish Villa Solbakken and the German embassy. The ambassadorial host, Ulrich von Hassel, was married to the daughter of the famous Grand Admiral Alfred von Tirpitz. *AELKZ*, 1929, col. 681.

29. This portion of the report is quoted verbatim in view of criticisms leveled later at Lutherans for alleged socio-ethical and political "quietism."

numbered between three and four million former members of the Uniate Church, many of whom were now seeking the ministry of the Lutheran church.

The report also listed certain policy and program principles that had emerged as guidelines for the committee during the years since Eisenach: (1) The continuation work of the Lutheran World Convention should be spiritual and churchly in character, being governed and determined by the truth as it is in Jesus Christ, revealed in the Holy Scriptures and witnessed to positively by Luther's Small Catechism and the Augsburg Confession. The discovery and furtherance of inner unity in the truth in loyalty to the confessional principle therefore would be a primary object; (2) The Lutheran World Convention should be of the nature of a free conference or a free association of Lutheran churches and organizations; (3) The complete autonomy of all existing organized Evangelical churches should be fully recognized and should under no circumstances be interfered with; (4) The Lutheran World Convention should exclude politics, national or international, from its programs of discussion and work, confining its activities to the spiritual interests of the church and the kingdom of God; (5) In all its work of serving love, the Lutheran World Convention and its committees should, so far as the means are available, assist the needy and deserving churches of the faith without respect to race, language, or political alignment; (6) Looking unto God for wisdom and strength, it should be the declared purpose of the Lutheran World Convention and its authorized committee or committees to become the servant of all in the gospel and in the faith that worketh by love; (7) Since the power is of God and his Word, the utmost simplicity in organization is right in principle and wise in the present situation.

Finally, the report offered a series of recommendations concerning the organizational character and the continuing ministry of the convention. These were referred to the Committee on Organization, which included three members of the executive committee who had been deeply involved in the preparation of the recommendations in the first place. They were Wilhelm von Pechmann (chairman), Lars W. Boe (United States), and Per Pehrsson (Sweden).[30] After suggesting

---

30. The original recommendations are to be found in *LWC . . . 1929*, pp. 174–76. The preparation of the report and especially the roles of von Pechmann and Boe have been mentioned above in Chapter 7.

some changes, the amended report was adopted by the convention.[31] A summary of the recommendations as finally accepted follows.[32]

Articles 1 – 4. The Fundamental Resolutions adopted at Eisenach were to be preserved. The nature of the convention should remain that of "a recurring assembly of delegates," "a free assembly, without binding power." (The definition of convention as a one-time event or as a theological debating forum, or a "free conference" as understood by the Iowa, Ohio, and Missouri synods, and conservatives in the Norwegian Lutheran Church of America, was clearly set aside.) Organizational changes should be minimal and made only when conditions urgently required them. The convention should assemble about every six years with delegations of approximately the same size and distribution as previously, except for altered conditions of churches in various countries, especially the appearance of self-supporting churches on mission fields. Special meetings of the convention might be called when deemed necessary by the executive committee.[33]

Articles 5–6. The six-member executive committee was to remain unchanged, its members being elected at each convention. The committee would elect its own officers: president, two vice-presidents, a treasurer, an assistant treasurer, and a secretary. The most fateful amendment occurred at this juncture. The original recommendation stated: "The office of president shall alternate among the three groups (Scandinavian, German, American) at regular intervals [*regelmässig*]." As adopted, the phrase "at regular intervals" had been altered to "as a

---

31. Ibid., pp. 206–7. Kurt Schmidt-Clausen sees the presentation and handling of the report as the work of a presiding officer who was "no amateur" in matters of this kind. The fact that only the English text of the twenty-page report was ready (why the German text was not at hand is an unexplained mystery) left the majority of the delegates at a disadvantage (cf. "Der lutherische Weltkonvent in Kopenhagen . . . Protokoll," p. 13, in LWF Archives, Geneva). This, according to Schmidt-Clausen, can only be interpreted as a Moreheadian "steamroller" tactic to assure the goals of the executive committee with minimal debate. Schmidt-Clausen, *Vom Lutherischen Weltkonvent*, pp. 120–21.

32. This summary is based in large measure on Willard D. Allbeck, "A Study of American Participation in Inter-Lutheran Cooperation Prior to the Formation of the Lutheran World Federation," prepared for the Department of Theology of the LWF, 1962, pp. 84–86, in ArCL.

33. The Second LWC (Copenhagen) was presented with an invitation from the Chicago Lutheran Pastoral Conference to hold the third world convention at Chicago in 1933, no doubt in view of the Chicago World's Fair ("A Century of Progress") to be observed in 1933–34. The disposition of the matter by the new executive committee, to which the invitation was referred, was predestined by the phrase "when deemed necessary." "Der lutherische Weltkonvent in Kopenhagen . . . Protokoll," p. 17, in LWF Archives, Geneva.

rule" [*in der Regel*].[34] This change must be noted, because it was the occasion for continuing tension between the Germans and Americans for leadership in the Lutheran World Convention. The committee was also empowered to elect individuals to fill vacancies in its membership between conventions. No reference was made to the creation of a central bureau. Instead, the committee was assigned all administrative duties to be carried out by correspondence, annual meetings at various places (to facilitate visitations of churches in adjacent territories), and the publication of news bulletins. The continuing support of weak and suffering churches remained a high priority. All these duties were underlined by the directive to "do everything possible to promote unity among Lutherans everywhere."

Articles 7–10. The First Lutheran World Convention's provision for a "Larger Committee" had been carried out in name and geography only. It was now to be replaced by the formation of "special" (national or area) committees, whose duties were to promote the cause of the Lutheran World Convention by raising funds and other activities appropriate to the convention's goals. Each national chairman was to report to the president of the executive committee. Member churches were obliged to contribute according to their ability to the expenses of the executive committee and the budget for relief work. The appointment of these so-called special committees on a geographic basis was really the origin of world Lutheranism's later "national committees," provisions for which were incorporated into the Lutheran World Federation constitution (1947).[35] To assure that these embryonic "national committees" would be established, the convention, at the urging of Lars W. Boe, provided a "Rule of Transition." It said: "The delegates to the Second World Convention are, within their own Churches and Church territories, responsible for the organization of the special committees. Until the organization of the committees they are personally responsible for the work to be entrusted to these."

The Committee on Nominations recommended the reelection of the current executive committee (Morehead, Boe, Ihmels, von Pechmann, Jørgensen, and Pehrsson). The recommendation was adopted.

The report of the Committee on Resolutions, likewise adopted,

34. *LWC . . . 1929*, pp. 175, 206; cf. the German minutes, *Lutherischer Weltkonvent . . . 1929*, pp. 164, 213.
35. For example, in America the NLC acted as the U.S. National Committee.

reaffirmed the Eisenach doctrinal paragraph, recognized the 400th anniversary of Luther's Small Catechism, urged continuation of "works of brotherly love," alerted the churches to the 400th anniversary (1930) of the Augsburg Confession, and, like the Committee on Organization, directed the executive committee to promote Lutheran unity along the lines suggested by Jørgensen's lecture and the subsequent discussion. Of special note was the resolution on "The Social Problem," which pressed upon the executive committee a thoroughgoing study and "comprehensive declaration" as to the attitudes of the Lutheran church toward social issues, emphasizing "the inner character of the Kingdom of God." This resolution was an oblique admission that the official presentations and discussions of this topic at Copenhagen were inadequate.[36]

When the business sessions were concluded, the assembly moved from its Bethesda headquarters to the Cathedral Church of Our Lady for the final service of thanksgiving and benediction. Short speeches were made by the dean of the cathedral, H. Ussing; a French delegate, E. Stricker (Strasbourg); bishop of Norway, Johan Lunde (Oslo); Ludwig Ihmels; and John A. Morehead. All spoke of the blessings received, voiced their thanks for the Danish hospitality, and expressed their hopes for continuing unity and greater manifestation of *una sancta* before the world. In this manner, the Second Lutheran World Convention came to a close.

Evaluations

Before examining the American reaction to the Copenhagen convention, mention should be made of the comments by Wilhelm Laible, editor of the *AELKZ*, the most widely read German Lutheran periodical in Europe.[37] In concluding his report he noted three unfulfilled hopes that he and others had held of a Lutheran world congress, standing as it did at a level where it could see the great temporal and ecclesiastical questions, enunciate clear guidelines, and sound a

---

36. The committee reports are in *LWC . . . 1929*, pp. 202–7.

37. Laible's coverage of the Copenhagen convention is the most extensive of any discovered by this writer. As an editor and official delegate, he was present in a dual role, and he did not hesitate to play both. For example, he showed understandable editorial pride and defensiveness when Jørgensen's lecture suggested the need for an organ that would be widely and commonly read throughout the Lutheran world. Laible huffed and puffed: "The *AELKZ* is being read in the entire world. A common periodical is already at hand!" *AELKZ*, 1929, col. 825n.

trumpet call in the conflicts of the present. He pointed to the "ethical witches' Sabbath," the problems of youth in a generation shot through with atheism, the "women's question," and the challenge of the church's missionary task. He was disappointed in the theological caliber of the lectures, which too often were monotonously doctrinaire and predictable, quite inferior to those delivered at the General Evangelical Lutheran Conference (AELK) in Hamburg in 1928. The reason, no doubt, was that with some exceptions the speakers had been chosen not on the basis of theological competence but on the basis of geographical representativeness. Likewise, the devotional periods were inadequate—they lacked what the Germans and Danes would call the quality of edification. Too often they failed to lead worshipers into "the depths of God's Word." Finally, the organizational matters were unsatisfactorily disposed of, the cause being the inability to move from the concept of "convention" to "federation."[38]

The American observations, as could be expected, were both positive and negative. Of the American delegations as such, only that of the United Lutheran Church in America (ULCA) published its comments.[39] Noteworthy were the following: (1) The Lutheran World Convention had become more ecclesiastical; the majority of delegations were officially appointed by their churches. (2) There was confessional advance over Eisenach, where the theological declaration had been presented with no little trepidation; at Copenhagen it was reaffirmed without question, a sign that Lutherans had learned to trust one another, exhibiting a greater sense of Lutheran solidarity. (3) The geographically ecumenical breadth of the convention was more evident. Although the German language still predominated (several of the non-Germans gave their addresses in German), there was much more use of both English and the Scandinavian languages. (4) Finally, the convention had enlarged the understanding of the magnitude of its worldwide tasks and the need for combining energies, thus underscoring the imperative of Lutheran unity.

The presidential report of Johan A. Aasgaard (NLCA) described the convention as "outstanding." The attention given to minority churches was noteworthy, and the movement away from theological liberalism

38. Ibid., cols. 898–900.
39. ULCA, *Minutes . . . 1930*, pp. 62ff.

was clearly evident, so much so that European liberals described this as an undesirable feature of the convention.[40] The Augustana Synod heard a similar account from one of its delegates, E. T. Ekblad, who said that Copenhagen testified that "the Lutheran Church throughout the world is one in matters of Faith."[41]

Several American Lutheran periodicals gave attention—some more, some less—to the event. *The Lutheran* (ULCA) gave extended narrative coverage without significant evaluation. *The Lutheran Standard* (Ohio) praised the program, the facilities, the services of worship, and the spirit of concord.[42] The Iowa Synod's *Kirchliche Zeitschrift* commented on the persistence of theological liberalism in some Lutheran circles but spoke positively of the convention's achievements: inner homogeneity had strengthened, willingness to learn from one another had increased, and the sense of common responsibility had grown.[43]

The Missouri Synod, which had declined invitations to both Eisenach and Copenhagen, decried the convention as "unionistic" and "liberal." Söderblom was described as one of the most notorious "radicals of today," and the failure of the convention to renounce freemasonry, scientific evolution, and biblical higher criticism served only to justify the synod's refusal to have any part in the world Lutheran movement.[44]

Summary Critique: The Issues

The issues at Copenhagen had been largely predetermined by the program worked out by the executive committee. Its plans had sought to incorporate topics that would address some of the internal problems of world Lutheranism and at the same time give serious attention to the socio-political context within which the church was experiencing centripetal forces. If one were to borrow vocabulary from the ecumenical movement, the main issues at Copenhagen could be subsumed under two headings: "faith" (doctrine) and "order" (organization).

---

40. NLCA, *Report . . . 1930*, p. 16.
41. Augustana Synod, *Minutes . . . 1930*, pp. 215–16.
42. Emanuel Poppen in *Lutheran Standard*, September 21, 1929.
43. J. Michael Reu, "Der zweite lutherische Weltkonvent," *Kirchliche Zeitschrift* 53 (December 1929): 671ff.; 54 (January 1930): 9ff.
44. *Lutheran Witness*, July 23, 1929. The editorial, signed "G," was no doubt written by Theodore Graebner.

The former included questions related to the distinctiveness of Lutheranism, the continuing search for unity, and the struggle to think clearly and act decisively on socio-ethical issues. The latter ("order") dealt primarily with the nature of the Lutheran World Convention and its future role.

Faith

Both internal problems and external pressures made it advisable for world Lutherans to ask again what made their confession distinctive. In the face of an increasingly secular culture, the emotional conflict between a waning liberalism and "a theology of crisis," and the persistence of a doctrinaire and even romantic nineteenth-century version of "Old Lutheranism," Copenhagen really addressed more than it could handle. What emerged was what might be expected: a diversity of answers reflecting individual convictions. One could not describe Copenhagen's theological profile as being shaped by confessional unity and theological uniformity. It was clear there was no theological uniformity, but it was likewise clear that the delegates were not of one mind about the meaning of Lutheranism's confessionality.[45]

Söderblom's attractively grand appeal to Luther's catechetical writing as the most evangelical and ecumenical expressions emanating from the era of the Reformation was a novel notion to many. Had the same thing been uttered by J. Michael Reu rather than the Swedish archbishop, it could well have been applauded, but the truth wrapped in a Söderblomian package might prompt some to say, "Beware of gifts borne by Greeks."

The address by Werner Elert, and in some measure that of Sam Stadener, was a reflection of a post–World War I interpretation of Lutheran confessionality growing partially out of the Lutheran renais-

45. One of the most severe critiques of the Copenhagen convention came from the editorial pen of Norwegian bishop Eivind Berggrav. He remarked that the delegates were besieged by "battalions of paragraphs" that were listened to by conservative and impassive delegates who were fearful of facing the world's realities. It was a congress without tension, and "congresses without tension are stillborn!" The spirit of Luther was not present (except for Söderblom's address); "it will take Luther to reform Lutheranism!" (Berggrav), "Redaksjonelle Noter," *Kirke og Kultur* 36 (1929): 385–87. Boe wrote to Johan Lunde (Oslo) that he agreed with Berggrav, but the real tragedy of Copenhagen was that such a convention was necessary at this late date in the history of Lutheranism. Boe to Lunde, December 21, 1921, Lars W. Boe Papers, box 33, folder 4, St. Olaf College Archives, Northfield, Minnesota.

sance and taking shape in response to the challenge of Barthianism. The proponents of the latter seemed to equate confessionality with what they judged to be German confessional legalism. Therefore they emphasized the personal, existential nature of confession as act, but were less enthusiastic about confession as a churchly guide to evangelical proclamation. Elert, in contrast, insisted on both personal confession and ecclesiastical confession, lest the removal of the dialectic throttle the New Testament witness.

The most limited understanding of Lutheran distinctiveness was voiced by Carl C. Hein, president of the Joint Synod of Ohio. His literal identification of the Word of God with the words of Holy Scripture and his virtual elevation of this identification to confessional status no doubt found favor among some of the delegates, but it only served to confirm numerous European theologians' suspicions that Americans were not only theologically superficial but also essentially fundamentalistic. Hein's view, surprisingly enough, was not now entertained by Reu, who held that the Bible's authority rests not on a theory of inspiration but on its instrumental character as a means of grace and on its soteriological message.[46]

Another confessional Lutheran, Olaf Moe, a member of the Independent Theological Faculty at Oslo, warned that the renewal of the church would not come by returning to the "orthodoxy" of the seventeenth century or to an "unhistorical biblicism." The evangelically confessional heritage, he asserted, requires theological change. To prevent theological revision within the evangelically confessional tradition would be to stifle religious renewal. The awakening, he said, would come "through the preservation of the churchly tradition in the ecumenical spirit."[47]

---

46. Reu was opposed to the merger between the Ohio and Iowa (also Buffalo) synods into what would be called the "American Lutheran Church" (1930). His opposition centered in Hein's view of inspiration and inerrancy, the struggle over which was carried on between 1926 and 1930. For details see Fred W. Meuser, *The Formation of the American Lutheran Church* (Columbus: Wartburg Press, 1958). For Reu's pre-1940 soteriological hermeneutical view, see his essay in *What Is Lutheranism?* ed. Vergilius Ferm (New York: Macmillan Co., 1930). In his later years Reu took an increasingly fundamentalist position on the Bible. His metamorphosis was complete by 1943. See his *Luther and the Scriptures* (Columbus: Wartburg Press, 1944).

47. *LWC . . . 1929*, p. 92. It is safe to assume that very few Norwegian-American Lutherans had heard of Moe or would have supported his views had they been apprised of them.

Much of this discussion was related to the question of church unity. Despite the chronic tension between Americans and Germans, there seemed to have been a growing Lutheran solidarity between Eisenach and Copenhagen. This "Lutheran" consciousness was evident in the prepared addresses, the subsequent discussion, and the official decisions of the convention. Illustrative of this tendency had been the question of choosing official delegates. The fact that the majority of the latter at Copenhagen were "churchly," that is, official representatives of their respective churches, was one mark of this attitude. The ever-present problem of the status of "Union" Lutherans had been solved by granting delegate status to individuals whose theological credentials were unimpeachable. However, their delegate status did not carry with it the implication that they represented their church (the Prussian Union church) or that their church was recognized as Lutheran. Only Lutheran churches were to be represented *qua* churches. This arrangement permitted the convention to hear the vigorous views of a Union Lutheran like Wilhelm Zoellner (Münster) and kept the Ohio and Iowa synods from withdrawing from the Lutheran World Convention on grounds of its alleged "unionism."

The Jørgensen lecture on unity among the Lutheran churches was an explicit statement of one of the purposes of Copenhagen: to consolidate both world and national expressions of Lutheranism. Although organizational or structural unity was of subordinate importance, certain practical and external means would serve to express and strengthen the sense of unity. To this end Jørgensen proposed a joint publication, an international theological faculty, a continuing ministry to the Lutheran diaspora, and a strengthened program of world, inner, and social missions.

Despite indisputable interest in Lutheran unity, none of the speakers demonstrated theological awareness of the positive connection between "inner" and "external" unity. It was symbolic of the Lutheran failure to understand Luther's teaching concerning "the two kingdoms," or two realms of God's activity. The tendency to separate the one from the other overlooked Luther's view that both realms are theonomous.

It was precisely this problem that frustrated the discussion of the lectures on the subject of the church and the world by Gustav M.

Bruce and Norway's bishop Maroni. With the clarity of hindsight and
the persisting anti-Lutheran prejudice refined by latter-day experience, modern critics of the Lutheran World Convention have been
shocked and dismayed to read that so little direct mention or general
discussion of the world's political problems took place. It seemed to
many that Lutherans existed in blissful isolation, ignoring the swirling
currents of atheistic Marxism, Italian fascism, and German nationalism. This, of course, was untrue. The threats of "isms" were headline
news in the daily papers, and Lutherans were quite as literate as
others. The dangers of demonic ideologies were not absent from the
minds of world Lutherans at Copenhagen. Yet they chose deliberately
to avoid confrontation. Why? There seem to be two answers. The first
was practical: The goal of world Lutheranism was unity. Since there
was nothing that seemed more destructive of unity than politics,
Lutheran leaders at Eisenach and Copenhagen and during the intervening years confined themselves to "spiritual" and "churchly" matters. They reiterated that it was not the business of the Lutheran
churches of the world to interfere with the internal affairs of governments or make public judgments on them. The report of the executive
committee at Copenhagen worded the policy as follows: "The Lutheran World Convention shall exclude politics, national or international, from its programs of discussion and work, confining its activities
to the spiritual interests of the Church and the Kingdom of God." This
was no policy of detachment; it was rather a somewhat feeble attempt
to transcend the world's conflicting ideologies by engaging in works of
serving love "without respect to race, language or political alignment."[48]

The second answer was unquestionably theological. Here the
Lutherans, who prided themselves on their theological astuteness,
exhibited a lack of understanding of their own theological heritage,
namely, Luther's doctrine of God's two realms of activity (the "two
kingdoms" doctrine). Traditional Lutherans had interpreted the latter
to mean that the church had its own sphere ("spiritual") and that the
state had its ("secular"). Since the state was of God, to criticize it was
to criticize God. Practically, this left the state free to go its own way
without divine or churchly interference. The doctrine of the two

48. Ibid., p. 174.

kingdoms seemed to lead to political absolutism. At the same time, the "new theology" of German "cultural Protestantism," Ritschlian ideas of an ethical, this-worldly kingdom of God, and the rise of the American "Social Gospel" led to the notion of the church's responsibility "to make the state (society) Christian." When Lutherans at Copenhagen listening to Bruce thought they detected the concept of "a Christian state," or a state ruled by the gospel, they saw a distortion of Luther's teaching and proclaimed all the more emphatically that the church had no business in the political realm. Wilhelm von Pechmann, who gave the clearest exposition of the necessity for keeping the two realms separate, argued effectively from quotations inscribed on two of Copenhagen's buildings. The exterior wall of the Bishop's Palace had been inscribed with the words of Philippians 3:20, "Our citizenship is in heaven." Only a short distance away, in Copenhagen's *Nytorv* ("New Market"), stood the Hall of Justice. Engraved on it were the words *"Med Lov skal man Land bygge"* (With justice shall one build the nation). While von Pechmann's argument had a "Lutheran" sound, its total impact left the impression that the two realms were separate, thus leaving secular authority sovereign in its realm, and the church as the only minister of God. Luther, however, would have seen these two quotations as dialectically related and descriptive of God's right- and left-handed work, the former creating God's *ultimate* kingdom of righteousness by faith in the gospel, the latter creating God's *penultimate* kingdom of civil righteousness by the law. It was not God's intention to create "a Christian state"; society on this earth could never be ruled by the gospel. Instead, civil righteousness, based on justice, was necessary for ordering human relationships. This was why Luther could vigorously denounce the injustices of magistrates with one breath and in the next breath praise them as needful ministers of God, but ministers using a tool that was powerless to provide a "heavenly citizenship." Copenhagen again showed, and the next two decades vividly demonstrated, that the muddy waters of traditional "Lutheran" social ethics required cleaning up. For this reason the report of the executive committee urged a thoroughgoing and comprehensive theological study of Lutheran social ethics.[49]

Before leaving this issue, it should be stated that although the

49. Ibid., p. 203.

convention itself took no positions regarding the current political ideologies of Marxism, fascism, and nationalism, one of the most prophetic utterances on the entire issue was made by another German, Wilhelm Zoellner. He warned that many of the world's desperate people were imagining a new hope on the horizon, where the "bloody and red" Soviet star was rising. Against this false hope there was yet another, equally dangerous, that a leader who understood the masses would present himself as a Nietzschian messiah, a "superman of today, who orders things according to his will, being beyond good and evil." (The reference was clearly to Nietzsche's *Jenseits von Gut und Böse* [1886].) This danger, he said, was compounded by modern technology, which, emancipated from God and serving the desire to master the world, would be insidiously demonic, leading to a new and fearsome thralldom. The road of this master would run inevitably through "blood and tears."[50] There was no indication that the speaker had in mind any specific individual, such as Hitler, who would fill the role of Nietzsche's "superman," but while Zoellner was speaking, a mustachioed Austrian had already (in 1926) won control of the National Socialist German Workers' Party and was urging all "nationalist" elements in Germany to accept him as their Führer in opposition to the Young Plan (1929).[51]

Order

The summary of organizational decisions taken at Copenhagen has already been made (see above pp. 250–51). At this juncture we need only list the most significant items which were to bear on the convention's future.

1. There was a general agreement that the Lutheran World Convention had established itself as an ongoing institution. There was no question that the convention was more than an ad hoc, one-time affair. Whether it was a "free conference" depended on how one defined the term. The consensus was that it was more than a global forum for debate, but surely less than a "superchurch" exercising some sovereignty over Lutheran churches throughout the world. It was also less

---

50. Ibid., p. 133. Churchill used this oratorical phrase, supplemented by "sweat," to defend Britain from the peril of Nazism.
51. Toland, *Adolf Hitler*, 1:229–49.

than a "federation" of churches; by definition it remained a "free conference or association" which recognized the "complete autonomy" of existing churches. In other words, Copenhagen did not invest the convention with any ecclesial character.

2. No action was taken on the frequently expressed desire of the Germans for a "central bureau." Instead, the executive committee would continue to be the focal point of administrative affairs, but the carrying out of its duties would be facilitated by the creation of special committees in specified geographic areas. These committees, as noted earlier, were to evolve into the so-called "National Committees," whose legitimacy would be recognized constitutionally at Lund in 1947.

3. Finally, the Committee on Organization altered the executive committee's proposal that the office of president be "regularly" rotated among the three main geographic groupings in world Lutheranism (Germany, Scandinavia, and America). The change from "regularly" to "as a rule" was to intensify the already strained relationship between the Germans and the Americans.

The Second Lutheran World Convention was now history. In view of its somewhat limited goals, its accomplishments were considerable. Although nobody could foresee the developments of the next decade, some of the Copenhagen decisions proved to be far-reaching, touching the lives of millions of people, and providing a transition to a new era in the story of world Lutheranism.

9

The Decade of Distress, 1929–39

In much of the Western world during the years immediately preceding Copenhagen there was a sense of well-being. By 1930, however, it had all but vanished. For most people the storm clouds that appeared at the beginning of the decade were associated with the Great Depression, the yet unveiled terrors of Marxist totalitarianism, the seductive appeal of Fascism and Nazism, and the distant Sino-Japanese struggle. The leaders of the Lutheran World Convention were not immune to the gloom that was beginning to engulf the world, but their experience of it was associated with specific occasions and relationships.

CLOUDS OVER ÖREBRO

The first instance of the approaching storm clouds was the reemergence of ill will between the Germans and Americans. The problem was rooted in the alleged postwar discrimination against the Germans. The Germans felt that they had done their penance and more, and it was now time that other Lutherans remembered that the German segment was the largest in world Lutheranism. It was proper, they reasoned, that they should be given roles of leadership commensurate with their strength.

The problem came to the fore immediately after the Copenhagen congress. The first meeting of the executive committee (the previous committee had been reelected) was to be held in connection with the 400th anniversary celebration of the Örebro (Sweden) Council of 1529, which had begun the reorganization of the Church of Sweden along the lines of the Reformation.[1] Before going to Örebro, the

1. Carl-Gustaf Andrén, "The Reformation in the Scandinavian Countries," in *The Lutheran Church Past and Present*, ed. Vilmos Vajta (Minneapolis: Augsburg Publishing House, 1977), pp. 59–60. Cf. Helmut Zeddies, "The Confession of the Church," in

committee met briefly at Copenhagen to discuss the agenda. It quickly became apparent that the Germans were intent on electing Ludwig Ihmels to replace John A. Morehead as president. When it also became obvious that Wilhelm von Pechmann and Lars W. Boe endorsed different candidates (von Pechmann's vote would be for Ihmels, and Boe's for Morehead), they entered a friendly agreement that neither should attend the meeting but would abide by the decision of the committee. With this arranged, von Pechmann returned to Munich, and Boe, who was ill with a severe cold, went to Oslo to recuperate for a few days and await the arrival of Morehead, with whom he was scheduled to sail back to America.

The Örebro meeting resulted in the election of Morehead as president, Alfred Th. Jørgensen and Per Pehrsson voting for Morehead. This led Ihmels to demand from the Scandinavians a written statement explaining their motives.[2] When von Pechmann heard the results, he was upset and suggested that the election was invalid. It had been agreed, he said, that Boe's vote and his own would cancel each other. "Why had not Morehead himself urged the appointment of Ihmels in view of the fact that world Lutheranism needed a rotating chairmanship?" The Copenhagen assembly had so indicated, he insisted, when it accepted the report of the Committee on Organization—of which he (von Pechmann) was chairman—even with the change in the wording of the election rule.

A flurry of letters among the members of the executive committee made it clear that four of the six members (the Americans and Scandinavians) were convinced that the interests of the Lutheran World Convention would best be served by the action taken at Örebro. Moreover, they felt that Ihmels and von Pechmann were not representative of the majority attitude even in the German church. The two Germans naturally rejected this interpretation, explaining that such

ibid., p. 106; and Morehead to von Pechmann, August 29, 1929, in the Archives of Cooperative Lutheranism, Lutheran Council/U.S.A., New York City (hereafter referred to as ArCL). The minutes of Örebro, July 6, 1929, are to be found in the Lars W. Boe Papers, box 101, St. Olaf College Archives, Northfield, Minnesota.

2. The explanation (in English, Swedish, and German) stated that von Pechmann, as chairman of the Committee on Organization, had agreed to the changed wording—from *regelmässig* ("regularly") to *in der Regel* ("as a rule")—and that the majority felt that world Lutheranism still needed the leadership of Morehead. See file on Örebro, John A. Morehead Papers, in ArCL.

important matters ought not to be decided by a majority vote. Rather, a solution representing the consensus of all parties should be sought. Lacking this, the Germans could very well withdraw their support of the Lutheran World Convention. Pehrsson replied that the responsibility for breaking up world Lutheranism would then rest exclusively on German shoulders.

If there was any substance to the threat of a German pullout, Jørgensen's presence and oral explanation at the Dresden meeting of the General Evangelical Lutheran Conference (AELK) served to settle the troubled waters, but not without evoking a letter of resignation from von Pechmann. With this action, the baron from Munich disappeared from inter-Lutheran affairs and ultimately converted to Roman Catholicism.[3] His replacement was August Marahrens, bishop of Hannover, who was to play a prominent role in German church affairs during the Hitler regime.

RUSSIAN CHURCH STATUS

The second instance of distress during the new decade was the worsening of the church situation in Russia. The 1930 meeting of the executive committee was held in Norway in connection with the 900th anniversary of the introduction of Christianity to that land.[4] Deputation visits to Sweden (Uppsala and Stockholm) and Finland (Abo, Helsinki, and Tampere) were made in late August prior to the official sessions scheduled for Trondhjem and Oslo.

High on the agenda was the desire of the executive committee to

3. Wilhelm von Pechmann's ancestors, including his father, were Roman Catholic. His mother, Ida Petersen, a Lutheran, reared him in her faith. He became a committed and active churchman whose Lutheran views were influenced by the "high church" confessionalism of August Vilmar and ecumenically shaped by Anglican friendships, sympathy for Nathan Söderblom, and lifelong Catholic contacts which were deepened during World War II. With the collapse of Germany, von Pechmann was increasingly disenchanted with Lutheranism and drawn to Catholicism. After his wife's death in 1945, he converted to Rome and in 1946 received the sacrament of confirmation from his friend Michael Cardinal von Faulhaber. Incidentally, both the latter and the Lutheran bishop of Bavaria, Hans Meiser, suffered for their anti-Nazi activities. See Friedrich W. Kantzenbach, ed., *Widerstand und Solidarität der Christen in Deutschland 1933–1945: Eine Dokumentation zum Kirchenkampf aus den Papieren des D. Wilhelm Freiherrn von Pechmann* (Neustadt/Aisch: Degener, 1971).

4. A copy of the official minutes, "Sitzungen des Exekutivkomitees in August und September 1930," is in the files of the LWC executive committee, in ArCL. The agenda, Morehead's excerpted report to the NLC, and the exchange of letters among the members of the executive committee are also in ArCL.

keep the church in Russia alive. The Russian delegates, not having been permitted to attend the Copenhagen assembly, had sent a message that presaged doom. This had prompted Morehead to send a memorandum to the executive committee in which he raised the question whether the time had not come to issue a declaration of concern to all governments to work for freedom to worship and to do religious work without persecution in Soviet Russia.[5] This proposal received scant attention, because just at this moment the question of the recognition of the Soviet government by America was under debate. In a second memorandum, Morehead suggested that "guarded, discreet and wise action be undertaken by members of the [Executive] Committee [individually, not officially] in their several countries" to interest their governments to exert pressure on behalf of religious freedom on the international level, especially in relation to Russia.[6] At this juncture Morehead approached the Danish count Carl Moltke, whose churchly role had blossomed at the Copenhagen congress and whose skills as an international diplomat were highly regarded. What did he think, asked Morehead, of requesting the League of Nations to work for religious freedom in Russia?[7] Moltke, like everybody else, had no clear solution to the problem. Though he continued to occupy himself with the issue for more than a year, his only suggestion was that the German foreign office be asked to collect information on the Russian church situation and to inquire regarding Soviet church policy. He expected that American recognition of the Soviet government would be posited on the guarantee of religious freedom, among other things.[8] Meanwhile, the conditions of the church in Russia deteriorated. Pastors and leading laymen were being banished or put under arrest, the Leningrad seminary was in jeopardy, and the entire picture was one of bleak despair.

The advisability of sending a delegation to Russia had been raised at the 1930 meeting of the executive committee. It was known, however, that as much as Theophil Meyer (Moscow) and Arthur Malmgren

5. Morehead to Executive Committee, October 25, 1929, in ArCL.
6. Morehead to Executive Committee, December 14, 1929, in ArCL.
7. Morehead to Executive Committee, January 24, 1930, p. 3, Boe Papers, box 99, folder 9.
8. See Armin Boyens, "Lutheranism in the Time of Dictators: The Lutheran World Convention 1923–1939," *Lutheran World* 23, no. 3 (1976): 232.

(Leningrad) desired this contact, they did not deem such a visit wise because it could easily result in further difficulties for those visited.[9] This seemed to indicate the futility of continued attempts at direct help. Perhaps the only recourse was to use Russian relief funds to assist the refugees who had been permitted to leave the Soviet Union. At the time of Morehead's memorandum, January 24, 1930, it was known that 1,100 of 5,700 refugees were Lutherans. This information had been supplemented by solid intelligence concerning the whereabouts of some of these refugees. Tucked away at the end of a relatively large budget ($6,400) for "Russian relief" was an item of $5,000: "For the temporary relief of distressed Russian Lutheran refugees in Persia and China."

In the light of future developments, the reference to China is significant. Four months after Morehead's January memorandum, Morehead received, through the office of Frederick H. Knubel, ULCA president, a letter from the spiritual leader of a group of approximately four hundred destitute persons who had escaped from Siberia into Manchuria and were living a desperate and precarious existence in a temporary refugee camp. The letter, written May 1, 1930, by a Pastor Ch. W. Kastler from Harbin (Manchuria), China, was a cry for help. The receipt of the letter began a long and complex series of negotiations to provide the refugees with money, food, and clothing and to arrange their ultimate settlement in Brazil.[10]

Since the case of the Harbin refugees was the last major effort undertaken by the ailing Morehead for the Lutheran World Convention, and since it represented a dramatic instance of Lutheran refugee service prior to the highly organized, well-financed, and efficiently operated refugee program of the Lutheran World Federation after World War II, it merits more than passing mention. The plight of the Harbin group came to the attention of American Lutherans at a critical

9. There is an obvious typographical error in the official minutes, which say that following the visit difficulties would be experienced *by the visitors* (*"Schwierigkeiten für die Besucher"*); obviously the minutes intended to say that difficulties would be experienced "by those visited." "Sitzungen des Exekutivkomitees in August und September 1930," p. 2, in ArCL.

10. The letters and documents relative to the Harbin refugees are largely to be found in ArCL and in Boe Papers, boxes 97 and 103. The most detailed study of this project in resettlement is Frederick K. Wentz, "Statesman on a Shoestring: John A. Morehead and the Harbin Refugees (1930–1932)," E. Clifford Nelson Papers, St. Olaf College Archives, Northfield, Minnesota.

time in their history. Morehead held two offices: president of the
Lutheran World Convention and executive director of the National
Lutheran Council. He now (1930) found it necessary to resign the
latter position to concentrate his energies on the duties of his office as
the first president of the convention (he had been merely chairman of
the executive committee since 1923).

Some of the Germans, still upset by the Örebro incident, suspected
that Morehead's resignation was a move to strengthen his own and the
general American hold on Lutheran world leadership. As a matter of
fact, Morehead's always delicate health had become even more fragile
by 1930. The future of the National Lutheran Council was in jeopardy
for at least two reasons: (1) depression-caused fiscal problems and (2)
inter-Lutheran tensions between two groupings in the council,
namely, the United Lutheran Church and the newly created federation, the American Lutheran Conference (formed in 1930 by the
American Lutheran Church, the Norwegian Lutheran Church, the
Augustana Synod, the Lutheran Free Church, and the United Danish
Lutheran Church). The split in the National Lutheran Council almost
caused its demise. It was clear, therefore, that if the NLC were to have
a future, it would require the full-time services of a healthy director.
Obviously Morehead could no longer give the leadership it required.
Named to succeed him, therefore, was Ralph H. Long, a member of
the former Joint Synod of Ohio, which in 1930 had become a part of
the American Lutheran Church.[11]

The Harbin problem not only put a strain on Morehead's health but
also tested all his skills as an international churchman, a hard-nosed
money-raiser, and a persuasive diplomat. Speedy assistance for the
refugees was urgent because of a threat that China might force them to
return to Siberia. Several major problems had to be faced. First, food,
clothing, and money had to be gathered and sent to support the
refugees while they awaited the disposition of their case. Second,
although the executive committee was reluctant to set a precedent by
engaging in a colonization program, there seemed to be no alterna-
tive. The problem, therefore, was to find a nation willing to admit the
refugees. Third, these people-without-a-country required passports to

11. For details, see E. Clifford Nelson, *Lutheranism in North America 1914–1970*
(Minneapolis: Augsburg Publishing House, 1972).

travel. Next, donations and a loan must be secured to finance the operation, and finally, the myriad of details of transporting and resettling these homeless pilgrims required an immense amount of work.

Morehead was able to secure subsistence help from LWC funds to tide the group over until more permanent arrangements could be made. Only three countries were willing to consider admitting the refugees, Canada, Australia, and Brazil; Brazil was chosen as the most suitable. The process of obtaining passports proved difficult and time-consuming. A request for Chinese passports was refused. The German government at first insisted that the Russian group come to Germany but finally decided to issue what Morehead called the "equivalent" of passports. Thus equipped, the refugees were prepared in 1932 to leave for Brazil. What was lacking was money. In this emergency situation, Morehead committed the Lutheran World Convention to help with transportation and a portion of the actual settling costs. He looked especially to the churches in the United States and Germany to carry this burden. In May 1932, Morehead transferred the details of the project to the German relief agency *Gotteskasten,* which in turn made arrangements with the Nansen International Refugee Office of the League of Nations in Geneva to facilitate the migration. An important part of the help received from the Nansen office was a loan of $11,000 to the Lutheran World Convention which was to be repaid by 1937.

The main reason for the transfer of responsibility to Friedrich Ulmer, the director of *Gotteskasten,* was Morehead's deteriorating health. In early May he suffered a breakdown (it was variously referred to as "an overtired heart," "stroke," or "spasm") and spent the summer and autumn recuperating in California. Meanwhile, his duties were left in the hands of three men, Frederick H. Knubel, Ralph H. Long, and Lars W. Boe. These men soon learned that Morehead's enthusiasm had exceeded not only his strength but also his authority. As a result, the Lutheran World Convention was deeply in debt. Boe, who was invariably loyal to Morehead, complained to his American colleagues that Morehead had acted precipitously and against the advice of Boe and others. But once the commitment to the Harbin-to-Brazil move had been made, there was no turning back.

When the resettlement in Brazil was completed and after More-head's health permitted him to return to his office, there was a general attitude of gratitude that the Harbin enterprise had been undertaken. Paying for the project during the Depression years was extremely difficult, but by 1934, Morehead reported, approximately $60,000 had been raised, one-third from Germany, one-third from America, and one-third from other lands. In addition to this, there was the indebtedness to the Nansen Fund, which was not repaid for several years. This concluded the Harbin saga, but the Lutheran church in Russia continued under its cross of suffering, and by the outbreak of World War II it was assumed that organized Lutheranism in Russia had ceased to exist.

WHAT ABOUT THE NAZIS?

The rise to power of National Socialism and Hitler in 1933 and the Great Depression confronted the Lutheran World Convention with special problems. Our intention is to deal in some detail with the German *Kirchenkampf* ("church struggle") and world Lutheranism in the next chapter. At this juncture we will note how these perplexities affected the work of the convention's executive committee.

The magnitude of the Great Depression had not yet been experienced when the executive committee met in 1930. Therefore the agenda was largely "business as usual."[12] The committee gave consideration to Jørgenson's proposal for an international theological faculty and the publication of a comprehensive Lutheran encyclopedia.[13] As noted earlier, the Russian situation received considerable attention, but one looks in vain for reference to the rising nationalism in Germany.

Morehead's illness and Boe's inability to leave St. Olaf forced postponement of the 1931 executive committee meeting to March 1932. By then, however, the full impact of the Depression was being

12. During the 1930 sessions at Oslo, August Marahrens was invited to lecture at Norway's Independent Theological Faculty (*Menighetsfakultetet*). In itself this was unimportant, but as a symbolic gesture it may have served to assure cautious Norwegian conservatives that the LWC, as reflected by Marahrens, was "soundly Lutheran."

13. This noble but expensive undertaking was throttled by the Depression and World War II. Finally, the three-volume *Encyclopedia of the Lutheran Church*, edited by Julius Bodensieck, was published in 1965 by Augsburg Publishing House in Minneapolis, Minnesota.

experienced, and the meeting had to be canceled.[14] Finally, after three years, the committee was able to assemble in Hannover in November 1933. Once again Morehead's poor health prevented his attendance, so he deputized Ralph H. Long, executive director of the National Lutheran Council, to represent him. Another strong leader was missing at Hannover: Ludwig Ihmels had died unexpectedly in 1933. His replacement was Hans Meiser of Munich.[15]

The Hannover meeting revealed the bewilderment and uncertainty of the executive committee regarding the Hitler phenomenon—this despite the fact that the non-German members had been sent a very confidential report from inside Germany by their Danish colleague Jørgensen, who had been present (as a regular member) at the AELK in Leipzig, June 8, 1933.[16] We shall return to this document later, but for the moment it is necessary to say only that Jørgensen stated that "everyone, without exception, is enthusiastic about Hitler." August Marahrens, he said, had been elected AELK president to fill the vacancy caused by Ihmels's death. His hour-long presidential address had discussed the church situation in the new Germany and provided a brief summary of the early struggle between the church and the so-called "German Christians" who had opposed the election of Friedrich von Bodelschwingh as Reich bishop. By political chicanery and propaganda they were able to unseat him in favor of their Nazi-supported candidate, Ludwig Mueller, Hitler's personal counselor in church matters. In other words, Jørgensen had already apprised the non-German members of the *Kirchenkampf* that was emerging in Germany.

14. Despite the absence of Morehead and Boe, the European members of the executive committee met for an "unofficial" and "nonbinding" consultation in Leipzig, November 7, 1932. Ihmels, Pehrsson, Jørgensen, and Marahrens were present. Most of the discussion revolved about the Russian situation. There was no hint of Hitler's rising star in Germany. It was assumed that the next convention would be held—perhaps in America—in 1935. See the minutes, "Geschehen in Leipzig . . . den 7. November 1932," in ArCL.

15. The 1930s marked the deaths of several leading personalities in the Lutheran world. Besides Ihmels there were Nathan Söderblom (1931), Theophil Meyer (1934), John A. Morehead (1936), Gustav A. Brandelle (1936), Charles M. Jacobs (1937), Carl C. Hein (1937), Sam Stadener (1937), and Johan Lunde (1938).

16. The archives in Geneva, Copenhagen, New York, and St. Olaf College (Northfield, Minn.) all have copies of communications written by Jørgensen after January 1933 to the non-German members (Morehead, Boe, and Pehrsson) and marked "confidential" or "very confidential." With the exception of this first letter (June 13, 1933), the customary salutation is: "*An die nichtdeutschen Mitglieder.* . . ."

When the committee members met at Hannover they were still perplexed by developments in Germany. As the meeting progressed they were instructed in at least two things that had been difficult to understand: (1) the obvious German fascination with Hitler, who was restoring both the spirit and economy of Germany, and (2) the anti-Semitic underside of the Nazi movement. As yet, they perceived the church's chief danger to be the "German Christians" rather than Hitler. It was from this perspective that they interpreted Jørgensen's warning: "On the one hand, we must be very careful and tactful in order not to hurt our German friends. . . . On the other, we must help them."[17] For the moment, the best procedure seemed to be to wait for the Hitler-mania to die down and for the anti-Christian character of the "German Christians" to become apparent to all.

The committee did not have long to wait for the latter. While the Hannover meeting was taking place, a huge rally of "German Christians" was held at Berlin's Sports Palace on November 13, 1933. It was reported that a resolution was passed requiring undivided loyalty of all pastors to National Socialism and universal application of the anti-Semitic Aryan law excluding Jews from public office.[18] In the light of this news, the committee was glad that it had accepted Marahrens's suggestion to call on Ludwig Mueller in Berlin after completing their business at Hannover. On November 17 the committee journeyed to Berlin. During the reception at Mueller's office, Marahrens gave a short greeting and introduced each of the committee members. The Reich bishop used the occasion to speak about his position on the Aryan Paragraph. Ralph H. Long reported later that Mueller "told us that the Aryan paragraph would not be carried out and that all the confessions of the churches would be kept inviolate. He stated that all religious societies would have to be confessional and that the so-called *Deutsch Glaubige* [*sic*] would soon disappear."[19] The members of the

17. Confidential letter: Jørgensen to Morehead, Boe, and Pehrsson, June 13, 1933, p. 6. The copy used by the writer is in the LWF Archives, Geneva, "Luth. Weltkonvent," v. 2, 1933–39.

18. This is the notorious "Aryan Paragraph," adopted on April 7, 1933. Henri Lichtenberger, *The Third Reich* (New York: Greystone Press, 1937), p. 149. Cf. Stewart W. Herman, *It's Your Souls We Want* (Philadelphia: [Muhlenberg] Fortress Press, 1943), pp. 139–41.

19. "The Executive Committee . . . Hannover . . . November 8–17, 1933," p. 11, in ArCL. The official minutes are in German: "Tagung des Exekutivkomitees . . . , Nov. 8–17, 1933," LWF Archives, "Luth. Weltkonvent," v. 2, 1933–39.

committee welcomed this statement as a portent of better things to come. Boe, for example, wrote Morehead that Mueller had declared that the executive committee could deal directly with the German churches without going through his office.[20] Thus the committee left Berlin with the impression that the Nazis' religious policy would henceforth be more favorably disposed to the church.

Only a short time elapsed before the executive committee realized that their optimism had been misplaced and that Mueller had no intention of carrying out his promises. News soon reached the outside world that Mueller and his legal counsel were seeking to force two of the so-called "intact" Lutheran churches, Bavaria and Württemberg, to join the newly created (1933) *Reichskirche* (a Protestant union church), which Mueller hoped to manipulate for Nazi ends. When the two Lutheran churches refused to join, the gestapo placed Theophil Wurm (bishop of Württemberg) and Hans Meiser (bishop of Bavaria) under house arrest (October 1934). Their offices were then occupied by Nazis.

Since the LWC executive committee at Hannover had decided to hold its 1934 meeting in Munich, the arrest of Meiser, the anticipated host of the meeting, placed the committee right in the center of the issue between the Nazis and the Lutherans of South Germany. In view of this the Bavarian governor, Ritter von Epp, wrote a letter to Berlin, warning that Christians throughout the world would be aroused. Protests had already arrived from the Anglican bishops of Chichester and Canterbury. A short time later, the United Lutheran Church in America, holding its convention in Savannah, Georgia, authorized its president, Frederick H. Knubel, to send a telegram of strong disapproval (October 23) to Hitler himself.[21] The German ministries of the interior and foreign affairs responded by urging that the proposed site of the meeting be changed to Hannover. But Meiser said that as long as he was deprived of his rights, there could be no meeting either in Munich or Hannover. At length, Hitler was induced to relent and agreed to meet with Marahrens, Meiser, and Wurm, bishops of the three "intact" Lutheran churches. Eventually Mueller fell into dis-

---

20. Boe to Morehead, January 5, 1934, in ArCL.
21. ULCA, *Minutes . . . 1934*, pp. 474–75.

favor with Hitler, and his functions were transferred in 1935 to a new Reich ministry for church affairs headed by Hanns Kerrl. Meanwhile the executive committee met in Munich, November 13–21, 1934, as originally planned.

One of the first items on the agenda was the next world convention. During the previous year's meeting (Hannover, 1933), Jørgensen had proposed Paris for the 1935 conclave. In 1934 there were two proposals: Paris and Munich.[22] It was reasoned that should the Germans be denied travel permits to Paris, the convention could be moved to Munich. The Third Lutheran World Convention, it was decided, would differ from the previous assemblies in Eisenach and Copenhagen in at least two respects. First, instead of a large and open congress of delegates and visitors, Paris should be "a small working convention." Second, unlike Eisenach and Copenhagen, which had dealt primarily with "the inner questions" of Lutheranism—confessional particularity and concern for Lutheran unity—Paris must address the question of "The Church and the World."[23] In reporting this to Peter O. Bersell, Boe said, "The time has come . . . to turn our faces outward, not because the Lutheran Church wishes to depart from its traditional attitude of keeping out of politics, but because political, economic and social developments have invaded the field of the Church to such an extent that it must speak or be pushed out of the field entirely."[24]

22. In addition to the official minutes (LWF Archives, Geneva) in German, there are several documents related to the Munich meeting: Morehead's report, "Annual Meeting of the Executive Committee . . . 1934," with attached German minutes, in ArCL; an unsigned (Jørgensen?) "Memorandum über die jüngste Entwicklung der kirchlichen Lage in Deutschland" (in LWF Archives), reporting the pressures on Meiser and Wurm and asking whether those outside Germany could help the German churches; a letter to Meiser from Boe (December 13, 1934) upon the latter's return to the United States; and finally a paper, "[Peter O.] Bersell Interviews Boe" (January 3, 1935). The last two items are in Boe Papers, box 97.

23. "Verhandlungen des Executive Committees . . . 1934," p. 1.

24. "Bersell Interviews Boe," January 3, 1935, p. 7. Although Boe could make a strong statement like this, he did not yet comprehend the situation in Germany. He saw the "church struggle" mainly as a conflict between the "German Christians" and the church, or between Reich Bishop Ludwig Mueller and men like Hans Meiser, August Marahrens, and Theophil Wurm. He seems to have been unaware that Mueller was Hitler's personal agent, holding this position until the Führer was embarrassed by Mueller's inept handling of growing church opposition. Boe's blind spot is revealed in a "thank you" letter to Meiser after the Munich meeting. Boe to Meiser, December 13, 1934, Boe Papers, box 97.

Boe's statement reflected accurately the hopes for the Paris convention. Its general theme was to be "Lutheranism and the Contemporary Crisis." The addresses and discussions were to deal with various aspects of this theme, including a main lecture on the subject "Lutheranism in Political Crisis." (Actually, at Paris the theme and lecture itself were less pointed: "Le Luthéranisme dans la crise du monde actuel," i.e., "Lutheranism in the Crisis of the Contemporary World.") Although there was a certain lack of specificity in the topics, there was no intention on the part of the executive committee to blunt the discussion by dealing in lofty generalities. For example, Hans Meiser argued at the Munich meeting that the rise of the Nazis required a thorough examination of such topics as the relation of church and people (*Volk*), church and state, and the Lutheran understanding of natural theology (in light of Barthian or "dialectical" theology).[25]

Finally, in light of the various crises the Paris convention would address the question of future organizational changes. American churchmen, especially Boe and Knubel, were eager for structural alteration. Among the problems were the question of a central bureau, the role of national committees, and the rotation of the presidential office. The latter question was especially acute in view of the election of a new president. Morehead's failing health and consequent inability to deal adequately with some of the pre-Paris arrangements—in addition to the disagreement over the Copenhagen and Örebro actions on the presidential office—made it a foregone conclusion that the Lutheran World Convention would have new leadership after Paris.[26]

---

25. "Verhandlungen des Executive Committees . . . 1934," p. 3. Neither the minutes nor the supplemental reports nor the letters bear out Boyens's contention that Marahrens was at odds with Meiser over these matters or that he warned against a discussion of church and state (see Boyens, "Lutheranism in Time of Dictators," p. 235). It is clear that Marahrens worked vigorously to preserve the "intact" character of the Lutheran confessional churches on the basis of "The Constitution of the German Evangelical Church, July 14, 1933." Cf. "Verhandlungen des Executive Committees . . . 1934," p. 15; and Jørgensen's confidential Danish report to Boe (with a request to translate for Morehead) of his trip to Germany and France in June 1935 ("Beretning om Besøg i Tyskland og Frankrig for at forberede det tredje lutherske Verdenskonvent," p. 2, Boe Papers, box 101). The constitution is printed in the Appendix of Arthur C. Cochrane, *The Church's Confession under Hitler* (Philadelphia: Westminster Press, 1962), pp. 224–28.

26. Boe, as the second American member of the executive committee, was distressed by two things: (1) his friend Morehead's evident deterioration, and (2) his fear that a German (Marahrens) would be elected president. Boe favored the election of a Swede. His copious correspondence with Knubel, Gustav A. Brandelle, president of the Augustana Synod, and Jørgensen revealed his concerns. See letters scattered throughout Boe's LWC papers, Boe Papers esp. boxes 97–101.

THE PARIS CONVENTION, 1935

A consideration of the Third Lutheran World Convention held in Paris, October 13–20, 1935, hardly fits the general theme of this chapter: special occasions of distress during the decade 1929–39. Nevertheless, it is both necessary and appropriate to be reminded that this assembly, which marked a turning point in the organizational procedures of the Lutheran World Convention, occurred in the context of severe economic, political, and religious crises.[27]

The themes that were discussed reflected the troubles of the times. The principal addresses were concerned with Lutheranism and (1) "The Contemporary Religious Crisis," (2) "Inner Missions of the Day," (3) "Current Foreign Missions," (4) "The Crisis in the Life of Nations," and (5) "The Coming Generation." In all this, there was no weakening of the confessional stance of the former conventions, but there was obviously a greater concern with practical and social issues confronting the church. This was in keeping with the design that this should be a "working convention."

Previous conventions in affirming loyalty to the Lutheran confessional writings had been concerned with their relevance to issues in the theological field. At Paris their insights were viewed in the light of "changes in economic, political and intellectual life." Their doctrines involved "rejecting all erroristic religious movements," which although not identified by name could be found in totalitarian lands. One of the more significant lectures in this respect was that delivered by the Swedish bishop, Sam Stadener. Without mentioning Hitler, Mussolini, or Stalin by name, the bishop drew clear and unmistakable

27. The official proceedings contain addresses in the languages in which they were delivered: German, English, and French. Denkschrift, *Lutherischer Weltkonvent zu Paris vom 13. bis 20. Oktober 1935* (Berlin, 1939). Morehead's handwritten notes, together with copies of numerous addresses and reports, are in ArCL. Brief summary reports used by the writer are Hanns Lilje, "Der Dritte Lutherische Weltkonvent," in Archiv des Lutherischen Kirchenamtes, Hannover, Germany (hereafter referred to as ALKH); Frederick H. Knubel, "Lutheran Officials in Conference," *The Lutheran*, November 21, 1935; Ralph H. Long, "The Story of the Lutheran World Convention," *The Bond*, January 1936; S. Grundmann, "Der III. Lutherische Weltkonvent," in *Der Lutherische Weltbund* (Cologne and Graz: Böhlau Verlag, 1957); and *The Lutheran World Almanac and Encyclopedia 1934–1937* (New York: NLC, 1937). Much of what follows, though supplemented in considerable detail by the above-named sources, is indebted to the outline in Willard D. Allbeck, "A Study of American Participation in Inter-Lutheran Cooperation Prior to the Formation of the Lutheran World Federation," prepared for the Department of Theology of the LWF, 1962.

Paris, France, 1935: Lutheran World Convention.

portraits of the people who were creating the crises "of the real world." The world had failed to learn the lessons of World War I, and today it "looks like a 'jungle' in which the weak are crushed between the jaws of the strong. . . . A modern State looks much more like a police organization than like a State organized on the basis of law. . . . Certain countries have grown so tired, disgusted and angry with economic or political strife, that one day, they swept away the existing government in order to give authority to a single man." The church has no human head to whom it gives total authority. Its task is rather to proclaim the absolute power of God to the world and to kneel in homage before him.[28]

A series of resolutions summed up the major problems confronting the church.[29] The first resolution sharply attacked ideologies seeking to shape the world in ways hostile to Christianity in general and to the evangelical authority of the church in particular. It insisted that, although details of church polity are of secondary nature, the government of the Lutheran church must be Lutheran in character. Related to it was the second resolution, which called for theological research and publication concerning "the nature and tasks of our Church in the present age." A third resolution insisted on the right of the church to give Christian training to its young people regardless of the demands of the state, a problem that was acute under dictatorships.

The fourth resolution, framed with reference to socialist political policies, declared that the Inner Mission "is to maintain the peculiar character impressed upon it by the Gospel and keep its independence over against the social service of the State, although co-operating intelligently with the state." As a sequel to this brief declaration, the fifth resolution concerning "The Church and Social Problems" presented a longer statement that was in effect an outline of the church's involvement in the social order. Because the church has a true understanding of the human predicament marked by the fact of sin and the need of grace, she is uniquely "equipped to contribute toward

28. "Le Lutheranisme dans la crise du monde actuel," in *Lutherischer Weltkonvent . . . Paris . . . 1935*, pp. 117–29.
29. The resolutions in German are to be found in the proceedings, ibid., pp. 159–66. An English translation is printed in *Lutheran World Almanac . . . 1934–1937*, pp. 33–35.

the solution of social problems." Her position is neither one of neutrality nor one of a religious socialism. Instead, she is sensitive to social ills, she ministers to those who suffer from them, she must be concerned with programs of social justice, and within her fellowship she must set an example of brotherly concern.

In the sixth resolution, the convention stoutly repudiated the assertion that foreign missions should be discontinued. It is not only true "that non-Christian peoples have a right to protection against the insidious effects of a de-Christianized culture, and against exploitation on the part of so-called Christian nations," but they also are entitled to "the proclamation of the gospel of salvation, which God continually offers anew to the world in the living Christ in order to make men children of God."

"Russia and the Ukraine" and "The Minority Churches" were the captions of the last two resolutions. Gratitude for faithfulness and for new opportunities for the spread of the gospel, especially in the Ukraine, was combined with sincere sympathy for Lutheran minorities suffering oppression, particularly in Russia. "The members of the Lutheran World Convention feel bound before God and the Christian Church to call upon the nations and their rulers to utilize every opportunity to make their influence felt in the proper place, so that the sufferings of our brethren for the sake of their faith may be brought to an end."

The business of the convention was concerned chiefly with improving its organizational structure. It was felt that the time had come when there could be an advance from the status of a free conference with a continuation committee to that approaching an agency or a confederation. Frederick H. Knubel had formulated his proposals. The absent Lars W. Boe had drawn up a list of suggestions for the executive committee to present to the convention looking toward a more stable and aggressive organization. At Paris the suggested plans for reorganization were presented by August Marahrens and Knubel, who concurred in many of Boe's proposals. Therefore, the resolutions were of threefold authorship.[30]

30. Although Boe was prevented from attending the Paris convention by his wife's illness, his carefully thought-out proposals were well received. Boe's suggestions are to be found in connection with a letter to Jørgensen, September 9, 1935; see Boe Papers

As a result of the propositions that were presented and the discussion that followed, the convention adopted the following eleven resolutions:[31]

1. The Lutheran World Convention confesses the truth which is in Jesus Christ as revealed in the Holy Scripture and as witnessed by Luther's Small Catechism and the Augsburg Confession. On the basis of this truth, the Lutheran World Convention declares its purpose to bring the Lutheran Churches and organizations of the world into an enduring and intimate relationship with one another in order to promote oneness of faith and confession and to ward off antagonistic and hostile influences. Those Lutheran Churches and groups which have special opportunities to witness for the faith shall be strengthened by the Lutherans of the world through the Convention. It shall also assume urgent definite responsibilities, especially at present those in the missionary and educational fields. Emergencies especially among oppressed Lutheran minorities shall be met.

2. The Lutheran World Convention shall meet every five years.

3. In addition to the six members of the Executive Committee, the Lutheran World Convention shall at each regular session elect six alternates, two from each of the three groups.

4. At its initial meeting, the Executive Committee shall first elect from its members a president, two vice-presidents, one treasurer, one associate treasurer and a secretary. The presidency shall rotate among the three groups.

5. The Executive Committee shall meet at least once each year. It shall decide as to the participation of any or all of the alternates in the meetings.

6. If necessary, the Executive Committee may call a meeting of the heads of all or part of the member-churches and affiliated organizations within the five-year period for special consultation with the Executive Committee and alternates.

7. For the sake of the continuity and efficiency of the work, the Lutheran World Convention regards it necessary to have an executive secretary and authorizes that he be appointed by the Executive Committee. His office shall, if possible, be located at the place of residence of the president and shall be supported by the member-churches of the Convention.

8. The Lutheran World Convention recommends the formation of special committees within the three main groups and also in the other areas, which shall promote its purpose.

---

and ALKH, Lilje, A/I. Knubel's clearheaded ecclesiastical sense was first expressed in outline form at a New York meeting of American church presidents on January 18, 1935, called by Boe to discuss proposals for Paris (see ArCL, LWC unit, box 24). The printed and fleshed-out version, "Organization of the Lutheran World Convention," delivered by Knubel at Paris on October 15, 1935, is to be found in ALKH, Lilje, A/I. Marahrens's lecture at Hannover, "Die Organisation des Lutherischen Weltkonvents," is also in ALKH.

31. As set forth in *The Bond* 12 (January 1936): 3.

9. In order that the interests of the small churches may be cared for, they may report to the Executive Committee, which will make one of its members responsible for this matter. In specially important cases representatives of smaller churches may be invited for personal consultations with the Executive Committee.

10. The Executive Committee shall present to the next meeting of the Lutheran World Convention a draft of an order of business. It shall provide for the nominations and elections of presiding officers at the beginning of each meeting.

11. The Executive Committee shall make full annual reports (including complete full annual financial statements) to all the Lutheran Church Bodies.

In accordance with these provisions, the convention chose the persons needed for an executive committee. The representatives of Central Europe were August Marahrens and Hans Meiser, with Karl Ihmels (son of the late bishop) and Ernst Sommerlath as alternates; for Scandinavia, Alfred Th. Jørgensen and Per Pehrsson, with Olaf Moe and Max von Bonsdorff as alternates; for America, Frederick H. Knubel and Ralph H. Long, with Abdel Ross Wentz and Lars W. Boe as alternates. The convention elected John A. Morehead as honorary president for life in recognition of his long and faithful service. The committee immediately elected its officers: Marahrens as president, Knubel as first vice-president, Pehrsson as second vice-president, Meiser as secretary, Jørgensen as treasurer, and Long as assistant treasurer. The office of executive secretary was to be filled later.

Though the program included no great public celebrations, there were several events of interest: Albert Lebrun, president of the French Republic, received the executive committee; the president of the city of Paris welcomed the entire convention; the executive committee placed a wreath of flowers on the grave of the unknown soldier at the Arc de Triomphe; and the Protestant theological faculty of the University of Paris conferred the honorary degree of doctor of theology upon Morehead and Jørgensen.

The American Lutheran response to the convention in Paris was modest both in scope and depth. This was no doubt due to the stark realities of everyday life rather than to any considered judgment that Paris was an insignificant event in the life of the church. Church people like other citizens were still struggling to emerge from the grip of the Great Depression. This meant a preoccupation with local church problems, bread-and-butter issues, and keeping the wolf away from the doors of church institutions, educational, missionary, and charitable.

Commentaries on Paris in Lutheran periodicals were largely reports without interpretation. There were exceptions, of course. Frederick H. Knubel noted a sense of inadequacy in the face of the dangers that threatened the world.[32] In their own strength, he said, Christians are always inadequate; they must never lose their dependence. Recognizing this, however, one must ask if Lutherans had sufficiently explored the practical implications of their confessional heritage. He thought not. But Knubel believed that in the area of organization there had been progress. It is surprising that he failed to mention one of the more important resolutions—one that bore the marks of Knubel's own thought regarding the organization of the church: ". . . All the details of Church polity are of secondary nature, nevertheless the government of the Lutheran Church must be Lutheran in character." This seemingly simple statement continued for decades to be hidden away in the Paris proceedings under the apparent assumption by all that their church governments were indeed "Lutheran in character." It was only in the 1960s and 1970s that the tip of the ecclesiological question began to be seen.

An extensive review of the convention was written by J. Michael Reu. He applauded the conservative Lutheran stance of two bishops, Hans Meiser and Simon Schöffel, but deplored the "unionistic" atmosphere brought to the convention by the presence of French Reformed Church dignitaries. He was especially upset by the celebration of Holy Communion, the first time this had occurred at a Lutheran World Convention. What disturbed him was not the innovation but the participation of both "liberals and conservatives."[33]

Ralph H. Long, writing in the publication of the Lutheran Brotherhood, a Minneapolis-based insurance company, described More-

32. *The Lutheran*, November 2, 1935, pp. 3–4.
33. Reu's commentary appears in successive issues of his journal, *Kirchliche Zeitschrift*, in February, August, and September 1936. Morehead too had been disturbed by the inclusion of Holy Communion on the program. Neither his nor Reu's criticism was based on the lack of or presence of an ecclesial character in the convention itself. In their minds, the "ecclesial character" was no doubt solved by the fact that the service was "sponsored" by a "church," St. Jean's Lutheran Congregation. Cf. Morehead to Boe, March 23, 1935, and April 24, 1935, Boe Papers.

head's farewell address as "a fitting climax," "the most impressive moment in the convention."[34] In one sense this was true. The man who was "Mr. Lutheran" to a large part of the church, and who had been described as the one "who had created world Lutheranism," had obviously delivered his valedictory.[35] He had come to Paris against the advice of his physician and arrived in a weakened condition. Temporarily revived by the warm greetings and display of gratitude and affection by his many friends gathered at Paris, he was able to preside at the first session, but that was all. It was but natural, therefore, that his message at the final session was one of high emotional appeal.

Upon Morehead's return to America, his already frail body began to manifest the legacy of years of physical and emotional strain. Despite his attempts at a brave exterior, he presented a tragic figure. Returning to Salem, Virginia, where he had been president of Roanoke College, both Morehead and his wife were taken critically ill. Mrs. Morehead died on May 29, 1936. Morehead, unable to attend the funeral, asked his nurse to inquire of his physician how much longer he would have. Three hours later he died. The date was June 1, 1936; he was sixty-nine years of age.

Morehead had been a tireless worker driven by a desire to effect a united world Lutheranism, to relieve human suffering, and to heal the wounds of war by cultivating transnational ties. He was, like so many southern Lutherans, a theological conservative and a deeply pious man. At the same time, he walked with the world's great men, counting many as personal friends. He was deluged with honors and decorations: two knighthoods (Denmark and Finland), several honorary degrees, the last of which was from the University of Paris in 1935.

34. *The Bond*, January 1936, p. 7.
35. Morehead's chronology from Samuel Trexler, *John A. Morehead* (New York: G. P. Putnam's Sons, 1938), p. 168:
    February 4, 1867—Born in Virginia
    1889—Graduated from Roanoke College
    1892—Graduated from Philadelphia Lutheran Seminary
    1892–98—Parish pastor
    1898–1903—President, Southern Seminary
    1903–20—President, Roanoke College
    1919–23—Chairman, NLC European Commission
    1923–30—Executive director, NLC, and chairman, LWC executive committee
    1930–35—President, LWC
    1935—Honorary president, LWC
    June 1, 1936—Death

En route to New York, 1936: Dr. Hanns Lilje of Berlin, Landesbischof Dr. August Marahrens of Hannover, and Landesbischof Dr. Hans Meiser of Munich travelled to the United States for the Executive Committee meeting of the Lutheran World Convention.

Four countries—Germany, Finland, Sweden, and Denmark—nominated him for the Nobel peace prize. Before the American President Franklin D. Roosevelt could submit Morehead's name to the committee in Oslo, Morehead had died. His monument was no doubt the Lutheran World Convention, which after his dominant direction was to confront new perplexities.

THE EXECUTIVE COMMITTEE: ISSUES, 1936–39

Under the provisions for altered governing procedures adopted at Paris, the new executive committee held four annual meetings before the outbreak of World War II: New York, 1936; Amsterdam, 1937; Uppsala, 1938; and Waldenburg, 1939.

It was not clear what the policy or influence of president-elect

Marahrens would be. We have noted Boe's questions about him. His reservations may have been shared by Morehead, Knubel, and Jørgensen. Nonetheless, when the committee elected officers at Paris, the American reluctance, if any, was not expressed. The minutes reveal that all agreed that the new president should be chosen from the "central group" (Germany). Since Marahrens and Meiser represented this "center," they were asked to leave the room. When they returned, it was announced that Marahrens had been chosen.[36] He accepted graciously and soon demonstrated his grasp of the situation and addressed his new executive responsibilities ably.

The annual meeting of the executive committee took place in New York, September 29–October 6, 1936.[37] This was the first time the committee had met outside Europe and also the first time that the Germans (Marahrens, Meiser, and Lilje) had visited America. The regular American members (Knubel and Long) together with the deputy members (Boe and Wentz) completed the roll. In the absence of the Scandinavians, a report from the northern countries was read.

By way of summary, only six matters require mention at this juncture. First, Hanns Lilje was elected executive (general) secretary with office in Berlin.[38] Second, a definitive declaration on "Lutherans and Ecumenical Movements" was prepared. Third, Marahrens reported on the condition of non-Aryan Christians in Germany, for whom special care was being solicited. The minutes have no other reference to the Nazi attack on Jews. Fourth, a memorial service with special tribute to Morehead by Boe was held in Holy Trinity Church in mid-Manhattan. Fifth, the Germans drew considerable attention from the

36. "Niederschrift . . . Exekutiv-Komitee . . . Paris, 19.10.1935," p. 1, in LWF Archives, Geneva.

37. "Protokoll der ersten Sitzung des Exekutiv-Komitees . . . 29. September 1936–6. Oktober, 1936, New York," Boe Papers, box 103, folder 7. A summary of the 1936 meeting, together with the full text of the important LWC document on ecumenical relations presented at New York, is to be found in Lutheran World Almanac . . . 1934–1937, pp. 35–38.

38. Johannes (better known as Hanns) Lilje (1899–1977) was an international figure in Christian circles from the 1930s to his death on January 6, 1977. His ecumenical career began when he was chosen general secretary of the Student Christian Movement in Germany. His involvement with organized world Lutheranism began in 1936 and continued to the end of his life. He was elected Bishop of Hannover in 1947 and became Abbot of Loccum on the death of Marahrens in 1950. He was elected president of the LWF in 1952. Arrested by the Nazi gestapo in 1944 for resistance to the regime, he was saved from execution by the American army in 1945. He served for many years on the Central Committee of the World Council of Churches and from 1968 to 1975 as one of the council's presidents.

American public. President Roosevelt received them in special audience, the *New York Times* published interviews on the situation in Germany, Lilje (the only one fluent in English) preached on the Columbia Broadcasting System's "Church of the Air," and the visitors traveled to the conventions of the American Lutheran Church in San Antonio, Texas, and the United Lutheran Church in Columbus, Ohio.[39]

The second annual post-Paris meeting was held in Amsterdam, August 24–28, 1937. Agreement was reached that Lutherans should present a united front in the proposed World Council of Churches and that they should press for confessional rather than geographical representation. Marahrens, who had been named by the Conference on Life and Work to the Committee of Fourteen, was requested to present this position at ecumenical meetings.[40] (The Nazis forbade his attendance at the 1937 Oxford Conference on Life and Work.) There was consideration of the Ukraine and other minority churches and of the Gossner Mission in India, which suffered loss of support when the Hitler government restricted the flow of money out of Germany. A budget of $51,000 for relief was adopted.

From the standpoint of the future structure of world Lutheranism, the most important action at Amsterdam was the discussion of a constitution and the decision that Lilje prepare a rough draft to be reviewed by Meiser, Pehrsson, and Knubel prior to the next meeting of the executive committee. The goal was to present a constitution for ratification at the next world assembly, which according to regulations adopted at Paris would take place in 1940 at a yet undesignated place.[41]

The committee's meeting in 1938 was held in Uppsala, Sweden,

39. For details, see *New York Times*, October 6 and 8, 1936; *Literary Digest*, October 10, 1936; *Evangelischer Pressedienst*, October 28, 1936. See also tapes of interviews with Lilje, October 30, 1974, conducted by E. Clifford Nelson; the tapes are on deposit in the St. Olaf College Archives, Northfield, Minnesota.

40. The official minutes: "Niederschrift . . . des Executivkomitees des Luth. Weltkonvents . . . Amsterdam . . . 24. bis 28. August 1937," in LWF Archives. Wentz's handwritten notes on this meeting's discussion of the ecumenical relations is in the LWC Papers, box 1, folder 17, in ArCL.

41. The embryonic stage of constitutional development is to be sought in the discussions and proposals prior to and at Paris, but world Lutheranism's constitutional history began to take shape in 1937 at Amsterdam and continued through 1939, when a draft was ready for the Philadelphia (1940) convention canceled by World War II. For the 1937 discussion, see the official minutes (n. 40, above), pp. 6–7.

May 21–25. Primary items for discussion were (1) the relation to the ecumenical movement, (2) the continuing work on a constitution for the Lutheran World Convention, and (3) the plans for the 1940 convention. Regarding the ecumenical movement, Knubel reported on the special Utrecht meeting (May 9–12, 1938), which adopted "The Basis" for the proposed World Council of Churches: "The World Council of Churches is a fellowship of Churches which accept our Lord Jesus Christ as God and Saviour." Utrecht also approved the principle of "regional" rather than "confessional" representation, despite vigorous opposition from Lutherans. The response to Knubel's report was the preparation of a resolution reaffirming the principle of confessional representation voiced by the executive committee at Amsterdam in 1937.[42]

Three different drafts of a constitution for the Lutheran World Convention were presented and discussed, but no action was taken.[43] With respect to the next assembly, it was decided to hold it at Philadelphia and to adopt the general theme "The Lutheran Church Today." Commissions were to be appointed by July 1, 1938, to prepare the three subtopics: Commission I—The Church, the Word, and the Sacraments (six Germans and three other members); Commission II—The Church and the Churches (six Scandinavians and three others); and Commission III—The Church in the World (six Americans and three others). At the conclusion of the meeting, Per Pehrsson, who had been a member of the committee since 1923, submitted his resignation, citing as reasons his age (seventy years) and the need for a younger person.

Between the 1938 and 1939 meetings of the executive committee, Hanns Lilje undertook a wide-ranging trip to the United States to assist the American commission in preparing for the Philadelphia assembly of 1940 and to visit Lutheran centers throughout the country. The six-week tour, from October 28 to mid-December, gave him

42. "Niederschrift . . . Verhandlungen . . . 21. bis 25. Mai 1938, Uppsala," p. 5, in LWF Archives. The Uppsala resolution was sent to all LWC churches by Lilje on July 6, 1938. See ALKH, Lilje A/V.

43. The three constitutional drafts (German, American, Scandinavian) are attached as exhibits to the official minutes. They are also reproduced in the appendix of Kurt Schmidt-Clausen, *Vom Lutherischen Weltkonvent zum Lutherischen Weltbund* (Gütersloh: Gerd Mohn, 1976), pp. 247–54.

firsthand experience of both the ecclesiastical scene and the general cultural scene in America. At the same time, it afforded the Americans an opportunity to become acquainted with the brilliant young German. Later, during World War II, they remembered his winsome qualities and were confident that the American church had a friend in Lilje. His role in the "church struggle" led eventually to his imprisonment by the Nazis. Seven years after the war, he was elected president of the Lutheran World Federation.[44]

The final meeting of the executive committee prior to World War II was held May 20–25, 1939, at Waldenburg in Saxony on the estate of Prince Günther von Schönburg-Waldenburg. Most of the members and alternates were present. Absent were Abdel Ross Wentz (United States) and Erling Eidem, Swedish archbishop, who had been named to the committee to replace Pehrsson.[45] If one were to rely on the official minutes alone, one might conclude that the meeting was held in a blissfully peaceful atmosphere, quite unaware of the political powder keg on which the world sat. One might be tempted to conclude, in a droll sort of fashion, that the business of the committee was more or less given over to the collapse of society and the passing of irrelevant resolutions in the framework of overall signs of disaster. That this was not the case was made evident by the appendix, which included a German translation of a statement signed by the presidents of the seven member churches of the National Lutheran Council. Entitled "These Momentous Times" (*In Entscheidungsvoller Zeit*), the document warned that the world was in imminent danger of war, that it was engulfed in an overpowering darkness out of which fearful cries were already being heard. On the one hand, nations were turning to communism, which said that all would be well with mankind if only bread were made available. On the other hand, fascism in its various forms sought security in "muscle" ("might makes right"). Moreover, signs were increasing that America too was in danger of seeking its

44. Lilje's report of the trip, "Bericht über eine Amerika-Reise," 1938, is in ALKH. An account of his imprisonment was published after the war: *Im Finstern Tal* (Nürnberg: Laetare Verlag, 1947); English translation: *The Valley of the Shadow* (Philadelphia: [Muhlenberg] Fortress Press, 1950). Lilje told the writer in October 1974 that during his 1938 visit with Lars W. Boe at St. Olaf College he was offered a position on the faculty but felt it his duty to remain in Germany.
45. "Niederschrift . . . Verhandlungen . . . 20. bis 25. Mai 1939 in Waldenburg," Boe Papers, box 102.

security in "bread and muscle." Lilje's report (not referred to in the minutes) noted that the Lutheran churches of the world were immediately affected by the world's political tensions.[46]

Despite the current threats to peace, the committee proceeded with plans for the 1940 Philadelphia convention, hearing the report that manuscripts of the topical studies would be in hand by January 1. Much of the remainder of the business was devoted to the new form of the proposed constitution. Although Boe, unlike his fellow American Knubel, felt that the time was not ripe, the proposal was adopted for presentation to the Philadelphia assembly.[47] Three months later the Nazis invaded Poland, and subsequent developments necessitated the cancellation of the 1940 convention. Nevertheless, an attempt was made to hold a meeting of the executive committee in Copenhagen during April 1940. Two Americans were prepared to make the trip, but with the Nazi invasion of Denmark and Norway on April 9, 1940, the meeting was canceled. Five bloody years elapsed before another meeting could be held, and seventeen years were to go by before world Lutherans could assemble on American soil, this time at Minneapolis in 1957.

Our rapid survey of the executive committee meetings between Paris and the outbreak of the war has given hints of the difficulties that faced the committee. Despite the distresses of the last half of the decade, the committee made some notable decisions which contributed solidly to the formation of the Lutheran World Federation after the war. At least three of these deserve elaboration: the establishment of a general secretariat under the leadership of Hanns Lilje; the adoption of a policy to guide Lutheran participation in the ecumenical movement; and the preparation of a constitution for world Lutheranism.

In Chapter 7 we reviewed the debate over the creation of a central bureau. When the question was affirmatively decided at Paris (1935), the selection of a general secretary to head the Central Bureau became

---

46. See Ralph H. Long's report in *The Lutheran*, June 28, 1939.
47. Knubel had pressed for the adoption of a constitution. See "Niederschrift . . . Amsterdam, 1937," p. 7, in LWF Archives. Boe's personal opinion did not prevent him from making the vote unanimous. "Niederschrift . . . Waldenburg, 1939," p. 6, Boe Papers, box 102.

a matter of considerable concern. Already at Paris, Knubel had backed up his support of a central bureau by urging informally the candidacy of Hanns Lilje.[48] Meiser wrote to Lilje that he was under the impression that Jørgensen desired the office and that Knubel was in favor of him.[49] Meiser's judgment in this matter was in error. Jørgensen and others were questioning the wisdom of locating the secretariat in Germany, where the severe limitations of life under Nazi dictatorship would restrict the church and link the Lutheran World Convention too closely to the fate of the German churches under Hitler. A neutral country might provide freedom of movement.

Scandinavian misgivings were concerned with Lilje, not as a person but as a German. There were countries where the executive secretary would not be welcome if he were a German. After Lilje was elected, Jørgensen, in a confidential letter, urged that someone other than Lilje represent the convention in certain nations:

> I beg you to understand that if we let one man represent the Convention in an independent way and as a constant factor, it will divide the Lutheran churches in Europe instead of unite them. You don't know how strong and how terrible the nationalistic feelings are in this moment. Only one example: I was in Czechoslovakia, invited by the Lutheran Slovaks who had a great festival. They had invited men from the . . . different churches, but none from the German church. From Czechoslovakia itself they had not invited the Czech Germans. They asked me not to speak German, but French. The only way to make progress is that the Executive Committee represents the Convention.[50]

The American members of the committee without exception desired Lilje as the first executive secretary. Knubel and Long (the regular members) and Boe and Wentz (alternates) had great confidence that Lilje could and would serve the whole Lutheran church. Long wrote to Jørgensen: "We believe that Dr. Lilje is eminently fitted to serve in this capacity."[51] Hanns Lilje's qualifications were indeed impressive. He possessed a winsome personality and a sense of humor, both of

48. See "Niederschrift . . . Exekutiv-Komitee . . . Paris, 1935," p. 4, in LWF Archives; and Knubel to Marahrens, November 21, 1935, in ALKH.

49. Meiser to Lilje, January 28, 1937, in Archiv der Landeskirche Bayerns in Nürnberg, Germany, Pers. XXXVI, No. 122. This letter shaped Lilje's somewhat unfavorable estimate of Jørgensen even after he learned the truth in the matter. Interview of Lilje by E. Clifford Nelson, October 30, 1974, Hannover.

50. Jørgensen to Long, November 18, 1936, in ArCL.

51. Long (for the American Section) to Jørgensen, December 4, 1936, in ArCL.

which added luster to his native intelligence, scholarly work, linguistic abilities, and ecumenical experiences. There were few, if any, who could match him. Only one American, J. Michael Reu, expressed any reservation. He said that he hoped Lilje would decline the appointment. Of course, he would not object to having a German in the office, but the executive secretary ought to be "an orthodox Lutheran." It was at this point, in Reu's opinion, that Lilje was unacceptable.[52]

The Americans in general, however, were not convinced that Lilje was theologically dangerous. Moreover, they entertained the conviction that an effort must be made to overcome nationalistic prejudices by emphasis on the great issues from which the Lutheran World Convention was constituted. If nationalism imposed limitations on Lilje's acceptability in certain quarters, perhaps a "discreet use of the members of the executive committee" would overcome these difficulties. Even so, it was felt, Lilje would disarm prejudices against himself or Germans in general.[53] Under these circumstances, Lilje took office January 1, 1937.

The second major contribution of the executive committee in the period between Paris and the onset of war in 1939 was the formulation of a policy statement on ecumenical relations. Bearing the title "Lutherans and Ecumenical Movements," the document arose in America when the question of Lutheran membership in the proposed World Council of Churches emerged out of the 1937 meetings of Faith and Order (Edinburgh) and Life and Work (Oxford). In anticipation of the decision that would have to be made, Frederick H. Knubel asked Abdel Ross Wentz to prepare a document to guide Lutherans. The paper was presented to the New York meeting (1936) of the executive committee, adopted by the committee, edited by Lilje, and then later approved by the absent Scandinavians.[54] The following summary, adapted from Willard D. Allbeck's research, emphasizes the main provisions under the various sections of the document.[55]

52. Reu to Long, December 7, 1935, in ArCL.
53. Long to Jørgensen, January 7, 1937, in ArCL.
54. The statement is printed in *Lutheran World Almanac . . . 1934–1937*, pp. 36–38. The most thorough study of Lutherans and the WCC has been made by Dorris A. Flesner, "The Role of the Lutheran Churches of America in the Formation of the World Council of Churches" (Ph.D. diss., Hartford Seminary, 1956).
55. Allbeck, "Study of American Participation"; used by permission of the author.

The statement notes as a sort of preface that at a time when many world organizations, both secular and religious, were being formed there was need for a fuller formulation of the Lutheran position. To begin with, there must be noted Lutheranism's ecumenical character both geographically and theologically, without limitation to race, nation, or temperament. The base from which Lutheranism operates is one which seeks expression for Lutheran ecumenicity and which endeavors to realize it in programs of missions and church relief. Thus there is a Lutheran solidarity that is actualized by putting into effect the resolutions of the Lutheran World Convention, by cultivating a truly Lutheran consciousness, by furthering Lutheran union, by forming a practical entente of Lutherans, and by presenting a common front toward other ecumenical movements. All this is nothing but a vigorous witness to the gospel as a scriptural heritage both in mutual Lutheran relations and in communications with others.

Following this prologue came a series of resolutions grouped under three headings. The first group was entitled "Concerning Evangelical Consciousness." It advocated all possible measures to deepen such consciousness in the churches and their members, calling attention to the grave dangers inherent in "such pernicious influences as atheism, secularism, syncretism, sectarianism, and politico-ecclesiasticism." The list of "isms" quite obviously viewed the crises not only in Russia and Germany but elsewhere as well.

"Concerning Lutheran World Solidarity" was the caption of the second group. These resolutions called upon the Lutheran churches to cultivate a sense of common interest and to foster it among their members. They encouraged the continued use of the Lutheran World Convention as an agent for cooperation. They urged the Lutheran churches to maintain this confessional solidarity in dealing with any associations tending to weaken it.

Having thus set the stage, the statement was ready for the third group of resolutions, under the title "Concerning Ecclesiastical Relations." Lutheran churches were encouraged to approach others without hostility but with a desire to cooperate "in works of Christian love." Lutheran churches should arrive at mutual agreements as to specific decisions involved in the ecumenical encounter. Participation by Lutheran churches in ecumenical movements is possible only when the following principles are observed: (1) guaranteed right and opportunity to testify for the faith and against error; (2) specific disavowal of any coercion upon participating churches to conform in thought or action; (3) assemblies of the ecumenical movement consisting of official representatives of the church bodies; (4) the purposes of the ecumenical organization exclusively those proper to the functions of the church without appeal to law enforcement; (5) acceptance by the ecumenical organization as fundamental doctrines the following: the fatherhood of God and human sonship by grace; Christ's deity, redemption, and continuing presence; the Holy Spirit's activity in calling and sanctifying; the supreme importance of Word and Sacraments; the authority of Scripture; the fact of sin and human inability to earn salvation; God's grace; the kingdom of God, the second coming of Christ in judgment and ultimate victory.

A final resolution urged the Lutheran churches "to maintain a united front in combating militant ecclesiasticism wherever it seeks to invade evangelical ranks or with politico-ecclesiastical measures to oppress evangelical minorities."

The basic principles of this 1936 statement have continued to be guidelines for Lutheran participation in ecumenical activities. Freedom to proclaim the gospel as Lutherans understand it is a necessary prerequisite. This is not a statement of isolation ("a Lutheran bloc") which views the situation in black-or-white terms of truth and error in which no compromise is possible. Rather, it is concerned with communicating with other churches regarding the essential content of the gospel, whereby misunderstandings are overcome and common convictions stressed. It insists that communication on the ecumenical level must be both confessional and responsible. Representation and participation on the basis of confessions rather than of countries is to recognize that the essential manifestation of a church is its faith rather than its nationality. It is appropriate in church matters that theology take precedence over geography. This is to recognize that the witness of the church is at once a heritage, a tradition, as well as a contemporary message. As for responsibility, the insistence upon official delegates not only guards against eccentric declarations by individuals who have no following, but at the same time makes possible such formulations as represent a consensus, affirmations truly typical of the fellowship of believers.

The statement served as a guide to Lutheran delegates to the World Conference on Faith and Order in Edinburgh in 1937. That conference and the Oxford Conference on Life and Work (also 1937) prepared to participate in the formation of a World Council of Churches by appointing a Committee of Fourteen, seven members from Life and Work, seven from Faith and Order, plus seven alternates, one of whom was Abdel Ross Wentz. The LWC executive committee meeting at Amsterdam, having adopted the statement of 1936 on ecumenical relations, gave support to August Marahrens, who had been invited to be a member of the Committee of Fourteen, by approving the following declaration:

1. We have learned with great interest of the plan evolved at Oxford and Edinburgh, July and August 1937, to unite the World Council on Life and Work with the World Conference on Faith and Order and so form a World Council of Christian Churches.

2. We urge the President of the Lutheran World Convention, Bishop Marahrens, to accept membership in the Constituent Committee that was set up at Oxford and Edinburgh and we instruct him to represent the interests of World Lutheranism in the formulation of plans for the future of the ecumenical movements as those interests are expressed in the action of the Executive Committee in New York on "Lutheranism and Ecumenical Relationships."

3. We express our conviction that representation in the proposed General Assembly, the proposed Central Committee, and the proposed Committees and Commissions, should be ecclesiastical and confessional and not territorial, and we instruct President Marahrens to insist upon this principle.

4. We instruct our President to communicate with all the Churches connected with the Lutheran World Convention, instructing them concerning the prospect of a union of Faith and Order and Life and Work, commending the general idea to their consideration, and securing their reaction thereto.

5. We prepare to approach with united front the completed plan for a World Council, and to that end we request all these Lutheran Churches to postpone their *final* action in this matter until they are instructed by President Marahrens concerning the general attitude of all the Lutheran Churches.[56]

When the organizing Committee of Sixty (the Committee of Fourteen plus an "advisory conference") met in Utrecht May 9–13, 1938,

56. "Niederschrift . . . Amsterdam 1937," p. 11, and addendum to the minutes, in Boe Papers, box 102.

Marahrens was not given a travel permit to leave Germany. Hence Knubel, the first vice-president of the executive committee, presented the Lutheran declaration. Though its position on confessional representation was not incorporated into the draft of the World Council of Churches constitution, a sentence was included making such representation a future possibility. In light of this, the LWC executive committee meeting at Uppsala (1938) devoted considerable discussion to the matter and adopted the following declaration, which was sent to member churches as well as to the World Council Provisional Committee (Committee of Twenty-eight), which had responsibilities for details until a general assembly of the World Council of Churches could be convened:

> The Executive Committee has heard the report of two of its members who participated in the ecumenical meeting at Utrecht from the 9th to the 13th of May, and records with satisfaction that the confession of our Lord Jesus Christ as God and Saviour was unanimously adopted as the basis of the proposed World Council of Churches. We would emphatically state that thereby agreement in faith was acknowledged as the unavoidable requirement for a true unification of the churches. If Jesus Christ is confessed in the fullest sense as our God and Saviour, it involves that He is the only mediator between God and man and that we are justified before God only through faith in Him, the crucified and risen One. Only where the Gospel of Jesus Christ is rightly and purely taught and the Sacraments are administered according to the institution . . . by Jesus will true church unity be maintained, according to the testimony of the New Testament as confessed by our church.
>
> In the organization of the World Council this principle was practically applied in the case of the Orthodox Church, which as such is to have special representation in the proposed new organization. This corresponds factually with the principle of confessional representation expressed in our Amsterdam resolution of 1937. Although this principle was carried through at Utrecht in the further arrangements for representation, we welcome the fact that the constitution provides for a possible change of the present territorial representation, and regard the present arrangement as only a temporary one, leading to such a change. The Lutheran World Convention believes that only on a confessional basis will participation in the work possess permanent and hopeful prospect.

Many of the leaders of the ecumenical movement looked upon the Lutheran confessional emphasis as a threat to "the ecumenical ideal." Therefore, they preferred that representation, with the exception of the Orthodox church, be national or geographic; that is, the allocation of seats in both the Assembly of the World Council and its Central Committee would be by territorial regions. For example, the U.S. representatives would be named by the Federal Council of Churches. The Lutherans saw this as a violation of the proposed constitution of the World Council of Churches, which described the council as "a fellowship of *churches*" (italics added). The logic of this seemed to be that representation should be by confessional churches as such rather than by regional segments of Christendom. The debate over this issue continued for the next decade, pending the adoption of the constitution of the World Council of Churches in 1948. By that time it had been agreed that delegates in the assembly would represent their respective churches. However, in allocating seats in the Assembly and the Central Committee, both confessional and geographical factors were to be taken into account.[57]

The third major achievement of the executive committee during the final years before World War II was the preparation and approval of a constitution for the Lutheran World Convention. Between 1923 and 1935, world Lutheranism had functioned within the limits of the Eisenach resolutions and, as we have seen, under the leadership of the executive committee. The Eisenach hope to have a "Larger Committee" as a kind of "interim parliament" to carry on the work between the general assemblies of the Lutheran World Convention was not realized, largely because Eisenach made no practical provision for its realization. In addition, the hope of some to have a central bureau or general secretariat, though much debated, was effectively delayed until 1935, when in the context of the whole question of reorganization a proposal for a secretariat was finally approved.

When Hanns Lilje accepted the office of executive (general) secretary, one of his first assignments was to give leadership to the executive committee's concern to provide a constitution for the Lutheran World Convention. It is quite evident that the chief architects of reorganization in the initial stages (1935–36) were Boe, Knubel, and

57. "Niederschrift . . . Uppsala 1938," p. 5, and appendix 2, in LWF Archives. Cf. Frederick H. Knubel, "Utrecht—Uppsala: World Council of Churches—Lutheran World Convention," News Bureau Release, NLC, no date (perhaps summer 1938), in ArCL. For a brief discussion of Lutherans in the ecumenical movement, see Abdel Ross Wentz, *A Basic History of Lutheranism in America* (Philadelphia: Fortress Press, 1964), pp. 361–71. Cf. Article V of the Constitution of the WCC (1948).

Marahrens. The actual constitutional drafts (1937–39) were largely the handiwork of Lilje and Wentz.[58] The executive committee's constitutional deliberations during the years to 1939 were in anticipation of presenting a completed draft for approval by the 1940 Philadelphia convention. Despite the fact that the latter was canceled, the constitutional draft of 1939 served as a guide in the preparation of the 1946 American-authored constitution for the Lutheran World Federation.

Meanwhile, in Germany, the repressive measures of the Nazis against the churches became steadily more severe. The years between 1933 and 1936 had been a time of sparring and tug-of-war between the church and the state. There was even some profoundly moving and memorable resistance, notably the Barmen Declaration of 1934. By 1937, however, the time for church action was past. One wonders, of course, what direct action could have been taken. William L. Shirer, the American news reporter in Berlin, asked German churchmen about this. The reply he received was in the form of another question: What action would he suggest? He admitted that he was at a loss to propose anything.[59] After all, what does one do within a totalitarian police state except obey or go to prison or the gallows? Of course, there were many who took the latter route. During 1937 more than eight hundred pastors were arrested (the most publicized in America was Martin Niemoeller's arrest) and church resistance continued to some extent. But popular interest in the "church struggle" (*Kirchenkampf*) had largely disappeared, and the physical and mental energies of church leaders were being sapped. Jørgensen wrote in one of his confidential reports to the non-German members of the executive committee that Marahrens especially showed the signs of strain: "For the first time in the many years that I have known Marahrens his nerves are

58. The various constitutional proposals before the executive committee in 1938, and the subsequent "final" proposal of 1939, are available in the appendix of Schmidt-Clausen, *Vom Lutherischen Weltkonvent*, pp. 247–57. Schmidt-Clausen provides an excellent analysis of the several drafts (pp. 202–14) and identifies the authors of each of the four proposals, which he labels A, B, C, and D. Lilje was the author of A; Wentz of B; the Scandinavians (von Bonsdorff, Moe, Jørgensen, and Pehrsson) of C; and the Swedish National Committee of D. Lilje worked through all the drafts and prepared a well-honed version for presentation to the 1939 meeting of the executive committee.

59. *The Rise and Fall of the Third Reich* (Greenwich, Conn.: Fawcett Publications, 1959), p. 321.

shattered."[60] So sure of their control of the church were the Nazis that they released from prison all but a dozen clergymen in December 1937. It was a hypocritical gesture of Christmas "peace on earth and goodwill to men."

Lars W. Boe had warned in 1935 that the election of Germans to lead the Lutheran World Convention would be a serious mistake. This was not to be construed, he insisted, as being anti-German. Rather, it was an indictment of the Paris convention for handing over the leadership of world Lutheranism to men (Marahrens and Lilje) who would not be free to act "as I know they would like to act." How much better it would have been had the destinies of world Lutheranism not been tied into the internal turmoils of the German churches. World Lutheranism was now shackled hands and feet. The election of Sam Stadener of Sweden, as Boe had proposed prior to the Paris assembly, would have left Lutheranism unfettered by its ties to immobilized German churchmen.[61] Boe's distress was only slightly mitigated by his personal hope that Lilje might be able to "do something" positive in a gloomy situation.

The possibility of effective service to the Lutheran World Convention by both the president and the executive secretary from their offices in Hannover and Berlin grew increasingly remote. When World War II broke out in 1939 and when the United States entered the conflict of 1941, Lutheran leadership from Germany ceased altogether. Although both Marahrens and Lilje retained their positions until after the collapse of Germany, practical leadership went by default to the "American Section" (as it was called) of the Lutheran World Convention. To this and to other topics we shall turn in the next chapter.

60. "An die nicht-deutschen Mitglieder . . . 31. January 1939." Abdel Ross Wentz Papers, in ArCL.
61. Boe to Knubel, March 16, 1937; March 20, 1937; August 6, 1937, in ArCL.

10

The Lutheran World Convention
in the Nazi Era, 1933–45

World Lutheranism was tragically yet fruitfully connected with the two world wars. In one way the wars obviously divided Lutherans; in another, they drew Lutherans together. The basic facts that Germany was the birthplace of evangelical Lutheranism and that a large percentage of its people were Lutherans—at least in name—immediately served to pit Germany's Lutherans against other Lutherans. Paradoxically, the very wars that divided Lutherans politically and militarily also released forces that created a heightened consciousness of confessional particularity and a broadened sense of unity and opened up opportunities for exhibiting Christian compassion and cooperation.

In the years immediately after World War I and in the era that ended with the collapse of Nazi Germany, strong confessional (although not necessarily institutional) loyalties worked to transcend ethnic, geographic, and patriotic boundaries. This was demonstrated in the formation of the Lutheran World Convention in 1923 and the increasing affection that member churches gradually bestowed upon it. Although the exigencies of the Nazi era and World War II created immense problems for organized world Lutheranism—for example, the LWC executive committee was largely immobilized because its president and executive secretary (August Marahrens and Hanns Lilje) resided in Germany—the LWC was saved from extinction by non-German Lutherans, especially the churches in America.

When war broke out in 1939, American Lutheranism possessed two cooperative agencies, the National Lutheran Council (for domestic affairs) and the American Section of the Lutheran World Convention (for international affairs).[1] In theory the two were separate entities; in actuality they were closely interlocked. This fact was acknowledged in 1941, when the National Lutheran Council adopted a statement that the two agencies were "coextensive." The NLC—whose executive director, Ralph H. Long, was also a member of the six-man American Section—was to carry out the day-to-day practical work of the American Section, while recognizing that it could not officially represent the American churches in their relationship to the Lutheran World Convention.[2] The American Section (as the members began to refer to themselves in 1937) consisted of the American members of the LWC executive committee—Frederick H. Knubel, Ralph H. Long, Lars W. Boe, and Abdel Ross Wentz. To prepare themselves for a possible emergency role, they held periodic meetings to deal with issues created by the worsening situation in Germany.[3]

The potentialities of this arrangement rested on the assumption that the confessional articulation of the gospel is an elemental fact of Lutheran life. Recognition of this, it was hoped, would transcend the current tensions and animosities that had already reached deeply and savagely into world Lutheranism. Practically, it was the only apparent way that organized global Lutheranism had a hope of survival. At the same time, it might provide a ministry of Christian compassion to the suffering members of "the household of faith" during persecution and war. Thus the American Section viewed the arrangement as an opportunity to cooperate with God as he did his work in a hostile world.[4]

1. These agencies represented only about two-thirds of American Lutheranism. The Missouri Synod and other ultra-conservative bodies were not members.

2. Frederick K. Wentz, *Lutherans in Concert* (Minneapolis: Augsburg Publishing House, 1968), p. 107.

3. The American Section published briefly (1937–39) a paper called *The World Lutheran* in order to provide information about global Lutheranism. The official minutes of the meetings of the American Section cover the years 1937–46; an informal meeting with representative American Lutherans within the NLC was held January 22, 1936, in Buffalo, New York. All minutes, as well as copies of *The World Lutheran*, are found in the Archives of Cooperative Lutheranism, Lutheran Council/U.S.A., New York City (hereafter referred to as ArCL).

4. Lutheran theology maintains that one cannot neatly exclude God from any event, even war. God is always there in the world's turbulence, not as Cause but as Presence. God "prevents" (the Latin means "to come or go before") people in that he is already present in the evil situation "preveniently" preparing them to heed the gospel. This was Luther's profound "theology of the cross": God's work (*opus dei*) is both "alien" or "strange" (*opus alienum*) and "proper" (*opus proprium*). His "proper work" is to save

The story of world Lutheranism in the 1930s and 1940s can now be resumed by describing (1) the ecclesiastical structures in Germany prior to Hitler's rule, (2) the "church struggle" during the Third Reich, and (3) the work of the American Section in the years leading to the collapse of Nazi Germany in 1945.

GERMAN ECCLESIASTICAL STRUCTURES

In Chapter 2 we traced the development of church structures in Germany on the basis of the familiar principle *cuius regio eius religio* that "settled" the church question after the wars of religion in the sixteenth and seventeenth centuries. The principle gave legal status to three churches: Roman Catholic, Lutheran, and Reformed (Calvinist). The Catholics were located chiefly in Bavaria, Austria, and the Rhineland (Hapsburg lands); the Lutherans dominated the north, the east, and the central territories; the Reformed—a distinct minority— appeared first in the regions closest to Switzerland, France, and the Netherlands. Far-reaching changes within the ecclesiastical troika of German Protestanism occurred when the Lutheran house of Hohenzollern switched its loyalties from the Lutheran faith to the Reformed. This was done without demanding that Lutheran subjects follow their leader into Calvinism. After the Napoleonic era, the Prussian Hohenzollerns gained the hegemony in Germany. Influenced by pietism, romanticism, and political aspirations over against the Catholic Hapsburgs, the Hohenzollern king Frederick William III of Prussia concluded that a united Evangelical church would provide Prussia with a religious as well as a political solidarity that could successfully challenge his Hapsburg rivals. This was the background of the Prussian Union church (1817), an administrative, liturgical, but nondoctrinal amalgamation of Lutherans and Calvinists in the Prussian territories. This model was adopted with modifications in some non-

---

and make alive; his "strange work" is to govern the world so it does not destroy itself and to crush and defeat the old Adam in us that by means of death the new Adam may be born, resurrected to new life. In this manner God turns an evil, like war, to his purposes so that in the end it becomes, in a sense, "the work of God" (*opus dei*). Thus the "strange work" serves the "proper work," the penultimate serves the ultimate, and the ultimate is the incorporation of humankind into Christ, the unity of all believers in him, and the consummation of his rule ("the kingdom").

Prussian "consensus union" churches (the latter united Lutherans and Reformed *doctrinally* as well as administratively and liturgically).[5]

Against this background, one can see quite clearly and understand quite sympathetically the sometimes tense relationships between the so-called "Evangelical" churches à la the Prussian Union and the Evangelical Lutheran *Landeskirchen* (territorial churches). The two lines can be traced from the mid-nineteenth century through the "church struggle" (*Kirchenkampf*) of the Hitler years to the reorganization of ecclesiastical structures after World War II. No one can adequately understand the "church struggle" unless he has these facts in mind.

The first line ("Evangelical") is associated with initiatives from Prussia and continued to emphasize the goals of the Old Prussian Union. The first step was a gathering of representatives from twenty-six churches in 1846 to engage in exploratory discussions of unity. This was followed by the formation of the Congress of German Evangelical Churches (Deutscher Evangelischer Kirchentag) at Wittenberg in 1848.[6] The third step was the Eisenach conference of church governments in 1852. No additional moves were made until 1903, when the Eisenach conference was succeeded by the Committee of German Evangelical Churches (Deutscher Evangelischer Kirchenausschuss), which served as an umbrella under which the various territorial churches could maintain ecumenical contacts. However, it possessed no authority to adopt resolutions binding on the *Landeskirchen*.

The second, or Lutheran, line grew out of the early nineteenth-century "awakening" and the parallel neo-confessional movement associated with Lutheran leaders like Wilhelm Loehe (Neuendettelsau), Theodor Kliefoth (Mecklenburg), Adolph G. von Harless, Johann C. K. von Hofmann, Gottfried Thomasius, and Franz H. R. Frank (all of Erlangen). If Friedrich D. E. Schleiermacher was the theologian of the Old Prussian Union and "the father of liberalism," these men

---

5. Brief but helpful summaries of the German church relationships are to be found in Heinz Brunotte, *The Evangelical Church in Germany* (Hannover: Verlag des Amtsblattes der Ev. Kirche in Deutschland, 1955); and E. Theodore Bachmann, "Lutheran Churches in the World: A Handbook," *Lutheran World* 24, nos. 2 and 3 (1977): 220–25.

6. The word *Kirchentag* connotes a congress, assembly, or ecclesiastical diet and carries a meaning akin to the usage in words like *Reichstag* and *Landtag*, the legislative assemblies of a nation and a provincial territory.

were the theological advocates of a revived and renewed Lutheranism that saw the New Testament evangel being compromised by "Evangelical unionists." This conviction produced a Lutheran reaction to Prussian political and religious aggrandizement in the 1860s. Although unable to halt the Prussian annexation of Hannover and other states, the Lutherans succeeded in keeping their churches "intact," that is, they were not absorbed into the Prussian state church ("The Union Church"); they retained their confessional and structural independence. In order to resist the unionization of the church along the lines of the Prussian Union and to strengthen the confessional proclamation of the evangel, leaders of the Lutheran *Landeskirchen* (e.g., Hannover, Schleswig-Holstein, Bavaria, Saxony) organized in 1868 the Allgemeine Evangelisch-Lutherische Konferenz (AELK, the General Evangelical Lutheran Conference) and published the widely read paper *Allgemeine Evangelisch-Lutherische Kirchenzeitung (AELKZ)*.

The bifocal character of German Protestantism, Evangelical Union and Evangelical Lutheran, continued beyond the establishment of the German Empire (1871)[7] through World War I to 1918, when the separation of church and state took place. The princes, who since the sixteenth century had been *summi episcopi,* or supreme heads of the churches, abdicated at the end of the war. Between 1919 and 1922 each territorial church provided itself with a new constitution reflecting the altered circumstance. In some instances, especially among Lutherans, the office of bishop was established to replace the secular princes who had been "emergency bishops" since the Reformation. The churches did retain the use of the tax machinery of the state to collect "the church tax," but this income was administered by the church without state supervision.

The separation of church and state left the churches free to continue and develop the interchurch structures, Evangelical Union and Evangelical Lutheran, which had originated in the last half of the nineteenth century. In 1922 the Federation of German Evangelical Churches (Deutscher Evangelischer Kirchenbund) was organized by

---

7. After the Franco-Prussian War, the south German states (Bavaria, Württemberg, and Baden) joined Bismarck's German Empire. The Protestant churches of Bavaria and Württemberg were "intact" Lutheran bodies, Baden was "Union."

the twenty-eight territorial churches for their common interests. The constitution provided three governing bodies: the Church Executive Committee (*Kirchenausschuss*), the Church Federal Council (*Kirchenbundesrat*), and the Church Assembly (*Kirchentag*). The latter was in the nature of a synod; the council consisted of representatives of the governing boards of the territorial churches; and the executive committee was composed of eighteen delegates from the council and the assembly. As its name indicated, it served as the executive group of the federation. The committee's president was always the chief administrative officer of the Old Prussian Union, a fact received by the majority (Lutherans) with something less than enthusiasm. The day-to-day affairs of the federation were carried out by the Church Federation Office (*Kirchenbundesamt*) in Berlin. Direct and indirect duties included safeguarding Evangelical interests as related to the state and to foreign countries, religious education in the public schools, and charities. In the two latter fields, specific action must originate with and remain under the aegis of the *Landeskirchen.* Moreover, the authority of the federation's Assembly (the synodical *Kirchentag*) did not extend to the confessions of faith, the constitutions, or the administration of the *Landeskirchen,* each of which zealously guarded its prerogative. In this way, the lines of demarcation between the heirs of the Prussian Union tradition and the confessionally concerned Lutheran churches were maintained. This situation existed through the years of the Weimar Republic and Hitler's Third Reich and persists to the present moment.

On the one hand, German Lutheran *Landeskirchen* after World War I were *ecumenically* related to others through the Federation of German Evangelical Churches (DEK), and after World War II through the Evangelical Church in Germany (EKD) and the World Council of Churches. On the other hand, they were *confessionally* related by membership in the AELK, the Lutheran World Convention, and, after World War II, in the United Lutheran Church of Germany (VELKD) and the Lutheran World Federation. A detailed explanation of the complicated structures and interrelationships of the German Protestant territorial churches will aid the reader in tracing the several stages of the "church struggle" during the Hitler era. We now turn to that story.

THE GERMAN "CHURCH STRUGGLE"

At the time the Nazis came to power, the population of Germany was divided religiously as follows: 62.7 percent as members of the Protestant *Landeskirchen* (Lutheran = ca. 31,000,000; United = ca. 22,000,000); 32.5 percent Roman Catholic (ca. 26,000,000); 4.1 percent Free Churches or sects: Lutheran, Reformed, Moravian, Methodist, Baptist, Pentecostal, Jehovah's Witnesses, no affiliation; and 0.7 percent Jews.[8]

Hitler and "Positive Christianity"

From the very beginning Hitler was on record as anti-Semitic.[9] However, his attitude toward Germany's traditional churches seemed favorable. In fact, as early as 1920 he had published his views in "The Program of the National Socialist German Workers' Party" (Munich, February 24, 1920) as follows:

> We demand liberty for all religious confessions in the State, in so far as they do not in any way endanger its existence or do not offend the moral sentiment and the customs of the Germanic race. The party as such represents the standpoint of "positive Christianity" without bending itself confessionally to a particular faith. It opposes the Jewish materialistic spirit within and without and is convinced that permanent recovery of our people is possible only from within and on the basis of the principle: General Welfare Before Individual Welfare (*Gemeinnutz vor Eigennutz*).[10]

Clearly, "religious liberty" was severely circumscribed by subservience to the state and to what the Nazis called "the general welfare." The Jewish "materialistic spirit" was singled out as if there were no Protestant, Catholic, Nazi, or "dialectical" (Marxist) materialism. Nevertheless, the emphasis on "positive Christianity" seemed reassuring to many.

As far as is known, Hitler himself never defined what he or the party meant by "positive Christianity." It remained a vague and even slippery phrase behind which Hitler could mask his true intentions

---

8. *Statistisches Jahrbuch für das deutsche Reich* (Berlin, 1935), p. 14; cited in Beryl R. McClaskey, *The History of U.S. Policy and Program in the Field of Religious Affairs under the Office of the U.S. High Commissioner for Germany* (Frankfurt am Main, 1951), p. 8.
9. Adolf Hitler, *Mein Kampf*, 35th ed. (Munich, 1933), pp. 335–36, 354, 356, 357, 369.
10. This is the famous Article 24 of "The Program."

while letting others make their own exegesis. And exegete they did! There was a veritable mélange of interpretations ranging from evangelical Christian to Germanic pagan religion. The famous Friedrich von Bodelschwingh of Bethel, writing the *aide memoire* of his thirty days as Reich bishop in 1933, admitted that Hitler had blinded evangelical Christians, "the common people" who understood "positive Christianity" as referring to the positive message of the Bible, with its emphasis on sin and grace, redemption through the crucified and risen Lord Jesus Christ. This "positive Christianity," they reasoned, would be a welcome sword with which to do battle against the negative influences of an unevangelical theological liberalism, the dangers of atheistic Marxist socialism, and the poisonous and mortally inimical virus which permeated the literature, art, theater, and permissive morality of the Weimar Republic intellectuals.[11]

When it became apparent that "positive Christianity" was not what simple, ordinary Christians thought it was, they nevertheless tended to blame the perversions of religion uttered in the name of "positive Christianity" on persons around Hitler, not on Hitler himself. Hitler was against atheistic communism, materialism, and immorality; therefore Hitler was on the side of the church. In this way, "positive Christianity" could be seen as the ethical side of traditional doctrinal beliefs. It meant that Hitler was dedicated to the social regeneration of the German people. The task of the church was to support the state in its attempts to alleviate social and economic distress. And what was that but part and parcel of "positive Christianity"? A Nazi aphorism declared: "Deeds are more important than words. Whoever stammers prayers in the presence of a child drowning in a rapid stream has, in truth, less religion than he who without prayers dives to the rescue in the river." What Christians overlooked—consciously or unconsciously—was that too often such high-sounding phrases were uttered by people who would "pause at the river's edge to ask whether the (drowning) baby is blond, blue-eyed, and Aryan."[12]

11. Friedrich von Bodelschwingh, "Dreissig Tage an einer Wegwende deutscher Kirchengeschichte," 1933, pp. 1–2, Bethel Archiv, Bethel bei Bielefeld, Germany; used by the writer through the courtesy of Alex Funke, Director of the Bethel Anstalt, Bielefeld, Germany.

12. Quoted in Stewart W. Herman, *It's Your Souls We Want* (Philadelphia: [Muhlenberg] Fortress Press, 1943), pp. 74–75. The phrase "Deeds are more important than words" was a reiteration of a theme that had been advocated by liberals who were heirs of the Ritschlian "kingdom of God" theology. It was the slogan of many at the 1925

Scant attention was given at the beginning to the Nazi advocates of a pagan "German religion." Alfred Rosenberg's *The Myth of the Twentieth Century* (1930) and Ernst Bergmann's theses on "German religion," it was thought, were but the expressions of extremists who were not to be taken seriously.[13] After all, had not Hitler come out unequivocally in support of the churches shortly after becoming chancellor? Indeed he had, but few churchmen saw behind the Hitlerian masquerade. The apparently favorable situation, as described by the American reporter William L. Shirer, was carefully contrived so as to win the confidence of the great forces and symbols of conservatism: Paul von Hindenburg, the army, the nationalistic elements including the Catholic Center, and the two chief churches, Protestant and Roman Catholic.[14] The main events of the 1933 scenario were the February 27 Reichstag fire (blamed on the Communists), the ceremonial opening of the first Reichstag of the Third Reich (March 21), and the first legislative session of the Reichstag (March 23).

The Reichstag fire, whoever may have been responsible for it, was cleverly exploited by Hitler. The constitution of the Weimar Republic had made provision (Article 48) for the president to set aside normal civil liberties in the event of emergency and "for the protection of people and state." Four days after the fire, Hitler persuaded von Hindenburg to issue an emergency decree that, among other things,

Stockholm conference, including American and British liberals, as well as some Germans. The chief executive of the Prussian Union, Hermann Kapler, seems to have been the author of the slogan. Cf. Ruth Rouse and Stephen Neill, eds., *A History of the Ecumenical Movement 1517–1948*, 2d ed. (Philadelphia: Westminster Press, 1967), p. 540. It is not strange, therefore, that some Prussian Union leaders were favorable to Hitler's "positive Christianity." This, of course, is not to suggest that Lutherans and Catholics were not also seduced.

13. Examples of Bergmann's theses published in 1934: *Thesis 15*—"The Ethics of the German Religion condemns all belief in inherited sin, as well as the Jewish-Christian teaching of a fallen world and man. Such a teaching is not only non-Germanic . . . it is immoral and non-religious. Whoever preaches this, menaces the morality of the people." *Thesis 16*—"Whoever forgives sin sanctions sin. The forgiving of sins undermines religious ethics and destroys the morale of people." *Theses 17 and 18*—". . . The German ethic is not for the salvation of the individual like the Christian ethic, but for the welfare of the people as a whole. . . . He who belongs to the German religion is not a slave of God, but lord of the divine within him." Ernst Bergmann, *Die 25 Thesen der Deutschreligion* (Breslau, 1934); English translation by F. W. Norwood, *The 25 Theses of the German Religion—A Catechism*, Publication no. 39 (London: Friends of Europe, 1936), pp. 20–22.

14. *The Rise and Fall of the Third Reich* (New York: Fawcett, 1968), pp. 274–75.

allowed him to order the arrest of anti-Nazis and especially leading Communists including the Communist members of the Reichstag. Therefore, acting legally under the Weimar constitution, Hitler with one bold stroke now enjoyed a parliamentary majority and saw the conservative political elements move into the Nazi camp.

The second act in the drama was the brilliantly staged ceremonial opening of the Reichstag. Planned by Hitler and his new minister of propaganda, Joseph Paul Goebbels, the event was to be a grandiose tribute to von Hindenburg and all he symbolized. A religious service was held in the Prussian Westminster Abbey, the Garrison Church in Potsdam, a shrine that evoked memories of Prussia's march to imperial greatness. It was reported that von Hindenburg was "visibly moved" as he walked slowly down the aisle, pausing to salute the empty seat of Kaiser Wilhelm II in the imperial gallery and then reading a brief speech in which he gave his blessing and support to the new chancellor. Hitler replied, "We pay you homage. A protective Providence places you over the new forces of our nation." It was a perverse genius at work.

The third act in this Faustian drama occurred in Berlin's Kroll Opera House, not far from the burned-out Reichstag building. This first session of the parliament heard Hitler promise that the roles of the Reichstag and von Hindenburg would remain unaltered, the provincial states would not be violated, and the rights of the churches would be respected. It was the latter declaration that churchmen perceived as Hitler's own understanding of more "positive Christianity." He had said:

> The national Government sees in the two Christian Confessions [Protestant and Catholic] the most important factors for the preservation of our nationality. . . . All other denominations will be treated with the same impartial justice. The national Government will provide and guarantee the Christian Confessions the influence due them in the schools and education. . . . The Reich Government sees in Christianity the unshakeable foundations of the moral and ethical life of our people. . . . The rights of the churches will not be curtailed; their position in relation to the State will not be changed.[15]

Not only did the churches take Hitler at his word, but the Reichstag proceeded to surrender to him its own powers of legislation—budget,

---

15. Arthur C. Cochrane, *The Church's Confession under Hitler* (Philadelphia: Westminster Press, 1962), p. 85.

treaty-making, and constitutional amendments—for a period of four years. This was the so-called Enabling Act—"The Law for Removing the Distress of People and Reich" (*Gesetz zur Behebung der Not von Volk und Reich*).[16]

"Gleichschaltung" and the Churches

Legally armed with dictatorial powers by the Enabling Act, Hitler and the Nazis now launched efforts to consolidate their position. The program was called *Gleichschaltung* ("coordination" or "synchronization"),[17] an attempt at total assimilation of all institutions and centers of power into the Nazi system, in order better to restore Germany's inner and external strength and to overcome the chief obstacles to this goal, namely, the Nazi nemeses international capitalism and international Bolshevism, both of which were allegedly controlled by international Jewry. Except for the churches, Hitler completed the *Gleichschaltung* between April 1933 and August 1934, when von Hindenburg's death gave him opportunity to take over the powers of head of state and commander-in-chief of the armed forces. The office and title of president were abolished, and Hitler designated himself Führer and Reich chancellor. Prior to this he had dissolved the trade unions and cooperative societies, neutralized the remnants of the Nationalists, outlawed all political parties except the Nazis, and controlled radio, press, and the arts. Moreover, industry and labor were won over because both prospered under the Nazi economic policies of government spending to finance social services, public works, rearmament, and general national welfare.

The Nazification of the educational system reached into all levels, including, of course, the appointment and dismissal of university professors. The control of the latter was relatively easy to achieve, because ever since the education act of 1899 Social Democrats had

---

16. The Enabling Act remained the legal basis for dictatorship until the end of World War II. Its passage was secured by the absence of twenty-six Social Democrats and eighty-one Communists, and the support of the Catholic Center, which was persuaded by Hitler's promises of freedom for the churches. It was later said that this act by which the parliament legislated itself out of business made of the Reichstag "the best paid male chorus in the world." Its duties were to sing the national and Nazi anthems once or twice a year and rubber-stamp Hitler's edicts.

17. Hitler's cleverness is apparent. He wished to achieve his goals in a legal and "equal" (*gleich*) manner. In this way there could be a smooth, synchronized "shifting of gears" (*Gleichschaltung*), bringing all elements under one "driver."

been denied professorships, thus making the universities in general centers of political conservatism. This explained why so many professors, though actually avoiding party membership, were sympathetic to National Socialism. Dissidents either resigned or were expelled, many emigrating to America.

Already by April 1933, Hitler felt secure enough to address the religious question. This involved plans to deal with Jews, Catholics, and Protestants. As far as Jews were concerned, it was not a question of *Gleichschaltung,* as in the case of the Christian churches. Jewishness was more than a religion, it was a matter of blood—blood that, according to Nazi racial theories, had corrupted the pure Aryan stock. The Nazi philosophy of anti-Semitism, therefore, simply could not allow *Gleichschaltung.* Rather, it demanded open hostility. Accordingly, on April 1, 1933, the Nazis instigated a four-day general boycott against Jews. This passed without serious incident but was followed by a series of laws calculated "to regulate the Jewish question." These included the notorious Aryan Paragraph of April 7 that forbade Jews from holding public office. Jewishness was also extended to include Christians who had one Jewish grandparent. Though hateful and reprehensible, this and subsequent regulations during the next few years might have been tolerable to most. However, these were but the beginning of terror. The anti-Semitism burst into violent ("spontaneous") manifestations on *Kristallnacht* (November 9–10, 1938). The fury of window-smashing (*Kristall*), destruction, beatings, arrests, and the eventual herding of Jewish "offenders" off to concentration camps adumbrated the demonic "final solution" begun in 1941–42 and continued until the Allies liberated the survivors of the Holocaust.[18]

The *Gleichschaltung* of the Roman Catholic church, like the overt persecution of Jews, began in April 1933. In a *quid pro quo* arrangement the Catholic Center party had voted for the Enabling Act because Hitler had guaranteed the rights of the Catholic church. The bishops formally declared that membership in the Nazi party was not incompatible with loyalty to the church and urged cooperation with the new regime. In view of these events, the Nazis had no difficulty negotiating a concordat with the Vatican. Signed by Catholic Nazi

18. See John Toland, *Adolf Hitler,* 2 vols. (Garden City: Doubleday, 1976), 2:587–98, 801–6, 809–14, 861–80.

Franz von Papen and Eugenio Cardinal Pacelli, later Pope Pius XII, on July 20, 1933, the document led Hitler to boast that he knew how to handle Catholics, "something Bismarck never learned." Superficially, the concordat granted the church the right to manage its own affairs, but it was not long before the Nazis subjected the Catholics to the same treatment accorded all potential foes of the National Socialist state. Pius XI, who had ordered the bishops to take the oath of allegiance to Hitler, finally found it necessary to publish a protest against Nazi ideology and practice. Issued on March 14, 1937, the papal encyclical carried the title in German translation *"Mit brennender Sorge"* (With Burning Anxiety) and served to encourage Cardinal Faulhaber of Munich and Bishop von Galen of Münster to speak out against Nazi violations of the concordat. In general, however, the church supported Hitler. On his fiftieth birthday, April 20, 1939, the pope sent his congratulations, and votive masses were celebrated in every church, including prayers for the Führer as "the inspirer and enlarger of the Reich." The next year, following Hitler's narrow escape from one of several assassination attempts, Cardinal Faulhaber instructed that the Te Deum be sung to thank God for protecting the Führer; once again the pope, now Pius XII, sent his personal congratulations. Somewhat less overt was the papal reaction to the Nazi invasion of Russia; nonetheless, the Vatican made it known that the Nazi fight against Bolshevism should be supported. Meanwhile, the hierarchy was painfully aware that the Nazis were cynically violating the 1933 concordat. Catholic schools were closed, church properties were confiscated, and religious orders were suppressed. In spite of clerical protests and a growing underground resistance, the Nazi subjugation of the church continued until the Allied victory in 1945.[19]

---

19. Brief surveys and data on Catholicism under the Nazis is readily available. See ibid., 1:331, 336; 2:617, 687, 774. Additional sources are David Childs, *Germany since 1918* (New York: Harper & Row, 1970), pp. 61–63; Herman, *It's Your Souls We Want*, pp. 188–206; McClaskey, *History of U.S. . . . . Religious Affairs*, pp. 11–13. The role of the popes, especially Pius XII, has been questioned. Rolf Hochhuth's *The Deputy* (New York: Grove Press, 1964) dealt with this subject. It is known that Pacelli's many years of service in Germany as papal delegate at Munich and nuncio at Berlin (and the co-signer of the concordat) had made him an admirer of Germany. "Pacelli Allé" in Berlin/Dahlem testifies that the admiration was mutual. One of the better works on Catholicism in Germany is Gordon C. Zahn, *German Catholics and Hitler's Wars* (New York: Sheed & Ward, 1962). See also Gordon C. Zahn, "Catholic Resistance? A Yes and a No," in *The German Church Struggle and the Holocaust*, ed. Franklin H. Littel and H. G. Locke (Detroit: Wayne State University Press, 1974), pp. 203–37.

The German "church struggle" is customarily associated with Hitler's attempts to bring about a *Gleichschaltung* of the Protestant clergy. In this effort, he had at hand a ready-made tool, the so-called "German Christians" (*Glaubensbewegung deutscher Christen*, or simply *Die deutsche Christen* [DC]). Although the DC—as they were designated—described theirs as a "faith movement," it was primarily an arm of National Socialism that sought to draw support from church members by shouting Nazi slogans.[20] The movement came to the fore even before Hitler became chancellor. Its "guiding principles" had been published on June 6, 1932, and provided a program that was unmistakably Nazi.[21] The DC received strong support in the territories of the Prussian Union and drew much of its initial leadership from these quarters. Like the party itself, the DC had its radicals, who boasted that they were "the storm troops of Jesus Christ."

Initially, Hitler kept his distance from the radical elements in both the party and the DC. In fact, he wished to present a picture of respectability, quite the contrast to the bullies and rowdies in the party. By April 1933, however, he felt he had sufficiently established himself so he could associate openly with the "German Christians," especially with their leader in East Prussia, Ludwig Mueller, an army chaplain whom Hitler had met in 1926. Mueller's moderate views suited Hitler better than the revolutionary spirit of the DC leader, a certain Joachim Hossenfelder, and as a result Mueller soon found himself a close and confidential friend and adviser of Hitler.[22]

In the optimistic atmosphere created by his political triumphs in the spring of 1933, Hitler invited Mueller to a quiet conversation at his retreat in Berchtesgaden on April 17. The discussion centered on

---

20. An excellent survey, "The Rise of the 'German Christians,'" is to be found in Cochrane, *The Church's Confession*, pp. 74–89.

21. The DC program has been printed as Appendix II in ibid., pp. 222–23.

22. Mueller has been described by two British historians, one of whom met him in Berlin in 1933, as "sincerely religious," "without theological acumen," "of no account," "devoid of the humility to acknowledge his own unfitness." A. S. Duncan-Jones, *The Struggle for Religious Freedom in Germany* (London: Victor Gollancz, 1938), p. 43; J. S. Conway, *The Nazi Persecution of the Churches 1933–1945* (London: Weidenfeldt & Nicolson, 1968), p. 34. German Lutherans were even less complimentary, perhaps because Mueller called them "stubborn goats" who ceaselessly talked about the church's confession. See Eberhard Klügel, *Die Lutherische Landeskirche Hannovers und ihr Bischof 1933–1945* (Berlin: Lutherisches Verlagshaus, 1964), pp. 37–38.

Article 2 of the "Guiding Principles" of the "German Christians," the subject of which was a union of all the *Landeskirchen* into a Reich church. Hitler was so impressed with Mueller's ideas that on April 24 he appointed him his personal deputy for church affairs ("Plenipotentiary for all questions concerning the Evangelical Churches") and charged him with the responsibility of creating a united Evangelical church. After all, the *Gleichschaltung* of *one* church would be easier than dealing with almost thirty autonomous *Landeskirchen*. The next day, April 25, Mueller appealed to the church leaders, calling upon them in the name of Hitler to cooperate in the building of one united Evangelical church.

The call for a united church was widely welcomed. In the first place, the "German Christians," as we have seen, had made union one of their primary goals. The motivation was political, not theological, but nevertheless the objective was appealing to many. In the second place, the call for a united church stirred the ecumenical instincts of most churchmen in all branches of the Federation of German Evangelical Churches. Their motivation was theological and revolved around confessional attitudes. The Union and Reformed churches, where the influence of Karl Barth was especially strong, tended to see the confessional statements as divisive rather than unitive. Therefore they urged union on the basis of a common confession of the lordship of Christ. The Lutherans saw their confessions as catholic statements guarding a particular understanding as well as a common confession of the gospel. It was this "agreement in the doctrine of the gospel" that manifested the already given unity of the church. Until the theological issue regarding gospel and sacraments was resolved, it would be better to form a federal structure within which the "intact" churches could preserve their confessional identity. It is against this background that the response of the churches to Mueller's call and the subsequent "church struggle" can best be understood.

The immediate response came from the executive committee of the Federation of German Evangelical Churches. This committee authorized Hermann Kapler, its president (the federation's 1922 constitution, it will be recalled, required that its president be the chief officer of the Old Prussian Union church), to appoint a three-man committee, including himself, to draft a constitution for a proposed "Reich church."[23] The Kapler Committee, as it was called, consisted of the leading Lutheran, August Marahrens, bishop of Hannover; Hermann Hesse of the Reformed church; and Kapler himself, representing the Prussian Union. Ludwig Mueller, as Hitler's deputy, was to be an ex-officio member of the committee. It was later learned that Mueller was seeking to be elected Reich bishop of the new church, a circumstance that fueled the "church struggle."[24]

The Resistance Movement

It has been said that the "resistance movement" went through several stages, from early warnings to virtual silencing of all opposition by 1937–45.[25] We shall mark four stages.

Stage I: The Reich Church 1933

At the beginning, most Germans, including the church leaders, did not detect the demonic nature of Nazism. Even such an outspoken critic as Martin Niemoeller had welcomed the end of the years of darkness and shame (the Weimar Republic) signaled by the emergence to power of the Nazis. In an appendix to the English translation of his *Vom U-Boot zur Kanzel,* we are informed that the former submarine commander rejoiced that National Socialism had finally created the "national revival" for which he himself had fought so long.[26] The Nazi

23. We have met Hermann Kapler in connection with Söderblom's 1925 Stockholm conference. Kapler, as president of the DEK, was that group's ecumenical representative, whose aphorism "Doctrine divides, but service unites" became a slogan in many ecumenical circles.

24. Jürgen Schmidt, *Martin Niemöller in Kirchenkampf* (Hamburg: Leibnitz Verlag, 1971), pp. 61–62. The best brief surveys of the early stages of the "church struggle," besides the above, are Jonathan R. C. Wright, *Über den Parteien. Die politische Haltung der ev. Kirchenführer 1918–1933* (Göttingen: Vandenhoeck & Ruprecht, 1977), pp. 209–30; *Dokumente zur Kirchenpolitik des Dritten Reiches,* 1:1933 (Munich: Chr. Kaiser Verlag, 1971); *Kirchliches Jahrbuch für die Evangelische Kirche in Deutschland 1933–1944,* ed. Joachim Bechmann (Gütersloh: C. Bertelsmann Verlag, 1948); and the autobiographical, unpublished memoir of Friedrich von Bodelschwingh, who relates the story of his thirty days as Reich bishop, in "Dreissig Tage."

25. Hanns Lilje, "The Church Struggle (*Kirchenkampf*)," *Encyclopedia of the Lutheran Church,* ed. Julius Bodensieck (Minneapolis: Augsburg Publishing House, 1965), 1:526–28.

26. Martin Niemoeller, *Vom U-Boot zur Kanzel* (Berlin, 1935), was published with English title, *From U-Boat to Pulpit* (Chicago: Willet, Clark & Co., 1937); see pp. 186–223. Niemoeller admitted his early Nazi sympathies at his trial in February 1938. He declared he had voted for the National Socialists in 1924 and preached a pro-Nazi sermon in 1933. See Duncan-Jones, *Struggle for Religious Freedom,* p. 151.

press praised him, and his book became a best-seller. But within months Niemoeller admitted his misjudgment and shortly became a central figure in the church resistance.

Although numerous persons experienced a similar movement from hope to disillusionment, only one major Protestant clergyman, Hermann Sasse, uttered a public warning to the church prior to 1933 regarding the anti-Christian character of the Nazis and their fellow travelers, the "German Christians." Already in 1932, before Hitler came to power, Sasse, as editor of the *Kirchliches Jahrbuch für die Evangelische Kirche in Deutschland,* had written a courageous and farsighted article, "Kirchliche Zeitlage," in which he pronounced Nazism to be utterly incompatible with and destructive of Christian faith. His attack on Article 24 of the Nazi Program (1920) grew out of his unyielding loyalty to the gospel as interpreted by the Lutheran confessions. Nazism's "positive Christianity" was neither "positive" nor "Christian." It was thoroughly inimical to the church's proclamation of sin and grace. He wrote:

> This article makes any discussion [by the Nazis] with the Church impossible. . . . The Evangelical Church would have to begin a discussion about [Article 24] with the frank admission that the [evangelical] doctrine is an intentional and permanent offense "to the moral and ethical conscience of the [Nazis'] Germanic race." . . . Let it be said that the evangelical doctrine of original (or inherited) sin [*Erbsünde*]—in contrast to the Catholic doctrine [as well as to Nazi doctrine]—does not admit the possibility of the Germanic, Nordic, or any other race being able by nature to fear and love God and do His will, that on the contrary a newborn child of the most noble Germanic descent with the finest racial characteristics of an intellectual and physical sort is just as liable to eternal damnation as a half-breed born of two decadent races and with serious hereditary defects. Furthermore, we must confess that the doctrine of the justification of the sinner *sola gratia, sola fide* is the end of "Germanic" morality as it is the end of all human morality.[27]

With hindsight today's interpreters of the "church struggle" readily admit that Sasse's sharp words were biblically prophetic and evangeli-

---

27. Quoted in *Kirchliches Jahrbuch 1933–1944*, pp. 2–3; the English translation, adapted and revised, is from Cochrane, *The Church's Confession*, p. 78. Another early protest, which showed the hand of Karl Barth and Hans Asmussen, was published in January 1933; cf. "Das Wort und Bekenntnis Altonaer Pastoren in der Not und Verwirrung des öffentlichen Lebens . . . 11. Januar 1933," in *Kirchliches Jahrbuch 1933–1944*, pp. 8–12.

cally confessional and that Sasse himself was prescient. Although numerous church people had assumed that it would be possible to work with Hitler, later developments proved them to be naive and Sasse to be wise. The first illustration of this fact was the difficulty surrounding the drafting of a constitution for the proposed merger of the *Landeskirchen* into one Reich church.

The Kapler "Committee of Three" (August Marahrens, Hermann Hesse, and Hermann Kapler), meeting on May 5, 1933, had several invited guests. One was Theodor Heckel, an expert in church law, who was to give assistance to the committee in drafting a constitution. The other three were "German Christians" whose Nazi ideas provoked a heated discussion and necessitated a second meeting on May 17. Meanwhile, one of the agreements reached on May 5—that there be a constitutional provision for a Reich bishop—caused a storm of controversy. On May 6 the "German Christians" asserted their demand that the bishop be named from among their membership.[28] In response to this, an informal group calling itself the Young Reformation Movement (*Jungreformatorische Bewegung*), among whose members were Hanns Lilje, Karl Heim (Tübingen), Walter Kuenneth (Berlin), Hermann Sasse (Erlangen), and Martin Niemoeller, urged that the Kapler Committee appoint a bishop from within the official church by whose authority the committee had been named (not from some "party" like the DC) and that this appointment be made immediately.[29] This group, made up of young theologians and pastors, organized itself on May 12 and became, in the words of Arthur C. Cochrane, "the forerunner of the Confessing Church."[30] The same day Ludwig Mueller, acting with Hitler's approval and sensing the growing church resistance, assumed the office of "protector" for the "German Christians," in order that a united Nazi front might exert its influence in the reorganization of the church. This meant that Mueller was no longer merely Hitler's liaison man with the church; he was the official representative of the "German Christians."

All this took place in the interval between the two meetings of the

---

28. Wright, *Über den Parteien*, pp. 9–10.
29. Ibid., p. 210.
30. *The Church's Confession*, p. 94. Cf. E. H. Robertson, *Christians against Hitler* (London: SCM Press, 1962), pp. 28–32.

Kapler Committee (May 5 and May 17). Meanwhile, Marahrens had invited the committee to hold its second meeting at the Lutheran Abbey of Loccum, a former Cistercian monastery located near Hannover and of which the Lutheran bishop of Hannover was ex officio the abbot.[31] In this quiet and secluded place, Marahrens hoped the committee could complete its assignment expeditiously.

On the evening of May 16, prior to the meeting at Loccum, the three committee members met in a Hannover hotel to discuss the proposed constitution with their legal adviser, Theodor Heckel. In a nearby hotel Ludwig Mueller met with "German Christian" advisers, chief of whom was the renowned scholar Emanuel Hirsch of Göttingen.[32] They prepared a moderate Nazi statement for presentation to the Kapler Committee with the hope of ingratiating themselves while at the same time laying plans to get a "German Christian" (Ludwig Mueller) named to the post of Reich bishop.

During the meeting at Loccum the main constitutional principles for a united "church" were agreed upon. But Marahrens, as a staunch Lutheran, had serious misgivings that the new organization could be called a "church." He maintained that only common "confession" of the gospel gave ecclesial character to an assembly of believers; the new constitution would be theologically impossible if it recognized three such "confessions." It was not until his advisers assured him that in this instance the word "church" was being used not in a theological but in a juridical sense that he agreed to a constitution that would erect a "church" (actually a federation) on the so-called three pillar theory (Lutheran, United, Reformed).[33] The new constitution, unlike the 1922 constitution, specified that the head of the church be a Lutheran who would be assisted by a council ("Spiritual Ministry" [*ein geistliches Ministerium*]) in which all three confessions would be represented.

At the conclusion of the Loccum meeting the committee issued a "Manifesto," which reported in general the conclusions reached by

31. On Loccum, see Erich Ruppel and Dieter Andersen, eds., *Loccum Vivum. Achthundert Jahre Kloster Loccum* (Hamburg: Furche Verlag, 1963).
32. Cochrane, *The Church's Confession*, p. 91. Hirsch (1888–1972), widely known as a Reformation and Kierkegaard scholar and the author of the massive five-volume history of modern theology, *Geschichte der neueren evangelischen Theologie* (1949–54), justified his support of the DC even into his old age.
33. Klügel, *Die Lutherische Landeskirche Hannovers*, p. 32.

the Kapler Committee.[34] The manifesto contained no hint of the sharp debate between the committee and Mueller. The latter was present, he claimed, as the representative of a legitimate party in the church, the DC, and as the personal representative of Hitler. In his "official" capacity, he argued heatedly against the opinion of the committee that the nomination and election of the Reich bishop was exclusively the business of the church. He insisted that the government be consulted for its concurrence prior to such action. The minutes of the session (May 18) report that "a very serious debate over the church-state relationship" took place.[35] On the basis of Article 137 of the Weimar constitution, which guaranteed the exclusive right of the churches to choose their own officers, the committee vigorously rejected Mueller's demand. He reluctantly agreed and finally signed the committee's formal "Method of Procedure," whereby the committee would be authorized to put the new church constitution in force when it had been approved by the leaders of the *Landeskirchen*, with whom they would also seek agreement on the person of the new Reich bishop. Only after these steps were taken would the committee announce to Hitler whom it had selected for the office. Mueller then told the committee that Hitler wished a meeting *before* the decision on the future bishop. The committee need not fear that the chancellor would insist on his own candidate. After all, this would be merely a courtesy call. With this understanding, the committee agreed to an audience with the Führer on May 24 at 6:00 P.M.[36]

While these decisions were being hammered out at Loccum, the battle lines between the "German Christians" and the church began to form. A conference of East Prussian "German Christians" at Königsberg on May 17 nominated Ludwig Mueller as the DC candidate for Reich bishop.[37] Two days later, as the Loccum meeting ended

---

34. See "Loccumer Manifest, Mai 1933," in *Kirchliches Jahrbuch 1933–1944*, pp. 15–16.

35. Quoted in Klügel, *Die Lutherische Landeskirche Hannovers*, p. 36.

36. Klügel, *Die Lutherische Landeskirche Hannovers*, pp. 36–37. Cf. Cochrane, *The Church's Confession*, pp. 92–93; and von Bodelschwingh, "Dreissig Tage," p. 14. It was clear to Marahrens and the others that Mueller wanted to be Reich bishop. Marahrens told Mueller to his face that he was unfit for the office. Klügel, *Die Lutherische Landeskirche Hannovers*, p. 37.

37. Von Bodelschwingh, "Dreissig Tage," p. 14; cf. Wright, *Über den Parteien*, p. 210; Schmidt, *Niemoeller*, p. 61; Wilhelm Brandt, *Friedrich von Bodelschwingh, 1877–1946. Nachfolger und Gestalter* (Bethel bei Bielefeld: Verlagshandlung der Anstalt Bethel, 1967), p. 119.

(May 19), the Young Reformation Movement, meeting in Berlin, called a press conference at which Walter Kuenneth announced that he and his colleagues were in favor of a bishop who possessed a deeply "spiritual character," a man who enjoyed the confidence of the congregations. Such a person was Friedrich von Bodelschwingh, director of the internationally famous Bethel Institutions at Bielefeld. The following day, May 20, Mueller announced, perhaps on Hitler's orders, that no further steps with regard to the Reich bishop should be taken until the Kapler Committee's audience with Hitler had been held.[38] The committee, meeting in Berlin on May 22, had not yet announced *its* choice. It had considered August Marahrens and Hans Meiser, but finally on May 24 settled on von Bodelschwingh.[39] It was agreed to keep the decision confidential for the time being.

Meanwhile, Mueller had informed the committee on May 22 that Hitler had canceled the audience scheduled for May 24 because he would be occupied with "foreign affairs." Moreover, said Mueller, he did not wish to create unrest for the man to be named Reich bishop.[40] In view of the mounting DC campaign for Mueller, the committee decided to prepare a press release that the committee, acting for the churches, had made its choice for Reich bishop but was not yet making the name public.[41] Mueller and the DC concluded immediately—and correctly—that Mueller was therefore not the committee's choice. This prompted them to create rumors that Mueller would be in fact the nominee of the committee. To give the rumors credence the semi-official Nazi press agency, *Conti-Büro*, announced that the authorized German Church Committee had agreed to name Mueller. This obvious propaganda ploy, calculated to influence the next day's meeting (May 26) of the representatives of the *Landeskirchen* who were to vote on the Reich bishop, forced the Kapler Committee to deny the *Conti-Büro* report of the previous day and to announce, with von Bodelsch-

---

38. Wright, *Über den Parteien*, p. 210.
39. Meiser was known to be somewhat sympathetic to Mueller; Marahrens did not allow his name to be presented. Although von Bodelschwingh was a member of a Union church, he was personally a committed Lutheran. Marahrens had assured himself on this point during a long conversation with von Bodelschwingh on May 24; see the latter's "Dreissig Tage," p. 15. Once convinced of von Bodelschwingh's confessional stance, Marahrens remained unswervingly loyal to him.
40. Wright, *Über den Parteien*, p. 211.
41. Ibid., p. 212.

wingh's agreement, that he was its nominee. To have permitted the DC propaganda to go unchallenged would have made it impossible for the churches to control their own affairs.

The tension between the church and the Nazis was clearly building to a climax, and the atmosphere in the assembly hall of Berlin's *Kirchenbundesamt* on May 26 was heavy with anxious forebodings. Attempting to defuse an explosive situation, the leaders agreed to permit Mueller—"as the chancellor's representative"—to make a twenty-minute address to the assembly. Von Bodelschwingh, who by his own choice was not present, expressed astonishment that Mueller was given this opportunity to speak.[42] Only the day before, von Bodelschwingh had written out a statement that he was withdrawing his name because of the mounting fury. This had so alarmed the churchmen that they told him that should he withdraw now he would surely leave the field open to Mueller and the Nazis. It would produce an impossible situation. He must therefore let his name stand, for the churches were behind him. The next day, when he learned that Mueller had been given an opportunity to address the convention, he was shocked into incredulity. Moreover, his friend Marahrens reported later that Mueller had turned his address into an election speech "with a revolver!"[43]

Von Bodelschwingh's dismay was not without foundation. The assembly's first vote (a straw vote) indicated only a small majority for him and a large number of abstentions. This was disquieting, but the next day (May 27), after much activity on the part of his supporters, especially Marahrens and Niemoeller, the final vote was 91 to 8.[44] After being informed of the result, von Bodelschwingh, accompanied by Marahrens, was ceremoniously led into the assembly hall and met

42. Von Bodelschwingh, "Dreissig Tage," p. 25.
43. Klügel, *Die Lutherische Landeskirche Hannovers*, p. 40. Marahrens's disgust was especially acute because he was one of the leaders who acquiesced to Mueller's appearance.
44. Von Bodelschwingh, "Dreissig Tage," p. 29. Meiser had been leaning toward Mueller. Knowing this, Niemoeller engaged him in a vigorous conversation, reminding Meiser that he (Niemoeller) was a thoroughgoing patriot but that his early association with the Nazis had convinced him of the danger posed by the Hitlerites. This personal testimony apparently persuaded Meiser to vote for von Bodelschwingh. Von Bodelschwingh concluded his account of the election day by saying that both Kapler and Hesse were shaky in their support and that the only man whom he could trust completely was Marahrens.

by Kapler, who presented him to the group as the Reich bishop. Thus in actuality the office was committed to him at that moment. In accepting the office, von Bodelschwingh declared that he would rather be called the "Reich deacon" (servant) than the Reich bishop. He added that he was grateful that God had given Germany a government that "strengthens the will to work mightily for a better future. . . . We Christians want to place ourselves heart and soul at its disposal in this service to the nation."[45] In a final conversation with the Kapler Committee, von Bodelschwingh was told that one of his immediate tasks was to work with the committee to complete the constitutional draft. When he asked whether he should assume the title of Reich bishop prior to the ratification of the constitution, the chairman replied, "I wouldn't print any calling cards yet!"

As it turned out this was sage advice; only thirty days later circumstances had so altered that von Bodelschwingh had no choice but to resign. An intimation of what was to come was the matter of an audience with Hitler. Ever since the Loccum meeting it had been agreed that after the church had made its decision Mueller was to arrange the audience. To this end the committee had made an appointment with Mueller for 7:00 on the evening of election (May 27). When Mueller failed to keep the appointment (Emanuel Hirsch and perhaps other DC men had advised him to break the appointment), it was clear that trouble lay ahead. The events moved so swiftly and the details were so involved that a clear and brief statement of them is impossible as well as unnecessary. A chronology of the most significant incidents must suffice.[46]

May 27   Mueller's evening speech over Radio Berlin was against the decision of the church leaders.

May 29   In a press interview, Mueller and Hirsch charged that the church election of von Bodelschwingh was illegal. The Nazi propaganda mill began a press, radio, and telegram campaign against the church and von Bodelschwingh.

45. Ibid., pp. 33–34.
46. The chronology has been compiled from several sources: Brandt, *Bodelschwingh;* Wright, *Über den Parteien;* Schmidt, *Niemoeller;* Cochrane, *The Church's Confession; Kirchliches Jahrbuch 1933–1944;* and Kurt Meier, *Der Evangelische Kirchenkampf* (Göttingen: Vandenhoeck & Ruprecht, 1976), vol. 1. The latter (in three volumes) is one of the most recent and detailed examinations of the German "church struggle."

June 4	Von Bodelschwingh preached the Pentecost sermon in Zion Church in Berlin. The sermon bore the title "The Church of the Word, Living and Free."
June 8	Mueller repeated the charge that the election was illegal; it violated the constitution of 1922, which did not provide for the office of Reich bishop; the new (1933) constitution was not yet ratified.
June 12	Hitler and Mueller announced a new general election. Should it sustain the earlier election, Hitler would legitimatize von Bodelschwingh as Reich bishop. Meanwhile, Hitler would have no audience with church leaders or von Bodelschwingh until after election.
Mid-June	Intrachurch debate over the constitutionality of election. Several *Landeskirchen* gradually withdrew support of von Bodelschwingh on legal grounds. Marahrens insisted that the Kapler Committee was fully authorized to draft a constitution and nominate the Reich bishop. He argued that the overwhelming vote of the churches (May 27) sustained the committee in its efforts to neutralize Mueller's power. Marahrens wrote Hitler (June 17) that a relationship of trust between church and state was impossible because of Mueller. The independence of the church, which Hitler had himself promised, was endangered.
June 21	Kapler resigned his office as president because of ill health.
June 22	Lutheran members of executive committee, meeting at Eisenach and unpersuaded by Marahrens's arguments, supported a new election on juridical grounds.
June 23	The executive committee, as a whole, followed Lutherans in moving away from von Bodelschwingh, who personally pleaded for their support.
June 24	Capitalizing on Kapler's resignation, Hitler's Prussian minister of education (Rust) appointed a Nazi lawyer, August Jaeger, as state director of church affairs in the ministry of education and commissar for the whole church. He immediately replaced all church-elected officials with "German Christians." This was outright

invasion of the church by the state. At 7:00 P.M. von Bodelschwingh announced that with the appointment of Jaeger he was deprived of the possibility of carrying out the office of Reich bishop.[47]

In retrospect these dramatic incidents stand out for what they were: tragic witnesses (1) to incredible political blundering on the part of church leaders in the face of powerful and sinister foes whose ruthlessness was yet unmeasured; (2) to the painful weaknesses of a disunited church failing to present a common front against a common foe; and (3) to the thoughtless haste of the churches in naming a bishop before a constitutional foundation was laid. Von Bodelschwingh himself said later, "We did not see the folly of building a house by beginning with the roof."[48] Perhaps the Kapler Committee had the legal right to take certain emergency steps prior to a national church assembly, but it was hardly justified in pressing for the election of a Reich bishop before the office was constitutionally defined and ratified by such an assembly. This has led some to conclude that the church leaders "were trying to beat the 'German Christians' at their own game" of politics. The amateurs pitted themselves against the professionals; predictably, the professionals won.

In the resulting confusion, Hitler and the Nazi "Christians" lost no time in consolidating their victory. With the help of the brown-shirted storm troopers, Mueller occupied the buildings of the Church Federation Office in Berlin and on Hitler's orders took over the administration of all levels of the church: the executive committee, the council, and the national assembly. A new committee completed the draft of the church constitution, which was ratified by representatives of the *Landeskirchen* on July 11 and confirmed by the government on July 14.

The church elections, which were set for July 23, were preceded by a Nazi propaganda blitz. The party newspaper, *Völkischer Beobach-*

---

47. The resignation ("Ein Wort an alle, die unsere deutsche evanglische Kirche lieben"), dated Eisenach, June 24, 1933, is to be found in Bethel Archiv, Bethel bei Bielefeld, Germany.

48. "Dreissig Tage," p. 12.

49. "Verfassung der DEK vom 11. July 1, 1933," in *Kirchliches Jahrbuch 1933–1944*, pp. 17–20. English translation: Cochrane, *The Church's Confession*, pp. 224–28.

ter, said, "Obviously it is the duty of every Evangelical to vote for the German Christians," and Hitler himself made a "surprise" radio appeal on the eve of the election, urging support of the DC. The result of the electioneering was a major victory for the "German Christians." In the light of this, Ludwig Mueller was appointed bishop of the Prussian *Landeskirche* on August 4. On September 27 in Wittenberg the national synod of the new Reich church elected him Reich bishop.

Stage II: The Confessing Church, 1934

Although many of the church leaders stood in opposition to this turn of events, the majority of the people, as indicated by the general church elections, favored this outcome. The victory of the "German Christians," though actually Pyrrhic, seemed to assure the rapid *Gleichschaltung* of the church into the "new Germany" of the Nazis. This assumption, however, was premature.

As if to celebrate their achievement, the "German Christians" held a massive rally at Berlin's Sports Palace on November 13, 1933, under the leadership of the man who had been prominent in the DC since the beginning, Joachim Hossenfelder. Although replaced in the affections of Hitler by Mueller, he had been awarded the positions of *Reichführer* for the DC, minister of church affairs, and bishop of Brandenburg. But it was really a minor Nazi layman, Reinhold Krause, who stole the show by saying that if the Nazi masses were to feel at home in the churches the Old Testament must be removed from the canon. Not only that, the Jewish theology of Rabbi Paul must be expurgated from the New Testament. The church must be built on the simple teaching of Jesus: "Love your neighbor as yourself."

A storm of opposition broke out all over Germany, and church leaders protested to "Reibi" (the nickname drawn from the title "Reich bishop") Mueller. Did not the "German Christians" know that Jesus was a Jew and that his command to love the neighbor as oneself was drawn from the Old Testament? Was the Reich bishop going to allow the rejection of the doctrine of atonement and justification by grace through faith? Was Jesus a universal savior, including Jews, or a Germanic savior? Was Luther a catholic Christian theologian or simply a Germanic hero? All this agitated Mueller into speaking from both sides of his mouth, at once rejecting the attack on the Bible and the confessions and at the same time giving support to Hossenfelder. This ambiguity soon led to a rekindling of opposition by pastors who saw the church's life being strangled by Nazi paganism and its rejection of the gospel.[50]

The unrest of 1933 set in motion a series of events that brought into being a strong movement that came to be called "The Confessing Church" (*die bekennende Kirche*).[51] As noted earlier, a group of young clergymen (Walter Kuenneth, Hanns Lilje, and Martin Niemoeller) had organized an anti-Mueller group in May 1933 calling itself the Young Reformation Movement (*Jungreformatorische Bewegung*). This movement declared that it was fighting for "a free church, a confessing church." In midsummer (July 17) the movement's headquarters were raided by the gestapo, which confiscated more than 600,000 pieces of "subversive" literature. By September the movement had virtually ceased to exist, but out of its ashes, phoenixlike, there arose "The Pastors' Emergency League" (*Pfarrernotbund*) under the leadership of Niemoeller, who made the league the spearhead of opposition to the Nazi Reich church. By early January its membership had grown to four thousand pastors and included Lutheran bishops in both North and South Germany, former leaders of the Union (Prussia), and some Reformed churchmen. Of major significance was the fact that several Lutheran leaders, who had originally deemed it possible to work with the Nazis, were now a part of the opposition, which sought the removal of "German Christians" from posts of leadership. Specifically they attacked Hossenfelder, who was eventually forced to resign.

The Pastors' Emergency League also demanded that Mueller withdraw from the DC, renounce his title as "Protector" (of the "German

50. Just at this time (November 1933) the executive committee of the Lutheran World Convention meeting in Hannover met with Mueller, who assured them that the "Aryan paragraph" would not be enforced and that the confessional stance of the churches would be respected. See Chapter 9, pp. 271–72, nn. 18, 19, 20.

51. A distinction should be made between "confessional church" (*Bekenntnis Kirche*), that is, Lutheran or Reformed, and "confessing church" (*bekennende Kirche*), a group within the "confessional" churches seeking "existential" expression of their faith amid the current conflict. Karl Barth's pamphlet *Theologische Existenz heute* (1933) set the tone for "existential" (*existenz*) confession. Hundreds of articles and books on "The Confessing Church" and its role in the "church struggle" have emerged. A well-researched and lucidly written volume is Cochrane's *The Church's Confession*, to which we have already made frequent reference.

Christian" movement), and reconstitute his cabinet ("the Spiritual Ministry"), which up to this time had been dominated by "German Christians." Ignoring promises to make changes, Mueller arbitrarily made laws to undercut his opposition. The pent-up fury of the churchmen was about to explode when von Hindenburg urged Hitler to use his influence to bring about peace. Always devious and cunning, Hitler allegedly set a trap and agreed to meet (on January 25) eight representatives of the Nazi Reich church, including Mueller, and eight representatives of the opposition. Chief among the latter were Martin Niemoeller, and August Marahrens, Hans Meiser, and Theophil Wurm, bishops of the three large "intact" Lutheran churches (Hannover, Bavaria, Württemberg). The church leaders proposed that Mueller be given a leave of absence and that Marahrens be appointed temporary administrator, so that what had been begun at Loccum in May 1933 could be concluded and thus restore peace to the church. Without saying so, the churchmen reasoned that in this manner the Mueller regime, like a bad dream, would be forgotten. At that moment, however, Hermann Goering, as if responding to a cue, rushed in and read a transcript of a tapped telephone conversation between Niemoeller and Kuenneth. The latter had phoned to learn why Hitler had called the meeting. Niemoeller explained that von Hindenburg was hoping for a peaceful solution of the church problem. In the middle of the conversation, some person (Niemoeller's secretary?) jokingly spoke into the telephone, saying that von Hindenburg was administering extreme unction to Hitler. Hitler, of course, exploded in anger and terminated the meeting. It is significant that Hitler never forgot and never forgave Niemoeller. When later arrested, Niemoeller was considered "the personal prisoner of the Führer."[52]

Although disheartened by this turn of events, the opposition to Mueller mounted. This was dramatically evident when bishops and pastors from all parts of Germany met in Ulm on April 22, 1934, to protest Nazi attempts to oust Wurm. The conference declared it would

---

52. Cochrane, *The Church's Confession*, pp. 130–31. There are various accounts of this incident; differing details do not materially alter its historicity. Cf. Ernst C. Helmreich, *The German Churches under Hitler: Background, Struggle, and Epilogue* (Detroit: Wayne State University Press, 1979), p. 155.

not identify itself with the Nazi church government but with the
Evangelical Church of Germany. This bold statement was read from
the pulpit of the Ulm cathedral by Hans Meiser to signal the gravity of
the occasion.

Some time later, the DC-dominated senate of the *Landeskirche* of
Hannover voted to approve the *Gleichschaltung* of its church into the
Reich church. August Marahrens vigorously opposed this on confessional grounds. So staunch was his stand that the church senate's move
was nullified by a vote of confidence in Marahrens by the clergymen of
the *Landeskirche*. Of the one thousand clergymen in the *Landeskirche*, 780 voted to support their bishop's stance. Only 71 nays
were registered; the remainder were abstentions. In this way Hannover retained its "intact" character, something it had treasured ever
since Bismarck had failed to bring the Hannoverian *Landeskirche* into
the Prussian Union at the time of the Prussian political annexation in
1866.[53]

Hitler continued to have difficulty with Marahrens, although the
bishop had the reputation with some of being "neutral" or even yielding in his relationship with the regime. His opposition to government
control of the church was always confessionally based. That meant that
Christians supported government when it exercised its proper role,
but the state had no right to dictate to the church. "The church must
always be the church" was a Marahrens dictum that constantly frustrated and angered the Nazis. This anger was intensified when they
learned that Marahrens had sharply warned that those were in error
who assumed that the state would allow them to preach the gospel
unhindered; that a "spirit of secularization" had been introduced by
the Nazis; and that "sooner or later" the freedom to affirm the gospel
and to repudiate hostile ideology would be lost. The churches were in
an "either-or" situation, a *status confessionis*, which forced a decision
either for the free confession of the church or control by the regime.[54]

Meanwhile, other *Landeskirchen* were less successful than Hannover in resisting *Gleichschaltung* into Hitler's Reich church. The
largest of the provincial churches, "the Old Prussian Union," had

53. "Der Kampf um die 'Eingliederung' in Hannover," in Klügel, *Die Lutherische
Landeskirche Hannovers*, pp. 122–56; the vote is recorded on p. 138.
54. Ibid., pp. 136–37.

fallen to Nazi control as early as March 2, 1934.[55] The next to be "incorporated" were the Union churches of Hesse-Nassau and of the Province of Saxony. Later during that year two large Lutheran *Landeskirchen* (Saxony and Schleswig-Holstein) and one smaller body (Oldenburg) were swallowed up. The steady destruction of constitutional authority within the *Landeskirchen* and the assumption by Mueller of increasingly dictatorial powers (hundreds of pastors were placed under disciplinary measures; many were also suspended or dismissed) led to two major protest meetings. The first was the Ulm Conference of April 22; the second was the famous Barmen Synod, May 29–31, 1934. The Ulm Conference had boldly served notice on Hitler and Mueller that the Reich church was *not* the Evangelical Church in Germany. The latter was now reappearing as a true "confessing church." Article I of the constitution of the Evangelical Church, recognized by the Reich government on July 14, 1933, stipulated that the "inviolable foundation of the . . . Church is the Gospel . . . as it is attested . . . in Holy Scripture and as it comes to light anew in the Confessions of the Reformation."[56] Since the Reich church completely disregarded the confessional character of the churches, the "Confessing Church" was the only legal and proper Evangelical Church in Germany. The story and the significance of the Barmen Synod and its widely subscribed "Confession" or "Declaration" have been the subject of hundreds of articles and books, so many, in fact, that this synod is the best-known aspect of the German "church struggle."[57]

The ingredients of the opposition which climaxed at Barmen, in addition to the Ulm Conference statement, were the activities of the Young Reformation Movement and its more aggressive successor, the

---

55. Ibid., p. 113.

56. Hans Asmussen, "An Address on the Theological Declaration [Barmen]." The original is found in Karl Immer, ed., *Bekenntnissynode der Deutschen Evangelischen Kirche Barmen 1934. Vorträge und Entschliessungen* (Wuppertal-Barmen: Kommissionsverlag Emil Müller, 1934), pp. 8–24.

57. A few of the better-known accounts are Karl Barth, *The German Church Conflict* (London: Lutterworth Press, 1965); Cochrane, *The Church's Confession;* Herman, *It's Your Souls We Want* (esp. chap. 8); *The Significance of the Barmen Declaration for the Ecumenical Church* (London: SPCK, 1943); Hans Asmussen, *Barmen!* (Munich: Chr. Kaiser Verlag, 1935); idem, *Kirche Augsburgischer Konfession!* (Munich: Chr. Kaiser Verlag, 1934); and E. Wolf, "Barmen" in *Die Religion in Geschichte und Gegenwart*, 3d ed. (Tübingen, 1957–65), 1:873–79.

Pastors' Emergency League, led by Niemoeller. The Swiss theologian Karl Barth, who was a professor at the University of Bonn, was the chief theological adviser to the Confessing Church. He said that the error in the current "German Christian" theology and church politics was rooted in neither Luther nor Calvin but in the theology of Schleiermacher and other nineteenth-century theologians, who violated both the Lutheran and Reformed confessions. The differences between Lutherans and Reformed must be taken seriously, but the current conflict in the church was centered not on these persisting differences "but on the first commandment and it is on this question that we have to 'confess' today."[58] Taking the initial steps that brought about the Barmen Synod were Barth (Reformed) and Hans Asmussen (Lutheran), and it was they who were largely responsible for the Barmen Declaration. Barth wrote the original draft, and Asmussen gave the main lecture interpreting it to the synod.

All groups within the Confessing Church (Lutheran, Union, and Reformed) agreed that Barmen was a significant and necessary event to expose the Nazi "German Christian" heresies and to protest the injustices and the usurpation of authority in the church. In spite of confessional differences, especially between the Lutherans and the Reformed, Barmen was able to speak a "common word" and to "confess" the gospel. Therefore, it referred to itself as the "Confessional Synod" and urged all who accepted its theological principles to be mindful of them in their church-political decisions.

Of the 139 delegates, only one found it necessary to exclude himself from the synod. This was Hermann Sasse, a professor at Erlangen who had been one of the members of the committee revising Barth's original draft of the Barmen Declaration. Sasse agreed with the overall intention of the declaration to protest the contra-confessional and outrageous activities of the Nazi "German Christians" (it will be recalled that he was the first theologian to speak out [in 1932] against the Nazi ideology), but he was unable to admit that a synod made up of churches of differing confessions could make decisions in matters of doctrine. It is important to note this, because within two years the Confessing Church was divided by this very principle into two wings, the "confessing" Barth-Niemoeller group and the "confessing" Lu-

---

58. Barth, *The German Church Conflict* (London: Lutterworth Press, 1965), p. 27.

theran group led by Marahrens, Wurm, and Meiser. Meanwhile Lutheran, United, and Reformed churches had spoken out against their common enemy, saying, "Precisely because we want to be and remain faithful to our various Confessions, we may not keep silent, since we believe that we have been given a common message to utter in a time of common need and temptation. We commend to God what this may mean for the interrelations of the confessional churches."[59] This modest assertion made it clear that Barmen had no purpose initially of altering the 1933 constitution of the German Evangelical Church, which defined itself not as a "church" in the theological sense but as a "federation of confessional churches." This meant, too, that the Barmen Synod had no intention of establishing a new "Union Church" after the pattern of the nineteenth century.

There is no question that Barmen was and continues to be a significant event. It not only pointed the way for Christians in Nazi Germany, but also set an example for Christians in other lands where hostile ideologies and governments threatened the life of the church. However, Lutherans in Germany and other countries resisted giving the Barmen Declaration status equal to the confessional statements of the sixteenth century. Whether Barmen was a "significant historic event" (Lutheran) or a churchly "confessional" statement (Confessing Church) was the subject of debate which caused a rift in Evangelical churches during the remainder of the Nazi regime and which extended into the era of postwar reorganization of German church life.

Stage III: The Confessing Church Divided, 1936

From Barmen to the silencing of the churches in 1937, the Confessing Church operated through its own national synods in opposition to the national synods of the Nazi church. The Council of Brethren (Bruderrat) served as the executive or standing committee of the Confessing Church. As such it continued the resistance to the Reich church and supported individuals and churches under Nazi pressures that were growing in intensity and frequency after Barmen. Two instances of this were the attacks on Hans Meiser of Bavaria and Theophil Wurm of Württemberg.

The Nazi church administration (Mueller and Jaeger) had sought

59. Cochrane, *The Church's Confession*, pp. 238–39.

unsuccessfully to force the "incorporation" of the Church of Hannover (see p. 326 above) and now tried by decree to bring the Lutheran churches of Bavaria and Württemberg into the Reich church. Both Wurm and Meiser refused to acknowledge the validity of the decree and published protests that won the support of their people. Nevertheless, Wurm and Meiser were placed under "house arrest," an act that provoked huge anti-Mueller demonstrations. These demonstrations were so vigorous that Mueller's attack collapsed completely. Bavaria and Württemberg, like Hannover, remained "intact," thus preserving the basic solidity of German Lutheranism. Wurm and Meiser, however, were kept under "house arrest" for the time being.[60]

In the autumn of 1934 the Second Synod of the Confessing Church was held in Berlin-Dahlem. Its main act of resistance was the proclamation of an "emergency law" for the whole German Evangelical Church, the intent of which was to declare Mueller's acts unconstitutional and to revoke his church laws and edicts. This led in time to the dismissal of the monstrous Jaeger and the demand for Mueller's resignation. Although the latter was not immediately forthcoming, it soon became apparent that the Reich bishop was losing the confidence of Hitler and the Nazis. In fact, as if to ease the tension, both Meiser and Wurm were released from house arrest. The next day they, together with Marahrens, were invited to an audience with Hitler. The Führer told them he was no longer interested in the conflict and would leave the church to solve its own problems. Although Mueller refused to resign, despite the continued attacks by the Confessing Church, it was clear that Hitler scorned his bishop's ineptitude. Thereupon Hitler appointed a "minister of church affairs," Hanns Kerrl, who without regard for Mueller arranged to control the churches by restricting the state's ecclesiastical subsidies. This prompted the Confessing Church to establish (on November 22, 1934) its own "Provisional Church Administration" under the leadership of Marahrens.

This bold step enraged Hitler, who promptly and conveniently forgot his promise to let the church settle its own affairs. He quietly made arrangements for the arrest of church leaders, provided Kerrl

---

60. For a detailed account, see Ernst C. Helmreich, "The Arrest and Freeing of the Protestant Bishops of Württemberg and Bavaria, September–October 1934," *Central European History* 2 (1969): 159–69.

with dictatorial powers, and saw to it that Mueller was more and more eased out of the picture. Meanwhile, in the face of these new measures and the increase in arrests of pastors, the Provisional Church Administration made a serious mistake in trying to win state recognition for itself rather than pushing for the immediate dismissal of Mueller. This failure, according to Hanns Lilje, led to the magnifying of tensions, political and theological, that had begun to manifest themselves within the Confessing Church.[61]

Seeking to capitalize on this advantage, Hitler and Kerrl tried a compromise: Mueller was dismissed and his administration of the Reich church was replaced (in 1935) by the Government Church Committee, the chairman of which would be the highly respected Lutheran leader of the Westphalian Union Church, Wilhelm Zoellner, an active supporter of the Confessing Church. This tactic was calculated to put a benevolent face on the regime and thus win the support of all parties in the church. This move proved abortive, however, in that it exacerbated the conflicting attitudes within the Confessing Church. The Lutheran wing thought it possible to work with the new Government Church Committee, especially under the leadership of the trusted Zoellner. The "intact" Lutherans (Hannover, Bavaria, Württemberg) sought to avoid Nazi control by compromising at times on matters they considered peripheral rather than central. They wished to prevent the total disorder and disruption that had taken place in the Prussian Union church when the latter failed to resist Hitler's *Gleichschaltung*. It is true that the stance of the Lutheran wing often weakened Protestant opposition to Hitler. In fact, the other wing (Niemoeller, et al.) was convinced that the Lutherans were guilty of capitulation. However, had the "intact" churches fallen to Nazi domination, the Berlin authorities could have carried out their program with greater speed and ruthlessness in the entire nation.

The open split between these two groups occurred at the Fourth (and last) Synod of the Confessing Church at Bad Oeynhausen, February 17–22, 1936. In order to comprehend what took place, we need to return to the immediate aftermath of the Barmen Synod two years earlier.

---

61. Hanns Lilje, "The Church Struggle,"p. 527. Both the narrative and documents of these days are to be found in *Kirchliches Jahrbuch 1933–1944*, pp. 77–85.

It is necessary to recall that Hermann Sasse, a "strict construction-
ist" of the Lutheran confessional tradition and an ecumenically respected scholar who had been active in Faith and Order, had refused
to sign the Barmen Declaration in 1934. This was done not because he
was "soft on the Nazis" but because he judged that the Barmen
Declaration would be elevated to confessional status (in the sense of
the sixteenth-century Lutheran and Reformed confessional documents). He reasoned that Barmen, which by its own admission did not
seek to create a new "Union Church," would actually lead to the
setting aside of the *magisterium* (the teaching office) of the Lutheran
confessional statements: "We believe, teach, and confess. . . ." He
argued that Barmen, as a synod of three confessions (Lutheran, Union,
and Reformed), had no "authority in matters of doctrine for Lutherans." Attributing such authority to the Barmen Declaration would
be a violation of Article VII of the Augsburg Confession, which
asserted that the true unity of the church required agreement in the
doctrine (teaching and preaching) of the gospel and administration of
the sacraments in harmony with such evangelical proclamation.[62]

Hans Asmussen, the chief Lutheran participant in the event of
Barmen, prepared the formal reply to Sasse. He wrote that the articles
set forth in the Barmen Declaration were not intended to be a common
confession of all Christian beliefs, thus abrogating the Lutheran
confessional writings, but simply "a defense of evangelical Christianity against a concrete enemy in a particular situation."[63] Unfortunately
the discussion between these two Lutherans, both of whom were anti-
Nazi, became acerbic and divisive. An increasing number of Lutherans, though not sympathetic with Sasse's defensive confessionalism, came to the conviction that some of Barmen's interpreters were
indeed drawing unwarranted confessional and ecclesiological conclusions from the Barmen Declaration. This led them to take steps
reminiscent of the year 1868, when the Lutheran "fathers" in the
German Church Federation had established the General Evangelical

62. Cochrane, *The Church's Confession*, pp. 193–95.
63. Cited in ibid., p. 195. That Asmussen was not entirely right and that Sasse's fears
were not without foundation was the action of the Prussian Synod of the Confessing
Church, May 10, 1937, at Halle, whereby the candidates for ordination were required to
pledge loyalty to the Barmen Declaration as well as to the Reformation confessions.
Herman, *It's Your Souls We Want*, p. 164.

Lutheran Conference (AELK) at Hannover. Once again in the same city on August 25, 1934, leading Lutherans organized "The Lutheran Council" which regarded itself as the Lutheran wing of the resistance movement.[64] Its membership consisted of leading figures in the Confessing Church: August Marahrens (Hannover), Theophil Wurm (Württemberg), Hans Meiser (Bavaria), Thomas Breit (Bavaria), Hugo Hahn (Saxony), Hanns Lilje (Hannover), and Niklot Beste (Mecklenburg).[65] It is worth noting that Sasse's name was not included.

By early 1936 the division within the Confessing Church had become overt, and the Fourth Synod of the Confessing Church (Bad Oeynhausen) experienced an ecclesiological rift between the "confessing" refugees from "the destroyed churches," notably the Union churches, and the "confessing" members of the "intact churches," notably the three large Lutheran *Landeskirchen* of Hannover, Württemberg, and Bavaria. The former were struggling to define themselves as a church, indeed a "confessional" (Barmen) church. As a matter of fact, they claimed "to be the one, true Church and repudiated the pretensions of the [Lutheran] confessionalists."[66] That they too might be pretentious apparently did not occur to them.

Despite the Lutheran repudiation of the "pretensions" of the other wing, Marahrens and others insisted that they had no intention to weaken or destroy the Confessing Church or to move to a position of neutrality regarding the Nazis. The confessional division at Bad Oeynhausen did not signal a Lutheran departure from the fold of the anti-Nazi Evangelicals. Rather, the Lutherans all along had thought of themselves as "the Lutheran wing of the Confessing Church," thus maintaining their identity within the resistance movement.[67] Nevertheless, the break had occurred and, in Hanns Lilje's words, this was a "tragedy" for the churches in Germany, which faced a common enemy

---

64. Klügel, *Die Lutherische Landeskirche Hannovers*, pp. 252–63. Cf. Erwin Wilkens, "Zur Vorgeschichte der Evang. Luth. Kirche Deutschlands," *Evangelisch Lutherische Kirchenzeitung* 10 (June 11, 1956): 239.

65. *Kirchliches Jahrbuch 1933–1944*, p. 126.

66. For reference to the "destroyed churches" and the "intact churches" see the introduction to the resolutions of the Bad Oeynhausen Synod, ibid., p. 117. Cf. Cochrane, *The Church's Confession*, pp. 203–5.

67. August Marahrens, "Rechenschaftsbericht . . . 15 April 1947," in Eberhard Klügel, *Die Lutherische Landeskirche Hannovers . . . Dokumente* (Berlin: Lutherisches Verlagshaus, 1965), p. 213.

whose power "both parties had underestimated."[68] Heinz Brunotte, who headed the German Evangelical Church chancellery after World War II, summarized the intrachurch conflict as follows:

> The issue was not (as is being claimed to the present day in some groups in Germany) whether the National-Socialist state was to be opposed more vigorously or less vigorously. The real question was how the second thesis [the christological article of the Barmen Declaration] was to be interpreted. Some interpreted it like Barth, in a "christomonistic" [or christocratic] sense, while others (the Lutherans) thought that Luther's properly understood doctrine of the two kingdoms was in jeopardy. It may be said that the [Barthians] have never caught the full seriousness of the Lutheran objection.[69]

It should be added that the "law-gospel" dialectic (closely interlocked with Luther's doctrine of the two kingdoms) was improperly interpreted by both the strict Lutheran confessionalists and the committed Barthians. The former tended to see the law as a static, eternal order, which in turn accounted for their "natural theology" and belief in "the divine orders of creation." Humankind is bound to the natural orders, like state, family, folk, soil, and race. For some Lutherans, therefore, the doctrine of law could be interpreted as giving divine sanction to Nazi ideology (one state, one folk, one blood). On the other hand, Barth and his Barmen disciples defined the law as *the form* of the gospel. The law like the gospel is gracious, granting a very definite freedom.[70] Hence law and gospel or, as Barth would reverse the dialectic, gospel and law, always have as their content grace. In this way these two are united and can be known only in Jesus Christ (christomonism). There can be, therefore, no "natural knowledge" of law which would make room for the "natural orders" (state, family, folk, blood), thus opening the door to Nazi racial theories.

The Lutheran objection to Barth during the Nazi era was not directed at this point. Rather, it charged Barth with uniting law and gospel, thus robbing the gospel of its unique character as the Word of God, the declaration to penitents of the forgiveness of sins for Christ's sake. To be sure, they would say, the two are united in that both are theonomous, both are gracious, but law is redemptive only in a

68. Lilje, "Church Struggle," p. 527.
69. "Barmen Declaration (1934)," in *Encyclopedia of the Lutheran Church*, 1:193.
70. Karl Barth, *Church Dogmatics* (New York: Scribner's, 1956–61), 2/2:585.

noneschatological sense; ultimate redemption or "spiritual righteous-ness" is God's gift through the gospel alone. Though the articulation of this anti-Barthian position by Lutherans during the Nazi era was often bumbling and cloudy, it was nevertheless this point of view that sought expression in the division of the Confessing Church during the years 1934–36.

Stage IV: The Shackled Church, 1937–45

Despite the tragic fact that evangelical Christians were unable to preserve an external unity, the "church struggle"—especially in the second and third stages—revealed that the substance of the church could not be destroyed by the Nazi regime. In fact, the substance, though wounded and enfeebled, survived the collapse of the Third Reich and emerged to a new life in 1945. But already in 1936 it was evident that little public success against the Nazis could or would be achieved.[71] Whether the disunity within the Confessing Church has-tened the shackling of the church is impossible to say. Given a totalitarian regime of the Hitler type, it is reasonable to believe that the *organized* church would not have been able to continue a united and public resistance, certainly not after the outbreak of World War II in 1939.

Up until 1936–37, Hitler purposely remained in the background as far as the "church struggle" was concerned. In fact, he posed as the benevolent arbiter between his own "German Christians" and the traditional churches. As we have seen, he used the "German Chris-tians" to entice "the reluctant sheep into the Nazi fold." During this period, which was coterminus with his four-year plan to rearm Germany, he was reaching for the church's throat with his "iron fingers in a velvet glove."[72] All this changed by 1937, when the Hitlerian deception ended. Further pretense of friendliness or even "neutrality" was no longer useful. The churches, reasoned Hitler, had not used the opportunity to align themselves with him and the party.

71. When Marahrens, Meiser, and Lilje were in New York for the 1936 meeting of the LWC executive committee (see Chapter 9, pp. 284–85), they made over-optimistic statements to the press regarding the German "church struggle," saying that the troubles were only temporary. Niemoeller, upon learning this, indicated that these men were wrong: "The fight is over and the church has lost." See *The Christian Century*, November 11, 1936.

72. Stewart W. Herman, *The Rebirth of the German Church* (London: SCM Press, 1946), p. 66.

The time had come therefore to withdraw the iron fist from the velvet glove and to carry out a systematic program to crush the churches, Roman Catholic as well as Protestant. To this end he employed Heinrich Himmler's *Sicherheitsdienst* (the SD) and the secret police, or gestapo. A secret directive set forth the steps by which the goal was to be achieved.[73] It was a plan of battle buttressed by the total resources of the regime. The strategy was to eliminate or force into silence all religious groups ranging from Protestant (Lutherans, Reformed, Union), Catholic, and sectarian societies to lodges like the Freemasons. Each was to be infiltrated by Nazi agents, who had instructions to ferret out subversive leaders, pastors, theological professors, church editors, youth groups, the Student Christian Movement, and other associations.

The Evangelical churches realized belatedly that their opponent was no longer (as if it ever had been!) the "German Christian Movement"; they now faced Hitler himself. The spokesman for the churches, Wilhelm Zoellner, quickly discovered this when he was forced by Nazi pressure to resign his chairmanship of the Government Church Committee early in 1937. He died a short time later, as his friends said, of a broken heart. This left Hitler's deputy, Hanns Kerrl, free to call upon the efficient and sinister gestapo and other arms of the state to carry out government directives without restraint. During the course of 1937, more than eight hundred pastors were arrested, and hundreds of others were placed under surveillance. Most publicized was the case of Martin Niemoeller, who was held incommunicado and awaiting a hearing between June 1937 and February 1938. Finally, in March 1938 he was given a secret trial, fined two thousand marks, and sentenced to seven months imprisonment, which in fact he had already more than served. Upon his release he was immediately arrested by the gestapo ("to protect him from an aroused public") and placed in the infamous Dachau concentration camp, where he remained until liberated by the Americans in 1945.[74] Not only were pastors persecuted, but students preparing for the ministry also were harassed and refused approval if they did not meet Nazi standards. Those who sought to supplement their university theological studies with classes

73. Ibid., p. 67.
74. Herman, *It's Your Souls We Want*, p. 174.

at a "secret" seminary like Finkenwald, conducted by Dietrich Bonhoeffer, were summarily expelled.[75]

Hanns Kerrl, who had already exercised fiscal pressure on the churches, now issued orders placing ecclesiastical finances under his direct control. Any action by local church authorities involving outlay of money required his approval. "Disobedient" pastors would have their salaries sharply reduced or even cut off. And contact with Christians outside Germany—the Vatican concordat theoretically permitted communication with Rome—was forbidden. The German delegates to the ecumenical conferences in Oxford and Edinburgh in the summer of 1937 were refused passports. The public press and radio were denied to church leaders.

In these and a hundred other ways the police state shackled Christian activities and fettered the church into immobility. So thoroughly and ruthlessly did Hitler carry out his program that virtually all resistance had crumbled by the end of 1937. Pastors had become weary of waging an unequal battle with an opponent whose demonic powers had restricted them to the ghetto of Sunday morning services. In fact, as the year drew to a close and Christmas neared, the Nazis were so confident of their control that they could afford to show the velvet glove again. With a maddening gesture of Yuletide generosity, all but a dozen of the imprisoned pastors were released on the order of a benevolent Führer.

The war years, of course, were but another opportunity to keep the church muzzled. Almost 50 percent of all clergymen were drafted for military service, leaving the spiritual care of congregations in disarray. The army and navy were allowed a severely limited number of chaplains. The air force had none at all. By 1941, the church press had been suppressed (the pretext was lack of paper); this meant that the printing of Bibles, catechisms, and other religious materials ceased. Confirmation instruction and youth work became all but impossible. The industrial and military war machine demanded the energies, loyalties, and time of young and old, male and female. The observance of Sunday was increasingly disregarded on the grounds that the necessities of war required it.

---

75. University professors were often under Nazi control. Exceptions like Karl Barth, Otto Piper, Paul Tillich, Gerhard Ritter, and Karl Jaspers had been pressured by the Nazis; some were dismissed, some resigned, others suffered in silence.

When 1943 drew to its close, the nationwide administration of the Protestant churches by the churches themselves had practically ceased. The Confessing Synod of the Prussian Church sought to issue occasional statements of spiritual encouragement to churches in North Germany, but according to the *Kirchliches Jahrbuch 1933–1944*, it was "unfortunately impossible to obtain wide distribution" of such documents.[76] In the south of Germany, Theophil Wurm wrote pastoral letters to the pastors of his *Landeskirche* which attempted not only to build up their faith but to sound the "word of the church" over against the Hitler regime. In this way he managed to keep alive a flickering hope for what was called "the church unity movement."[77]

The regime was patently pleased that there was no longer a unified leadership of the church. However, the government kept up a semblance of church contact through Hitler's lackey Kerrl, who already in 1939 had ensconced a lawyer, Friedrich Werner, as the director of the German Evangelical Church chancellery. The idea was that *administrative* leadership rested with Werner; spiritual leadership would ostensibly be exercised by the bishops and superintendents of the *Landeskirchen*.

With the invasion of Poland (1939), Werner appointed several leading churchmen to the so-called Spiritual Trust Council of the German Evangelical Church (*Der Geistliche Vertrauensrat der Evangelischen Kirche*).[78] The leading churchman on the new "Trust Council" was none other than August Marahrens, who for reasons best known to himself accepted this dangerously exposed position. His acceptance led to severe criticism from many of his friends in the Confessing Church, who now suspected him of complete capitulation to Hitler.[79] Marahrens did allow his name to be inscribed on several compromising documents that gave credence to the charges against

76. *Kirchliches Jahrbuch 1933–1944*, p. 382.

77. Ibid., pp. 412ff., 440ff.

78. Ibid., p. 472. The translation of the council's official name is cumbersome and difficult. The question lies in the word *Vertrauensrat:* What was a "spiritual trust"? Was it analogous to a trust department in a bank? If so, who managed the trust, the church or Hitler? The circumstances of the appointment clearly indicate the latter.

79. About this time Kerrl boasted to Hitler that he had all the bishops under his thumb. Hitler responded: "I have no interest in any of them except in that oak in Lower Saxony [Hannover]." The reference, of course, was to Marahrens. Interview of Lilje by E. Clifford Nelson, October 30, 1974, Hannover.

him and ultimately led to his being discredited. After World War II he resigned his two chief positions: the leadership of the *Landeskirche* of Hannover and the presidency of the Lutheran World Convention. To the very end, however, he insisted that he had always acted "in conscience" as a confessional Lutheran. In the final report of his ecclesiastical stewardship and in letters to friends, he gave a detailed interpretive account of his role in the German church since 1933. From the ascendancy of Hitler, he declared, his every act was determined by his confessional convictions and his desire to awaken the consciences of those in authority. Never, he held, did he waver from his purpose to preserve the rights of the church over against the state and, he said, he did this in a legally unassailable manner. This meant he often had to walk a tightrope. Sometimes his statements and decisions gave the impression of conceding too much to the Nazis. He freely admitted that he made mistakes, but bishops too are fallible, even when acting in conscience.

Illustrative was his signing of "The Five Principles" issued in connection with the Godesberg Declaration (1939).[80] This document, prepared by "German Christian" church officials acting under Kerrl, sought a declaration of principles purporting to manifest the unity of the churches in support of the regime. When only a relatively small number of persons affixed their signatures, it was apparent that Kerrl's scheme had misfired. In order to salvage something out of a bad situation, the DC changed their tactics by shifting attention to the current Anglo-German political polemic surrounding Hitler's march into Czechoslovakia. They issued a sharp denunciation of Cosmo Gordon Lang, archbishop of Canterbury, who had addressed the British House of Lords on March 20, 1939, five days after Hitler's takeover of Prague. In his speech, the archbishop had virtually "blessed" the Russian Bolshevik regime.[81] This incensed the Germans and provided the DC and the government press with an opportunity to

---

80. See Ernst C. Helmreich, *The German Churches under Hitler: Background, Struggle, and Epilogue* (Detroit: Wayne State University Press, 1979), pp. 232–34.

81. "Threat to Civilized Order: Primate on Moral Issue," *The Times* (London), March 21, 1939, p. 8. For Marahrens's comment on the archbishop's address, see the supplement to the LWC executive committee minutes, 1939: Hanns Lilje, "Bericht . . . die Sitzung . . . vom 20. bis 26. Mai 1939 in Waldenburg/Sachsen," pp. 3–4, LWF Archives, Geneva, Switzerland, vol. 2, 1933–39.

call for renewed support of Hitler's anti-Soviet "protection" of Czech-oslovakia.

In this atmosphere, Kerrl moderated his position and recast the original Godesberg Declaration into "Five Principles" for the reorganizing of church-state relations. Interlarded with numerous references to Luther, the document was presented to Marahrens, who in turn submitted it to a conference of church leaders. They reformulated the principles along more acceptable theological lines. This only angered Kerrl, who replied that his promised church reforms would not be undertaken unless the Five Principles were accepted without revision. Moreover, he demanded that Marahrens sign them. Apparently convinced that this was a last chance to reach a settlement, Marahrens acquiesced, but not without first preparing a commentary explaining his action. Later, in his own defense, he said he never referred to the principles apart from his "Commentary."[82] Nonetheless, Marahrens's action tended temporarily to breach the united front of the Lutheran wing of the Confessing Church. His fellow bishops, Meiser and Wurm, refused to sign Kerrl's statement, and pastors within his own *Landeskirche* were critical.

After the war, Marahrens confessed publicly that he had been wrong, not only in the Kerrl episode but also in the group signing of a telegram to Hitler at the beginning of the Russian campaign in 1941. He indicated, however, that he was aware of the ambiguous nature of his situation. He said that he was always conscious of his role before both God and man, and each step of the way he prayed that God would forgive him wherein he may have done wrong.[83] Although Marahrens had apparently acted in conscience when he accepted the leadership of the Kerrl-Werner appointed Spiritual Trust Council, he had risked too much. Despite his conscious exposure to manipulation by the regime and the anticipated criticism of his colleagues, his attempts

82. "Rechenschaftsbericht D. Marahrens vor der Hann. Landesynode vom 15. April 1947," in Klügel, *Die Lutherische Landeskirche Hannovers. Dokumente,* p. 215. Willem A. Visser 't Hooft, general secretary of the World Council of Churches, wrote about the Godesberg affair that Marahrens had signed reluctantly and with a personal commentary that received little publicity. See his *Memoirs* (Philadelphia: Westminster Press, 1973), pp. 96–97. Cf. also Visser 't Hooft's dismay regarding Canterbury's "political" stance. Cited in Armin Boyens, *Kirchenkampf und Ökumene 1933–1939* (Munich: Chr. Kaiser Verlag, 1969), pp. 262–63.

83. "Rechenschaftsbericht D. Marahrens . . . 15. April 1947," pp. 212–13.

to be a buffer between church and state were futile. As the war went on, the sorrows of the people multiplied and the cold terror of Nazism mounted. The last drastic attempts to extirpate the Jews and the promulgation of euthanasia on physically and mentally retarded persons were but further evidence of demonic forces running wild.[84]

THE AMERICAN SECTION THROUGH WORLD WAR II

The American members of the executive committee of the Lutheran World Convention began to refer to themselves as "The American Section" in 1937. They were led to this by the ominous news that had reached them through the normal media since 1933. Moreover, personal contact with the German members at the meetings of the executive committee provided them with firsthand information of a disquieting nature. Even more illuminating were the highly confidential reports of committee member Alfred Th. Jørgensen, whose personal contacts with the church situation in Germany continued unbroken until the invasion of Denmark in April 1940. Between June 1933 and May 1937 these reports were addressed to the Americans and Scandinavians by name and marked either "Highly Confidential!" or "Strictly Confidential!" Then in mid-1937 the reports were altered by omitting the personal salutation and simply addressing them thus: "To the *non-German* members."[85] This change coincided with the worsening church situation in Germany, which precipitated the decision by the U.S. members to assume the name "The American Section." Illustrative of the altered mood in the four-year period are quotations from Jørgensen's reports of June 13, 1933, and May 27, 1937. The occasion for both letters was his attendance at meetings of the AELK, of which he was a member. In the first, he wrote about the unexpected death of Ihmels and the election of Marahrens as his successor. He continued:

84. The story of the courageous resistance of Christian leaders like von Bodelschwingh to the government's program of euthanasia is told in Brandt, *Von Bodelschwingh*, pp. 186–211.
85. The Jørgensen reports are on file in the Danish Royal Archives, Rigsarkivet, Copenhagen, Denmark. Copies of most, if not all, are also in ArCL and the Lars W. Boe Papers, St. Olaf College Archives, Northfield, Minnesota.

I will now attempt—very confidentially—to give you my impressions. Increasingly the situation for the Lutheran World Convention is becoming sad and difficult. Everyone without exception is enthusiastic about Hitler [this was 1933]. Only one acquaintance [von Pechmann?][86] spoke of his grief over the persecution of the Jews. But one must remember how terrible the Communist danger was and how thankful the Germans and the rest of us must be that Hitler has struck them down. The Jews in the large cities also represented a danger, especially since many had come from Russia. Of the 3,000 physicians in Berlin only thirty were non-Jewish. On the other hand, the Nazis are exercising a harsh rule. Freedom of the press has totally disappeared. . . . Only Hitler is untouchable, nobody goes against him! . . . [Jørgensen here reviews the struggle over von Bodelschwingh and the triumph of Hitler's "German Christians."] Let me say to you, my three honorable colleagues, that the situation in Germany is terribly difficult not only for the German Lutherans but also for us outsiders. On the one hand, we must be very tactful and careful lest we harm our friends. . . . On the other hand, we must help them; they are counting on it. . . . We can strengthen them in their confessional loyalty; perhaps we can even show the government leaders that Lutherans of the world, quite like Catholics, are watching developments within Germany.

Jørgensen's letter of May 27, 1937, was written following a trip to Leipzig, where he once again had attended the session of the AELK:

The mood was extraordinarily depressed and the situation more critical than before. Especially tragic was their plea not only to be very careful in our letters to Germany but also in our reports to our own newspapers and journals. As in Russia, the situation for the Confessing Church becomes more difficult when those abroad express their sympathy for them. [Jørgensen mentions that the regime has prevented Marahrens from attending the ecumenical meetings in Britain and has not been permitted to speak in Thuringia or Mecklenburg, both of which were strongly "German Christian." He also refers to the split in the Confessing Church, the "radical" Niemoeller wing and the Lutheran wing.] The best news [he continues] that I can report is the organization of "the Lutheran Council," representing all the "intact churches" (Bavaria, Württemberg, Hannover). . . . Unfortunately the foreign newsmen, United Press and other correspondents who view the situation from their offices in Berlin, limit their reports to news of the Niemoeller wing. Hence they are often one-sided and polemical.

In Jørgensen's last report prior to the Nazi invasion of Denmark—

---

86. Cf. Friedrich W. Kantzenbach, ed., *Widerstand und Solidarität der Christen in Deutschland 1933–1945* (Neustadt/Aisch: Degener, 1971).

dated January 24, 1940—he said that never before had Lutheranism in Europe been so threatened by enemies without and within. Humanly speaking, Americans represented the last hope for world Lutheranism. Therefore, those European Lutherans who had not yet been overcome by the Nazis must stand by the side of the American brethren and struggle to preserve Lutheranism. He reported that just before Christmas (1939) he had met with August Marahrens and Hanns Lilje in Germany. Marahrens wondered whether he should remain as president, in view of the fact that his term would have expired during 1940 had the Philadelphia assembly not been canceled. Jørgensen advised that this was a question for the executive committee to decide; meanwhile, the Lutheran World Convention ought not to be without a president. Lilje thought the German members could attend a meeting of the executive committee if it were held in a neutral country. But it was unlikely, under the present circumstances, that Americans could travel to Europe.

This was the last communication (via Jørgensen) from within Germany. Marahrens and Lilje remained in office until 1945. Meanwhile, the American Section became the functioning head of world Lutheranism.

As noted earlier, the American Section and the National Lutheran Council were closely interlocked in programs, personnel, and headquarters. Since they served the same Lutheran churches in America, the two agencies for all practical purposes could be looked upon as being coextensive. The sole exception was that the NLC was not to take over the American Section's "representative" responsibility within world Lutheranism; the council would serve as the agent in gathering funds. With this understanding, a common program quickly emerged. This consisted of support of orphaned missions, European relief, and a ministry to refugees and prisoners of war.[87]

87. The following summary has been drawn primarily from *The World Lutheran*, published by the American Section between 1937 and 1939, and the minutes of the meetings of the American Section, 1937–45. Both are in ArCL. Supplemental accounts are in Wentz, *Lutherans in Concert*, and Osborne Hauge, *Lutherans Working Together: A History of the National Lutheran Council* (New York: NLC, 1945). It should be noted that the American Section of the executive committee voted on March 23, 1944, to enlarge itself to eight members. Strictly speaking, this action was unconstitutional, but it was justified by "necessity knows no law." The four "legal" members were Frederick

The question of "orphaned missions" had already been encountered shortly after World War I, so this was no novelty to American Lutherans.[88] But the problem was intensified after 1933, when the Hitler government imposed currency regulations that tended to cut off support of German mission societies. By 1934 the financial ax had fallen on the Gossner Mission Society (Berlin) and its field in India. Because American Lutherans had preserved this German work after World War I, it was but natural that they step into the new crisis that threatened Gossner, one of the largest Lutheran missions in the world.[89] By June 1939 the German missions in India, East Africa, New Guinea, China, and Jerusalem were completely orphaned. In addition, missions operated by Finnish Lutherans were threatened with extinction as a result of the "winter war," when Russian troops invaded Finland.

Faced with these realities, representatives of the NLC churches met on October 2, 1939, to coordinate and direct efforts to assume these new responsibilities. A campaign to raise funds was authorized. Called the Lutheran Emergency Appeal and directed by Oscar C. Mees, the campaign raised $238,000 by the spring of 1940.[90] The drain on this sum of money was sharply increased in April 1940, when the Nazis invaded Norway and Denmark, thus isolating their mission fields. This had the effect of making American Lutherans responsible for all Lutheran mission fields in the world, with the exception of those sponsored by groups in Sweden.

Although the United States was not at war, the members of Lutheran churches in Canada were immediately involved. This prompted Ralph H. Long to call a conference of Canadian Lutherans at Winnipeg on

---

H. Knubel, Ralph H. Long, Lars W. Boe (who died in 1942 and was succeeded by Johan A. Aasgaard in 1943), and Abdel Ross Wentz. The new members ("associates") were Theodore G. Tappert, Ethan Mengers, John Wargelin, and Peter O. Bersell. See "Minutes . . . American Section . . . March 23, 1944," p. 1; and June 14, 1944, p. 1.

88. See Fred W. Meuser, "Facing the Twentieth Century, 1900–1930," in E. Clifford Nelson, ed., *The Lutherans in North America* (Philadelphia: Fortress Press, 1975), p. 411.

89. *The World Lutheran* 1, no. 1 (1937?): 1–2.

90. Hauge, *Lutherans Working Together*, p. 73; and Wentz, *Lutherans in Concert*, pp. 106–7.

April 2, 1940. At this meeting the Canadian Lutheran Commission was organized to supervise the wartime service of the dominion churches. Approved by all groups except the Missouri Synod, the commission undertook a broad-gauged ministry, including services for German prisoners of war in Canadian camps. Initially the project received financial subsidies from the National Lutheran Council, but by 1942 it was self-supporting.

The service to personnel in the armed forces and the support of war-orphaned missions soon became parts of a massive overall project. The Lutheran Emergency Appeal of 1940, as we have seen, had been undertaken primarily for the benefit of orphaned missions. Consequently there were no funds on hand to engage in a ministry to men and women in the armed services. In 1941 the annual meeting of the National Lutheran Council heard a report of a survey trip made by Nils M. Ylvisaker and Clarence E. Krumbholz among forty-two military camps and forty-eight communities adjacent to the camps. On the basis of the report, the NLC voted to initiate a comprehensive program and named Ylvisaker as director. So that the work might get under way immediately, Johan A. Aasgaard arranged for the Norwegian Lutheran Church of America to make a direct appropriation of $100,000; the Lutheran Brotherhood insurance company donated office space at its headquarters in Minneapolis. Thus almost overnight the National Lutheran Council embarked on what was soon to be a vast program of wartime services. The responsibilities of the Service Commission included maintaining close touch with the chaplains, establishing centers for service men and women (in 1944 there were forty-four full-time pastors at these centers), and encouraging local parishes to keep in touch with their members in the armed services.

The program of the National Lutheran Council in 1941 to raise $500,000—one-half of which was to be used for the newly formed Service Commission, the remainder to support orphaned missions and the program of aid to war refugees—was named Lutheran World Action (LWA). The supervision and direction of Lutheran World Action fell chiefly upon the shoulders of two of the ablest men in American Lutheranism, Ralph H. Long and his assistant, Paul C. Empie. The latter had served on a part-time basis until he was elected assistant

director of the NLC in 1944.[91] Thereafter Lutheran World Action was
Empie's full responsibility, one which he discharged with imagina-
tion, efficiency, and dedication. When Long died unexpectedly in
1948, it was only natural that Empie be asked to succeed him as
executive director. Under Empie, Lutheran World Action became a
household word in the congregations, the vast majority of which gladly
cooperated in the program. Symbolized by a strong arm thrusting the
cross forward ("Love's Working Arm"), the Lutheran World Action
appeal became an annual event for the next quarter-century. Some
called it the Lutheran churches' Marshall Plan during the postwar
reconstruction. The 1941 LWA goal of $500,000 was supplemented by
a gift of $200,000 from the exiled Norwegian government in London
and earmarked for orphaned Norwegian missions. This gift, administered by Johan A. Aasgaard, president of the Norwegian Lutheran
Church in America, was especially timely, because the program of the
Service Commission and mission needs exceeded the early estimates.[92]

In subsequent months and years, new needs and programs were
thrust upon the Americans. The ministry to war refugees, though
actually begun in 1938, reached new heights after 1939–40. The
homeless victims of war and the stream of Jewish Christians fleeing
Nazi Germany, especially after *Kristallnacht* in 1938, provided the
Americans with a new challenge. Although service to refugees was a

91. Ralph H. Long, executive director of the NLC and member of the American
Section of the LWC, was chosen to direct the LWA appeal for $500,000 and was given
authority to select an assistant director ("Minutes . . . American Section . . . July 16,
1940," p. 1). Shortly thereafter, Long selected Paul C. Empie, superintendent of the
Lutheran Home for Orphans and Aged in Germantown, Philadelphia, and former
chairman of the Committee on Arrangements for the canceled 1940 Philadelphia
assembly of the LWC; he was to give part-time assistance to LWA. Meanwhile, since
both Long and Empie were occupied with these pressing obligations, Frederick H.
Knubel proposed that an administrative assistant for Long be called ("Minutes . . .
American Section . . . November 19, 1940," p. 5). This was discussed again on January
20 and May 21, 1941. At the latter meeting, Knubel reported that Carl E. Lund-Quist,
campus pastor at the University of Minnesota, had been approached, but action was
deferred for the time being. Meanwhile, by 1944 Empie was called to be assistant
director of the NLC, succeeding to the directorship upon Long's death in 1948. He held
this office through 1966, when the NLC was succeeded by the Lutheran Council in the
U.S.A. Empie continued to be active in Lutheran and ecumenical affairs until his death
in 1979. Lund-Quist became executive director of public relations for the NLC from
1946 to 1950. In 1951 he went to Geneva to be the assistant to Sylvester C. Michelfelder,
the first executive secretary of the LWF (1947–51). When Michelfelder died, Lund-
Quist succeeded him. He held the office until his resignation for reasons of health in
1960. He died in 1965.
92. "Minutes . . . American Section . . . September 5, 1941," p. 2.

special project of the American Section, the actual performance of the task was delegated to the NLC's Department of Welfare. By the end of 1941 more than 1,600 refugees had been "processed" and 1,118 had been provided employment.

By 1942 another wartime service was emerging. Prisoners of war were being placed in camps in Europe, Canada, and the United States. Most of these were Germans, and more than half were at least nominally Lutheran. In order to begin a ministry among them, the American Section urged the National Lutheran Council to appropriate $15,000 for the prisoner-of-war program of the YMCA.[93] By 1943–44 the number of prisoners had increased to more than 400,000, thus enlarging the responsibilities and necessitating the establishment of a Lutheran Commission for Prisoners of War.[94] The task of that commission was to locate among the prisoners Lutheran pastors who could lead the services of worship, to provide German hymnals, prayer books, and other literature, and generally to foster the welfare of the prisoners.

The use of America's most powerful shortwave radio, Station WRUL Boston, was offered to the American Section in the spring of 1941 (seven months before the Japanese attack on Pearl Harbor). A series of weekly broadcasts sought to reach the Lutherans of the world. Six languages—English, German, Norwegian, Swedish, Danish, and Finnish—brought news and religious programs to an audience estimated by WRUL at 70,000,000. Although there was no way of obtaining accurate figures, occasional reports smuggled from occupied countries indicated profound gratitude for the broadcasts.[95]

The dramatic operation of the American Section in rescuing missionaries in those portions of China threatened by Japanese troops was a story in itself. Directed by Daniel Nelson, the China program established a Lutheran Center in Chungking, which housed a congregation and an exiled seminary. After the war, Nelson's exciting rescues of

---

93. "Minutes . . . American Section . . . January 29, 1942," p. 2.

94. Hauge, *Lutherans Working Together*, p. 107. This commission was one of a few enterprises in which the Missouri Synod found it possible to cooperate. One of the NLC members was Michelfelder, who was a close personal friend of Long and who later went to Geneva as the postwar deputy of the American Section to reestablish relationships with the German church and to work with the WCC (in process of formation) in European reconstruction.

95. Ibid., p. 80. Cf. "Minutes . . . American Section . . . January 29, 1942," p. 3.

missionaries and hairbreadth escapes in a reconditioned airplane christened *The St. Paul* became legendary.

These extensive programs quite naturally placed heavy demands on American churches, but under the effective leadership of Empie, the Lutheran World Action appeals in 1943 and 1944 raised $1,319,723 and $1,536,128, respectively. These results could not have been achieved without the tireless cooperation and goodwill of a large corps of regional and group workers, who reached into every congregation of the member churches of the National Lutheran Council.

Together with Lutheran World Relief (not an incorporated part of the NLC), which was the material aid program of the council, and the Missouri Synod's Board of World Relief (after 1953), Lutheran World Action elicited the admiration of both ecclesiastical and governmental leaders. In fact, the manner in which American Lutheranism mobilized its resources for overseas aid both during and after the war did as much as anything else to enhance its stature in ecumenical circles. Voices in Asia, Africa, the Middle East, and Western Europe were raised in unstinted praise. A few were critical of what they termed American Lutheranism's "confessional imperialism." Martin Niemoeller, for example, was credited with the remark "Cuius dollar eius religio" (Religion is controlled by those who supply the money). Most people, however, recognized Lutheran World Action as an outpouring of Christian compassion.

By 1944 the possibility of an early termination of the war in Europe prompted the American Section to make even larger plans for postwar relief. The 1945 Lutheran World Action campaign goal was set at $2,500,000. Arrangements had been made (1944) with the Missouri Synod's Emergency Planning Council to cooperate with the National Lutheran Council in the vast program of postwar reconstruction. The Missourians agreed that the joint services of American Lutherans would be offered in the name of the Lutheran World Convention, although Missouri Synod President John W. Behnken said this must not be construed as "becoming a member of the Lutheran World Convention." It was also agreed that there would be a single treasury for the disbursement of funds.[96] A resolution was adopted to appoint a

96. "Minutes . . . American Section . . . January 29, 1944," p. 8; June 13–14, 1944, pp. 2–5; September 18–19, 1944, pp. 3–6, and appendix, pp. 1–2.

representative of the American Section to go to Geneva, and tentative plans were made to establish a fact-finding commission to go to Europe as soon as conditions permitted and as soon as transportation was available. The commission would include a representative of the Missouri Synod, who turned out to be Lawrence B. Meyer, director of the synod's Emergency Planning Council. After extended negotiations with the U.S. Department of State, the commission members (Long and Bersell from the American Section and Meyer from the Missouri Synod) were granted passports. The decision was then made to depart for Sweden in early 1945.[97]

The members of the American Section were aware that the doors to Europe might open more speedily than anticipated. They knew that once inside the doors, they would face tasks of an overwhelming nature. It was only wisdom, therefore, to give careful thought to the work that lay before them. Two basic premises undergirded the European phase of their program: (1) the rehabilitation of church life by relief, reconstruction, and restoration of the spiritual functions of crippled and distressed congregations; and (2) the reestablishment of the all-but-destroyed Lutheran World Convention, perhaps even changing its nature and goals to meet the new challenges. To this story we turn in the next and final chapter.

---

97. "Minutes . . . American Section . . . October 13, 1944," p. 1; January 22, 1945, pp. 1–2. Long had expressed concern that passports could not be secured. Meyer was confident that three passports would be permitted. His confidence may have been based on information secured from an employee of the State Department. In any case, Meyer's confidence proved to be well based. Meyer makes no mention of cooperation with the NLC and the American Section, except for the service to prisoners of war, in his account "The Emergency Planning Council," in Lawrence B. Meyer, *Missouri in Motion* (St. Louis[?], 1970), pp. 81–83.

11

The Rebirth and Reconstruction of World Lutheranism, 1944–47

The postwar commissioner of the American Section, Sylvester C. Michelfelder, had set up his office at Geneva in July 1945. On June 19, 1946, he wrote to the American members of the executive committee who were planning to attend the Uppsala meeting in July:

> Our tasks . . . are enormous. . . . Pray for the success of this meeting. Come prepared with helpful suggestions. We dare not reconstruct merely what once was. We must do more—we must construct a new world organization of Lutherans, that by the guidance of the Holy Spirit we may make our rightful contribution in these difficult days.[1]

This appeal by one of the leading figures in the rebirth and reconstruction of world Lutheranism after World War II summed up the convictions of many. Of course, the immediate aims, as after World War I, were the relief of suffering and the kindling of hopes of people caught in the enormous destruction and widespread dislocation at war's end. The longer view, however, led to the belief that world Lutheranism would no longer be served adequately by a simple continuation of the Lutheran World Convention. A new structure was needed, and it emerged in the minds of churchmen as they began in 1944 to make specific postwar plans and as they faced the actual problems in 1945–46.

This chapter will attempt to chronicle the story in three parts: the plans and events of 1944–46; the reassembling of the Lutheran World

---

1. "Advance Information to Members of Executive Committee, LWC, for Meeting at Uppsala, July 24–26, 1946," p. 2, in "Minutes and papers of the American Section," Archives of Cooperative Lutheranism, Lutheran Council/U.S.A., New York City (hereafter referred to as ArCL).

Convention and the birth of the Lutheran World Federation at Lund in 1947. The Epilogue sets forth an assessment of the federation's self-understanding as it faced the future.

"ALL THE KING'S MEN":
PUTTING WORLD LUTHERANISM TOGETHER AGAIN

After 1939 the American Section of the Lutheran World Convention and the National Lutheran Council were engaged in immense efforts to meet the challenges that confronted the churches. When it became evident in 1944 that Hitler's war machine was being overcome, the pace and scope of plans for postwar relief quickened. Although the Missouri Synod had not associated itself with either the National Lutheran Council or the Lutheran World Convention, the occasion seemed propitious to explore the possibility of cooperation. Missouri possessed a large German-American constituency and in prewar years had established relationships with Lutheran Free Churches in Germany. It was only natural that the American Section propose informal discussions regarding cooperation in postwar relief. This was initiated in January 1944 and led to an arrangement whereby Missouri's Emergency Planning Council felt it could work with the American Section "in externals" without compromising its theological position.[2]

The carefully worded statement of agreement, adopted on September 19, 1944, made provision for Missouri's exit, in case it should conclude that "cooperation" was going beyond "externals."[3] The statement read:

> 1. The conviction and conscience of all those participating in the program of relief and reconstruction of Lutheran churches in Europe shall be respected at all times. Any participating body shall have the privilege

---

2. Records of the negotiations with the Missouri Synod are found in "Minutes of the American Section" in ArCL; see January 29, 1944, p. 8; March 23, 1944, pp. 2–3; June 14, 1944, pp. 2–5; September 18–19, 1944, pp. 3–6; October 13, 1944; January 22, 1945, pp. 1–2. John W. Behnken, Louis Sieck, and Lawrence B. Meyer were the Missouri negotiators.

3. The struggle over the artificial distinction between *res externae* and *res internae* had been joined in the NLC shortly after its birth in 1918. Lars W. Boe and Ralph H. Long—in addition to Frederick H. Knubel and Abdel Ross Wentz—had long since agreed that the distinction was impossible to maintain. See E. Clifford Nelson, *Lutheranism in North America 1914–1970* (Minneapolis: Augsburg Publishing House, 1972), pp. 125–26.

to withdraw all support for any phase of work in the general program which is contrary to its conviction and conscience.

2. The program of relief and reconstruction shall be administered under the name of the American Section of the Lutheran World Convention.

3. There shall be an administrative committee of five members, three to be appointed by the American Section of the Lutheran World Convention and two to be appointed by the Missouri Synod.

4. It shall be the responsibility of the administrative committee to direct the program of relief and reconstruction in accordance with principles agreed upon by the American Section of the Lutheran World Convention and the Missouri Synod as outlined in the minutes of the joint committee held in Detroit in June 14, 1944, and such regulations as may be made by the participating bodies from time to time.

5. A common treasury shall be established out of which all relief funds for the joint program as agreed upon from time to time are to be drawn.

6. The treasurer shall be elected by the American Section of the Lutheran World Convention.

7. The selection of representatives to administer relief in Europe shall, as far as possible, be in the ratio of two from the constituency of the American Section of the Lutheran World Convention and one from the constituency of the Missouri Synod.

8. Any member finding it necessary or expedient to withdraw from cooperation with the American Section of the Lutheran World Convention shall be entitled to withdraw its remaining proportionate share of funds contributed to the common treasury.[4]

Armed with this "basis for cooperation," the executive director of the Missouri Synod's Emergency Planning Council, Lawrence B. Meyer, joined Ralph H. Long, executive director of the National Lutheran Council, and Peter O. Bersell, president of the NLC (and of the Augustana Synod), in a six-week fact-finding journey to Europe between late February and early April 1945. Bersell declared exuberantly and optimistically that Missouri's participation marked a new day. For the first time it was no longer necessary to say apologetically, "We represent only two-thirds of the Lutherans in America"; the commission would be the voice of virtually all American Lutherans.[5]

---

4. "Minutes . . . American Section, September 18–19, 1944," pp. 5–6.

5. Peter O. Bersell, "We Saw Europe," *The Lutheran Standard*, May 19, 1945, p. 14. Bersell's optimism about Missouri was to be short-lived. Shortly after this trip, cracks in the agreement began to appear. See "Minutes . . . American Section . . . April 18, 1945," pp. 5, 6. Later on, Missouri resumed its traditional posture regarding other American Lutherans and rejected membership in the LWF. This attitude has been maintained to the present (1981).

On a bleak winter day, February 28, 1945, the three commissioners left Washington, D.C., in a U.S. army transport command airplane for Europe via Labrador and Iceland. The journey was described by Bersell as "hazardous." German V-1 and V-2 bombs were still falling on London when the Americans reached the British capital.[6] It was clear to them that, despite the dangers of travel, they were being afforded a welcome and perhaps unexpected opportunity to realize the fivefold purposes for which they had been commissioned. Bersell described them as follows:

First, [we were] to observe and evaluate conditions, to learn as much as possible of the state of the Lutheran churches and their present and postwar needs. The magnitude of this prime objective of our mission is quite evident when we remember that eighty-five percent of all Protestants on the continent of Europe are Lutherans, and that no church has suffered as much as ours.

Second, to contact as many Lutheran church leaders as possible in order to set in motion and implement a worldwide program of Lutheran action looking to the reconstruction and rehabilitation of the Lutheran church and its work in all lands.

Third, to contact other Christian leaders, especially the World Council of Churches' Reconstruction Committee in Geneva, for the purpose of coordinating and integrating this work of the Lutheran Church with the work of other churches that are also ready to launch out on great reconstructive and eleemosynary programs, involving the expenditure of millions of dollars. It is obvious that by the very ecumenical character of this worldwide church relief work the Lutheran Church will be the greatest beneficiary. Proportionately the free Lutheran churches should also be the greatest contributors.

Fourth, to contact the United States Army and Navy chaplains, their chiefs and staffs, for the purpose of extending as widely as possible our American Lutheran spiritual ministry to our servicemen abroad. As a result, a chain of Lutheran Service Centers, such as we have in America, will soon become a reality, not only in London (491 Oxford Street) but also in Paris, perhaps Berlin or some other German city, Manila, and Chungking (already established). [Meetings with chaplains and service pastors were held while the committee was in London.]

Fifth, to contact those in charge of the prisoners of war work on the continent and in England, namely, the civilian organizations such as the

---

6. The most detailed account of the commissioners' experiences and actions has been recorded by Bersell. He kept the "Protocol" of meetings and wrote reports that were later published in *The Lutheran Companion* (March 23, 1955, p. 8) and *The Lutheran Standard* (May 19, 1945, p. 14). A copy of the "Protocol" is in the E. Clifford Nelson Papers, St. Olaf College Archives, Northfield, Minnesota.

Y.M.C.A. and World Council of Churches, and the military command, for the purpose of learning how our American Lutheran Commission for Prisoners of War can best cooperate in this service wherein we have already given such a large contribution.[7]

After nine days of meetings in Britain the survey team obtained a flight to Stockholm aboard a converted Boeing Flying Fortress. This part of the journey took them on a cloudy, moonless night over the North Sea and German-occupied Norway. Once in Stockholm they plunged immediately into a round of discussions with government leaders (including King Gustav V and Count Folke Bernadotte) and churchmen from Sweden, Norway, Denmark, and Finland. The latter provided significant information on church relief needs, orphaned missions, and reconstruction of church property (the devastation in the northern Norwegian province of Finnmark was almost totally due to the "scorched-earth policy" of the retreating Nazi forces).

The two most important meetings regarding the immediate future of world Lutheranism were held at Sigtuna, Sweden (March 17, 1945) and Geneva, Switzerland (April 2, 1945). The former laid the foundation for the rebirth of the Lutheran World Convention (Bersell maintained that the Lutheran World Federation was "conceived" at Sigtuna and "born" in Lund [1947]); the latter established the principles by which Lutherans were to do joint work with the World Council of Churches (WCC, in process of formation), and thus embark on a path that led a confessional body into serious ecumenical encounter.

The details of the first meeting have been carefully recorded in handwritten minutes as well as in report articles in American Lutheran church papers.[8] The site of the meeting was the Sigtunastift-elsen (Sigtuna Foundation), a conference and retreat center about twenty miles south of Uppsala.[9] In addition to the three Americans, members of the Swedish Section of the Lutheran World Convention were present. They were Erling Eidem, vice-president of the LWC,

---

7. *The Lutheran Standard,* May 19, 1945, p. 14.

8. "Protocol of meetings held in Sigtuna, Sweden, March 17, 1945," recorded by Bersell; for published articles see n. 6, above.

9. The Sigtuna Foundation was established in this twelfth-century center of Swedish church life in 1915 by Manfred Björkquist. It set the pattern for the post–World War II German evangelical academies that fostered dialogue between the Christian faith and modern culture.

Edvard Rohde, Per Pehrsson, Lars Wollmer, Yngve Rudberg, and Thore Borgvall.

Three major topics were addressed. The first spoke to the relationship between the American Section and the Swedish Section, especially pertaining to relief work. It was quickly apparent that there was a difference of opinion between the Swedes and the Americans. The former took the position that responsibility for relief work should be divided: the Swedes would care for the Scandinavian churches, especially Norway and Finland (Denmark had suffered little destruction), while Americans would carry the responsibility for continental Europe. The Swedish proposal, the Americans protested, would undercut one of the hopes of the American Section, namely, the resuscitation of the Lutheran World Convention. They pleaded, therefore, that all relief work be a cooperative enterprise on the part of all Lutherans who were financially able to participate, so that there would be "no cleavage between the Lutheran churches of the world." To accept the Swedish proposal would be to damage Lutheran world solidarity.

The Swedish reply led to the second major topic, the current leadership of the Lutheran World Convention. Since the executive officers (August Marahrens and Hanns Lilje) were located in Germany, the Lutheran World Convention was in reality impotent. Therefore, said the Swedes, the American proposal was irrelevant. The Americans responded that prior to their departure the presidents of eight American Lutheran church bodies—members of the National Lutheran Council—had voted to ask for the resignation of August Marahrens, who, according to Bersell's account, had officially "blessed" Hitler's armies in their "push to the east." After considerable urging by the Americans, the Swedes agreed to take a similar stand. Erling Eidem stated, somewhat reluctantly, that he would contact Marahrens and request his resignation "in the name of the Lutherans in the U.S.A. and Sweden."[10] Upon the receipt of the

---

10. The first consideration by the Americans of the possible resignation of Marahrens and Lilje is recorded in "Minutes . . . American Section . . . March 20, 1940," pp. 4–5. In the event this became necessary, the vice-president, Eidem, would be asked to assume the presidency, and Paul Sandegren of India, who was on furlough in Sweden, would be asked to take over as general secretary for one year.

resignation, Eidem would call a meeting of the executive committee to discuss reorganization of the convention. Despite this decision, the Swedes let it be known that they had but little interest in the future of the Lutheran World Convention.

The third topic under discussion at Sigtuna flowed out of the previous two. If the twin problems of relief and reorganization of the Lutheran World Convention were to be addressed effectively, some provision for implementation and coordination must be made. To this end a "Lutheran World Convention Liaison Committee" was created. Initially its membership would include two Swedes and "one or two" Americans. The committee would continue the survey of needs and propose plans of operation to its constituencies. Edvard Rohde was named chairman and Erling Eidem honorary chairman. Other members were Thore Borgvall and Ralph H. Long. The second American member, Franklin Clark Fry, was chosen at the next meeting of the American Section.[11]

The agreements reached at Sigtuna included a proviso by the Church of Sweden that the proposed plans be shared with the World Council of Churches, still in the process of formation. The Swedish Church had already made commitments to participate ecumenically in reconstruction and was eager to avoid misunderstandings. Therefore the three-man American committee agreed to report the Sigtuna proposals to Willem A. Visser 't Hooft, WCC general secretary, as soon as they arrived in Geneva.

The Americans journeyed to Geneva via England and France. On April 2 they met with Visser 't Hooft and representatives of the WCC Department of Reconstruction and Inter-Church Aid. They learned that the Geneva office had already made contact with various prominent church people, from whom reports on conditions within their own countries had been received. Thus when Allied military restrictions would be lifted, representatives of relief agencies such as the World Council of Churches and the Lutheran World Convention would have some idea of what to expect.

The accounts of the meeting revealed that a high degree of mutual

---

11. "Minutes . . . American Section . . . April 18, 1945," pp. 2, 7.

respect and desire for cooperation characterized the consultation.[12] Visser 't Hooft, for example, wrote Erling Eidem that he had made it clear to the Lutheran delegation that the new World Council of Churches would not interfere in the internal affairs of churches within the same confessional family. Like the Lutherans themselves, the WCC was interested in collaboration so as to eliminate competition and overlapping. He indicated, moreover, that the council was eager to avoid giving the impression of seeking centralization. He wished the Lutherans to know that his office and staff stood ready to offer consultative services in the huge task of reconstruction, and he was happy that Eidem had accepted the honorary presidency of the Lutheran Liaison Committee. As such, the archbishop would be a personal link between the World Council of Churches and the Lutheran churches. "The more links of this kind . . . the more surely will we avoid any friction." The official minutes show that the American commissioners accepted this ecumenical arrangement with gratitude and expressed their desire for close cooperation with the WCC Department of Reconstruction and Inter-Church Aid. In fact, it was agreed that a representative of the American Lutheran churches should come to Geneva to serve in a liaison capacity and to be a member—with voice and vote—of that department's staff. This position was soon filled by Ralph H. Long's close friend, Sylvester C. Michelfelder of Toledo, Ohio.[13]

When the American delegation returned to the United States, it reported the results of its investigations to a hastily called meeting of the American Section (plus Missourians John W. Behnken, Louis

---

12. Official minutes of the meeting were kept by Bersell: "Minutes of a meeting between the Delegation of the American Lutheran Churches . . . and Representatives of . . . the World Council of Churches . . . , Geneva, Switzerland, April 2, 1945." Cf. *The Lutheran Standard*, May 12, 1945, and Visser 't Hooft to Eidem, April 7, 1945. The latter is in the WCC Archives, Geneva, Switzerland, box 284, Eidem correspondence file. The WCC representatives in addition to Visser 't Hooft included Hanns Schönfeld, Nils Ehrenström, and Adolf Freudenberg.

13. The agreements reached in Geneva are in Bersell's handwritten minutes, April 2, 1945. A summary of the NLC News Bureau was distributed in the U.S. Cf. "American Lutheran Commissioners Make Plans with World Council," *The Lutheran Standard*, May 12, 1945, p. 15. The first choice of the American Section for the post in Geneva had been Abdel Ross Wentz, who was unable to accept. Michelfelder was initially called for a period of one year. "Minutes . . . American Section . . . April 18, 1945," p. 2.

Sieck, and Lawrence B. Meyer) in Chicago on April 18, 1945.[14] The
report elicited a protracted discussion of the tentative agreements with
the World Council of Churches. Although it was apparent that the
Missouri Synod representatives had reservations not only about the
WCC arrangements but also about the original Plan of Cooperation
(June 14, 1944, and September 18, 1944) with the American Section,
the recommendations were adopted.[15] With this accomplished, the
Missourians were excused, and the American Section continued in
session to transact its business. Among the major items were the
election of Ralph H. Long and Franklin Clark Fry to serve on the joint
American-Swedish Liaison Committee and the appointment of Sylvester C. Michelfelder as its Geneva representative.[16]

The long-range results of "the fact-finding" survey were impressive.
First, the channels of communication had now been established for
the rapid assumption of relief and reconstruction activities *outside*
Germany.[17] Second, the directions of postwar interchurch relationships were outlined, at least for the two-thirds of American Lutherans
in the American Section of the Lutheran World Convention. That is,
the *confessional* direction was indicated at Sigtuna when tentative
steps were taken to reactivate the Lutheran World Convention; the
ecumenical direction was adumbrated when agreements were made
with the representatives of the World Council of Churches to coordinate the work of reconstruction and interchurch aid. In these ways the
American Section was preparing the way for participation in the Lund
assembly of the Lutheran World Federation (1947) and the Amsterdam
assembly of the World Council of Churches (1948).

On July 3, 1945, the troop ship *Mariposa* set sail from Boston bound
for Le Havre. Only a few days earlier it had brought 6,300 American
servicemen from the European theater of war. It was now returning to

---

14. "Minutes . . . American Section . . . April 18, 1945," p. 2. Awareness of the
imminent collapse of Nazi Germany (Hitler committed suicide on April 30) is indicated
by a document attached to the minutes: "The Geneva Memorandum: Suggestions for
Immediate Relief Action." More than $100,000 was set aside for pressing needs.
15. Ibid., pp. 5–6.
16. Ibid., pp. 7–8.
17. Official Allied policy was to enforce "a hard peace" (the Morgenthau Plan) on
Germany. It was not until 1946 that an aroused public sentiment led President Harry
Truman to relax the policy so as to allow American voluntary agencies to send relief *into*
Germany.

Boston, 1945: Dr. and Mrs. S. C. Michelfelder bound for Europe following his appointment as liaison to the World Council of Churches in Geneva.

En route to Europe, 1945: The three-man delegation to Europe sent by the American Section of the Lutheran World Convention. R. H. Long, F. C. Fry, and J. A. Aasgaard.

France carrying the first large contingent of civilians bound for postwar Europe. Among the 380 passengers were numerous representatives of the United Nations Relief and Rehabilitation Agency, some diplomats returning from the United Nations meeting in San Francisco, and a number of church-related groups and individuals. Among the latter were two Lutheran couples, Dr. and Mrs. Sylvester C. Michelfelder and Dr. and Mrs. Stewart Herman, who had been pastor of the American Church in Berlin between 1936 and 1941 and during the war had been associated with the U.S. Office of Strategic Service. Because of his church and government experience and general knowledge of the German situation, Herman was quickly sought out at war's end by the World Council of Churches to be associate director of its Department of Reconstruction with many duties in Germany.

After arriving in Geneva, Herman received military clearance speedily and within a month was on his way into Germany, where he made contact with churchmen at the historic Treysa Conference, August 27–September 1, 1945. The conference was convoked by the Lutheran bishop of Württemberg, Theophil Wurm, to replace the Nazi-dominated church organization. It produced a new Evangelical Church (Federation) in Germany (EKiD). On this occasion Herman was able to make contact with men like Theophil Wurm, Hans Meiser, August Marahrens, Hanns Lilje, Martin Niemoeller, Martin Dibelius, and others.[18] He reported later that a letter written by Michelfelder from Geneva, where he was impatiently waiting for a permit to enter Germany, was read to the Treysa Conference by Theophil Wurm and received with great enthusiasm. In fact, Michelfelder's plea that Germans make a confession of guilt—something that they were hearing from all sides—was mitigated by his acknowledgment that "before the throne of God all of us have sinned and gone astray." This emphasis enabled them to make an unforced, genuine confession of sin by which they could make a clean break with their past and begin anew in the context of the Lutheran understanding of *sola gratia.* [19]

---

18. Herman has published his account of Treysa and other postwar ecclesiastical events in his *The Rebirth of the German Church* (London: SCM Press, 1946). Cf. "Konferenz in Treysa," in Wilhelm Brandt, *Friedrich von Bodelschwingh, 1877–1946. Nachfolger und Gestalter* (Bethel bei Bielefeld: Verlagshandlung der Anstalt Bethel, 1967), pp. 243–49.

19. Michelfelder's letter is found in his "Diary and Impressions," a typescript covering July 1 to October 4, 1945, pp. 13–14. The writer obtained a photocopy while

The Michelfelders and the Hermans had arrived in Geneva on July 18, 1945. Michelfelder's visa troubles gave him the opportunity to "settle in" for the one-year assignment.[20] The immediate problems were to learn the operations of the World Council of Churches, to continue efforts to gain entry into Germany, and then to set up the channels whereby relief could be administered to war sufferers. It was a gargantuan task that only slowly yielded to constant expenditure of time, energy, and patience. Michelfelder wrote in his diary that he was exasperated with the endless "red tape" in dealing with embassies and military governments. Meanwhile, reports from all over Europe flooded into Geneva. Most disconcerting was the fact that the Lutheran World Convention, the World Council of Churches, and other private agencies had no access to UNRRA funds. The United Nations had realized that the administration of physical aid to prostrate Europe was beyond the abilities of voluntary agencies. Hence the United Nations Relief and Rehabilitation Agency (UNRRA) had been organized to help areas and peoples liberated by the Allied armies. Financed by contributions from member nations in the amount of 1 percent of their national incomes, UNRRA was able to provide millions of dollars for the liberated areas. Unfortunately, these funds were not available for relief work inside Germany or any of the nations associated with that country, including Finland. The vengeful Morgenthau Plan and the Potsdam Agreement, plus the huge movement of expellees and displaced persons from the East, had reduced the population of Germany to a near-starvation level of 1,550 calories per day (the average American diet contained 3,000 calories). When Michelfelder finally was able to visit Germany, he was appalled by what he saw and sent reports to America attacking the policy of deliberate starvation. Others were likewise seeking to stir up public opinion and urging humanitarians and church people to proclaim that this was no way to achieve a "just and enduring peace."

These actions, together with other considerations, prompted both

---

examining the LWF Archives in Geneva. Cf. Kurt Schmidt-Clausen's favorable comments re Michelfelder in *Vom Lutherischen Weltkonvent zum Lutherischen Weltbund* (Gütersloh: Gerd Mohn, 1976), pp. 234–35.

20. Michelfelder had received a leave of absence from his congregation, St. Paul's, in Toledo, Ohio. At the end of one year, however, it was deemed best that he resign from his parish position and remain in Geneva to carry on the vast work he had begun. He continued in his assignment as the representative ("commissioner") of the American Section of the LWC until his sudden death in 1951.

the Federal Council of Churches and the American Section of the Lutheran World Convention to send deputations to Germany in the autumn of 1945. Franklin Clark Fry, successor to Frederick H. Knubel of the United Lutheran Church, was a member of both commissions. Other members of the FCC group were Methodist bishop G. Bromley Oxnam and Episcopal bishop Henry Knox Sherrill. This commission was given a "guided tour" by American officials—who were inclined to suggest that the Germans were getting what they deserved—and returned with a report that gave little hope that American Protestants could be of much assistance because private relief shipments to Germans were banned. Fry was indignantly opposed to this and took occasion publicly to denounce the American use of "starvation as an instrument of foreign policy." Under mounting criticism, President Harry Truman finally in 1946 lifted the ban and thus opened the way to the Council of Relief Agencies Licensed to Operate in Germany (CRALOG), of which Lutheran World Relief (established in 1945) became an important member.[21] It was in this context that Michelfelder was given an additional responsibility: He became the organizer and director of the Material Aid Division of the World Council of Churches.

The way was now prepared for additional American Lutherans to join those already in Europe. Clifford Ansgar Nelson of St. Paul, Minnesota, arrived to serve as short-term assistant to Michelfelder; Carl Schaffnit of Detroit, Michigan, became the Lutheran representative for CRALOG; Julius Bodensieck, president of Wartburg Seminary, Dubuque, Iowa, served as commissioner to Germany for the LWC American Section; and Bodensieck's remarkable wife, Justine, was soon engaged in service to displaced peoples (DPs). Still another American Lutheran, E. Theodore Bachmann, came to Europe to serve as the WCC's "liaison person" with the German churches in 1946–47.

It was the so-called "spiritual ministry" to displaced peoples that at the outset engaged the attention of Michelfelder's associates. In April 1946, Michelfelder and Howard Hong[22] made contact with the head-

21. For a lively account of Fry's meeting with Truman see Stewart W. Herman's article in *Franklin Clark Fry: Palette for a Portrait*, ed. Robert Fischer. This publication is a supplementary number of *The Lutheran Quarterly* 24 (1972); Fry's letter to Herman is on pp. 171–72.

22. Hong, professor of philosophy at St. Olaf College, had arrived in Europe during December 1945 under the auspices of the YMCA's program for prisoners of war.

quarters of UNRRA. Clifford A. Nelson surveyed the needs of the displaced peoples and "the Lutheran churches in exile." Carl Schaff-nit, completing his assignment with CRALOG, moved directly into DP work. Justine Bodensieck, now attached to the WCC staff, was similarly engaged. Howard Hong returned to St. Olaf College to resume his teaching duties in September 1946. The following January the annual meeting of the American Section of the Lutheran World Convention in Detroit approved a recommendation from Michelfelder that a permanent service to refugees be established and that Hong be appointed director to take up his duties in June 1947. The intervening months afforded Hong time to project some plans, one of which was to gather a cadre of volunteers to serve in Germany as a sort of Lutheran early-day Peace Corps. One month after Hong's appointment, the LWC American Section approved the use of college and seminary student volunteers to staff the program. In April the first of these had been signed up, Kenneth Senft, Gettysburg Seminary, and James Anderson, St. Olaf College. During Hong's imaginative administration no less than sixteen other workers joined the refugee service.[23]

Meanwhile, the second commission of which Franklin Clark Fry was a member, the three-man delegation from the American Section of the LWC, had arrived in Europe in November 1945. Its members (Johan A. Aasgaard, president of the Norwegian Lutheran Church of America; Ralph H. Long, director of the National Lutheran Council; and Franklin Clark Fry) had been given a fourfold task: (1) the reactivating of the executive committee of the Lutheran World Convention (the Swedish members of the Liaison Committee, including Erling Eidem, had thus far failed to arrange a meeting of the executive committee); (2) the setting up of effective relief and welfare agencies in war-stricken Europe; (3) the securing of European Lutheran support for confessional rather than geographic representation in the World Council of Churches; and (4) the determining of the future program for American-supported orphaned missions.

It will be recalled that the earlier team of American Lutherans to visit Europe had held a meeting with Swedish churchmen at Sigtuna in March 1945. At that time the Liaison Committee (Swedish-Ameri-

---

23. Interview of Hong by E. Clifford Nelson, November 13, 1969. Cf. Richard Solberg, *As Between Brothers* (Minneapolis: Augsburg Publishing House, 1957), pp. 143–44.

can) for the Lutheran World Convention had been formed. When the second American trio arrived in Britain, they chanced to meet Eivind Berggrav of Oslo, who was in London to receive from the archbishop of Canterbury the Lambeth Cross for his outstanding Christian witness.[24] Berggrav had been a staunch opponent of the Nazis during the German occupation of Norway and as such had become a national hero as well as a prominent figure in ecumenical circles. The American commissioners apparently used the occasion to ask the bishop about circumstances in Norway and to inquire about his relationship to the Liaison Committee. They had learned in July that Thore Borgvall, a Swedish member of the committee, had visited Norway in June 1945, at which time he had a long visit with Berggrav and Olaf Moe, chairman of the Norwegian Committee of the Lutheran World Convention.[25] Borgvall's written report to the American Section had indicated that Berggrav was critical of the Swedes for their neutral stance during Norway's struggle against the Nazis. For this reason, Berggrav was not inclined to accept an appointment, along with Bishop Fuglsang-Damgaard of Denmark, to membership on the LWC Liaison Committee. Borgvall asserted, however, that once Berggrav had ventilated his feelings he said, "When God has such great common tasks for us in these times, we must in the future disregard national bagatelles." The Swede commented that the conversation continued in this spirit, and he predicted that Berggrav and Moe would join the Liaison Committee after Norway's immediate exigencies had been dealt with.[26]

At the time that the American commission was conferring with Eivind Berggrav in London, the Liaison Committee was already in a shambles. Thore Borgvall and Lars Wollmer were being attacked by the Swedish press for alleged pro-Nazi views during the war. This led them to resign from the committee.[27] Moreover, they had done very little to prepare for the restoration of the Lutheran World Convention. Even Erling Eidem, vice-president of the LWC, had found

---

24. Fry to Wentz, December 7, 1945, Geneva, p. 4, Abdel Ross Wentz Papers, in ArCL. Cf. *The Lutheran Standard,* December 22, 1945, p. 19.
25. See Borgvall to the LWC American Section, July 3, 1945, p. 1, in ArCL.
26. Ibid., p. 2.
27. Long had learned of this trouble before the commission left the States. See Michelfelder to Long, October 13, 1945, Ralph H. Long Papers, in ArCL.

little time or inclination to reactivate organized world Lutheranism and had done nothing to secure the resignation of LWC president August Marahrens. It was a special blow to learn that Berggrav himself had disassociated himself from the Liaison Committee.[28] Nevertheless, despite this discouraging information, the Americans were heartened by Berggrav's willingness to urge his personal friend Eidem to issue a call for a meeting of the executive committee of the LWC to be held at Copenhagen, December 16–17, 1945.

Meanwhile, Long and Aasgaard went on to Geneva (Fry went to Paris) to consult with Michelfelder in his "gate house" office on the campus of the World Council of Churches. He briefed them on his role and activities as the European commissioner of the American Section and staff member of the WCC Department of Reconstruction. A quarter of a century earlier, when American Lutheran commissioners had come to Europe for their post–World War I survey, there had been no ecumenical center to which they could relate their concerns and activities. Michelfelder's dual role after World War II and the WCC activities of his fellow American, Stewart Herman, served in large measure to determine the location of the future headquarters of the Lutheran World Federation. The resulting relationship between the World Council of Churches and world Lutheranism was symbolized by the fact that both joint and separate endeavors were directed from offices in close proximity at 17 route de Malagnou.

This fruitful cooperation was supported by the conviction of the Lutherans that their contribution to the ecumenical movement could best be made only by maintaining their identity as a confessional body. Already in September 1945, American Lutherans had gone on record in favor of "confessional" rather than "geographic" representation in the World Council of Churches. All three Americans—Aasgaard, Fry, and Long—had been present at a meeting in Columbus, Ohio, on September 6, 1945, where the decision was reached to approach "the Provisional Central Committee of the World Council in process of formation" and to insist that the WCC constitution be amended to provide "confessional representation."[29] Although the Lutherans were

28. "Berggrav forlater verdenskonventet," *Norsk Ungdom* 33 (October 1945): 1.
29. For a report of the Columbus meeting see ULCA, *Minutes . . . 1946*, pp. 219–22. This meeting came as a result of action taken by the ULCA's Committee on Inter-

to meet considerable resistance to this principle prior to the WCC's constituting assembly at Amsterdam in 1948, the situation in the autumn of 1945 was conducive to genuine cooperation at the ecumenical center in Geneva.[30]

The American trio was likewise apprised, while at Geneva, that the Missouri Synod was moving away from the cooperative relief program that had been planned in conjunction with the American Section of the Lutheran World Convention. The agreement between Missouri and the American Section, as we have noted, provided for Missouri's withdrawal in the event it judged cooperation to be inimical to its theological position. When representative American Lutherans had met at Columbus in September 1945, the Missouri Synod president, John W. Behnken, was present, but he warned that "the contemplated step" (membership in the WCC) would not be approved by his church.[31] It was clear to Michelfelder and his visiting colleagues that the earlier optimism about Missouri's growing spirit of cooperation was without foundation. In fact, the synod had now begun to initiate its own relief programs and was working assiduously to bring Germany's Lutherans into the Missouri orbit. Michelfelder confided to his diary: "I am of the opinion that the best way to get along with Missouri is to ignore them and let them find out that they may get lonesome."

The Lutheran survey team—Long and Aasgaard accompanied by Michelfelder—left Geneva for Germany on November 27.[32] Fry, as we have noted, was a member of both American committees, and this made for some difficulties. In the first instance Fry, accompanied by Stewart Herman, spent much of his time with the FCC team. His

---

Lutheran Interests (Fry, Henry H. Bagger, P. H. Krauss, and J. K. Jensen), which had asked the executive board to instruct Fry to invite representatives from all Lutheran bodies in America to assemble at Columbus to urge "confessional" rather than geographic representation in the WCC.

30. For details on the question of ecumenical relationships see Abdel Ross Wentz, "Lutheran Churches and the Modern Ecumenical Movement," in *World Lutheranism Today: A Tribute to Anders Nygren* (Stockholm: Svenska Kyrkans Diakonistyrelses Bokförlag, 1950), pp. 406–17. Cf. Dorris A. Flesner, "The Role of the Lutheran Churches of America in the Formation of the World Council of Churches" (Ph.D. diss., Hartford Seminary, 1956). See also Wentz's article in *Franklin Clark Fry: A Palette for a Portrait*, pp. 100–102; and Fry to Wentz, December 7, 1945, Abdel Ross Wentz Papers, in ArCL.

31. ULCA, *Minutes . . . 1946*, p. 221.

32. Michelfelder, "Report on Conditions in Germany as Seen on a Visit November 23 to December 15, 1945," p. 4, Long Papers, in ArCL.

itinerary only occasionally coincided with that of his Lutheran colleagues. Although Fry was unhappy and frustrated by this arrangement, he realized the necessity of this division of labor.[33] Consequently, Fry had traveled from London to Paris, where he met Herman on November 24. These two then went to Frankfurt, where they were to have been joined by Bishops Oxnam and Sherrill. The latter, however, were fogbound for three days in the Azores.[34] Faced with this delay, Fry and Herman drove to Hannover to seek out Lilje and Marahrens. Some background for this meeting is required.

One of the major problems of the Lutherans, apart from assessing the overwhelming physical needs, was the task of reactivating the Lutheran World Convention. Involved in this, so they mistakenly thought, was the necessity of obtaining the resignation of LWC president August Marahrens, who by this time had become the subject of severe emotional attacks from ecumenical churchmen. All three American Lutherans, quite uninformed about Marahrens's actual situation, shared the conventional anti-Marahrens opinions and, breathing fire, planned to accost him with his "sins" at the first opportunity. It was with this in mind that Fry took Herman with him to Hannover in late November.[35] A second visit to Marahrens was held sometime after November 27 and prior to the mid-December Copenhagen meeting of the executive committee.[36] On this latter occasion the entire team—Fry, Aasgaard, and Long—was present. Thus the

33. Sources include Fry's letter from Geneva to Wentz, dated December 7, 1945, in the Wentz Papers, ArCL; and Herman's diary entries summarized in a letter to E. Clifford Nelson, June 15, 1979, Nelson Papers, in St. Olaf College Archives.

34. While in Frankfurt, Fry and Herman chanced to meet Behnken and Meyer of the Missouri Synod. Behnken denied that Missouri was trying to "steal a march" on other Lutherans in their contacts with the German church. Fry was not convinced by the disclaimer.

35. Stewart Herman, "Conversation with Dr. Hanns Lilje in Hannover, November 27, 1945" (typescript, December 12, 1945, in WCC Archives, box 284 [43], Germany, General Reports, Geneva).

36. The date of this meeting was probably December 12, 1945. Aasgaard wrote to Thaddaeus F. Gullixson, Luther Seminary, St. Paul, Minnesota, on December 11, 1945: "Leaving American Zone today to go to Hannover, Bremen and Kiel and thus to Denmark for meeting of Ex. Com. Luth. World Conv. 16 & 17 Dec." It is clear that the Americans were in Copenhagen on December 14, 1945 (Fry to Herman, December 14, 1945). Allowing a day for the trip from Hannover to Copenhagen (December 13), the meeting at Hannover doubtless occurred on December 12. Cf. Aasgaard to Gullixson, December 11, 1945; American Lutheran Church Archives, Luther-Northwestern Seminaries Library, St. Paul, Minnesota.

Lutheran commissioners had ample opportunity to hear at first hand Marahrens's version of what had transpired. Despite this, they were to return to America with their prejudices intact and report what they had done to remove the "guilty" bishop from office. In this manner, the 1945–46 oral tradition of *one* confrontation (an unpremeditated conflation of the two meetings) with the bishop became the "official version" of the Marahrens case and remained unaltered to the present.[37]

In order to recapture the emotional atmosphere and the not surprising distortions that characterized the postwar weeks and months, it seems best to let documents from the participants in the drama recreate the sequence of events and relate what actually took place. The unpublished reports of the first meeting—the Fry-Herman trip to Hannover on November 27, 1945—were properly and innocently filed away in the New York and Geneva archives, where they have remained largely unknown to this day. One might say that this cunning (or accident?) of history provided the time to evoke a more sympathetic appraisal of Marahrens. Be that as it may, a brief report of the *second* meeting was published in 1972 and perpetuated quite unintentionally the "inside story" of Marahrens's recalcitrance when asked to relinquish his office as president of the Lutheran World Convention. Fry sent a letter from Copenhagen just two days before the sessions of the executive committee (December 16–17, 1945). He wrote:

> Long gave Marahrens both barrels about M's dealing with the Nazis and the handicap which he has become to the church but the old man mountain didn't budge an inch. I am almost despairing about him! Meanwhile I wrote long memos to Lilje about all that was said at Geneva.[38]

The proper question now must be, What was being "said at Geneva"? If this can be determined, it will help us to clarify *l'affaire*

---

37. The writer vividly recalls speeches delivered in 1946 by members of the survey team who castigated Marahrens. There seemed to be no reason to question the assessments made by respected church leaders.

38. Fischer, ed., *Franklin Clark Fry: A Palette for a Portrait*, p. 173. All three Americans (Long, Fry, Aasgaard) were present. Cf. Marahrens to Ernst Sommerlath, January 19, 1946; cited by Schmidt-Clausen, *Vom Lutherischen Weltkonvent*, pp. 237–38.

Marahrens and to understand why Hanns Lilje said in 1973 and 1974 that the cliché interpretation of Marahrens's role during the war years was false and needed now to be set aright.[39] A clue to what was emanating from Geneva is to be found in Marahrens's final report to the synod of the Hannoverian church in 1947.[40] In it he referred to a news release issued in July 1945 by the ecumenical press service in Geneva, which maligned him as a Nazi sympathizer. This release was quickly picked up by the international press services and spread abroad by secular and ecclesiastical newspapers, journals, and radio. Marahrens said that this report had been sent out by people who could not possibly have known his situation and that the vilification had persisted as a credible verdict because he had not been given an opportunity by the originators of the release to make a public reply through the same channels. "I am convinced," he said, "that a later more objective writing of the history of the church will . . . be different from the current religio-political gossip columns with their, in part, horribly inaccurate exposes."[41] He went on in his report to give the rationale of his actions (he freely admitted having made serious mistakes), to give the theological basis of his stance, to elaborate on his pastoral motivations ("The decisive thing for me was the following: My goal was to lead the church through its period of greatest danger from the state and to assure the parishes that the gospel would be preached"), and to deny emphatically any collaboration, sympathy, or

39. Hanns Lilje, *Memorabilia. Schwerpunkte eines Lebens* (Stein/Nuremberg: Laetare Verlag, 1973), pp. 138–42. Lilje reiterated this to the present writer in taped interviews at Hannover, October 29–30, 1974 (Nelson Papers, St. Olaf College Archives). This opinion is supported by the highly regarded ecumenical leader in post–World War II, Heinz Brunotte, president of the chancellery of the Evangelical Church in Germany. He wrote in 1952 that the time had come to undertake a "demythologizing" of Marahrens's alleged wrongs. See his "Im Kirchenkampf," in Walter Ködderitz, ed., *D. August Marahrens. Pastor Pastorum* . . . (Hannover: Feesche Verlag, 1952), p. 86.

40. "Rechenschaftbericht D. Marahrens vor der Hann. Landessynode vom 15. April 1947," in Eberhard Klügel, *Die Lutherische Landeskirche Hannover und ihr Bischof 1933–1945. Dokumente* (Berlin: Lutherisches Verlagshaus, 1965), pp. 205–15.

41. Ibid., pp. 211–12. The offending press release stated: "Such church leaders as have come to terms with National Socialism must be dismissed. To quote one special example, the Confessional Church might lay emphasis on the efforts of the Church leaders in Germany, aiming at the speedy resignation of Dr. D. Marahrens, Bishop of Hannover. For if this man were to remain, confidence in the German Evangelical Church would be shaken . . . he allowed himself to be used by Nazi propaganda in an irremedial manner." *International Christian Press and Information Service*, no. 29, July 1945, pp. 1–2. This release naturally fueled the wartime prejudices that the American survey team carried to Europe in the autumn of 1945.

encouragement of the Hitler regime. Illustrative of Marahrens's defense was his account of one of the most frequently leveled charges, his refusal to approve the assassination attempt of July 20, 1944. In a letter to Ernst Sommerlath he explained:

> I believe unspeakable harm would have befallen our country if it had succeeded. However, God prevented it because—to express it more concretely—Hitler was supposed to play out his role to the end. Then people would realize his true nature and be convinced of the evil of the entire [Nazi] system, something they had not been at that time. If Hitler had fallen victim to the assassination attempt, he would have become a hero for the masses. All those who considered [Nazism] dangerous and destructive would have been blamed for his death. . . . [As it was] how many splendid persons, indispensable for the life and health of our people, have fallen victim to [Hitler's] revenge! But all this does not prevent me from saying that the assassination attempt was irreconcilable with Luther's views.
>
> We must understand that our Scandinavian and ecumenical friends did not seem to understand this and are inclined to reproach me, as Jørgensen has done. . . . He cannot claim any lack of information about my attitude [to the Nazis], because I had made provision for the eventuality that the Nazis might do away with me. I sent him a telegram that was intended to call forth an outcry from the Lutheran World Convention. I made the same arrangement with President Knubel. So far I have never spoken of these letters lest I be suspected of making self-serving statements. [42]

Hanns Lilje, who had suffered intensely under the Nazis, likened Marahrens's situation to that of faithful Lutheran Christians (pastors and laity) under the present-day dictatorship of the Communist regime in East Germany. To experience the demonic difficulties of life under either the Nazis or the Communists would give the lie to facile judgments of Marahrens. [43] Furthermore—and finally—Lilje said that it

42. Marahrens to Sommerlath, March 5, 1947; cited in Schmidt-Clausen, *Vom Lutherischen Weltkonvent*, p. 239.

43. Today (1979–81) some churches in Communist-dominated Eastern Europe feel compelled to negotiate the terms of sheer survival. Others engage in confrontation while hoping against hope for support from Christians in the West. These latter "witnesses" are profoundly suspicious of those who negotiate with Communist authorities. The ambiguity of this situation has been addressed by a pastor residing in the German Democratic Republic. Writing in 1976 he said: "The churches . . . have not yet found a universally applicable formula for their testimony and service in the socialist order. *Nor will they find one.* . . . Shunning opposition and opportunism, the churches in East Germany are trying to tread the narrow path of the church within, not against, the socialist order. They know that in this way they are pledged to the Gospel." Gerhard Thomas, "The Lutheran Church in the German Democratic Republic: A New Minority in Search of Greater Fellowship," *Lutheran World* 23, no. 3 (1976): 218, italics added. East German Christians, having lived under Nazi totalitarianism, have had the "benefit" of experience as they now seek to live in a Communist totalitarian state.

was simply "absurd" to conclude that Marahrens was taken in by Hitler or had any Nazi sympathies.[44] For our purposes there is no need to go into further detail about the attacks on Marahrens. Suffice it to say that, as of now, circumstantial evidence points to the Niemoeller-Barth wing of the Confessing Church as the source upon which the controversial Geneva press release was based. It was this judgment that had largely influenced the opinion of Fry, Long, and Aasgaard.

It now becomes our task to retrace the steps leading to Marahrens's resignation. Early in the war, in 1939–40, Marahrens had raised the question with Alfred Th. Jørgensen whether he should resign. He thought it proper to step aside because his term as president would have expired at the 1940 Philadelphia assembly had it not been canceled. At that time, however, Jørgensen advised that this was a matter for the executive committee to decide. For Marahrens to resign before the executive committee could meet would leave the Lutheran World Convention without a president. There was to be no opportunity for the executive committee to meet between 1939 and 1945, and consequently Marahrens and Lilje remained in office.[45]

Within weeks after the war ended, Marahrens became aware of the attacks being made on him. He wrote his friend Ernst Sommerlath of Leipzig that when he attended the Treysa Conference (August 1945) it was apparent that the Niemoeller wing of the Confessing Church was hostile to him and that this hostility had been spread abroad by the press release from Geneva. Marahrens concluded that, although he could not understand or admit the reproaches made against him, he

---

Marahrens had no such prior experience to guide him. In his situation, he looked to the New Testament and the pre-Constantinian church, which had been enjoined, despite persecution by Roman totalitarianism, to pray for dictator Caesar. It was this position that Marahrens and his supporters articulated in the early days of the resistance movement: "The church must remain the church; the church must become the church." See Klügel, *Die Lutherische Landeskirche Hannovers*, p. 20.

44. *Memorabilia*, pp. 141–42. The vulnerability of Marahrens's defense lay in his heavy emphasis on Paul's teaching in Romans 13 on obedience to temporal "authority," without giving attention to countervailing New Testament passages like Acts 5:29 ("We must obey God rather than men") and Revelation 13 (demonic political authority as an enemy of God's people). Hanns Lilje's *The Last Book of the Bible*, trans. Olive Wyon (Philadelphia: [Muhlenberg] Fortress Press, 1957), written just as World War II erupted and revised by him while he was in a gestapo prison (1944–45), indicates that he perceived clearly the significance of Revelation 13 for Christians in a totalitarian police state (pp. 192–97).

45. See Chapter 10, p. 343, for an account of the Jørgensen conversation with Marahrens and Lilje.

felt he must resign his office lest he be a hindrance to his fellow Lutherans. In view of this, he reported, he had written to Erling Eidem, vice-president of the Lutheran World Convention, announcing that he was stepping aside so Eidem could take over as president.[46] This letter to Eidem, dated October 31, 1945, urged Eidem to call a meeting of the executive committee. Marahrens reminded Eidem: "I have already occupied the office of LWC president five years beyond the normal term. During the war I have repeatedly called attention to this extraordinary circumstance. I am now resigning."[47] Unaware of this development, Franklin Clark Fry and Stewart Herman had gone to Hannover in late November to see Lilje and Marahrens.[48] During this significant conference, which took place on November 27, Fry was given "the written resignation dated October 31, 1945, of Bishop Marahrens as president of the Lutheran World Convention." This was without doubt a copy of Marahrens's letter to Eidem of the same date.[49]

The following day (November 28) Fry and Herman joined Bishops Oxnam and Sherrill in Frankfurt to begin their survey of the German situation. On December 12, as noted above, Fry joined his Lutheran colleagues in order to meet again with Marahrens prior to the executive committee meeting in Copenhagen. Marahrens so informed Ernst Sommerlath, saying that he had been visited by "Dr. Long, Dr. Frey [*sic*] and the leader of the Norwegian-American Synod [Aasgaard]." He added that these gentlemen had made it quite clear that they accepted as true the anti-Marahrens statement in the July press release from Geneva.[50] It was this visit that Fry reported in his letter from Copenhagen on December 14, 1945, in which he described Long as giving Marahrens "both barrels about [his] dealings with the Nazis." It is clear from this sequence that the subject of conversation at this

46. The letters to Sommerlath are in Schmidt-Clausen, *Vom Lutherischen Weltkonvent,* pp. 237–39.

47. Marahrens to Eidem, October 31, 1945, Archiv der Landeskirche Bayerns in Nürnberg, Pers. XXXVI, No. 187.

48. Fry to Wentz, December 7, 1945, in ArCL. Herman, "Conversation with Dr. Hanns Lilje in Hannover, November 27, 1945" (see n. 35, above). Cf. also summary of Herman's diary entries in Herman to E. Clifford Nelson, June 15, 1979, Nelson Papers, St. Olaf College Archives.

49. Herman, "Conversation with Lilje" (see n. 35, above).

50. Schmidt-Clausen, *Vom Lutherischen Weltkonvent,* p. 238: "That became very clear in the course of a recent visit by [Long et al.]."

second meeting was not the demand for Marahrens's resignation (Eidem already had his voluntary resignation, and Fry reported that he too had a copy of it in his own pocket to carry to Copenhagen). Rather, Marahrens was refusing to admit the truth of the charges leveled against him. On this "the old man mountain wouldn't budge an inch." In other words, here was evidence of how deeply the Americans had been influenced by Geneva's ecumenical links with the Niemoeller wing in the Confessing Church.[51] All this raises an interesting question: Did Eidem, residing in a neutral country, know more about Marahrens's actual situation during the war than did the Americans?

The scene now shifts to Copenhagen, where the long-awaited meeting of the executive committee was to be held December 16–17, 1945.[52] There had been some unexplained delays in issuing a call for the meeting. Agreement had been reached at Sigtuna, Sweden, seven months earlier that Erling Eidem, as vice-president of the Lutheran World Convention, should call the meeting. Two weeks before the American delegation left New York (November 11, 1945), no word had yet been received from Eidem. Thereupon a cablegram was sent requesting him to set the date and place. When Aasgaard, Fry, and Long arrived in London, they were dismayed to learn that nothing had been done. It was then (November 20) that they chanced to meet Eivind Berggrav, who agreed to try to persuade Eidem to action. When the ecclesiastical primate of Norway got through to his Swedish counterpart, there was prompt action, and the long-delayed call for the meeting went out immediately.

The churchmen assembled in Copenhagen in mid-December and discovered that only four of the twelve regular members had been able to come. They were Jørgensen, Long, Fry, and Aasgaard. Absent were the four German members and two representatives from Norway and America, Olaf Moe and Abdel Ross Wentz. Also absent were Eidem (recovering from recent surgery)[53] and Aleksi Lehtonen, archbishop of Finland. The former was represented by Edvard M. Rohde,

51. It is significant that Martin Niemoeller was a close friend of Karl Barth, whose delight in Luther but distaste for Lutherans is well known. Cf. Eberhard Busch, *Karl Barth* (Philadelphia: Fortress Press, 1976), p. 366.

52. LWC Executive Committee, "Minutes . . . December 16–17, 1945," in ArCL.

53. See *The Lutheran*, January 9, 1946, pp. 8–9.

a member of the defunct Liaison Committee; Lehtonen was represented by his chaplain Toivo Harjunpää. Two American members had died, Lars W. Boe in 1942 and Frederick H. Knubel in 1945. According to the Copenhagen minutes, Aasgaard, who succeeded Boe in the American Section, was reckoned an alternate for Knubel, while Fry, who had been named to succeed Knubel was counted as an alternate for the absent Wentz.

Jørgensen, the only surviving member of the original 1923 executive committee, was chosen to preside, and Børge Andersen, who accompanied Jørgensen and Bishop Fuglsang-Damgaard, was asked to be recording secretary. The limited attendance and awkward and improvisational character of the meeting (actually there was no quorum) made the sessions little more than a joint meeting of some members of the American Section and their Scandinavian counterparts. Nevertheless, they proceeded through the agenda as if acting for the full committee.

The first action was the acceptance of August Marahrens's resignation as president. This decision was accompanied by the request that he also resign as a member of the executive committee. The absent Erling Eidem was then elected president, and Olaf Moe (Norway) was chosen vice-president. The former Liaison Committee was then replaced by a "Relief Committee" whose members were Franklin Clark Fry and Ralph H. Long (United States), Edvard Rohde and A. Johansson (Sweden), and Bishop Fuglsang-Damgaard and Alfred Th. Jørgensen (Denmark). Norwegian and Finnish representatives were to be selected later. Sylvester C. Michelfelder was elected to two positions: secretary of the Relief Committee and executive secretary for the executive committee. The latter action was subject to the approval of Eidem.

Among the items on the agenda was the American proposal for confessional representation in the World Council of Churches. After discussion, it was decided to delegate to the American Section the drafting of a communication for referral to the member churches of the Lutheran World Convention. This action and the generally favorable attitude of the group did not constitute the endorsement and authorization that Abdel Ross Wentz, the chief author of the American proposal, desired to have in hand when he made his presentation to the upcoming meeting of the WCC Provisional Committee. The net effect of this development was that the petition for confessional representation presented by Wentz in February 1946 at Geneva was only "an American proposal," rather than one by the whole Lutheran World Convention, as the Americans had hoped it might be.[54] It also meant that the entire matter would have to wait for the next official meeting of the executive committee.

Ralph H. Long reported that the American Section had expended $2,000,000 ($600,000 in 1945) to support orphaned missions, and that the Norwegian and Danish mission societies had announced that they would need no help after January 1, 1946. The situation of the German missions, of course, was unclear.

Eulogies for Lars W. Boe (d. 1942) and Frederick H. Knubel (d. 1945) were spoken by Jørgensen, and memorial tributes for each were attached to the minutes.

In looking to the future of the Lutheran World Convention, the committee elected Long and Jørgensen together with Rohde to consider the place, time, and program of the next Lutheran World Convention and then resolved that the next meeting of the executive committee be held in 1946 at the call of Eidem.

Manifestly, the Copenhagen meeting had been but a small beginning in the attempt to resuscitate the Lutheran World Convention. Numerous problems remained to be addressed. The task of obtaining a united front among world Lutherans on the issue of "confessional representation" was unfinished. Although Marahrens had submitted his resignation as president, he nevertheless considered himself a member of the executive committee to which he had been nominated in 1930 by the German churches. Until they named a successor, he counted himself an officially designated representative of the German churches. In addition, Hanns Lilje had not yet officially resigned as executive secretary.[55] To complete this list of potentially troublesome matters, Erling Eidem, upon receipt of the Copenhagen minutes, had

54. Flesner, "Role of the Lutheran Churches," p. 136.
55. Marahrens wrote to the director of the Leipzig Mission Society, Karl Ihmels, on April 19, 1946, noting that although he had resigned the presidency he had not left the committee. Neither he nor Lilje had been invited to the 1946 meeting of the executive committee. Archiv der Landeskirche Bayerns in Nürnberg, Pers. XXXVI, No. 187.

ruled the actions of the meeting invalid because a quorum of regular members was not present.[56] This was no doubt a proper judgment. Eidem officially called the full executive committee to meet at Uppsala, July 24–26, 1946, at which time the Copenhagen decisions would be reconsidered.

THE BIRTH OF THE
LUTHERAN WORLD FEDERATION

Of crucial importance to the future of organized world Lutheranism were the Uppsala meeting of the executive committee in the summer of 1946 and the first assembly of the Lutheran World Federation at Lund in the summer of 1947. We must now examine the decisions reached on these occasions.

Executive Committee, Uppsala 1946

Sylvester C. Michelfelder and Erling Eidem had agreed on the agenda for the Uppsala meeting and communicated it to American, Scandinavian, and German church leaders.[57] Chief items in the proposed agenda were a review of the actions at Copenhagen (1945), the role of the executive (general) secretary, reports by Wentz on the new constitution and confessional representation in the World Council of Churches, and selection of place and time for the next convention.

It was not a large group that came together in the beautiful old university and cathedral city of Uppsala in late July 1946, but it was a company of farsighted individuals committed to the cause of world Lutheranism.[58] They agreed with Michelfelder, who in his "Brief Report" urged his fellow Lutherans to build a new body on the

---

56. "Minutes . . . American Section . . . March 22, 1946," p. 3.

57. Michelfelder, "Advance Information to Members of the Executive Committee, Lutheran World Convention for Meeting at Uppsala, July 24–26, 1946," dated June 19, 1946, in ArCL.

58. *From Scandinavia:* Erling Eidem (Sweden), Alfred Th. Jørgensen (Denmark), Olaf Moe (Norway), and Max von Bonsdorff (Finland). *From America:* Johan A. Aasgaard, Franklin Clark Fry, Ralph H. Long, and Abdel Ross Wentz. *From Geneva:* Sylvester C. Michelfelder. *From Germany:* Hans Meiser, Ernst Sommerlath, and Karl Ihmels (the Germans encountered travel difficulties: Meiser of Munich arrived on July 26; Ihmels and Sommerlath, traveling from the Russian Zone, did not arrive until after the meeting had adjourned). *Visitors:* Edvard Rohde, Anders Nygren, Ernst Newman, Harry Johannson (all from Sweden), and Julius Bodensieck and Clifford Ansgar Nelson (United States).

Uppsala, Sweden, 1946: Executive Committee meeting of the Lutheran World Convention.

Front row, S. C. Michelfelder, E. M. Rodhe, A. R. Wentz, E. Eidem, O. Moe, J. A. Aasgaard.

Second row, F. C. Fry, A. Nygren, H. Johannsson, E. C. Newman, Deaconess Marthe, A. Th. Jørgensen, J. Bodensieck.

Rear row, C. C. Rasmussen, C. A. Nelson, R. H. Long, Pastor Carlstrom, M. von Bonsdorf.

---

foundations established at Eisenach after World War I. What had been begun so well in 1923 and directed so wisely by men like John A. Morehead had been reduced by World War II to little more than a name. Now this committee must seize the opportunity to reshape the old agency in order to "meet the new and more challenging problems of this age." He suggested that the ways in which this could be done were already before them in the agenda.[59]

Before reconsidering the decisions of the invalidated Copenhagen

59. "A Brief Report," July 24, 1946, Wentz Papers, in ArCL.

meeting of 1945, the committee elected Abdel Ross Wentz as a "primary member" of the executive committee (he and Boe had been appointed "alternates" at the 1935 Paris convention) to succeed Frederick H. Knubel, who had died, and Johan A. Aasgaard and Franklin Clark Fry to replace "alternates" Lars W. Boe and Wentz. A resolution to include the memorial tributes to Boe and Knubel in the official record was adopted. The committee elected the following officers: Erling Eidem, president; Olaf Moe, first vice-president; Abdel Ross Wentz, second vice-president; Sylvester C. Michelfelder, recording secretary. The chairman appointed Harry Johansson as assistant to the secretary.[60]

The committee, still in its first session, turned to the sensitive question of Marahrens's resignation, which had been submitted to Eidem on October 31, 1945, and accepted by the "rump" meeting at Copenhagen in December. After the Copenhagen minutes had been read by Long, and Eidem had explained his decision to present them for official ratification by this meeting, Michelfelder took the floor to report how he had "interpreted" the Copenhagen actions to Marahrens, Meiser, and Lilje. The Uppsala minutes do not record what Michelfelder said, but we do have his letter to Lilje (May 10, 1946) and can assume that it reflects what was written to the other two Germans. After mentioning Eidem's decision not to recognize the Copenhagen resolutions as official, he went on to say that Eidem did, however, inform Marahrens "that his resignation as president presupposes his resignation as a member of the Executive Committee. . . . For this reason he did not receive an invitation to the [Uppsala] meeting." Lilje had replied that this action violated the right of member churches to name their candidates for the executive committee. This principle had been ignored at Copenhagen; it must not be repeated at Uppsala. Said Lilje: "I consider it proper that the Lutheran World Convention officially request the Lutheran Council in Germany [*Der Lutherrat*] to name its members for the Convention and the Executive Committee. Furthermore, the *Lutherrat* should decide who should occupy the seat hitherto held by Bishop Marahrens."[61]

---

60. LWC Executive Committee, "Minutes . . . Uppsala . . . Samariterhemmet, July 24–26, 1946," pp. 1–2, items 2, 4, 5, Wentz Papers, in ArCL.
61. Michelfelder to Lilje, May 10, 1946; and Lilje to Michelfelder, July 15, 1946, quoted in Schmidt-Clausen, *Vom Lutherischen Weltkonvent*, p. 240.

After hearing Michelfelder's recital of these matters, Marahrens's letter of resignation was accepted. In so doing, the committee acted on the assumption that the bishop was resigning from the committee as well as from the presidency of the convention. That this was the posture of the committee was evident in the resolution to ask the Lutheran Council of Germany to nominate Marahrens's successor on the executive committee. When Eidem would receive the nomination, he would in turn inform the members of the committee. If there were no objections, the nominee would be invited to attend the next meeting of the executive committee.[62]

The wounds caused by the exclusion of Marahrens healed slowly in Germany, where to this day the American Lutherans are seen as acting precipitously under the influence of the emotional postwar circumstances and the attitudes of the left wing of the Confessing Church in Germany. That the Church of England, whose archbishop of Canterbury had provoked the German Godesberg Declaration of 1939 against the British, now saw things differently is intimated in a 1947 comment of Lilje's: "The retirement of our Bishop Marahrens took place with such dignity and episcopal bearing that our English friends, for instance, were deeply impressed by it."[63]

The resignation of Marahrens virtually concluded his career. His last major statement was the account of his stewardship before the 1947 synod of Hannover.[64] Shortly thereafter he retired and was succeeded by Lilje. Marahrens died in 1950.

Meanwhile the executive committee in Uppsala discharged the Relief Committee and asked that reconstruction and relief matters be coordinated through the office of the executive secretary. But what about the office of executive (general) secretary to which Hanns Lilje had been elected in 1936? No pressure had been exerted on him to resign, but the minutes record that his resignation had been submitted. It was now read and accepted. The letter itself, which was not

---

62. LWC Executive Committee, "Minutes . . . Uppsala . . . July 24–26, 1946," items 6, 7. Meiser informed Michelfelder in March 1947 that Sommerlath (with Lilje as alternate) had been named by the *Lutherrat.*

63. There had been close ties between the Church of England and the Church of Hannover ever since the days of the Hannoverian kings of England. In keeping with this tradition, Anglican guests were apparently present for Marahrens's retirement. See Lilje's letter, May 1, 1947, LWF Archives, Geneva.

64. See n. 40, above.

included in the minutes, has been discovered in the Geneva archives of the Lutheran World Federation. Lilje wrote:

> May I finally add a personal word in regard to my position as General Secretary. . . . I have not the slightest doubt that I cannot continue this work. In view of the present German situation, I could not possibly make any significant contribution. It is not feasible today to have a German president or a German general secretary. I hope, therefore, that the Executive Committee will act accordingly. In order to avoid misunderstandings, I will state clearly that I would sincerely welcome such a decision by the Executive Committee.[65]

Before Lilje's resignation was accepted "with regrets," the committee spread upon the minutes a resolution of warm appreciation "for his [Lilje's] untiring service in the work of the Lutheran World Convention throughout the years." The absence of such a resolution with respect to Marahrens makes more poignant the declaration of the aged bishop to the Hannoverian synod: "We accept all of this and place it at the disposal of Him who will judge correctly."[66]

After a thorough discussion of the new position, Sylvester C. Michelfelder was elected executive secretary (American bureaucratic vocabulary preferred "executive secretary" to the European "general secretary") of the Lutheran World Convention to serve until the next assembly. The American Section offered to pay his salary during that time.

The next item of business was the report of the Committee on Constitution, of which Abdel Ross Wentz was chairman.[67] Prior to the war, both Wentz and Lilje had prepared drafts for a constitution.[68] When the American Section met in Chicago on June 6, 1946, it expected that Uppsala would discuss and recommend a constitutional draft. Wentz's 1939 version was circulated with the request that comments be submitted prior to the Uppsala meeting. Wentz's proposal became the outline for his committee's consideration. It was, therefore, Wentz's reworked proposal that was presented, discussed,

---

65. Lilje letter, July 15, 1946. Cited in Schmidt-Clausen, *Vom Lutherischen Weltkonvent*, p. 241.
66. "Rechenschaftsbericht D. Marahrens vor der hann. Landesynode vom 15. April 1947," in Klügel, *Die Lutherische Landeskirche Hannover. Dokumente*, p. 212.
67. Eidem had appointed Wentz to select a committee to propose a constitution. Michelfelder, "Advance Information."
68. The various drafts are printed in the appendix of Schmidt-Clausen, *Vom Lutherischen Weltkonvent*.

and finally adopted for recommendation at Uppsala. A comparison between Wentz's 1939 version and the Uppsala version reveals several alterations and questions, chief of which were as follows:

1. Wentz had proposed the name "Lutheran World Council"; Uppsala changed this to "Lutheran World Federation."

2. Wentz described the nature of the organization "as a free association of Lutheran Churches" which would have "no power to interfere with the complete autonomy of the individual churches." Uppsala added the phrase "it shall have no power to legislate for the Churches belonging to it or to interfere, etc."

3. Wentz's list of purposes was altered to begin with a general statement "To bear united witness before the world to the Gospel of Jesus Christ as the power of God for salvation." Specific purposes included "To achieve a united Lutheran approach to ecumenical Christian movements. . . ." (Question: Did this imply a "Lutheran bloc" in the ecumenical movement?)

4. The 1939 version declared that the world organization "definitely excludes politics, both national and international, from its programs. . . ." The Uppsala version showed the influence of the war years 1939–45: "The Lutheran World Federation may take action on behalf of member churches in such matters as one or more of them may commit to it."

5. The 1939 draft had no general paragraph on organizational structure. Uppsala specified that the LWF should function through (a) the assembly, (b) the executive committee, (c) national committees, (d) special commissions. It then went on to describe the specific functions of each segment of the structure, including those of the executive secretary, who was to be chosen by the executive committee.

It was this constitutional draft that would be placed before the next assembly in 1947. As was to be expected, the careful preliminary work of 1939 and 1946 would be honored by the 1947 convention by acceptance of the general proposal with only a few alterations at specific points. These will be noted in our consideration of the Lund assembly.

The next major item for consideration by the executive committee was the issue of confessional representation in the World Council of Churches. Once again Abdel Ross Wentz, who was the author of and spokesman for the Lutheran proposal, was called upon by Eidem to introduce the Petition Concerning Confessional Representation to the executive committee.[69] Wentz had personally presented the petition to the Geneva meeting of the WCC Provisional Committee in February 1946. Meanwhile, the document had been circulated among member churches of the Lutheran World Convention, several of whom had sent letters endorsing the American Lutheran position. According to Flesner,[70] the most serious criticism of the American proposal came in a communication from Eivind Berggrav of Oslo. He raised the question whether Lutherans in America and elsewhere would not thus gain their representation at the expense of the Lutheran churches in Scandinavia. Also, he expressed apprehension lest the channeling of the Lutheran witness through one route would tend to obliterate breadth of viewpoint and thus actually impoverish the Lutheran testimony in the World Council. He suggested that Lutherans might have a stronger voice "as a chorus than as a solo." He voiced opposition to "bloc-building" by a confessional group, convinced that such a development would be destructive of the Christian unity being sought.[71]

In answer to these objections, Wentz pointed out that the proposed action would not prevent any Lutheran church from electing representation on a geographical basis, should that be preferred. The LWC executive committee was being asked only to help secure representation along confessional lines for those Lutheran bodies of the world desiring thus to be represented.

Noting that the American Lutheran petition was mistakenly viewed in some quarters as a request for LWC membership in the World Council of Churches, Franklin Clark Fry made it clear that such an arrangement was neither contemplated nor desired. It asked only that a proportionate number of seats be reserved for the Lutheran churches of the world and that these churches be permitted to have the

---

69. A copy of the document, entitled "To the Provisional Committee of the World Council of Churches: A Petition concerning Confessional Representation," is included in "Minutes . . . American Section . . . June 6, 1946," pp. 6–8, in ArCL.

70. A detailed account of the discussion at Uppsala is given in Flesner, "Role of the Lutheran Churches," pp. 150–55. Flesner has graciously permitted this writer to quote extensively from his dissertation.

71. *The Lutheran*, August 14, 1946, p. 4.

Lutheran World Convention serve as allocating agent for distributing such seats among the individual bodies. Only the churches themselves would be members of the WCC, and each church would name its own delegates.

The Lutheran witness in the World Council of Churches would not be impoverished, as Berggrav feared, nor would breadth of viewpoint be obliterated, since each Lutheran body would retain full freedom of expression. Nor would a united Lutheran approach to the council constitute bloc-building contrary to the ecumenical spirit. The real peril in a world wrecked by nationalistic conflict was the formation of national blocs rather than confessional or ecclesiastical alignments on a voluntary and consultative basis.

After the position of the Lutheran churches of America had been interpreted at some length, and objections to their proposal answered, Erling Eidem declared: "We had not completely understood before. . . . Our misgivings rested on misunderstanding." He added that Berggrav also had misunderstood the significance of the American proposal. From the explanations given it was now clear that "bloc-building," against which the Norwegian primate had mainly objected, was not involved at all. Eidem further observed that he himself actually felt much more at home among Lutherans than he did in the geographically constituted Continental Section of the World Council of Churches. Indicating a deep desire to have all Lutheran churches of America participate in the World Council of Churches, the LWC president asked what influence the proposed change in constitution would have on their entry. Johan A. Aasgaard replied that the Norwegian Lutheran Church of America would probably not join unless the change were made. If representation would be along confessional lines, possibly all but one of the Lutheran groups in America would affiliate. In response to a further appeal by Fry that the LWC executive committee support the American proposal and recommend it to all Lutheran churches of the world, Eidem replied: "We of the northern countries are willing to recommend this proposal with gladness to our brethren and to our Churches. This is not just a gesture of compliance. We agreed because it is right and expedient."

Others at the meeting also expressed hearty approval. Said Alfred Th. Jørgensen of Denmark, "We must support the American brethren.

'The strong must support the weak' and this is a case. It will not be merely charity but right and wise." Edvard Rohde indicated he too was now in favor of the proposal and would uphold it before the Swedish bishops. Olaf Moe of Norway joined in the endorsement, adding that he thought Berggrav would now understand the real significance of the American petition and rally behind it. Max von Bonsdorff, Finnish bishop, admitted that until now he had not been clear on the matter. Noting Aleksi Lehtonen's favorable attitude, even earlier, he stated that he himself now also gave full assent. Approval of the proposal would result in stronger Lutheran representation in the World Council of Churches. He added that he would be sorry to see the Lutheran churches of America fail to participate in the council, as Aasgaard had indicated would probably be the case if representation were continued on a geographical basis. When a vote was finally taken it was unanimously agreed to "support the petition of the American Lutheran Churches—and recommend it to the Committee on Arrangements of the World Council for favorable action."[72]

Franklin Clark Fry reviewed the Uppsala decision in an address delivered before the American Lutheran Conference at Rockford, Illinois, November 13–15, 1946. In it he said that the action taken at Uppsala was

> an epochal victory for world Lutheran unity. . . . July 25, 1946, was one of those pivots on which history is swung. Although the future recorder may not have the acumen or the information to detect it, it was a decisive date for ecumenical Lutheranism. A momentous issue was in the balance at Uppsala. The Executive Committee of the Lutheran World Convention had been meeting affably. Now it had to make up its mind. Should the Lutheran Churches of the world adopt a common stand in relation to the emerging World Council of Churches? A more powerful Lutheran unity or a potential cleavage waited on the choice. The verdict on that day would affect the future decisively.[73]

The arrival of Hans Meiser of Munich on the last day of the meeting provided the most emotional moment at Uppsala. All three German members experienced travel difficulties in reaching Sweden. Meiser's

---

72. LWC Executive Committee, "Minutes . . . Uppsala . . . 1946," item 4, afternoon session, July 25, 1946.
73. Franklin Clark Fry, "A Crisis in Lutheranism," *The Lutheran Outlook,* January 1947.

two countrymen, Karl Ihmels and Ernst Sommerlath from Leipzig in the Russian Zone, encountered so many Russian military travel restrictions that they did not arrive until after the committee had adjourned. Meiser also encountered problems in his trip through the American and British zones, but managed to reach Uppsala on Friday, June 26. The exchange of greetings between Eidem and Meiser after the morning prayer was high drama and profoundly religious:

EIDEM: First I would like to bring a hearty greeting to you from all the members of this Committee. I shall speak to you in your own mother tongue. We are grateful that you have come, even if you were delayed. We are glad to meet you and see you.

There are meetings in life, dear Brother, when we must meet with sad hearts. A heavy burden has fallen upon us and upon all mankind. We want to do what St. Paul said in the lesson which we have just read: "Bear ye one another's burdens." We know that your country is bearing heavy burdens. All of us must bear our share of the responsibility. We do not wish to judge. "Love rules our hearts." I want you to be firmly convinced of this that we receive you in our midst with brotherly love.

MEISER: You must believe me that I have come here with a deep feeling of gratitude and am now deeply moved that I can be here and hear these words of welcome.

You cannot imagine how I have missed the broken relationship in the past years. We know of so much injustice that has been done by our people, and we could not hinder it. We fully realize that the collapse of the Hitler regime was possible only through the terrible destructions which had to come. We have documentary evidence now, that should Hitler have been victorious the real difficulties of the Church would have just begun. We trembled at what would follow, if Hitler would have won. With the collapse there came a real religious experience. It was evident amongst our people. Never were the churches so crowded before. Now we must place ourselves before the judgment of God. We dare not confess the faults of others, but only our own. We accept all this as the judgment of God because our nation treated the Jews as we did. As our own churches burned and were destroyed we remembered that the German people first set fire to the Jewish synagogues.

Now nations are divided, but we Christians dare not allow that which has divided the nations to divide the churches. We are in condemnation with others for the catastrophe which has come to us. We did speak and tried to awaken the conscience of our people. Some day we hope to publicize the steps which we took and the protests which we made. For us the difficult question has been and still is, how far can the church go in causing the death of the tyrant. Is this the way of Lutheran ethics? I do not even know if this is an open question. We might ask who was right in the days of persecution: the Salzburgers, the secret Austrian Protestants or the Huguenots? We could not have settled this question finally though we could have spoken more and more, but I do not believe that this would have made any difference in the outcome. Certainly we knew of some of the terrible conditions which prevailed in our own concentration camps, some knew much more than others. Now we must come to a full realization of how we can repent and ask God to forgive.

Forces were loosed in our country which could not be controlled even by those who . . . released them. Demonic were the powers that reigned and we seemed powerless before them. We simply could not offer effective political resistance.

You must believe us that what we declared as our confession of guilt at Stuttgart was a sincere declaration. We will not modify that statement in any way, we say it once for all and hope it will not be necessary to repeat it constantly. It was no tactical move on our part but was intended as an earnest declaration to be taken just as it was spoken.

All of us have felt the fellowship of Christians. Not only have the Christians of the world spoken but they have acted and proven their fellowship and love. I cannot miss this opportunity to thank you for all that you have already done for us. Now love alone can heal the broken ties. The material aid which has been given so generously is at the same time spiritual aid.

The church was the only real opposition which held out against the Nazi régime. A Gauleiter in Munich admitted to me that the church in its opposition had got a real victory. We do not want a substitute social Gospel, but we realize that a physical preparation must be made for spiritual reconstruction. We on our part are prepared to make all amends necessary to restore a real Christian fellowship. But we must not forget that we must prepare not only to preserve life for this world but also for the life to come. We can only ask that you will forgive the wrongs which we have committed.[74]

After the minutes of the previous day were read, Meiser expressed his strong approval of what had been done, especially regarding confessional representation in the World Council of Churches.

The last major item of business dealt with the time, place, and program of the next assembly. Earlier in the meeting (Thursday, June 25) the committee had received the invitation of Edvard Rohde to hold the first assembly of the Lutheran World Federation in Lund, Sweden, June 30–July 6, 1947. Logically, the assembly ought to have met in America, where its 1940 convention in Philadelphia was canceled because of the war, but postwar economic and political factors did not make it feasible for most churches to send delegates to America. In

74. LWC Executive Committee, "Minutes . . . Uppsala . . . July 24–26, 1946," item 3, morning session, July 26, 1946.

these circumstances the committee gratefully accepted the Swedish invitation and heard a report on the suggested items and topics for the assembly. The Program Committee quite obviously sought continuity with the prewar assembly plans and patterned its proposal along the lines of the Philadelphia program. The following outline makes this clear:

THE LUTHERAN CHURCH IN THE WORLD TODAY

I. The Faith by which she lives
   a. The Word
   b. The Sacraments
   c. The Church
II. The Mission she should fulfill
   a. Evangelism
   b. Foreign Mission
   c. Helping one another
III. The Problems she must face
   a. Relations to other churches
   b. Relations to the state
   c. Secularism[75]

After a thorough discussion, Eidem appointed the permanent Program and Commission Committee for Lund, consisting of Alfred Th. Jørgensen, Anders Nygren, Hans Meiser, Ralph H. Long, and Sylvester C. Michelfelder. The committee was instructed to arrange an assembly of six days, in addition to a Sunday. Morning sessions should be devoted to topics like "The Word," "The Sacraments," "The Relation of Church and State." Afternoon sessions could be given over to practical problems. This committee was empowered to choose the themes, select speakers, appoint commissions, and arrange other pertinent matters.

On the day following adjournment, Sommerlath and Ihmels finally arrived in Uppsala, having been en route for ten days. Weary from the tension and vicissitudes of travel in the Russian Zone, they allowed themselves a day of rest. On Sunday, July 28, the American delegates and the executive secretary, Michelfelder, met with them in Stockholm, thus providing an opportunity to review not only the decisions of the Uppsala meeting but also to inquire about the situation of the church in East Germany under Soviet occupation.

As the Uppsala meeting became history, it was understood that the

75. Ibid., item 5, afternoon session, July 26, 1946.

Abdel Ross Wentz

Gustav A. Brandelle

Carl C. Hein

J. Michael Reu

Johan Arndt Aasgaard

S. C. Michelfelder

Ralph H. Long

Carl E. Lund-Quist

Peter O. Bersell

Franklin Clark Fry

Eivind Berggrav

Erling Eidem

Hans Meiser

Theophil Wurm

August Marahrens

Anders Nygren

Hanns Lilje

Paul C. Empie

Lutheran World Convention—to a large degree this meant the American Section and the new executive secretary in Geneva—would provide the formal continuity between the past ministry of world Lutheranism and the gestating entity whose birth was expected at Lund in midsummer 1947.

After following the long and sometimes bewildering path from the birth of the Lutheran World Convention at Eisenach in 1923 to the emerging Lutheran World Federation at Uppsala, one is attracted by the manifest similarities of circumstances that attended these occasions. Both events occurred in the somber milieu of postwar worlds. Both instances were testimonies to the growing influences of Americans in world Lutheranism. The historical leadership of European Lutherans, not least in the field of theological scholarship, was giving place to the practical wisdom and organizational expertise of the Americans. Both Eisenach and Uppsala-Lund demonstrated that world Lutheranism owed much of its organizational structure and its workable expression of unity to the encouragement given by American Lutherans whose initiative, vision, and money flowed in generous amounts across the seas to strengthen their brethren in the faith. Even such a small matter as the language in which the minutes of executive committee meetings were recorded testified to the sudden ascendancy of the Americans. Between Eisenach and Waldenburg (1939)—including New York (1936)—the minutes were in German. The first official minutes after World War II were written in English. When one looks beyond 1947, the American influence, though considerable, was consciously diminished by farsighted leaders who sought successfully to broaden the base of support and to increase the involvement of international personnel.

The Lund Assembly, 1947

Our purpose in this final section is to concentrate on the birth of the Lutheran World Federation, the *terminus ad quem* of our study. After a brief look at the birthplace, we shall be spectators at the preassembly meeting of the executive committee. This will prepare us to observe the birth of an infant, already twenty-four years old, by examining the constitution itself rather than trying to listen to and interpret the conversation of the attending doctors. Having done that, we will leave behind the travail of birth and try to recapture the "joy that a child is born into the world" (John 16:21). In other words, we shall try to characterize the mood of Lund: the atmosphere of gracious reconciliation, of theological vigor, and of dedicated stewardship that pervaded this joyful—but still wounded and suffering—fellowship of Lutheran Christians. As an epilogue to Lund and what preceded it, we will ask the question *Quo vadis?* or What was the Lutheran World Federation's self-understanding as it faced the future?

Like Uppsala, Lund has a long and rich religious and cultural tradition. In both cities this tradition is symbolized by cathedral and university. Lund, the focal city of the area known as Skåne,[76] was for many of its earliest years a part of the archdiocese of Bremen-Hamburg. By the middle of the eleventh century it was separated from the north German ecclesiastical jurisdiction and received its own bishop. In 1103 the pope raised the bishopric to an archdiocese whose head received the primacy for all of Scandinavia, a rank which it lost in the sixteenth century. Politically the province was associated with Denmark until the seventeenth century, when the Danish king was forced to cede Skåne to Sweden.

The Romanesque Cathedral of Lund, where the opening service and other services for the first assembly of the Lutheran World Federation were held, ranks with cathedrals at Uppsala, Roskilde, Aarhus, Trondheim, Stavanger, and Turku as among the most impressive in Scandinavia. Its crypt, often likened to that at Canterbury, is of unusual interest architecturally and historically. The university (founded in 1688) provided the other focus for the assembly, most of whose sessions were held in the Great Hall of the Academic Union.

It was to this picturesque city in southern Sweden that the executive committee came for its preassembly meeting, June 28–29, 1947.[77] The purpose of the meeting was clearly to review the agenda for the assembly, appoint assembly committees, and make last-minute decisions. Of the latter, two were of long-range significance. The first was the welcome to the newly elected bishop of Hannover, Hanns Lilje, who arrived on the second day of the meeting. The bishop was immediately elected a member of the executive committee, having

76. The name is undoubtedly related to the Latin *Scandia*.
77. See "Minutes . . . Executive Committee . . . June 28–29, 1947," Wentz Papers, in ArCL. Attached to these minutes are the minutes of meetings of the committee held during and after the assembly, namely, July 2, July 5, July 6, and July 7, 1947.

been nominated by the National Committee of Germany. Five years later at the Hannover assembly (1952), he was to be chosen president of the Lutheran World Federation. By the time of his death in 1977, Lilje had been associated with world Lutheranism for almost forty years, longer than any other individual.

The second item was the appointment of Carl E. Lund-Quist as official recorder of minutes. Lund-Quist was present at the meeting in his capacity as director of public relations for the National Lutheran Council in New York. Fluent in Swedish, this former campus pastor at the University of Minnesota was to be called to Geneva as Michelfelder's assistant in 1951. When the latter died unexpectedly during preparations for the Hannover assembly, it fell to Lund-Quist to carry on. This began a close association with Lilje, a relationship which increased in mutual respect and confidence when Lund-Quist was chosen by the executive committee to succeed the deceased Michelfelder. Lund-Quist served as executive secretary under two LWF presidents, Lilje and Fry, until ill health led him to resign in 1960. He died in 1965.

Another matter faced by the executive committee was the task of seeking a successor to Erling Eidem, who announced that he had neither the time nor the strength to continue as the federation's president. The nominating committee chosen by the group was chaired by Lilje.

Next on the agenda of the executive committee was a review of the proposed constitution. Abdel Ross Wentz and others interpreted the meaning of various sections. Emphasis was placed on the stipulation that only Lutheran "churches" (not federations or councils of churches) could be members of the Lutheran World Federation. Moreover, it was decided that when the assembly had adopted the constitution, the chairman of the delegation from each church would affix his signature to the document as a formal gesture of accepting membership. The official text of the constitution for consideration by the assembly was to be English.

The problem of finances was another matter of concern. The committee discussed the proposed budget for 1947–48 and finally recommended that the new executive committee give it further study. The budget of $20,000 would provide salaries, rental expenses, and travel funds for the office of the executive secretary in Geneva. It also

Lund, 1947: S. C. Michelfelder and Landesbischof Theophil Wurm at the Lutheran World Federation Assembly.

Lund, 1947: F. C. Fry, A. R. Wentz, H. Meiser, and J. A. Aasgaard; S. C. Michelfelder between Wentz and Meiser.

Lund, Sweden, 1947: Dr. J. P. Vanheest of Holland signing the charter of the Lutheran World Federation at the first Assembly. Also seated, A. R. Wentz and Hanns Lilje; among the observers, R. E. Tulloss and E. Eidem.

projected an item of $4,000 for a Lutheran world quarterly, the need for which the committee discussed at some length. As an indication of the relative postwar financial strength of the churches, the finance report showed that half the budget ($10,000) would be supplied by the U.S. National Committee. The other half was to be allocated as follows:

U.S.	$2,000*	Czechoslovakia	$200
Canada	2,000	Hungary	200
Sweden	1,000	India	200
Germany	2,000	China	200
Denmark	600	South America	100
Finland	600	Romania	100
Norway	600	Yugoslavia	100
Holland	300	Iceland	100
France	300	Austria	100
Poland	200	Others	100

The asterisk (*) indicates that the allocation was over and beyond the contribution by the U.S. National Committee. Moreover, it was understood that the U.S. National Committee would pay the amounts for those churches who found it impossible to meet their apportionments out of the reconstruction funds that the Lutheran World Federation had made available for them. A majority of these funds, of course, likewise came from the United States.

It was manifest on June 30 and the following days of the Lund assembly that the executive committee had done its work well. After the opening service in the cathedral and the ceremonial events at the first session, the officers and delegates of the assembly addressed their common tasks without delay and moved through the agenda with a sense of assurance born of confidence in the executive committee's preparatory deliberations. This was no more evident than in those sessions devoted to the main items of business, the consideration of the constitution and the subsequent actions to implement the new constitutional structure.

The surprising physical growth, the vigorous enterprise, and the exciting global mission that would characterize the Lutheran World Federation during the next two decades were made possible by the relatively rapid adoption of the modest and uncomplicated constitution submitted by the executive committee. Moreover, it was appropriate that Abdel Ross Wentz, who had been involved in the constitutional studies since the late 1930s, presented the document for official consideration.[78]

The assembly examined each of the thirteen articles, the chief of which require mention. Article I specified the name: The Lutheran World Federation (incidentally, this was the proposal of John A. Morehead twenty-seven years earlier). The other main articles were Doctrinal Basis (Article II), Nature and Purpose (Article III), Membership (Article IV), and Organization (Article V). The doctrinal article was that of Eisenach 1923, and Article V specified that the LWF should exercise its functions through (1) the assembly, (2) the executive committee, (3) national committees, and (4) special commissions. The remaining articles spelled out the details of this structure and provided, finally, that amendments might be made "by a two-thirds vote of those present *at any regularly called Assembly, provided notice of intention to amend shall have been made the preceding day*" (italics added).

The executive committee realized that changes were already being advocated, perhaps for good reason. However, it wisely decided to press for adoption of the recommended draft, thus officially bringing the Lutheran World Federation into formal existence, and then, according to Article XIII ("Amendments"), to entertain revisions the next day. This explains the statement in the minutes that the "Constitution was unanimously adopted without alteration" on July 1, 1947, at 12:25 P.M. This was followed by a joyous singing of the long-meter doxology ("Praise God from whom all blessings flow") and the decision that there should also be an official German text of the constitution.[79]

---

78. *Proceedings . . . LWF, Lund . . . June 30–July 6, 1947* (Philadelphia: United Lutheran Publication House, 1948), p. 15. Wentz made no reference to his involvement. He mentioned that early on the LWC executive committee had asked Knubel and Marahrens to prepare a constitution. As it turned out, Knubel delegated his assignment to Wentz, and Marahrens gave the task to Lilje. Thus the constitutional drafts were a joint American-German undertaking, but the 1946–47 draft was largely the work of Wentz.

79. Ibid., pp. 15–21. The minutes have a photocopy of the signatures that were affixed by church presidents and bishops on July 3. The event was recorded on sound film. Ibid., pp. 22–23.

On July 2, opportunity was given to the delegates to discuss the question of amending the adopted constitution. There were two substantive issues. One spoke to the ecumenical stance of the Lutheran World Federation and Lutheran confessional identity according to Article III. The other addressed the imbalance in representation between the traditionally strong Lutheran churches of northern Europe and North America on the one hand, and the "younger churches" of what today is called the Third World on the other hand. Leaders in the discussion were Stewart Herman, whose relation to the ecumenical movement was deep and of long standing, and S. W. Savarimuthu of Madras, India, who pointed out the constitution's demeaning attitude toward the "younger churches" as shown by their placement without name under the category of "other countries." This was "pejorative anonymity" and called for constitutional alteration.[80]

The amendments were submitted to the executive committee, which met right away and quickly approved the changes. These were reported to the plenary session on July 4 and adopted by unanimous vote. The first amendment altered Article III. The original draft described the ecumenical stance in these words: "To achieve a united Lutheran approach to ecumenical movements. . . ." In order to avoid the implication that Lutherans were primarily interested in a "Lutheran bloc or front," the amendment was phrased more positively: "To foster Lutheran participation in ecumenical movements." Then, in order to pick up the other concerns of the original draft, the amendment added this statement: "To develop a united Lutheran approach to responsibilities in missions and education." In this manner both concerns, ecumenical and Lutheran, were clearly and positively stated.

The second change occurred in Articles VI and VIII, both of which dealt with the question of representation. Instead of specifying the number of assembly delegates from each country, as in the original, the amendment said: "The allocation of the representatives in the Assembly shall be made to the member churches by the Executive Committee with the advice of National Committees, and due regard shall be given to such factors as numerical size of the churches,

---

80. For a personal account of this debate see Stewart W. Herman, "The Inside Story: How the LWF Began," *The Lutheran Forum* 7 (February 1973): 6–11. See also *Proceedings . . . Lund . . . 1947*, p. 22.

geographical distribution by continents and countries, adequate representation of the younger churches and minority churches, and the right of each completely independent member church to have at least one representative in the Assembly." The alteration in the provisions for representation in the executive committee (Article VIII) repeated the essential part of the phrase above but limited the committee to sixteen members, including the president.

According to the official version of the constitution published by the Lutheran World Federation in December, the amendments would become effective one year later, that is, on July 4, 1948, "unless objection has been filed with the Executive Committee by churches embracing in the aggregate one-third of the constituency of the Federation."[81]

Article VII stated that the president of the Lutheran World Federation must be chosen by ballot of the assembly. On July 4, Hanns Lilje, reporting for the nominating committee, announced with regret that Erling Eidem had declined to serve as president for the next term of five years. The committee, therefore, was now proposing the name of Anders Nygren, a professor at Lund University. The ballot showed that Nygren received 90 percent of the votes cast. In accepting the office, the famous member of the so-called Lundensian school and author of the internationally acclaimed book *Agape and Eros* (1932–39) spoke simply: "What I have seen during this Assembly has filled me with a deep sense of joy. The work is great and we are small. Therefore we need the power of God." The nominating committee made its second report on July 5. This time Lilje presented the committee's nominations for members of the executive committee. The following were elected:

United States: Johan A. Aasgaard, Franklin Clark Fry, Ralph H. Long, Abdel Ross Wentz

Scandinavia: Anders Nygren (ex officio as president of the LWF), Sweden; Alfred Th. Jørgensen, Denmark; Aleksi Lehtonen, Finland; Johannes Smemo, Norway

Germany: Hans Meiser, Ernst Sommerlath, Nikolot Beste, Hanns Lilje

---

81. *The Constitution of the Lutheran World Federation* (Lausanne: La Concorde, 1947), p. 10.

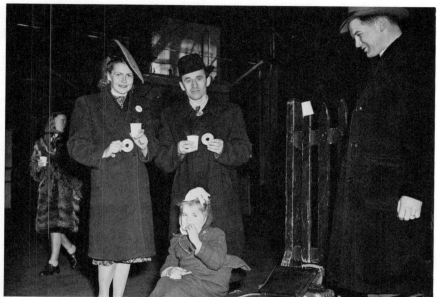

New York, 1949: Displaced persons from Baltic Europe are assisted at pier-side by Pastor Ross Hidy.

New York—Maryland, 1949: En route to a Maryland farm are displaced persons from Latvia who were under the sponsorship of the Lutheran World Federation.

Other countries: Charles Delbruck, France; Lajos Ordass, Hungary; Joel Lakra, India; Teodor Grünbergs, Latvia in Exile.

The new executive committee met on July 6 and elected its officers as follows:

First vice-president:	Abdel Ross Wentz
Second vice-president:	Lajos Ordass
Treasurer:	Ralph H. Long

Acting under the constitution, the committee also elected Sylvester C. Michelfelder as executive secretary for a term of five years.[82]

Finally, in order to complete the constitutional structuring of the new federation, the assembly adopted a resolution to authorize the executive committee to create the following "commissions or departments":

1. A Commission or Department of Missions
2. A Commission or Department of Work on Behalf of Displaced Persons and Refugees
3. A Commission or Department of Relief
4. A Commission or Department of Youth Activities
5. A Commission or Department of Social Welfare[83]

When Erling Eidem closed the last plenary session of the assembly, it was already clear to the 184 delegates that they had been participants in a memorable occasion. The birth of the Lutheran World Federation was a historic moment fraught with far-reaching significance. Said Eidem: "We must not forget each other. We must pray for each other."

Before closing this report on Lund, a word should be said about the mood that characterized the assembly. The first characteristic mark was reconciliation. The delegates strove to exhibit that World War II was over. The hostilities and suspicions that had been generated among Lutherans on opposite sides during the Nazi era were consciously laid aside. The Germans asked forgiveness for their nation's iniquities and for themselves personally; the opposite side refrained

---

82. LWC Executive Committee, "Minutes . . . July 6, 1947, 2 o'clock," Wentz Papers, in ArCL. This action was reported to the assembly by the president. *Proceedings . . . Lund . . . 1947,* p. 34.
83. *Proceedings . . . Lund . . . 1947,* p. 33.

from castigating the German brethren and confessed that non-Germans were not without sin. As Stewart Herman has said, "At no other such meeting which I have ever attended—including . . . five LWF assemblies and four out of five WCC assemblies—was reconciliation so overridingly the chief concern."[84]

The second characteristic mark was theological confidence. Although Lutherans had always prided themselves on their theological concern, conservative Lutherans during the first half of the twentieth century were inclined to be theologically defensive. Their doctrinal system was regarded as a "mighty fortress" from behind which embattled Lutherans looked out at the world with increasing but unspoken insecurity. Lund, however, was a theological pivot. There was no turning away from the tradition; rather, there was a deepened understanding of the evangelical heart of the confessional tradition. The mood was not repristinationist in a sloganeering way ("Back to the Bible," "Back to the confessions," "Back to Luther"); instead, it recognized that the church's strength in every time of trouble—as in the war years—lay in the Word of God witnessed to in the Holy Scriptures, in the gospel that was the throbbing heart of the confessions, and in the prophetic testimony of Luther. Section I of the assembly, the report of which bore the unmistakable marks of its most prominent member, Anders Nygren, declared: "Our Evangelical Lutheran Church may not surrender anything of what was given to it at the Reformation." Nygren himself raised this question: Can the Lutheran church recover its original testimony, or can she speak only in secularized terms? He answered his own question by calling the church not "Back to Luther" but "Always forward to Luther."[85]

Authentic heroes like Hanns Lilje, Lajos Ordass, and Eivind Berggrav echoed these convictions. The latter's lively words were heard by all: "It was a joy to sling Luther in the face of the Gestapo. . . . His theology was our best weapon in the fight against the Nazis. . . . God was so near . . . we felt as though we became contemporaries of the Apostles. . . ."[86] The mood at Lund was one of newborn theological vitality.

84. *The Lutheran Forum*, February 1973, p. 11.
85. *Proceedings . . . Lund . . . 1947*, pp. 58–140.
86. Cited by Stewart Herman in *The Lutheran Forum*, February 1973, p. 8. Cf. Eivind Berggrav, *Man and State*, trans. George Aus (Philadelphia: [Muhlenberg]

Finally, Lund was characterized by a profound sense of steward-ship. This was manifested in several ways; two areas require special mention. The first was the resolution that emerged out of the sectional report "Lutheran World Missions Today." It urged common support of orphaned missions, but with a view to restoring them to their parent bodies. It also urged the formation of united Lutheran churches in the various mission fields.[87] The second resolution was related to the report of Section III, "Facing the Problems in a Troubled World." The focus of this action was the unimaginable tragedy of refugees, expel-lees, and displaced persons. All Lutheran relief and social agencies were urged to place their resources at the disposal of a common effort to mitigate and to resolve, if possible, this huge international prob-lem.[88] The dramatic story of the carrying out of this resolution has been competently told in original documents, published articles, and books by participants—Stewart Herman, Howard Hong, Richard Solberg, to name a few—in the Lutheran World Federation Service to Refugees.[89]

A mere recital of these resolutions can never convey the personal and institutional dedication that characterized individuals, congrega-tions, Lutheran denominations, and agencies that found themselves deeply engaged in the prodigal and far-flung activities of the Lutheran World Federation. To quote Stewart Herman again: "There is no belying the plain fact that the tone and structure of the Lutheran World Federation was indelibly marked—up to the fifth assembly at Évian in 1970—by two predominant concerns, namely, an integrated, global mission enterprise and the needs of destitute and homeless people." Those who know the story best will only say "Amen!"

Fortress Press, 1951). With reference to the church's anti-Nazi stance, Berggrav's postwar comment was highly significant. He remarked that the church began to realize the positive role of law. Although law is redemptive in only a noneschatological sense, it is an essential part of God's economy for the world and his church. "What helped us reach a decision was the experience of a *lawless* society. . . . We came to see that right and justice have more than merely human value. Justice belongs to God." Berggrav, "Experiences of the Norwegian Church in the War," *Lutheran World Review* 1 (July 1948): 42–43.

87. *Proceedings . . . Lund . . . 1947*, pp. 70, 94–95.

88. Ibid., pp. 86–96.

89. See especially Richard Solberg, *As Between Brothers* (Minneapolis: Augsburg Publishing House, 1957); Howard Hong, "Displaced Persons," in *The Encyclopedia of the Lutheran Church*, ed. Julius Bodensieck (Minneapolis: Augsburg Publishing House, 1965), 1:710–12; and E. Theodore Bachmann, *The Epic of Faith* (New York: NLC, 1952), pp. 36–44.

Epilogue

What was the self-understanding of the Lutheran World Federation as it turned from Lund to face the future?

It was self-consciously Lutheran in its theological stance. This meant that it saw Luther as a giant figure: a teacher and preacher of the gospel, a prophet who was being appreciated anew in "his own country" (the Lutheran church), and an authentic church father in the catholic tradition. This meant also that the confessional tradition was not merely a fortress to defend but also a treasury for evangelical proclamation, an arsenal for warfare against evil, and an incentive for ecumenical outreach.

It was self-consciously committed to Lutheran unity. The children of the Reformation who had lived apart for four hundred years were now encouraged to recognize the family connection. The factors that had blocked communication and life together (nationalisms, languages, liturgies, polities, and even mutual theological mistrust) must be acknowledged as sub-Lutheran in the post-Lund world.

It was self-consciously oriented to the world. World War II had thrust this communion, as well as others, into the maelstrom of the world. Although horizons were still limited, there was no denying that political, social, economic, and cultural concerns impinged upon the church. The question that troubled many, if not all, was how the church was to retain its integrity, how it was to be "in the world, not of it," how it was to be faithful to the hortative "let the church be the church."

It was self-consciously committed to the ecumenical movement. Although the Lutheran World Federation was pressing the World Council of Churches to approve the Lutheran-sponsored petition for confessional rather than geographic representation, and although the

LWF as such could not and would not be a member of the World Council, its constitution stipulated that one of its purposes was "to foster Lutheran participation in ecumenical movements." This was not hollow rhetoric. Ever since the early days of the modern movement to find ways to manifest before the world the oneness of the church of Jesus Christ, Lutheran theologians had been conspicuous in ecumenical deliberations. In fact, leaders of the federation occupied roles of leadership in the World Council. The ecumenical conviction was genuine and ran deep.

While the Lutheran World Federation was certain about its stance in the above-mentioned areas, it was uncertain, even nervous, about its own nature. That is to say, the LWF had not yet thought through the ecclesiological question. What was this global assembly of Lutherans? Was it a church? Or was it merely an agency of "churches"? Was it more than a relief organization, a sort of religious Red Cross? Just what was it? The assembly apparently settled the question by calling itself a federation, "a free association of Lutheran churches." In fact, like the Shakespearean character of whom it was said "the lady doth protest too much," the LWF said of itself, "It shall have no power to legislate for the churches . . . but shall act as their agent in such matters as they assign to it." The very emphasis by which the LWF denied its ecclesial character measured the power and significance of the ecclesiological problem. That there was ambivalence and uncertainty about the nature of this phenomenon had been evident in the various names suggested: Lutheran World Movement, Lutheran World Council, Lutheran World Conference, Lutheran World Convention. The matter was to continue as an unresolved issue in the years after Lund, as was illustrated in the ecclesiological studies of the Department of Theology in the early 1960s and the discussion at the Helsinki assembly in 1963. From that time to the present, the debate has not been pursued in depth. Significant for our epilogue, however, is the fact that shortly after the delegates returned from Lund to their homes the question surfaced in two journals, *The Lutheran Church Quarterly* and *The Lutheran World Review*.[1] Thaddaeus F. Gullixson, president of Luther

---

1. Thaddaeus F. Gullixson, "Achievements at Lund in Retrospect," *Lutheran Church Quarterly* 21 (October 1948); and Abdel Ross Wentz, "Future Tasks of the Lutheran World Federation," *Lutheran World Review* 1 (October 1948).

Theological Seminary in St. Paul, wrote in retrospect of Lund: "The Lutheran World Federation . . . is and must remain 'a free association of churches.' " In the same month, Abdel Ross Wentz wrote in the LWF's own journal: "It is easier to define a free association than to define a Lutheran church. . . ." Although neither writer went on to spell out the ecclesiological question, it was clear that uncertainty prevailed.

Perhaps by the time some hardy soul has written the history of the Lutheran World Federation, it will have discovered the confessional description of what and where the church is and decided whether world Lutheranism is "a free association of Lutheran churches" or a genuinely ecclesial entity on the global level.

Bibliographical Note

No attempt has been made to provide a bibliographical listing of all the individual works used in the preparation of this book. Such a list, even a selective one, would be both unnecessary and unwieldy. Scholars who are interested in further research will find full bibliographical data on primary and secondary sources in the footnotes. Nonetheless, the reader may find helpful the following lists of libraries and archives whose resources were made available to the author, and the main bibliographical headings together with brief notes.

LIBRARIES

Ecumenical Center Library, Geneva, Switzerland.
Gullixson Library, Luther-Northwestern Seminaries, St. Paul, Minnesota.
Krauth Memorial Library, Lutheran Theological Seminary, Philadelphia, Pennsylvania.
The Lutheran Council/U.S.A. Library, New York, New York.
Rølvaag Memorial Library, St. Olaf College, Northfield, Minnesota.
Wartburg Seminary Library, Dubuque, Iowa.
University of Minnesota Library, Minneapolis, Minnesota.

ARCHIVES

Archives at St. Olaf College, Northfield, Minnesota.
Archives of Cooperative Lutheranism, Lutheran Council/U.S.A., New York, New York.
Archives of The American Lutheran Church, Luther-Northwestern Seminaries, St. Paul, Minnesota.

Archives of The American Lutheran Church, Wartburg Seminary, Dubuque, Iowa.

Archives of the Lutheran Church in America, Lutheran School of Theology, Chicago, Illinois.

Archives at the Krauth Memorial Library, Philadelphia, Pennsylvania.

Rigsarkivet (National Archives), Copenhagen, Denmark.

Archiv des Lutherischen Kirchenamtes, Hannover, Germany (Archives of the Church of Hannover).

Archiv der Landeskirche Bayerns (Archives of the Church of Bavaria), Nürnberg, Germany.

Bethel Archiv (Bethel Institute Archives), Bethel bei Bielefeld, Germany.

Archives of the Lutheran World Federation, Geneva, Switzerland.

Archives of the World Council of Churches, Geneva, Switzerland.

Of the archives noted, the most useful by far were the Archives of Cooperative Lutheranism in New York City and the St. Olaf College Archives in Northfield, Minnesota. They contain papers (or copies thereof) of many of the leading people in the movement toward Lutheran world unity, notably the papers of the first two American members of the executive committee of the Lutheran World Convention, John A. Morehead (in New York) and Lars W. Boe, president of St. Olaf College (in Northfield). Moreover, the New York and Northfield archives possess between them copies of letters, minutes, and sundry papers, the originals of which are in other archives, especially in Germany and in Scandinavia.

GENERAL BACKGROUND BOOKS

Bachmann, E. Theodore. *The Epic of Faith.* New York: National Lutheran Council, 1952.

Boyens, Armin. *Kirchenkampf und Ökumene 1933–1939.* Munich: Chr. Kaiser Verlag, 1969.

Cochrane, Arthur C. *The Church's Confession under Hitler.* Philadelphia: Westminster Press, 1962.

Fischer, Robert, ed. *Franklin Clark Fry: A Palette for a Portrait.* Gettysburg, 1972. (Supplementary number of *The Lutheran Quarterly* 24 [1972].)

Fleisch, Paul. *Für Kirche und Bekenntnis. Geschichte der Allgemeinen Evangelisch-Lutherischen Konferenz.* Berlin: Lutherische Verlagshaus, 1956.

Grundmann, Siegfried. *Der Lutherische Weltbund.* Cologne: Böhlau, 1957.

Hauge, Osborne. *Lutherans Working Together: A History of the National Lutheran Council.* New York: National Lutheran Council, 1945.

Helmreich, Ernst C. *The German Churches under Hitler: Background, Struggle, and Epilogue.* Detroit: Wayne State University Press, 1979.

Herman, Stewart W. *It's Your Souls We Want.* Philadelphia: [Muhlenberg] Fortress Press, 1943.

———. *The Rebirth of the German Church.* London: SCM Press, 1946.

Hetle, Erik. *Lars Wilhelm Boe: A Biography.* Minneapolis: Augsburg Publishing House, 1949.

Klügel, E. *Die Lutherische Landeskirche Hannovers und ihr Bischof 1933–1945.* 2 vols. Berlin: Lutherisches Verlagshaus, 1964–65.

Ködderitz, Walter, ed. *D. August Marahrens. Pastor Pastorum . . . .* Hannover: Feesche Verlag, 1952.

Lilje, Hanns. *Memorabilia. Schwerpunkt eines Lebens.* Stern/Nürnberg: Laetare Verlage, 1973.

———. *The Valley of the Shadow.* Philadelphia: [Muhlenberg] Fortress Press, 1950.

The Lutheran Churches of the World. Edited by Alfred Th. Jørgensen, et al. Minneapolis, Gunzenhausen, Geneva, 1929–77.

Meier, Kurt. *Der Evangelische Kirchenkampf.* Göttingen: Vandenhoeck & Ruprecht, 1976.

Nelson, E. Clifford, ed. *The Lutherans in North America.* Philadelphia: Fortress Press, 1975.

Rouse, Ruth, and Neill, Stephen, eds., *A History of the Ecumenical Movement 1517–1948.* 2d ed. Philadelphia: Westminster Press, 1967.

Schmidt-Clausen, Kurt. *Vom Lutherischen Weltkonvent zum Lutherischen Weltbund.* Gütersloh: Gerd Mohn, 1976.

Solberg, Richard. *As Between Brothers.* Minneapolis: Augsburg Publishing House, 1957.

Sundkler, Bengt. *Nathan Söderblom: His Life and Work.* Lund Gleerups, 1968.

Tappert, Theodore G., et al., eds. *The Book of Concord.* Philadelphia: Fortress Press, 1959.

Trexler, Samuel. *John A. Morehead.* New York: G. P. Putnam's Sons, 1938.

Visser 't Hooft, Willem A. *Memoirs.* Philadelphia: Westminster Press, 1973.

Wadensjö, Bengt. *Toward a World Lutheran Communion: Developments in Lutheran Cooperation up to 1929.* Uppsala: Verbum, 1970.

Wentz, Abdel Ross. *A Basic History of Lutheranism in America.* Rev. ed. Philadelphia: Fortress Press, 1964.

Wentz, Frederick K. *Lutherans in Concert.* Minneapolis: Augsburg Publishing House, 1968.

ENCYCLOPEDIAS, ALMANACS, DICTIONARIES

Aschehougs Konversasjonsleksikon. Oslo: Forlagt av H. Aschehoug & Co. (W. Nygaard), 1974.

Encyclopaedia Britannica. 11th ed. Cambridge: University Press, 1910 and 15th ed. Chicago: H. H. Benton, 1974.

The Encyclopedia of the Lutheran Church. Edited by Julius Bodensieck. Minneapolis: Augsburg Publishing House, 1965.

Evangelisches Kirchen Lexikon. Göttingen: Vandenhoeck & Ruprecht, 1956, 1961.

Kirchliches Jahrbuch für die Evangelische Kirche in Deutschland 1933–1944. Edited by Joachim Beckmann. Gütersloh: C. Bertelsmann Verlag, 1948.

The Lutheran Cyclopedia. Edited by Henry Eyster Jacobs and John A. W. Haas. New York, 1899.

The Lutheran World Almanac and Encyclopedia. New York: National Lutheran Council, 1921–37.

The New Schaff-Herzog Encyclopedia of Religious Knowledge. New York, 1908–12.

The Oxford Dictionary of the Christian Church. New York: Oxford University Press, 1974.

Real-Encyclopedie für protestantische Theologie und Kirche. Leipzig, 1877–88.

Die Religion in Geschichte und Gegenwart. 3d ed. Tübingen, 1957–65.

Salmonsens Konversationsleksikon. Copenhagen, 1915–30.

Svensk Uppslagsbog. Malmö, 1947–55.

PERIODICALS

Most American Lutheran official church papers contain articles and reports on world Lutheranism. These periodicals include, among others, *The Lutheran, The Lutheran Herald, The Lutheran Companion, The Lutheran Standard, The Lutheran Outlook,* and *The Lutheran Witness.* Scholarly journals include *The Lutheran Quarterly, The Lutheran Church Review, The Lutheran World Review,* and *The Lutheran World.* The most frequently consulted German periodical was *Allgemeine Evangelisch-lutherische Kirchenzeitung.* Other periodicals, English as well as non-English, have been cited in the footnotes.

PUBLISHED MINUTES AND REPORTS

The libraries of most Lutheran colleges and seminaries in North America and Europe contain the official printed reports and minutes of church bodies and their subdivisions. The North American records of agencies such as the National Lutheran Commission for Soldiers' and Sailors' Welfare, the National Lutheran Council, the Lutheran Council in the U.S.A., the Lutheran World Convention, and the Lutheran World Federation are most readily available at the Archives of Cooperative Lutheranism in the Lutheran Center, 360 Park Avenue South, New York, New York.

UNPUBLISHED MATERIALS

Indispensable are the collections of personal and official documents, manuscripts, reports, correspondence, minutes, and so on in the papers of individuals who were prominent in world Lutheranism, especially those who were members of the National Lutheran Commission for Soldiers' and Sailors' Welfare, the National Lutheran Council, the Allgemeine Evangelisch-Lutherische Konferenz, and the executive committee of the Lutheran World Convention. Special mention should be made of the following collections:

The John A. Morehead Papers, Archives of Cooperative Lutheranism, Lutheran Council/U.S.A., New York City (ArCL)

The Lauritz Larsen Papers, ArCL

The Frederick H. Knubel Papers, ArCL

The Ralph H. Long Papers, ArCL

The Abdel Ross Wentz Papers, ArCL

The Lutheran World Convention Documents: General Papers (1923–47) and American Section (1936–47), ArCL

The Lars W. Boe Papers, St. Olaf College Archives, Northfield, Minnesota

The Alfred Th. Jørgensen Papers, Rigsarkivet, Copenhagen

The Wilhelm von Pechmann Papers, Archiv der Bayerischen Landeskirche, Nürnberg

The Hans Meiser Papers, Archiv der Bayerischen Landeskirche, Nürnberg

Lutheran World Convention Papers, Archiv der Bayerischen Landeskirche, Nürnberg

The August Marahrens, Hanns Lilje, and Lutheran World Convention Papers (fragmented during World War II), Archiv der Bischofskanzlei and Archiv des Lutherischen Kirchenamtes, Hannover

In these collections the letters are of special importance as aids to interpretations of related documents. The diary of Sylvester C. Michelfelder (LWF Archives, Geneva), as well as unpublished autobiographical items like Friedrich von Bodelschwingh's "Dreissig Tage . . ." (Bethel Archiv) and manuscripts like Dorris A. Flesner's "The Role of the Lutheran Churches of America in the Formation of the World Council of Churches" (Ph.D. diss., Hartford Seminary, 1956) and Willard D. Allbeck's "A Study of American Participation in Inter-Lutheran Cooperation Prior to the Formation of the Lutheran World Federation" (New York: National Lutheran Council, 1962), provide extra dividends to the scholar who is seeking to organize and to understand data.

References to the remaining hundreds of documents utilized in this study are stored in the footnotes.

Index

LUTHERAN FAMILY IN NORTH AMERICA

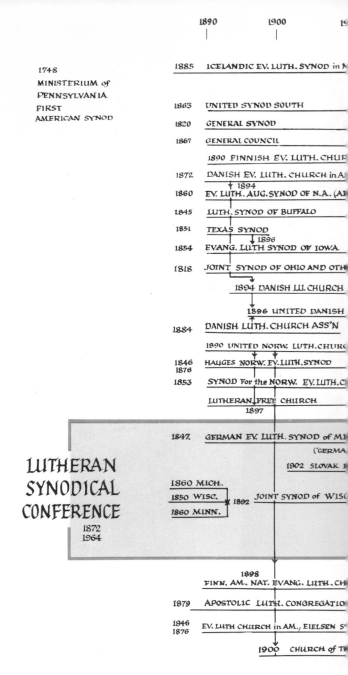

1890   1900   19

1748
MINISTERIUM of
PENNSYLVANIA
FIRST
AMERICAN SYNOD

1885   ICELANDIC EV. LUTH. SYNOD in N

1863   UNITED SYNOD SOUTH

1820   GENERAL SYNOD

1867   GENERAL COUNCIL

1890   FINNISH EV. LUTH. CHUR

1872   DANISH EV. LUTH. CHURCH in A
        1894
1860   EV. LUTH. AUG. SYNOD OF N.A. (A

1845   LUTH. SYNOD OF BUFFALO

1851   TEXAS SYNOD
        1896
1854   EVANG. LUTH. SYNOD OF IOWA

1818   JOINT SYNOD OF OHIO AND OTH

1894 DANISH LU. CHURCH

1896 UNITED DANISH

1884   DANISH LUTH. CHURCH ASS'N

1890 UNITED NORW. LUTH. CHURC

1846   HAUGES NORW. EV. LUTH. SYNOD
1876
1853   SYNOD For the NORW. EV. LUTH. C

LUTHERAN FREE CHURCH
1897

1847   GERMAN EV. LUTH. SYNOD of M
        ("GERMA
        1902 SLOVAK

LUTHERAN
SYNODICAL
CONFERENCE
1872
1964

1860 MICH.
1850 WISC.   1892   JOINT SYNOD of WISC
1860 MINN.

1898
FINN. AM. NAT. EVANG. LUTH. CH

1879   APOSTOLIC LUTH. CONGREGATIO

1846   EV. LUTH CHURCH in AM., EIELSEN S
1876

1900   CHURCH OF T

Source: ECN, *Lutheranism in*